How Children Learn the Meanings
of Words

LDCC **Learning, Development, and Conceptual Change**
Lila Gleitman, Susan Carey, Elissa Newport, and
Elizabeth Spelke, editors

From Simple Input to Complex Grammar, James L. Morgan, 1986

Concepts, Kinds, and Cognitive Development, Frank C. Keil, 1989

Learnability and Cognition: The Acquisition of Argument Structure, Steven Pinker, 1989

Mind Bugs: The Origins of Procedural Misconception, Kurt VanLehn, 1990

Categorization and Naming in Children: Problems of Induction, Ellen M. Markman, 1989

The Child's Theory of Mind, Henry M. Wellman, 1990

Understanding the Representational Mind, Josef Perner, 1991

An Odyssey in Learning and Perception, Eleanor J. Gibson, 1991

Beyond Modularity: A Developmental Perspective on Cognitive Science, Annette Karmiloff-Smith, 1992

Mindblindness: An Essay on Autism and "Theory of Mind," Simon Baron-Cohen, 1995

Speech: A Special Code, Alvin M. Liberman, 1995

Theory and Evidence: The Development of Scientific Reasoning, Barbara Koslowski, 1995

Race in the Making: Cognition, Culture, and the Child's Construction of Human Kinds, Lawrence A. Hirschfeld, 1996

Words, Thoughts, and Theories, Alison Gopnik and Andrew N. Meltzoff, 1996

The Cradle of Knowledge: Development of Perception in Infancy, Philip J. Kellman and Martha E. Arterberry, 1998

Language Creation and Change: Creolization, Diachrony, and Development, edited by Michel DeGraff, 1999

Systems That Learn: An Introduction to Learning Theory, second edition, Sanjay Jain, Daniel Osherson, James S. Royer, and Arun Sharma, 1999

How Children Learn the Meanings of Words, Paul Bloom, 2000

How Children Learn the Meanings of Words

Paul Bloom

A Bradford Book
The MIT Press
Cambridge, Massachusetts
London, England

Third printing, 2001

This book was set in Palatino by Achorn Graphic Services, Inc. and was printed and bound in the United States of America.

Library of Congress Cataloging-in-Publication Data

Bloom, Paul, 1963–
  How children learn the meanings of words / Paul Bloom.
    p. cm.
  Includes bibliographical references and index.
  ISBN 0-262-02469-1 (hc: alk. paper)
  1. Language acquisition. 2. Semantics. I. Title.
P118.B623   2000
401'.93—dc21   99-23901
                                                                         CIP

For my brother, Howard Bloom

Contents

Series Foreword

This series in learning, development, and conceptual change includes state-of-the-art reference works, seminal book-length monographs, and texts on the development of concepts and mental structures. It spans learning in all domains of knowledge, from syntax to geometry to the social world, and is concerned with all phases of development, from infancy through adulthood.

The series intends to engage such fundamental questions as:

The nature and limits of learning and maturation: the influence of the environment, of initial structures, and of maturational changes in the nervous system on human development; learnability theory; the problem of induction; domain-specific constraints on development.

The nature of conceptual change: conceptual organization and conceptual change in child development, in the acquisition of expertise, and in the history of science.

Lila Gleitman
Susan Carey
Elissa Newport
Elizabeth Spelke

Acknowledgments

This book contains everything I know about how children learn the meanings of words. This is a topic I have studied for over a decade, and it has been immensely rewarding. The child's ability to learn new words is nothing short of miraculous. And the study of this ability bears on the most central questions in cognitive science. What is the nature of human learning? How are language and thought related? How do children think about the people and objects around them? We are far from answering any of these questions, but I think that the study of word learning can provide us with some valuable and unexpected insights.

I would have never started down this path without the good luck to have John Macnamara as my mentor when I was an undergraduate at McGill University. He has had a profound influence on my work, and much of what I say here is based on John's theory of word learning, as outlined in his book *Names for Things* and elsewhere. My debts to John are many. It was because of him that I decided to become a psychologist and went on to do my graduate work with Susan Carey at the Massachusetts Institute of Technology. And, on a more personal note, it was at a party at his home that I met my wife (and occasional collaborator) Karen Wynn.

Amy Brand at MIT Press encouraged me, many years ago, to write this book, and I finally had the chance to do so while on sabbatical at the Medical Research Council's Cognitive Development Unit in London. I am very grateful to the people there for providing such a stimulating and hospitable environment. In particular, I thank Uta Frith, Mark Johnson, Annette Karmiloff-Smith, and John Morton. Down the road at Birkbeck College, Lolly Tyler and Heather van der Lely provided further moral and intellectual support.

Karen Wynn gave me extensive and insightful comments on a very rough first draft. I could not have completed this book without her encouragement and advice. I am also grateful to Susan Carey, Eve Clark, Gil Diesendruck, Susan Gelman, Gary Marcus, and Lori

Markson for taking the time to give me valuable comments on the entire manuscript. Susan Carey deserves particular mention, as her penetrating commentary motivated me to rethink and rewrite a large portion of this book.

I thank Uta Frith, Gregory Murphy, and Sandeep Prasada, all who provided helpful comments on chapters in their areas of expertise. Other colleagues took the time to answer specific questions and offer helpful advice, including Elizabeth Bates, Felice Bedford, Larry Fenson, Tim German, Francesca Happé, Bill Ittelson, Deborah Kemler-Nelson, John Allen Paulos, Mary Peterson, and Steven Reznick. Writing this book on sabbatical required long-distance help with references, xeroxing, and the like, and I thank Lori Markson for her expert and cheerful assistance.

The opportunity to write this book was provided by a grant from the Spencer Foundation, a grant that also funded most of my own research described within. I am very grateful for this support.

My son Zachary was born during the final revision, giving me an excellent excuse to miss my deadline. His older brother, Max, began to speak as I started to write the book and went on to provide me with many illuminating anecdotes about early word learning. I thank both of them.

How Children Learn the Meanings of Words

Chapter 1

First Words

It looks simple. A 14-month-old toddles after the family dog, smacking it whenever she gets close. The dog wearily moves under the table. "Dog," the child's mother tells her. "You're chasing the dog. That's the dog." The child stops, points a pudgy hand at the dog, and shrieks, "Daw!" The mother smiles: "Yes, dog."

Many parents—and many philosophers and psychologists—would say that word learning is as simple as it looks. It can be explained in part by the processes of association and imitation and in part by the efforts of parents who want their children to learn how to speak. A child starts by listening to her parents use words and comes to associate the words with what they refer to. When she starts to use words herself, her successful acts of naming are rewarded, and her mistakes are gently corrected.

From this perspective, word learning is the easiest part of language development. The rest of language emerges without the support of "negative evidence"; children do not receive consistent feedback on the grammaticality of what they say (Brown & Hanlon, 1970; Marcus, 1993). But word learning may be a different story. While parents tend to be unconcerned if their child says "goed" instead of "went," they are likely to notice, and react, if their child was to use *dog* to refer to a chair. Another difference is that much of language is productive. An understanding of syntax, for instance, allows us to produce and understand a potential infinity of new sentences. But word learning is merely the memorization of a series of paired associates: *dog* refers to dogs; *water* refers to water, *Mommy* refers to Mommy, and so on.

This is one picture of word learning. This book presents another. I will argue that a careful consideration of what children know and how they come to know it reveals that word learning is actually far from simple. Children's learning of words, even the simplest names for things, requires rich mental capacities—conceptual, social, and linguistic—that interact in complicated ways.

John Macnamara defends this alternative in the first paragraph of his 1982 book *Names for Things*. He remarks that the learning of simple names

> is a surprisingly complicated matter. And much of the complexity has eluded the abundant literature on language learning. Complexity is as much a nuisance as gout, but sometimes just as real and inevitable. Like gout one avoids introducing it to the system, but confronted with it one has no reasonable alternative but to deal with it. So far psychologists have failed to deal with what strikes me as the very real complexity of name learning.

I think this is basically true, with two qualifications. First, the situation in psychology has changed over the last several years (largely as a result of Macnamara's own work), and there has been renewed interest in the topics he lists as being unfairly neglected—reference, meaning, intentionality, hierarchies, and the role of grammar. And second, a better analogy for complexity might be cholesterol; gout is always a nuisance, but there is bad cholesterol and there is good cholesterol. Some psychological problems are complex in bad ways: they cut across domains in a chaotic and messy fashion; they have no clean answers; and their solutions, to the extent they have any, impart no illumination about the mind in general. But a reader of Macnamara's book is drawn toward the conclusion that the learning of names is complex in a different, more positive, sense. Word learning is complex because it involves different cognitive capacities working together in an elegant fashion. Hence the study of word learning might provide insight into these capacities and how they interact in the course of development.

This brings us back to the question of how word learning relates to other aspects of language acquisition. In the sections that follow, I suggest that deep similarities exist between word learning and other aspects of language development. But there is one major difference. Under many analyses, systems such as syntax and morphology have a highly modular flavor; they are self-contained, with their own rules and representations, and interact in a highly circumscribed fashion with perceptual and motoric systems, as well as with other aspects of language. In contrast, it is impossible to explain how children learn the meaning of a word without an understanding of certain nonlinguistic mental capacities, including how children think about the minds of others and how they make sense of the external world. To the extent that Leibniz was right in saying that language is "a mirror of the mind," he was talking about words.

The Problems of Word Learning

Word learning, and especially the learning of names for things, certainly *seems* like a simple process, at least to scholars who are not directly engaged in its study. To take a typical example, in the midst of an otherwise fine discussion of primate drawing abilities, Maureen Cox (1992, pp. 17–18) makes the following remark: "Now, chimps cannot speak because they lack the necessary vocal apparatus, but they can be taught to use sign language. They may not be able to use it in quite the same creative way as humans, but at least they can use it to name things."

I am not concerned (not here, at least) with the empirical claims about what chimps can or cannot do. And while I believe that naming really is a creative act, it is reasonable to say that it is not creative in the same sense as other parts of language. The part of this passage that grates is the phrase "at least." To me this is like saying that chimps can't play checkers—but at least they can play chess! If chimps could use signs for the act of naming, it would show that they have remarkable mental powers.

What is so impressive about word learning? In a classic discussion, Willard V.O. Quine (1960, p. 29) asks us to imagine a linguist visiting a culture with a language that bears no resemblance to our own and trying to learn some words: "A rabbit scurries by, the native says 'Gavagai,' and the linguist notes down the sentence 'Rabbit' (or 'Lo, a rabbit'), as tentative translation, subject to testing in further cases."

Quine goes on to argue that it is impossible for the linguist to ever be certain such a translation is right. There is an infinity of logically possible meanings for *gavagai*. It could refer to rabbits, but it could also refer to the specific rabbit named by the native, or any mammal, or any animal, or any object. It could refer to the top half of the rabbit, or its outer surface, or rabbits but only those that are scurrying; it could refer to scurrying itself, or to white, or to furriness.

The linguist could exclude some of these interpretations through further questioning (assuming some means of figuring out when the native was saying yes or no). For instance, if the native denies that a rat is *gavagai*, the linguist could be confident that the word does not refer to all animals; if he agrees that *gavagai* could be used for a gray rabbit, then it could not mean white, and so on. Other interpretations are harder to exclude. How could the linguist know that the native isn't using the word *gavagai* to refer not to rabbits but to time slices of rabbits—to entities that exist only for the instant that the word is used? Or that the native isn't talking about, as Quine puts it, "all and sundry undetached parts of rabbits"?

There are actually several different problems here. The first is how the linguist knows that *gavagai* is a name at all, as opposed to the native clearing his throat, or making a noise to warn the animal away, or talking to himself, or saying the equivalent of "Look!" or "I'm bored." How does the linguist know that it is one word and not two—*gava* and *guy*? This segmentation problem is a real one when one considers less idealized examples of translation. People do not typically use words in isolation; most words are used in the context of sentences. Even if the linguist can be certain that an act of naming is going on, he or she has to somehow parse the utterance so as to extract the name (which might itself be more than one word, as in *chinchilla rabbit*).

A more serious problem was noted above: How can the linguist know what the word is describing? It could be the whole rabbit, the rabbit and the ground it is on, a part of the rabbit, its color, shape, size, and so on. And this raises the final problem—figuring out how to extend this word in the appropriate way in new circumstances. Suppose the linguist can be sure that *gavagai* is a name and that it refers to the whole rabbit. How should the word be used in the future?

This problem of generalization is a specific instance of a more general dilemma. Nelson Goodman (1983) has pointed out that for any act of induction, there is an infinite number of equally logical generalizations that one can make, each equally consistent with the experience one has had so far. If you burn your hand on a large white stove, for instance, one has to decide which objects to be more careful around. The right answer is *stoves* and not *large things* or *white things*. Goodman points out that there is no logical reason to favor this conclusion over any of these alternatives, as well as over some truly bizarre hypotheses, such as *stoves—but only to the year 2000, then carrots.*

Word learning is a paradigm case of inductive learning. Something has to explain why the linguist, as well as any child, should favor the hypothesis that *gavagai* should be extended to other rabbits as opposed to the hypothesis that it should be extended to other white things, or other rabbits plus the Eiffel Tower, and so on.

These problems of reference and generalization are solved so easily by children and adults that it takes philosophers like Quine and Goodman to even notice that they exist. If we see someone point to a rabbit and say "gavagai," it is entirely natural to assume that this is an act of naming and that the word refers to the rabbit and should be extended to other rabbits. It would be mad to think that the word refers to undetached rabbit parts or rabbits plus the Eiffel Tower. But the naturalness of the rabbit hypothesis and the madness of the alternatives is not logical necessity; it is instead the result of how the human mind works.

Some Facts about Words and How They Are Learned

Since humans learn words, we somehow solve the problems sketched out above. But how often and under what circumstances? If children knew few words, for instance, and had to learn each word under extensive tutelage, this would motivate a different psychological theory of their abilities than if they knew many words and could learn them under very impoverished circumstances.

How many words do people learn? This is a hard question to answer. It requires a robust notion of what a word is, some understanding of what it is to know a word, and a good method with which to test whether such understanding exists. If you simply ask educated people how many words they know, you will get very low estimates (Seashore & Eckerson, 1940), and they are even stingier when estimating the vocabularies of others. Jean Aitchinson (1994) remarks that one respected intellectual in the nineteenth century claimed that peasants have a vocabulary that does not exceed 100 words; they make do with such a small lexicon because "the same word was made to serve a multitude of purposes, and the same coarse expletives recurred with a horrible frequency in the place of every single part of speech." The linguist Max Müller proposed that highly educated people use 3,000 to 4,000 words, other adults know about 300 words, and "the child up to the eighth year probably confines himself to not more than 150 words" (cited by Nice, 1926). More recently, the writer Georges Simenon explained that he makes his books so simple because most Frenchmen know fewer than 600 words. (Simenon also claims to have slept with 10,000 women in his life, leading Aitchinson to suggest that he suffers from a general problem with numerical cognition.)

More sensible estimates emerge from studies that use the following methodology (Miller, 1996). Words are taken from a large unabridged dictionary, including only those words whose meanings cannot be guessed using principles of morphology or analogy. (Even if you never learned *restart*, for instance, you can guess what it means, and so it shouldn't be included in a test of how many words you learned.) Since it would take too long to test people on hundreds of thousands of words, a random sample is taken. The proportion of the sample that people know is used to generate an estimate of their overall vocabulary size, under the assumption that the size of the dictionary is a reasonable estimate of the size of the language as a whole. For example, if you use a dictionary with 500,000 words, and test people on a 500-word sample, you would determine the number of English words they know by taking the number that they got correct from this sample and multiplying by 1,000. The typical test is a multiple-choice question with four or five alternatives (which introduces a chance factor that must be controlled for); studies with young children use other, more sensitive, methods as well (see Anglin, 1993).

This procedure yields estimates of about 45,000 words for American high school graduates (Nagy & Herman, 1987). This is roughly the same number as those found by scholars in the late 1800s and early 1900s, though they used somewhat cruder methods (Nice, 1926). It is inevitably a low estimate, as it excludes proper names for people and places, idiomatic expressions, and undecomposible compounds. Taking these into account, the estimate jumps to 60,000 or 80,000, and people who do a lot of reading might know twice this many (Aitchinson, 1994; Miller, 1996).

Children start to produce words at about the age of 12 months, which, if we stick to the more conservative estimate of 60,000, equates to about 10 new words a day up until the end of high school. Steven Pinker (1994b, p. 151) remarks that this sort of learning of arbitrary pairings is unprecedented: "Think about having to memorize a new batting average or treaty date or phone number every ninety minutes of your waking life since you took your first steps." And while the recovery of most arbitrary facts is slow and hard, access to words and their meanings is fast and effortless. In normal speech, we produce about three words a second and can recognize a word about one-fifth of a second after its onset (Marslen-Wilson & Tyler, 1980).

What about the circumstances under which words are learned? Consider the example that began this chapter, in which a child interacts with a dog, hears it called "dog" as she is looking at it, and is rewarded (and corrected) in her efforts to name the animal. How much of this is necessary? That is, how much can we take away from this situation and still have children learn the meanings of words?

First, words can be learned without a strict spatial and temporal cooccurrence between the word and the meaning. It is true that in many Western cultures parents often speak to their children in contexts in which the referents of words are easily recoverable. In particular, they often use words to refer to what the child is attending to at the moment the word is spoken, and for one-year-olds this may be the case as much as 70 percent of the time (Collins, 1977; Harris, Jones & Grant, 1983). But if so, this still leaves 30 percent of cases in which no such cooccurrence occurs. Some of the time that children hear "Time for your milk" they will be looking at their milk, and it would be reasonable to map the word onto the substance, but some of the time they will be looking at a fork or a person's face, and a mapping based on a sensitivity to spatiotemporal association would lead them into grief. It is revealing, then, that children are capable of learning words on the basis of a single trial and that serious mistakes—such as a child thinking that *milk* means "fork"—virtually never occur.

Moreover, while parents might name objects ("This is a cookie"), they do not name actions. Most of the time that adults use verbs, the actions that the verbs refer to are not taking place (Gleitman, 1990; Tomasello, 1992). As Lila Gleitman (1990, p. 19) puts it,

> When, every evening, Mother opens the door upon returning from work, what does [the child] hear? I would venture that he rarely hears her say *Hello, Alfred, I am opening the door!*, but very often hears *Hello, Alfred, whatcha been doing all day?* . . . In short, any scheme for learning from observation must have some machinery for dealing with the fact that caretaker speech is not a running commentary on scenes and events in view.

This point is worth stressing, since the standard scenario that finds its way into discussions of word learning is that the child is observing a scene and hearing words that describe it. But as Gleitman points out, this isn't typically what happens: opening often occurs without anyone using the word *opening,* and the word *opening* often occurs without anything being opened. As we will see later, there is also experimental evidence that children are able to learn words for objects and actions that are not observable to them at the time the words are being used.

Second, children do not need a full complement of sensory abilities to learn words. Deaf children learning a signed language such as ASL do so at exactly the same pace as hearing children learning spoken languages; the age of milestones of word learning, such as the first word and the first 50 words, is identical (Petitto, 1992). More surprising, given the tradition of viewing visual experience as a driving force in language learning, is how well blind children learn language. Such children cannot identify objects that are not within reach, cannot follow the direction of a parent's gaze, and cannot use pointing as a cue. Yet one extensive longitudinal study of the language development of three blind children found that two of them showed only a small initial delay in the onset of word use—which may be in part due to a more general lag in motor development found in blind children—and the third was actually linguistically precocious (Landau & Gleitman, 1985). By each of the children's third birthday, their language was indistinguishable from that of sighted children.

Landau and Gleitman also explored in detail certain aspects of the lexical knowledge of one blind child named Kelli. In one set of studies, they found that her knowledge of color words was similar to that of sighted children of the same age. That is, she knew that color words belong to a single domain, that they apply only to concrete objects, and that they map onto a property that she could not herself identify. At the very least, these observations suggest that visual perception might not play as large a role in language development as many have suggested.

Third, children do not need feedback to learn word meanings. Although some Western parents correct their young children if they use words incorrectly, this is not universal; there are cultures in which adults do not even speak to children until the children are using at least some words in a meaningful manner (see Lieven, 1994, for review). Yet such children nevertheless come to learn language. Consider also studies of children who for various reasons cannot speak but can hear and are otherwise neurologically intact. In one study of a four-year-old who could produce only a few sounds, it was found that he could understand complex syntactic structures, could make appropriate grammaticality judgments, and had a normal vocabulary (Stromswold, 1994). Needless to say, if someone cannot talk, they cannot get feedback on their speech, and so the fact that this child developed a normal language proves that parental reactions such as correction cannot be necessary for vocabulary development.

Fourth, children do not need ostensive naming for word learning. The paradigm case for the study of word learning—both in philosophy and psychology—is the sort of example that began this chapter: the child is looking at a dog, someone says "dog," and she somehow connects the word with the object. But, just as with feedback, this pattern of naming is not a human universal; children can learn language without it. For example, Bambi Schieffelin (1985, pp. 531–532) describes the cultural context of children acquiring Kaluli. These children grow up in a rich linguistic environment, surrounded by adults and older children who are talking to one another, including making observations about the infant himself, as in: "Look at Seligiwo! He's walking by himself." Furthermore, Kaluli adults explicitly teach children *assertive language,* such as teasing, shaming, and requesting, by modeling the appropriate sentence to the child and adding the word *elema*—an imperative meaning "Say like that." (Appealing or begging for something is never part of an *elema* sequence; according to Kaluli ideology, assertiveness has to be taught, but begging is innate.) But object labeling is never part of an *elema* sequence; there is no naming of objects and no labeling interactions: when a child names an object for an adult, the adult's response is disinterest. This lack of object labeling has been observed in other cultures as well (Lieven, 1994).

All of these considerations show how robust the word learning process is. Nobody doubts that for children to learn words they have to be exposed to them in contexts in which they can infer their meanings:

this is a truism. But the words do not need to be presented in a labeling context (they can be learned from overheard speech), nor do children need to be able to see what the words refer to or have their efforts at using the words encouraged and corrected. And children learn words over and over again, coming to build a vocabulary in the tens of thousands, each word available in an instant for production and understanding.

Finally, consider the nature of what is learned. Noam Chomsky (1993, p. 24) has often maintained that vocabulary acquisition poses learning problems akin to those posed by the acquisition of other aspects of language: "The pervasive problem of 'poverty of stimulus' is striking even in the case of simple lexical items. Their semantic properties are highly articulate and intricate and known in detail that vastly transcends any relevant experience."

To take a simple example (see Keil, 1979; Pustejovsky, 1995), consider the word *book*. This can refer to a material entity, as in the sentence *There are five books on the floor*. But if you say that "John wrote a book," *book* refers to an abstract entity, one that need not correspond to any material object. (All of the five books on the floor might be copies of the book that John wrote). If you say that you are "beginning a book," it will normally be taken as meaning that you are beginning to read a book and will have a different interpretation than the phrase *beginning a sandwich*. Similarly the adjective in *a hard book* or *a long book* has a different meaning than it does in *a hard cookie* or *a long flagpole*. An adequate theory of language acquisition must explain how we come to know all this without any explicit tutelage. Similar puzzles arise when we consider the subtle ways in which verbs and prepositions are used to denote both concrete and abstract relations and events (e.g., Jackendoff, 1990; Lakoff, 1987; Pinker, 1989).

One particular case of interest that is discussed later on is the use of words to name representations of what the words depict. We use *dog* to refer not only to dogs but to statues of dogs, photographs of dogs, and drawings of dogs—including those that bear no resemblance at all to actual dogs. As we will see, this common use of words poses some surprisingly complicated problems from the standpoint of learning and development.

A further aspect of the poverty-of-stimulus problem is our grasp of word meanings that correspond to things that do not exist. As an example, Chomsky (1995, p. 25) cites John Milton: "The mind is its own place, and in itself can make a Heaven of Hell, a Hell of Heaven." One can find this perfectly intelligible, even true, without being committed to the idea that any of these names actually refer either to things in the natural world or to entities in some abstract mental world.

How Children Learn the Meanings of Words

An argument often made in the cognitive sciences starts by describing how hard a task is (such as object recognition, for instance) and then uses this consideration to argue that there is a dedicated part of the mind that does this task. This is not the argument I am making here. To the extent that this book has an overarching theme, it is this. Word learning really is a hard problem, but children do not solve it through a dedicated mental mechanism. Instead, words are learned through abilities that exist for other purposes. These include an ability to infer the intentions of others, an ability to acquire concepts, an appreciation of syntactic structure, and certain general learning and memory abilities. These are both necessary and sufficient for word learning: children need them to learn the meanings of words, and they need nothing else.

This proposal is not original. Many scholars who look at word learning from the standpoint of social cognition argue that word learning is the product of children's ability to figure out what other people are thinking when they use words. And scholars interested in syntactic cues have made a similar claim for the role of syntax, just as those discussing the cognitive prerequisites of word learning have been concerned with the conceptual and logical underpinnings of the process. I argue that a complete explanation for how children learn the meanings of words requires all of these capacities.

There are two ways in which such a proposal could be wrong. It might be attributing too much to young children. It could be argued, for instance, that children do not need an elaborate theory of mind to determine which objects words refer to because they can use statistical information instead. Perhaps a theory that posits fewer resources on the part of the child can explain the developmental facts just as well.

Alternatively, the capacities I have proposed might not be enough. Perhaps lexical constraints (or principles, assumptions, or biases) specifically earmarked for word learning are needed to explain how children learn the meanings of words. There has been a proliferation of these constraints over the last decade or so. They include the whole-object bias, the taxonomic bias, and the mutual-exclusivity bias (Markman, 1989), the noun-category linkage (Waxman, 1994), the shape bias (Landau, Smith & Jones, 1988), the principles of contrast and conventionality (Clark, 1993), and the principles of reference, extendibility, object scope, categorical scope, and novel name-nameless category (Golinkoff, Mervis & Hirsh-Pasek, 1994).

When some of these constraints were first proposed, critics, such as Nelson (1988), argued that they attributed too much preexisting mental structure to young children. These criticisms have been taken to heart by developmentalists. Few proponents of the constraints view are rash enough to propose that they are innate. Instead, they are said to be learned (or better, to develop or emerge), although—with the important exception of the shape bias (Landau, Smith & Jones, 1988)—nobody has much to say about how this learning, development, or emergence supposedly takes place. In fact, even the mild suggestion that constraints on word learning exist at all is seen as an extreme view, and researchers are careful to insist that they mean *constraint* in a weak sense, not at all like the sorts of principles that linguists talk about (e.g., Golinkoff, Mervis & Hirsh-Pasek, 1994).

All of this caution reflects the empiricist prejudices of the field, and it seems to me to be unjustified. There is nothing biologically implausible about innate constraints on language learning, and we would be unsurprised to find innate constraints underlying the development of analogous systems in other species, such as bee dance, monkey cries, or birdsong. My objection to these special constraints isn't that they are nonbiological or not developmental enough; it isn't that there is some *a priori* reason to believe that they cannot exist. It is that the evidence suggests that, in fact, they don't exist.

By rejecting the idea of special constraints, I am not denying that young children know a lot about words—about their phonology, morphology, syntax, and meaning—and that this knowledge can facilitate the learning of language. For instance, two-year-olds have a tacit appreciation that words referring to objects are typically count nouns. This is part of their understanding of the relationship between meaning and form, and it can help them learn new words. I am not denying that such knowledge of language exists or even that some of it might be innate. The proposal I am arguing against is that there exist *additional* constraints of the sort proposed by Markman and others, constraints whose sole role is to facilitate the process of word learning.

Note also that a rejection of the special-constraint proposal does not entail rejecting the view that children must be constrained as to the inferences they make. This point is often misunderstood. For instance, Roberta Golinkoff and her colleagues (1995, p. 192) discuss Lois Bloom's position that lexical constraints are the inventions of researchers, not actually mental entities on the part of the child, and they suggest that her view "begs the question of how children determine the meanings of words without considering a myriad of hypotheses." But Bloom doesn't beg the question; she just denies that its answer lies in special constraints on word learning.

Elsewhere, Golinkoff, Mervis, and Hirsh-Pasek (1994) suggest that lexical principles "enable the child to avoid the Quinean (1960) conundrum of generating limitless, equally logical possibilities, for a word's meaning." But the problem of "limitless, equally logical possibilities" arises for any act of induction. If a dog jumps onto a stove and gets burned, it is likely to infer that stoves are hot—not that undetached stove parts are hot or that stoves until the year 2000 are hot, and so on, even though these alternatives are logically consistent with its experience. So at least *some* constraints on induction are independent of language learning. The issue, then, isn't whether children's inferences about word meaning are somehow constrained (they must be, since word learning is a form of inductive learning); it is whether these constraints are special to the learning of words.

I suggest in the chapters that follow that the phenomena that such constraints have been posited to explain (such as children's tendencies to treat words as object names, to avoid words with overlapping references, and to generalize object names on the basis of shape) are better explained in terms of other facts about how children think and learn.

Preliminaries

The question "How do children learn the meanings of words?" needs clarification. I briefly discuss each of its four content words—children, learn, meanings, and words—to make clear some foundational assumptions and to raise some of the issues that are discussed in subsequent chapters. Meaning is the thorniest issue of all and so is saved for last.

Children

Most research on word learning focuses on two-year-olds to five-year-olds. Why? Why study young children at all, instead of older children and adults?

This would be a silly question to ask about other aspects of language. By the time children are about four, they have mastered just about all of the phonology, syntax, and morphology they are ever going to know, at least for their first language. If you want to study these aspects of language learning, there is no alternative to studying children. But words are different. A six-year-old knows about 10,000 words (Anglin, 1993)—which is less than one-sixth of the number she will know when she graduates from high school.

Nevertheless, most studies on this topic, including my own, follow the practice of developmental research in general and focus on two- to five-year-olds. Such children are the right blend of the exotic and the accessible: they are different in their mental habits from adults, with funny beliefs and immature patterns of thought, and yet they are easy to find, relatively good company, and can be studied without expensive and time-consuming procedures. And by looking at their capacity to learn words, one can gain insight into the different components of the word learning process, particularly if these emerge at different points in development.

In the end, every age is relevant. Prelinguistic infants are interesting because they lack whatever capacities are necessary to start talking, one-year-olds are interesting because they are word-learning novices, older children and adults are interesting because they are word-learning experts, and preschoolers are interesting because they represent an illustrative midpoint between novice and expert. And by any account, children at these different age groups really do differ in their patterns of word learning. If you look at how many words children learn per day, the difference between a one-year-old and a two-year-old is striking, as is the difference between a two-year-old and a four-year-old, and a four year old and 10 year old. And when you get to adults, the rate of word learning often drops to close to zero, perking up only for the learning of proper names and names of cultural and terminological innovations, such as *Internet, karaoke,* and *Tickle Me Elmo.*

Why do these age differences exist? This is an issue that is discussed in detail in the next chapter, but one obvious consideration is that as children get older, they have increasing access to information concerning what words mean. One-year-olds start off with little or no syntactic knowledge to guide their interpretation of a new word. And before they have learned their first word, they are obviously not going to be able to learn new words from linguistic context. Slightly older children have more syntactic understanding and know a few more words; once their vocabulary and syntax takes off, they can learn words by hearing them used in sentences. They hear words in more diverse contexts; in some cultures, this includes exposure to television and videos and, most important, through literacy.

Learn
Talk about learning has an old-fashioned flavor, and many scholars prefer expressions such as development, emergence, growth, and acquisition. Some argue that there is no such thing as learning—that the notion reflects an out-of-date way of looking at mental processes. The argument often goes like this. We know from the biological sciences that the brain, and all that the brain can do, emerges from the interaction of genes and environment. Since there is no sense in which the environment can have an effect on the brain that is not strongly constrained by our genetic endowment, the whole idea of something being *learned* (as opposed to the ethological notion of being *triggered,* for instance) is an archaic idea that should be expunged from the cognitive sciences.

This is the nativist attack on learning; ironically, the empiricist attack is similar. We know from the biological sciences that the brain, and all that the brain can do, emerges from the interaction of genes and environment. Since there is no sense in which genes can have an effect on the brain that is not strongly constrained by the environment, the whole notion of something being *innate* (as opposed to its *developing* or *emerging*) is an archaic notion that should be expunged from the cognitive sciences. And since nothing can be unlearned (which is the usual meaning of *innate*), then the notion of learning either is incoherent or applies to every aspect of human knowledge. Either way, we should get rid of it too.

If we were to accept these arguments, it would have dramatic consequences and, I think, unfortunate ones. It would be a poor psychology that insists that the same developmental story be told about the emergence of Down syndrome and how people come to learn the word *rabbit*. In fact, even though both arise from the interaction of genes and environment, it is nonetheless entirely reasonable to conclude that Down syndrome is innate and the meaning of the word *rabbit* is learned. There is a sensible dichotomy that should be maintained.

The problem with the arguments does not lie in their premises. It is true that any effect of the environment on how one thinks can occur only if the right innate abilities are in place (some "instinct to learn"), and it is also true that the action of genes on brain and behavior comes about through considerable interaction with all sorts of environments, from the cell to the society. Nobody has ever doubted this. The arguments go wrong in concluding that these facts show that nothing can be explained as caused by the environment or caused by the genes. This doesn't follow; the notion of causal responsibility, both in science and in normal usage, is more sophisticated than that. If Fred throws a cup to the floor and it breaks, this breaking is a profoundly interactionist affair; the cup would not have broken if gravity didn't exist, if the floor hadn't been made of a hard surface, if the cup wasn't made out of a fragile material, if Fred's parents hadn't decided to have sexual intercourse at a certain time, and so on. But none of this takes away from the banal fact that it was Fred who caused the glass to break, not his parents and not the person who built the floor.

By the same token, the interaction between genes and environment does not make it any less reasonable to say things like "Down syndrome is caused by certain genetic factors" or "Joe knows the word *rabbit* because he heard his father use it to refer to Flopsy." These are reasonable things to say; in fact, they are true. Some things are caused by the genes, and others by the environment. There are even genuine cases of interaction, in which both sources play a substantial causal role; cases like alcoholism and syntax come to mind. This division between genetics and environment is more than common sense; it is good science. If you want to see why a child has Down syndrome, you would look for a genetic cause, but if you want to see why he or she thinks rabbits are called *rabbits,* you would look toward the environment.

Distinguishing between genes and environment is not enough to save the notion of learning, however. After all, bullet wounds and tenure are caused by the environment, but there is no sense in which they are learned. The notion of learning picks out a subset of environmentally caused events, those in which the organism comes to store and represent information through a rational process (Fodor, 1981) of interaction with the environment. The caveat of "rational" is present to capture the intuition that not any interaction counts: if you get smacked in the head and miraculously come to know the rules of baseball, this wouldn't count as learning. But if you come to know baseball by observing other people play the game or by having someone explain the rules to you, then this does count as learning—even though, of course, this process would be impossible without the innate ability to learn.

This is a crude definition, but it captures the sense in which word learning counts as learning. In fact, word learning is the clearest case of learning one can imagine. Nobody was born knowing the meaning of the English word *rabbit.* Everyone who knows the word has heard *rabbit* used in a context in which its meaning could be recoverable from the environment using a rational process; that is, everyone who knows the meaning of *rabbit* has learned it. If you can stomach the terminology, I suspect this might be the least controversial claim in the study of language development.

Words

There are different notions of what a word is, not all of them appropriate for the study of word learning. One notion is that of a syntactic atom, something that can be a member of a category such as a noun or a verb and that can be the product of morphological rules (Pinker, 1994b). This notion is what morphologists have in mind, and it corresponds roughly to our intuitive notion of a word: a sound or sign that, if written down, corresponds to a string of letters that has spaces or punctuation marks on either side (Miller, 1996). Under this definition, the sentence *John stayed in the poker game until he got cleaned out* has 11 words, and this assessment is confirmed by the word count tool of my word processor, which uses this algorithm.

But this notion of word is unsuitable for certain psychological purposes, particularly if you are interested in what children have to learn. For instance, children do not have to learn the word *stayed.* What they do need to have learned is the verb *stay* and the morphological rule that adds *-ed* to transform verbs into the past tense. In general, it is clear that we can use and understand far more words (in the morphological sense) than we have learned. As soon as one learns the verb *stay*, then *stayed*, *staying*, and *stays* all come for free.

Idioms pose another problem. To understand the above sentence, it is not enough to have learned the verb *clean* and the preposition *out*; you also have to learn something else; the meaning of the idiom *clean out*, which means, roughly, to be totally deprived of something, usually money. As with many idioms, the meaning of the whole bears some relationship to the meaning of the parts (Gibbs & Nayak, 1989), but to fully understand the idiom you have to learn its meaning in much the same way as you would learn the meaning of the syntactic atoms *clean* and *out*.

Finally, consider *poker*. From a learning perspective, the string of letters is at least two words—a card game and a fireplace tool—and each meaning has to be learned separately. The individuation of words, then, must make some reference to meaning. This point is sometimes missed. As Miller and Wakefield (1993) point out, when studies ask how many words children and adults know, they often mean by *word* what lexicographers call a *lemma*—a listing in a dictionary. This has the advantage that *stay*, *stays*, *stayed*, and *staying* count as a single word, as do *zeugma* and *zeugmas*. But it has the disadvantage that *poker* is also counted as one word, despite its ambiguity.

The relevant sense of *word* from the standpoint of language acquisition should include all and only those forms whose meanings must be learned. This sense corresponds to *listemes*, units of a memorized list (Di Sciullo & Williams, 1987), or *minimal free forms* (Miller, 1996) or "the smallest semantic units that can move around in an utterance" (Clark, 1993) (though note that the second and third definitions exclude idioms). All these definitions have as their basis the notion of a Saussurian sign (Saussure, 1916/1959)—an arbitrary entity that has on one side a concept and on another, a form.

This is the sense I adopt here; when I talk about children learning words, I mean Saussurian signs. *Dog* is a word, then, but so is *clean out, hat trick, capital gains, kit and kiboodle,* and *Citizen Kane. Poker* has to be learned twice; it is two separate words. On the other hand, certain units that are words from the standpoint of other theories do not count as words for the purposes here, as they are not Saussurian signs. So while I will have a lot to say about how children come to know *dog*, I have nothing to say about how they come to know *dogs* or *dogcatcher*.

What makes this complicated is that words do not come with tags that they are Saussurian signs. A child who hears *poker* used to refer to a game and then, days later, *poker* used to refer to a tool has to figure out that these are two words and not one. A child who knows the meanings of *clean* and *out* and who hears that someone was "cleaned out" in a poker game has to figure out that this expression is an idiom and hence a sign that has to be learned. And a child who hears *stayed* has to realize that this is not itself a word that has to be learned, though it includes one. (Phonology is a good cue here, but the child does have to be wary; the adjective *staid* sounds the same as the verb, but it really is a Saussurian sign.)

In the end, then, both senses of *word* are relevant. The morphological sense—the sense that people use when they count the number of words in a manuscript—describes the input to the child. Long before learning the meanings of words, children have partially solved the problem of segmenting the sound stream into words in the morphological sense (Jusczyk, 1997). But what they have to *learn* are words in the Saussurian sense, arbitrary signs. This makes the task of word learning even more complex.

Meaning

What is it to know the meaning of a word? Some philosophers say there is no such thing. Quine did not use his Gavagai example to encourage developmental psychologists to search for cognitive constraints on children's inferences (though when Macnamara, 1972, introduced this example to the developmental community, this was ironically its effect); he used it to argue against the very idea of meanings in the head. What the problem of radical translation shows, Quine argued, is that the only robust notion of meaning is the behaviorist one of *stimulus meaning*—a person's disposition to respond to certain sensory stimulation. Other philosophers share this skepticism about meaning, and still others propose that while sentences have meanings, such as their truth conditions or their methods of verification, words do not.

Since I am talking about how children learn word meanings, this commits me to the view that such things as word meanings exist and can be learned and known. In particular, to know the meaning of a word is to have

1. a certain mental representation or concept
2. that is associated with a certain form.

Under this view, two things are involved in knowing the meaning of a word—having the concept and mapping the concept onto the right form. This is the sense of "knowing the meaning of a word" implicit in most discussions of language development, both scientific and informal. Saying, for instance, that a two-year-old has mixed up the meanings of *cat* and *dog* implies that the child has the right concepts but has mapped them onto the wrong forms. On the other hand, saying that the two-year-old does not know what *mortgage* means implies that the child lacks the relevant concept. People can also possess concepts that are not associated with forms. A child might have the concept of cat but not yet know the word, and even proficient adult users of a language can have concepts, such as of a dead plant or a broken computer, that they don't have words for.

If a concept is to constitute a word's meaning, it has to include some aspects of knowledge but not others. Consider what it is to know the meaning of *dog*. I once owned a dog named *Bingo*, but this knowledge cannot be part of the meaning of *dog* (at least as we normally talk about meaning) since someone could know *dog* even if they've never heard of Bingo. More generally, if the meaning of *dog* were determined by all thoughts related to dogs, then there would be no sense in which two people, or even a single person over time, could ever have the same meaning of a word. This is an undesirable consequence of an extremely holistic theory of meaning (Fodor & LePore, 1992).

Intuitively, then, only some aspects of knowledge are relevant to meaning. What are they? The traditional view, emerging first in Aristotle, is that the meaning of a word is what determines its reference. A word like *dog* has an extension (which entities the word refers to—dogs) and an intension (what the entities share—what all dogs have in common). Meaning is identified with the intension. While the intension of a word is not itself a psychological entity (Frege, 1892), it can be learned and understood. Hence the meaning of *dog* determines which things are and are not dogs, and knowing the meaning of *dog* entails knowing what things are and are not dogs.

As Murphy (1991) points out, this conception is implicit in almost all psychological discussions of the learning and representation of word meaning. One traditional view, for instance, is that meanings are pictures. The meaning of *dog* is a picture of a dog, and you know the meaning of *dog* if you have a mental representation of that picture that lets you tell the dogs from the nondogs. Another view is that meanings are identified with sets of necessary and sufficient conditions. The meaning of *bachelor* is said to be "unmarried man" because all and only bachelors are unmarried men, and hence you know *bachelor* when you map the form onto a concept that includes this definition. A currently popular notion is that meanings are sets of weighted feature and hence knowing the meaning of *dog* is to have a mental representation of the appropriate feature set, which will allow you to judge the extent to which different objects in the world are dogs. Other views include the idea that meanings are mental models, nodes in a semantic network, or sets of specific exemplars. These accounts all share the assumption that knowing the meaning of x involves being able to tell the differences between those things that are x and those things that are not.

There is, for instance, debate over how well prototype theory can explain our knowledge of words such as *chair* and *mother* (e.g., Armstrong, Gleitman & Gleitman, 1983; P. Bloom, 1996a; Malt & Johnson, 1992; Rosch et al., 1976), but the one thing that is agreed by all sides is that for prototype theory to work it must adequately capture patterns of categorization: it has to explain why we think that some things, but not others, are chairs and mothers. And when developmentalists talk about constraints on word meaning (Markman, 1989), inductions about word meaning (Soja, Carey & Spelke, 1991), or cues to word meaning (Gleitman, 1990), they are talking about constraints, inductions, and cues that pertain to the sorts of things children think words refer to.

This fits our commonsense idea of what it is to know the meaning of a word. If someone consistently uses *dog* to talk about tables, then this person does not know the meaning of this word. Conversely, if someone uses *dog* to talk about dogs and only dogs, then they do know the word, even if they have a lot of otherwise bizarre beliefs about dogs. Anyone who believes that dogs are expert chess players has a serious psychological problem, but we would not usually say that their problem is a *lexical* one. We are comfortable translating a word from an ancient Greek text into the English word *star*, even though the ancient Greeks believed that stars were holes in the sky. It is enough that we all use the word to refer to the same things; further cognitive overlap is not necessary.

For these reasons, relating word meaning to categorization seems like a reasonable strategy, and it is the one that I adopt throughout the discussions that follow. But serious objections to this view have been raised, and these have important ramifications for any psychological theory of concepts and meanings.

The main problem is this. It is true that when we talk about knowing the meaning of a word, we are usually thinking in terms of sameness of reference: we and the Greeks both mean the same thing by *star* because we are referring to the same things. But there are many cases in which our mental representations do not determine reference, and so if reference is central to meaning, then meaning is not determined by mental representation.

Consider some examples from Hilary Putnam (1975, 1988), which I slightly modify for my purposes here. Imagine a normal eight-year-old girl who uses the word *water* to refer to the stuff that she drinks, washes with, and swims in. She has clearly learned the meaning of the

English word and uses it to refer to the stuff that happens to be made up of H_2O (though she doesn't know this). Now imagine that there is another world, Twin Earth, that is exactly the same as ours, except that instead of being composed of H_2O the stuff that they call *water* is made up of different chemicals: XYZ. The eight-year-old will have an identical twin on Twin Earth, who uses *water* to refer to the substance that she drinks, washes with, and swims in. But her word does not refer to H_2O; it refers to XYZ (though she doesn't know this). If reference determines meaning, then the two girls use the words with different meanings, and, as Putnam (1975, p. 227) famously put it: "cut the pie any way you like, 'meanings' just ain't in the *head!*"

One can find the same situation without resorting to science fiction. Consider two boys, one raised in Boston, the other raised in London, and assume that they each have the same concept associated with the word *robin*; they each believe that robins are red-breasted birds, and this is all they know about them. The twist here is that *robin* in American English and *robin* in British English refer to different species of red-breasted bird. So which meaning do the boys have associated with *robin*—the American one or the British one? The most natural solution is that the Boston boy knows the American English meaning of the word and the British boy knows the British English meaning of the word. But this would again imply that there is more to meaning than human psychology.

One might be tempted to argue that neither boy knows the meaning of *robin* because this requires the actual ability to determine its precise reference; incomplete knowledge is not enough. But by these standards, most people do not know the meanings of many words: Can *you* tell robins from nonrobins? Or consider the word *gold*. Many people who use the word do not know what distinguishes gold from other metals and have no ability to make the distinction in practice. Similarly, I know the name *Moses* and so do you, but we might have entirely different beliefs about who the person is, and it is perfectly possible that we could discover that all of our beliefs about Moses are false (Kripke, 1980). Still, although we might lack the knowledge to pick out the unique substance that is gold or the unique person that is Moses, we nonetheless know the meanings of both words and use them to talk about the substance gold and the person Moses.

Matters get worse when we try to make sense of what is meant by *the* meaning of a word. What is the meaning of *disinterested?* One possibility is that it means "unbiased," as most dictionaries say; another is that it means "uninterested," as many English-speaking adults believe. Whatever the answer is—assuming that there is an answer—is not going to be solved by neurological and cognitive research. It is more of a sociological issue, related in complicated ways to notions of authority, expertise, community standards, and so on (Chomsky, 1995).

What moral should we draw from these cases? Putnam (1988) takes them as showing that a psychological theory cannot capture certain basic facts about meaning and reference. Hence such approaches are inherently limited; better to study word meanings in a social and embodied context. Chomsky (1995) draws the opposite conclusion. He argues that the above examples show that trying to build up a theory of semantics from notions such as reference is a waste of time. The only scientific theory will be an "internalist" one, the same sort that holds for aspects of language such as phonology and syntax. This point has been elaborated and extended by Ray Jackendoff, who distinguishes I-concepts (internal concepts) from E-concepts (external concepts) and who sees only the former as "a fruitful framework in which to conduct scientific inquiry" (1989, p. 100).

In either case, the conclusion is that there are two ways to think about meaning—the psychologist's way (as something identified with mental representations) and the philosopher's way (as something identified with reference). And, as David Lewis (1972, p. 170) remarks: "Only confusion comes from mixing these two topics."

But this seems rather extreme. After all, any adequate philosophical theory of reference and meaning must explain what it is about people that enables us to use words that have semantic properties. The fact that I can use the word *gold* to refer to gold, while not entirely explainable in terms of my cognitive structure, plainly has *something* to do with it. Conversely, one of the motivations for a psychological theory of concepts and meaning has always been to explain how we can think about, talk about, and categorize entities in the external world. It may well be that Chomsky and Jackendoff are correct that this is a wrongheaded approach. But there is not, at present, any worked-out alternative.

So what is meant by *the meaning of a word*? Following the lead of *two-factor theories* of semantics (e.g., Block, 1986), we can assume that there are two aspects (or determinants) of the meaning of a word—an internal psychological aspect, sometimes called *narrow content*, and an external social and contextual aspect, sometimes called *broad content*. These work together to determine what words refer to. In what follows, I use the expression *meaning of a word* to correspond to narrow content—to the psychological aspect of meaning. In the end, nothing rests on the terminology, and philosophical purists should feel free to replace my expression *meaning of a word* with the unwieldy but more modest expression *knowledge associated with a word that is relevant to explaining people's intuitions about reference and categorization*.

Still, even if one does adopt a two-factor theory, the phenomena pointed out by Putnam and others still seriously constrain any account, however internalist, of the meanings of words. They show that while possession of a concept might be intimately related to categorization ability, it does not reduce to it. One cannot say that children have learned the meaning of *gold* only when they can tell gold from nongold or have learned a proper name like *Moses* when only they can correctly pick out the person referred to by the name. By these standards, nobody knows the meanings of such words. The psychological part of knowing the meaning of a word has to be more subtle than this.

One final point. The program of relating word learning to issues of reference and categorization works best for common nouns like *dog* and *gold* and proper names like *Moses* and *Fido*. And it can be readily extended to some adjectives and verbs. But it works very poorly for words such as determiners, prepositions, and modals. The semantics of these terms is substantively different; these words get their meanings not by reference but by the roles that they play in modulating the meanings of other, referential, terms. It does complicate matters to say that there are (at least) two types of word meanings, one for *dog* and one for *the*. But the alternative—that all words are understood and learned in the same way—is not very promising.

Outline

Each of the following chapters is self-contained enough to be read on its own, but they do have a logical progression, and each rests to some extent on evidence and arguments introduced earlier.

The next chapter explores fast mapping—the rapid acquisition of the meanings of new words. It presents some data about the nature and scope of fast mapping and then turns to questions about the time course of word learning and individual differences in how words are learned. Why does word learning start when it does? Why does it speed up in the years to follow and slow down in adolescence? How do people differ in their word learning, and why?

Chapter 3 discusses children's appreciation of the mental states of others. Evidence is presented that this understanding underlies several aspects of the learning process, including how children know which entities in the world certain words refer to. When an understanding of intentions of others is partially absent, as with autistic children, there are devastating results.

Once children know what the word refers to, they have the further problem of figuring out whether the word is a common noun, referring to the kind (as in *rabbit*), a proper name (*Flopsy*), or a pronoun (*her*).

Common nouns are the topic of chapter 4, and pronouns and proper names are dealt with in chapter 5. While these chapters focus mostly on object names, they also discuss more abstract expressions, such as *family* and *London.*

Chapter 6 concerns the conceptual foundation of word learning—the nature of the concepts that constitute certain word meanings. Chapter 7 focuses on an important case study for any theory of concepts and naming—visual representations.

The idea that there are linguistic cues to word meaning is introduced early in the book, as such cues help explain how children learn names for objects, substances, and specific individuals. But they are far more important when it comes to learning the meaning of more abstract nouns, such as *mortgage* and *idea,* as well as for learning other parts of speech, such as verbs like *think* and adjectives like *blue.* This is the topic of chapter 8.

Chapter 9 addresses the learning of number words. These words show an interesting pattern of development and illustrate both the importance of linguistic cues and their limitations. Toward the end of this chapter, I explore the idea that the learning of number words might affect how we think about numbers. This raises the more general question, addressed in chapter 10, of how the words we learn affect our mental life. I suggest that language can affect thought, but only in certain circumscribed ways. The chapter concludes by arguing that the rich mental life of humans is the foundation of word learning; it is not the product of it.

Chapter 11 contains a brief summary and some general remarks.

Chapter 2

Fast Mapping and the Course of Word Learning

The average American or British high school graduate has learned about 60,000 words (Aitchinson, 1994; Miller, 1996; Pinker, 1994b). This is a rough estimate, and there are considerable individual differences. Some people learn many more words, others somewhat fewer, and those who know two or three languages might know two or three times as many. But 60,000 is a good conservative number. Since word learning starts at about 12 months of age, this averages to learning 3,750 new words a year, or 10 words a day—a word every waking 90 minutes.

This statistic is impressive, but it is misleading in a number of ways. Learning the precise meaning of certain words, especially verbs, might be a long process requiring many trials, as shown by the fact that even some relatively frequent verbs, such as *pour* and *fill*, are not fully understood until middle childhood (Gropen, Pinker, Hollander & Goldberg, 1991). On any given day, then, it might not be that children are learning 10 words; they might instead be learning one-hundredth of each of a thousand different words.

Also, word learning does not proceed at an even pace. It does take some of the drama away to realize that, despite what is often said in language-acquisition textbooks, three-year-olds are not learning even close to 10 words a day; it is more like 10 words a week. But in another sense this somewhat slow start makes the word-learning task all the more impressive—because it means that older children have to learn words at an even faster rate, such as 12 or 15 words per day, a word every waking hour.

Sixty thousand words are a lot to learn and remember. Learning a word requires memorizing an arbitrary relationship between a form and a meaning, and the rote learning of paired associates is notoriously slow and difficult. Consider how hard it is to learn the capitals of different countries or the birthdays of particular people. The recall of such arbitrary facts is also relatively slow. What is the capital of Spain? When is your mother's birthday? If it took you a half second to answer these questions, this is much slower than it took you to access the meaning of each of the words you are now reading. And although the vast majority of words we know are not frequently encountered, once heard or read—*putrid, centrifuge, apostle, fawning*—they are immediately understood. There is no denying the impressiveness of word learning.

This chapter addresses three general issues. The first concerns the nature of the word-learning process. How much input do children need to learn a new word? Do children learn words better than adults? And to what extent does word learning differ from other types of learning? The second issue is the time course of word learning—when it starts, when it stops, and what happens in between. And the third issue is individual differences: What differences exist, what causes them, and what do they tell us about the process of word learning?

Fast Mapping

Young children can grasp aspects of the meaning of a new word on the basis of a few incidental exposures, without any explicit training or feedback—in fact, even without any explicit act of naming. In the first experiment to systematically explore this phenomenon, Carey and Bartlett (1978) casually introduced a new color word to three- and four-year-old children who were involved in another, unrelated activity. The children were asked by the experimenter to walk over to two trays, a blue one and an olive one, and to "Bring me the chromium tray, not the blue one, the chromium one." All of the children retrieved the olive tray, correctly inferring that the experimenter intended "chromium" to refer to this new color. When tested a week later on their comprehension of the word, over half of the children remembered something about its meaning, either that it named olive or that it named a color that resembled olive. In another study, children were taught the word, tested after a week, and then given a production test five weeks later. Even six weeks after hearing the new word, children typically retained some understanding of its meaning, if only that it was a color term (Carey, 1978). Susan Carey (1978) has dubbed this process of quick initial learning *fast mapping*.

Heibeck and Markman (1987) expanded on this research in certain ways, obtaining some interesting results. First, even two-year-olds can fast map new words. Second, fast mapping is not limited to color words; children can fast map shape and texture terms as well. Shape is easiest of the three to learn, texture hardest, and color falls in between. Finally, explicit linguistic contrast is not necessary. Children don't need to hear something like "Bring me the chromium tray, not the blue one," in which the novel word is explicitly contrasted with an existing color term; they do just as well if they simply hear "Bring me the chromium tray, not the other one."

There is one way in which the Heibeck and Markman (1987) study was quite different from the original Carey and Bartlett (1978) study. In the original study, children were tested after a gap of one week and six weeks. For Heibeck and Markman, the gap between teaching and testing was 10 minutes. This short gap is common in word learning research, even in studies that are specifically designed to study fast mapping (e.g., Dollaghan, 1985; Rice, 1990). In fact, given the prominence of the Carey and Bartlett study, and even though there have been countless subsequent studies in which children have been taught new words and then tested for what they think these words mean, there are almost no experiments that replicate one of the most interesting features of the original study—the long delay between exposure to the new word and testing for its retention. Teaching children new words and immediately testing them on what they think the words mean is a fine way of exploring their conceptual and linguistic biases. But it tells us little about the retention capacity so manifest in normal word learning, and so certain basic questions about word learning that were raised by the Carey and Bartlett study remain unanswered.

First, color names constitute a relatively narrow domain, with universal constraints on the terms that exist and the order in which they are acquired (e.g., Berlin & Kay, 1969). In contrast, there are thousands of object names, and these show vastly more variability across cultures, as their referents include foods (*apple, bagel*), animals (*dog, snake*), artifacts (*clock, car*), and so on. It is a natural question whether fast mapping applies for these words as well.

Second, is there any difference between children's and adults' abilities to fast map? One might expect adults to be better, since they have had more experience acquiring words and are usually more adept at learning and memory tasks. Nevertheless, young children are notably superior to adults at successful acquisition in the linguistic domains of phonology, morphology, and syntax (Newport, 1990), and it is conceivable that a similar critical period might exist in lexical acquisition.

Finally, is the ability to fast map limited to word learning? Children's capacity to quickly learn new words on the basis of limited experience is frequently cited as showing how good they are at language learning. But it is possible that this capacity emerges through more general capacities of learning and memory. This issue can be addressed by seeing whether fast mapping of arbitrary information occurs with equal force in contexts other than word learning.

Lori Markson and I have addressed these questions in a series of studies designed to be similar to the original Carey and Bartlett study.

In one study (Markson & Bloom, 1997), three-year-olds, four-year-olds, and adults first participated in a sequence of activities in which they measured different objects in a variety of ways. There were 10 kinds of objects—six of them novel (in the sense that adults found them unfamiliar and were not able to name them) and four of them familiar (such as pennies). Subjects were asked to use some of the objects to measure other objects. For instance, in one of the tasks, subjects were requested to use pennies to measure the circumference of a plastic disk.

Children were told that this was a game, and adults were told that this was a game designed to teach young children how to measure objects. The experiment was structured so that the subjects spent equal time playing with and interacting with all the objects.

In the course of this training phase, all of the subjects were exposed to a new word applied to one of the unfamiliar objects that was presented in a context such as the following: "Let's use the koba to measure which is longer. . . . We can put the koba away now." Subjects were not asked to repeat the word, and no effort was made to ascertain whether they even noticed that a new word was being introduced.

In addition to the new word, half of the subjects were given a linguistically presented fact in precisely the same way. They were told that one of the novel objects was given to the experimenter by her uncle: "Let's use the thing my uncle gave to me to measure which is longer. . . . We can put the thing my uncle gave to me away now."

The other half of the subjects were given a visually presented fact (this was based on a similar condition by Dollaghan, 1985). They watched as a sticker was placed on one of the unfamiliar objects and were told, "Watch where this goes. This goes here [placing the sticker onto one of the objects]. That's where this goes."

One-third of the subjects were tested immediately after this training phase, one-third after a one-week delay, and one-third after a one-month delay. During the test phase, subjects were presented with the original array of 10 items used during the training phase. They were asked to recall which object was the koba ("Is there a koba here? Can you show me a koba?"). Those subjects taught the linguistically presented fact were also asked, "Is there something here that my uncle gave to me? Can you show me something that my uncle gave to me?" Subjects exposed to the visually presented fact were handed a small sticker and told, "Put this where it goes. Can you show me where this goes?"

Before turning to the results, consider what counts as chance performance. There are 10 objects shown during the test trial. If subjects forget the word, the obvious prediction is that they should be correct only about 10 percent of the time. But there is a subtlety here that applies to the word task. Four of the objects that they see in the test phase have familiar names. Since people tend to infer that a novel word refers to something that does not already have a name (Markman & Wachtel, 1988; see chapter 3), they might assume that the word must refer to one of the six unfamiliar objects, even if they have no memory of having heard it before. Here, then, chance for the word task should be calculated as a more conservative one sixth, or 17 percent. The results are shown in figure 2.1.

In the new word task, children and adults in all three delay conditions performed significantly above chance. Adults were better than children when tested immediately, but after a week and a month, three-year-olds and four-year-olds were doing as well as adults, and all age groups remembered which object was the koba over half of the time, far better than chance. In the linguistically presented fact task, the results are basically identical. All age groups again performed significantly better than chance in all delay conditions. There were no age differences and no significant decline across delay conditions. In contrast, in the visually presented fact task, adult performance was considerably diminished after a week and a month, and the three-year-olds and four-year-olds, taken together, showed a significant decline over time and did significantly worse than in the koba and uncle conditions. Only the adults performed significantly better than chance after a one-month delay; the children's performance was indistinguishable from guessing.

We can now return to the three questions raised earlier. First, fast mapping does apply to object names. Even after a one-month interval, most children and adults retained the meaning of an object name that was presented to them in an incidental context. Second, there does not appear to be a critical period for fast mapping: adults and children tend to perform equally well. Finally, fast mapping is not limited to word learning. Children and adults were as good at remembering an arbitrary linguistically presented fact about an entity as they were at remembering what the entity was called. Nevertheless, fast mapping does not apply to any arbitrary memorization task, as illustrated by the children who, after a one-month delay, were unable to recall which object a sticker was applied to.

One possible objection to this experiment is as follows. Suppose children really are better at fast mapping words than facts. This difference could be obscured in the experiment above because learning the new word condition involves storing novel phonological information (the sound *koba*) while the uncle condition does not. If the uncle condition also involved memorizing a novel sound, perhaps learning the word would be easier.

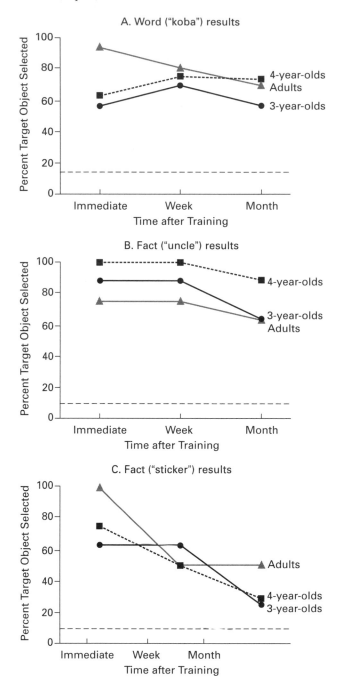

Figure 2.1
Three-year-olds', four-year-olds', and adults' recall of novel words (A) and novel facts (B, C) (from Markson & Bloom, 1997)

Table 2.1
Children's and adults' recall of a fact that contains a novel word

| | Percent Correct | |
	Children	Adults
"koba" (from original study)	65%	69%
"uncle" (from original study)	75	63
"came from a place called Koba"	77	60

To test this, we ran another experiment in which children and adults were taught an arbitrary fact that included an unfamiliar word (Markson & Bloom, 1997). Specifically, they were taught that one of the unfamiliar objects "came from a place called Koba." They were tested on their memory of the new fact after a one-month delay by being asked to recall which object "came from a place called Koba."

The results are shown in table 2.1. Children and adults performed significantly above chance in this condition, and there were no significant differences between participants' ability to recall which object "came from a place called Koba" and their performance on the koba and uncle conditions. This alleviates the above concern about task complexity.

What did subjects learn in these studies? They might have learned that a specific word or fact is mapped onto an object. But another, less interesting possibility is that they just learned that such-and-so object has *some* novel word or fact associated with it, without remembering which one. For instance, when, during testing, subjects were asked to find "the koba," they might have had no memory of the specific word. But they did remember that a certain object had some novel name associated with it, and since *koba* is certainly a novel name, they guessed correctly.

To explore this, another group of subjects was asked about words and facts that were different from the ones they were taught. If people do not remember the specific word or fact that they were taught, then their responses should not differ from those in the original study; they should still pick the original object. On the other hand, if they do remember the specific word or fact, then they should recognize that the item they are being asked about is different and should not choose the original object.

Subjects were taught either a new word ("koba") or a new fact ("the one my uncle gave me"). They were tested a month later; they were asked to "show me a modi" or "give me the one my sister gave me." The results are shown in table 2.2.

Table 2.2
Children's and adults' choice of the original object when asked about words and facts different from those that they were originally taught

	Percent Choice of the Original Object	
	Children	Adults
Taught "koba," asked for "koba" (from original study)	69%	65%
Taught "koba," asked for "modi"	19	19
Taught "from uncle," asked "from uncle" (from original study)	75	93
Taught "from uncle," asked "from sister"	13	13

Table 2.3
Two-year-olds' recall of novel words and novel facts

	Percent Correct	
	Immediate	One-Week Delay
Word	81%	81%
Fact	88	75

When tested on a word or fact that was not originally taught, subjects tended not to choose the original object. These results show that, in general, when tested a month after hearing a specific word or fact applied to an object, subjects tend to remember what that word or fact is (Markson, 1999).

What about fast mapping by younger children? A group of two-year-olds was tested on a simpler version of the original study, using only four objects, all of which were novel. They were tested either immediately or after a week delay, and the results are shown in table 2.3. In all conditions, children did significantly better than chance, and there was again no difference between the new word and the new fact (Markson, 1999).

What do these findings tell us about the mechanisms of word learning? It is conceivable that two distinct capacities or mechanisms explain our results—one explaining performance on the new word task and the other explaining performance on the nonlexical uncle task. But this is an unparsimonious way to explain the data. Given two patterns of learning that are virtually identical, it is simpler to see them as emerging from one mechanism and not two. More generally, since children and adults seem to have a general ability to fast map, there is no motivation to posit a separate mechanism that applies only in the domain of word learning.

One might object that similarities in how words and facts are remembered do not directly bear on the question of how words and facts are learned. Perhaps words are learned in an entirely different way from facts; it is just that in both cases the information is stored in the same sort of memory.

This is a valid point, but one needs to keep in mind that fast mapping, as I have been using the term here, includes not only the ability to store information for a long period of time but also the ability to learn the information in the first place. So there are two parallels between words and facts: one has to do with memory; the other has to do with learning. In the studies above, the fact conditions were virtually identical to the word conditions. Most notably, the facts and the words were taught in the same linguistic and pragmatic context ("Let's use the _____ to measure which is longer"). The finding that both types of information could be learned under these quite minimal circumstances suggests that the cognitive mechanisms that underlie word learning also apply more generally.

This isn't to deny that words have special properties. They do, and some of the next chapter discusses what they are and how children learn about them. But the findings reviewed above do suggest that the act of learning and storing words in memory—the act of fast mapping—involves cognitive mechanisms that apply to facts as well.

What is the scope of fast mapping? What sorts of information can be fast mapped? Given how little we know about the process, and since we only have one reliable case in which fast mapping does not fully apply (the sticker condition, in which the fact is learned but not recalled after a long delay), there is no shortage of possibilities. Perhaps it applies only to information conveyed through language. Or perhaps salience is the key factor, and our subjects simply found the name of the object and its origin to be more *interesting* than the placement of the sticker and hence easier to remember. A third possibility (independently suggested by Dare Baldwin and Susan Carey) is that fast mapping applies only in circumstances in which the information is seen as relevant to the category that an object belongs to. This would be consistent with the notion that fast mapping is intimately tied to our understanding of categories or kinds, and it raises the intriguing possibility that fast mapping should not apply to proper names, as these refer to individuals and not to kinds.

A different possibility is that fast mapping applies only to information that cannot be accessed through observation. There is, after

Table 2.4
Three-year-olds' and adults' recall of a novel word, a hidden fact, and an observable fact

| | Percent Correct | | |
	Word	Inside Color	External Color
Three-year-olds	87%	81%	50%
Adults	63	75	44

all, a functional motivation for a fast-mapping mechanism to apply in exactly these cases. The location of a sticker is an observable property; this information is "stored in the world," and there is no need to store it in the head. If you forget where the sticker is, just have another look. And in fact, adults are often oblivious to dramatic changes across a visual scene, even for objects that are the direct focus of attention, a phenomenon known as *change blindness*. In one striking demonstration of this, an experimenter started a conversation with a pedestrian and then, during a distraction, was surreptitiously replaced by a different experimenter. Only about half of the pedestrians noticed the change (Simons & Levin, 1998). Unless there is conscious encoding, most observable information does not enter memory.

An object's name and where it comes from, however, are social and historical facts, accessible only through attending to what others say. If you forget this information, you might never encounter it again. For these sorts of facts, fast mapping could be crucial.

We have just begun to test this hypothesis, but one finding is promising. In one study, we showed three-year-olds and adults a novel object, commented on its external color ("You can start with the blue one"), its name ("This is a koba"), and its internal color, which could not be observed ("which is white on the inside"). A week later, subjects were shown a black-and-white picture of the object and asked about its name and its internal and external color. In this situation, more information was actually given during training about the external color: subjects were told about it *and* they could see it. But our prediction was that, since the external color was available to perception and the internal color was not, it would be the internal color that would be fast mapped. The results are as shown in table 2.4.

Subjects tended to recall the object's name and its internal color but did significantly worse on its external, observable, color. These findings are consistent with the view that fast mapping emerges from a general capacity to learn socially transmitted information—including, but not limited to, the meanings of words. This connects nicely with evidence for the role of social cognition in word learning, something that is a theme throughout this book.

The Course of Word Learning

One account of word learning goes like this. Children's first words are not really words in the adult sense; they are nonsymbolic and nonreferential. Children have no initial appreciation of notions such as reference and meaning; first words are learned through a simple associative process. Then, at about 16 months, or after learning about 50 words, a sudden acceleration occurs in the rate of word learning—a word spurt. This marks the point at which children are serious word learners, capable of acquiring and understanding words in a mature fashion. From 18 months on, they can pick up new words on the basis of a single trial, learning them at the rate of five, 10, or even 20 new words a day.

I suggest that all the above claims are false. There is no evidence that children's words differ from adults' words or that they learn these words in a substantially different way. And there is no sudden acceleration in word learning. The word spurt is a myth.

First Words

Children show some understanding of words before they start to speak. In one study, Larry Fenson and his colleagues (1994) asked parents to report how many words their children produced and how many they understood. Based on these reports, Fenson et al. concluded that eight-month-olds have a median receptive vocabulary of about 15 words, with children in the top 10 percent understanding over 80 words. Ten-month-olds are said to have a median receptive vocabulary of about 35 words, with children in the top 10 percent understanding over 150 words. These numbers are a bit astonishing, and it is a legitimate concern that they could be inflated by enthusiastic parents, who might have overly generous criteria as to what counts as understanding a word (Tomasello & Mervis, 1994). There is, after all, a difference between recognizing a word as familiar, something that even five-month-olds can do (Jusczyk, 1997), and knowing what the word means. Nevertheless, there is little doubt that before children start to talk, they know the meanings of at least some words.

Children start using words at about 10 to 14 months (Bates, Bretherton & Snyder, 1988; L. Bloom, 1973; Dromi, 1987; Fenson et al., 1994). These words have aberrant phonologies: they sound funny. They are seen as corresponding to words in the adult language largely because of the contexts in which they are used. For instance, if a child points and says "daw" when a dog enters the room, this would be counted, by a parent or a psychologist, as showing that he or she has learned the English word *dog*. This method of attribution is what Lois Bloom (1970) calls *rich interpretation*.

Considerable debate has been engaged in over the nature of children's earliest words. Many investigators have suggested that the word spurt said to occur later in development is caused by a dramatic change in the ability to learn and understand words; this change makes adult-like word learning possible. Prior to the word spurt, children's first words differ radically from those of adults (e.g., Dromi, 1978; Nelson, 1988). They are not semantically constrained in the right way and are learned in a slow associative fashion, without the support of lexical constraints.

This sort of discontinuity between early and later words is sometimes proposed from the standpoint of a constructivist theory of development, in which children gradually learn, though experience with language, just how words work. But a discontinuity is also consistent with the idea that there is a distinct language capacity that underlies word learning, one that emerges through neural maturation. Such a capacity might not have matured by the time children start to speak. Noam Chomsky (1975, p. 53), for instance, suggests that "It is possible that at an early stage there is use of language-like expressions, but outside the framework imposed . . . by the faculty of language—much as a dog can be trained to respond to certain commands, though we would not conclude, from this, that it is using language."

But does such a discontinuity really exist? Consider the claim that early words have bizarre meanings. Lois Bloom (1973) reports that Allison used the word *car* only when watching cars move on the street below the living room window. Melissa Bowerman (1978) notes that Eva used *moon* to talk about, among other things, a half grapefruit, the dial of a dishwasher, and a hangnail. Eve Clark (1973) gives the example of a child who called a doorknob *apple*. My son, Max, at 20 months, put a slice of yellow pepper on his head during dinner one evening, and said "hat." A month later, when we were perusing a book called *Trucks*, I pointed to the ice cream cone affixed to the top of an ice cream truck, and asked him what it is. I expected him to say "ice cream," a word he knows well, but instead he said "pee-pee," which is his word for penis. And indeed, the cone *was* shaped like a penis, though I hope that wasn't the intent of the illustrator.

First words are also said to blur the semantic distinctions between objects, properties, and actions. Children have been observed to use *hot* to talk about both the property of being hot and also to refer to certain objects, such as ovens and radiators. Esther Dromi (1978), in her careful diary study of the acquisition of Hebrew, found that her daughter's early words frequently referred to both objects and actions, such as the use of the verb meaning "to fly" to refer to birds.

These funny utterances may be signs of an incomplete understanding of word meanings, either because children have not yet figured out how words work or because they possess an immature faculty of language. But there are other interpretations.

First, all these examples are based on observations of productive speech, not comprehension, and some might be speech errors, slips of the tongue. There is independent evidence, after all, that children have greater problems with lexical retrieval than adults and are more error prone in their speech (Marcus et al., 1992).

Second, some of the examples might not be errors at all. When one takes into account that these children don't know many words and have no productive syntax, many of these utterances might be perfectly reasonable. For instance, children have been observed to point at a cookie jar and say "cookie." One might say that this reflects a profound confusion: the child thinks that the word refers not only to cookies but to all cookie-related entities. But perhaps the child thinks that there is a cookie in the cookie jar, doesn't know the words *jar* and *in*, and is expressing her thought in a sensible way (Huttenlocher & Smiley, 1987). Similarly, a child who says "cookie" only while in a highchair might have a bizarre contextualized meaning for the word, in which it can be used only in a certain situation—but might also know that the highchair is the place for eating, and requesting, cookies. And there is nothing at all wrong about calling a stove "hot" or saying "flying" about a bird, so long as one is expressing the opinions that the stove is hot and the bird is flying. After all, if I see a nice car go by, I might say "Nice!" This doesn't mean that I have my object names and property names mixed up.

Related to this, it has often been pointed out that when children call a doorknob "apple," it could mean that they are observing that the doorknob is *like* an apple. Overextensions are especially likely if children don't know the right word for what they wish to talk about. As Lois Bloom (1973, p. 79) puts it, using another example: "It is almost as if the child were reasoning: 'I know about dogs, that thing is not a dog, I don't know what to call it, but it is like a dog!'"

Sometimes it is clear that children are using words in a nonliteral fashion, as when a two-year-old says that wheeling searchlights on top of a building are "like a helicopter" (Macnamara, 1982). And I suspect that when Max put the pepper on his head, he didn't think it was *really* a hat. He found the situation extremely amusing, after all, much more so than normal hat-wearing and hat-naming. His naming is plausibly seen as an early instance of pretend play or, to use a more weighted expression, metaphor. This is also true for the ice cream truck; when his mother asked him to name the depicted object about an hour later, he said "pee-pee" again, but that was the last time. When asked again several days later, he went back to "ice cream." As Macnamara notes, even Shakespeare was a baby once.

It is a fair objection to point out that just about any error on the part of children can be explained (or explained away) as an honest mistake, a speech error, a metaphor, and so on. And in the end, it may well be that some of children's early word meanings really do not conform to the sorts of meanings that older children and adults have. It is hard to disprove such a claim. But there are by now large-scale studies of child language that tell a different story. On the basis of one extensive study of the speech of 10 children, systematically examining the contexts in which the words were used, Janellen Huttenlocher and Patricia Smiley (1987, p. 82) conclude that "from the earliest usages, the extensions of children's object names are like those of adults. . . . we find no evidence of restriction of word use to objects in particular location or action contexts. Furthermore, while words are sometimes used in the absence of category instances, we have presented evidence that these utterances do not reflect overgeneral complexive meanings."

Similarly, Leslie Rescorla (1980, p. 334) reports the results of an analysis of the speech of six children from 12 to 20 months of age and concludes that "normal extension and overextension are two aspects of the same basic process. In both cases, extension is generated in the same manner, is based on many of the same criteria of application, and takes place over the same period. . . . While children do make some errors in their early application of words, these errors are generally rule-governed and systematic."

In other words, overextensions do occur, but they are typically reasonable ones, honest mistakes. For instance, a child who calls a cat "dog" might genuinely think that the cat belongs to the category of dogs. This is wrong, but it is not perverse. It is the sort of mistake that an adult who had very limited experience with dogs and cats might make. The same holds for more taxonomic errors that are not based on shape, as when a child names a sock as "shoe" (Dromi, 1987) (see chapter 6 for discussion).

One final piece of evidence for early sophistication with words emerges from Katherine Nelson's landmark study of 18 children's first 50 words (Nelson, 1973). As she points out, one sign that children know what words are is pointing at things and asking about their names. Two-year-olds can ask "What's that?," but younger children can ask the same question by pointing and saying something like "Wha?," "Tha," or "Eh?" Interestingly, this sometimes occurs early in lexical development. Most of the children Nelson studied had a deictic pronoun that was used in just this way by the time they learned 50 words—and six of the children had one such pronoun among their first 10 words. Going back to Chomsky's speculation about the nature of early speech, it's worth noting that asking about the names of things isn't something that dogs do.

What about the children's ability to learn words? As we will see, young children learn new words at a much slower rate than older children. But it is not clear that they learn words in a different way. There is evidence that when the task is made easy enough, fast mapping occurs even with very young children. In a study by Oviatt (1980), one-year-olds were introduced to a live animal, such as a rabbit, and told its name ("rabbit") When later asked a question such as "Where's the rabbit?," half of the 12- to 14-month-olds looked and gestured toward the rabbit—but they did not do so when asked about a nonsense word: "Where's the kawlow?"

In another set of studies, 13- and 18-month-olds were told the name of a novel object nine times in a five-minute session ("That's a tukey. See, it's a tukey. Look, it's a tukey."). Another novel object was present and commented on ("Oooo, look at that. Yeah, see it? Wow, look at that.") but was not named. When the children were later asked to point out "the tukey," even 13-month-olds could do so better than chance. Remarkably, they even succeeded with a 24-hour delay between being taught the new word and being tested (Woodward, Markman & Fitzsimmons, 1994).

The Word Spurt
After the first words are acquired, there is often said to be a dramatic change in how words are learned. As Dorothea McCarthy (1954, p. 526) wrote, "After the appearance of the first few words used consistently with meaning in appropriate situations, there occurs a rapid increase in vocabulary." This is sometimes said to occur just with names (in which case it is called a *naming explosion*) or with vocabulary as a whole (and called a *word burst, word spurt,* or *vocabulary spurt*). It is said to occur once children have learned about 50 words, at the age of about 16 to 19 months (Benedict, 1979; Goldfield & Reznick, 1990; Nelson, 1973), though some investigators have found it occurs later, sometimes just prior to the emergence of productive syntax (Dromi, 1987; Mervis & Bertrand, 1995). This spurt might be caused by—among other things—the child's insight that language is symbolic (Dore, 1978; McShane, 1979), the emerging ability to categorize in a mature fashion

(Gopnik & Meltzoff, 1986), the onset of word-learning constraints (Behrend, 1990), or the nonlinear dynamics of a connectionist learning procedure (Plunkett, Sinha, Møller & Strandsby, 1992).

The existence of a word spurt is often presented as an undisputed fact. Several studies look at longitudinal data, find when the word spurt occurs, and then explore its relationship to other facets of language and cognition, such as children's object sorting or their understanding of syntax. But these studies have an odd definition of what counts as a spurt. They count children as going through a spurt when they learn words at a certain *rate*, such as 10 or more new object names in a three-week period (Gopnik & Meltzoff, 1986), 12 or more new words in a three-week period (Lifter & Bloom, 1989), 10 or more words in a two-and-a-half week period (Goldfield & Reznick, 1990), or 10 or more new words in a two-week period, at least five of which are object names (Mervis & Bertrand, 1995). Reznick and Goldfield (1992) have a similar criterion for a word spurt in comprehension: two new words in 2.5 weeks, taken from a list of words that are expected to be difficult.

What's wrong with these criteria? Note first that, by adult standards, children who have had a word spurt according to these investigators are still learning words at a relatively slow rate—less than a word a day. If they stuck to this rate, they would end up with an adult vocabulary of about 4,500 words—a far cry from the 60,000 estimate. So when one defines *word spurt* in this way, it is no longer an empirical question whether it exists. Its existence is a mathematical necessity, simply because 17-year-olds know far more than 4,500 words.

A more serious problem is that the criteria above have nothing to do with a spurt (or burst or explosion) in any normal sense of the term. To see why, consider figure 2.2, which represents the rate of vocabulary development in two imaginary children.

Using the Mervis and Bertrand (1995) criteria, both children go through a word spurt in the period right before they reach 18 months; they each learn 10 new words. But only Zack undergoes a spurt in any meaningful sense of the term. Zoe shows a gradual increase in the rate of word learning. The criteria used by these investigators tell us when children start to learn words at a certain rate (something that may be of interest for other purposes); they tell us nothing about the nature of the change in vocabulary growth.

This is more than a quibble about terminology; it really matters. The theories of the word spurt mentioned above all assume that *something interesting* happens at the point of the word spurt. This seems true for Zack. But it is not at all true for Zoe; nothing interesting happens to her prior to 18 months, nothing that distinguishes this point in time from the period before and the period after.

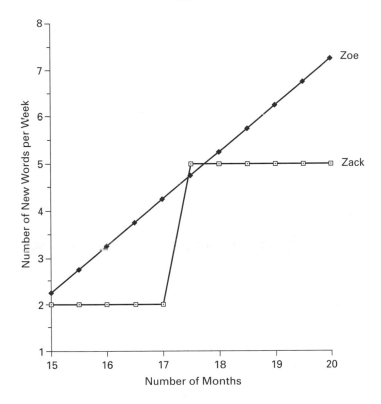

Figure 2.2
Changes in the vocabulary growth of two imaginary children

Consider an analogy. If Joe has eaten 40 french fries in 10 minutes, there has to be some period of time in which he eats french fries at the rate of more than 2.5 per minute. But this does not entail a "starch spurt" or "french fry explosion." One *might* occur: Joe might nibble at his fries at a leisurely rate for the first nine minutes and 30 seconds and then gobble down the rest in the remaining half minute. But it is also possible that Joe could eat his fries at a constant rate. Or he could eat one fry in the first minute and then slowly speed up his rate of fry eating. There would be no spurt, just a gradual increase. To point to the moment he starts eating fries at the rate of 2.5 per minute and say "Aha! That's an eating explosion" is worse than bad terminology. It leads to bad theorizing, since it gives the false impression that something special is happening at this point, something that has to be explained.

In a perceptive discussion of these issues, Jeffrey Elman and his colleagues (1996) suggest that vocabulary development might in fact

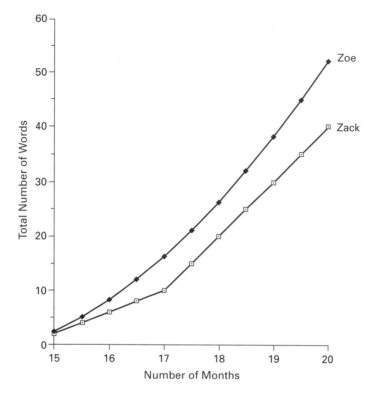

Figure 2.3
Changes in the vocabulary sizes of two imaginary children

exhibit a gradual linear increase in rate (see also Bates & Carnevale, 1993). Studies of vocabulary growth typically present their data in terms of overall vocabulary *size*, not rate of acquisition, and figure 2.3 depicts how the data from the imaginary children look when they are transformed into such graphs. The precise shapes of the curves depend on arbitrary choices about how fast the imaginary children learn words. What isn't arbitrary is that if a child has a gradual increase in the rate of word learning, it will show up as a smoothly accelerating function in vocabulary size. If a child actually has a word spurt, it will show up as a sudden increase in the *slope* of the line that corresponds to vocabulary size.

An examination of the available data supports Elman et al.'s hypothesis that the development of vocabulary is similar to Zoe, not to Zack (e.g., Benedict, 1979; Dromi, 1987). This isn't to say that word learning always shows a gradual linear increase in rate. Nothing in life is that elegant. If a child is sick, for instance, she might spend a day in bed and be exposed to no new words; if she goes to a zoo, she might be exposed to exciting new animals and learn several words. Some children go through long periods in which their rate of word learning remains constant, like Damon (Clark, 1993), while others show a gradual exponential increase in rate, like Keren (Dromi, 1987).

Note also that estimates of vocabulary size are indirect; they are based on observations of what children say, which is an imperfect reflection of what they know. This fact might account for some otherwise puzzling facts about word learning. For instance, some scholars have discovered *dips* in the rate of the vocabulary growth of their children (Dromi, 1987). These are sometimes explained in terms of children's shifting of resources away from word learning to learn syntax (van Geert, 1991), but there is a simpler account: the dips are statistical artifacts. Children can produce only a finite number of words each day, and so, as their vocabulary increases, any single new word is less likely to be uttered and hence less likely to be noticed by an observer. This is clear enough when you consider extremes. Suppose, for instance, that a child has a vocabulary of 20 words and begins to add new words at a rate of five per week. She goes from 20 words to 25 words. Compare this to an adult who is doing a lot of reading and increasing her vocabulary at the same rate. She goes from 85,000 words to 85,005 words. Which change is more noticeable?

Nothing in what I have said above precludes the possibility that a word spurt could happen for some children. It would not be difficult to see if it did occur. One could graph the child's vocabulary growth and look for a dramatic (or at least statistically significant) change in the slope of the line denoting rate of growth. (Note that the graph has to be of an individual child, not aggregate data, and has to be of rate, not size.) This is a simple criterion, but, as far as I know, no evidence is available that any child has ever met it.

Later Word Learning
By the age of 17 months, children are learning words at the rate of about five per week. This rate speeds up in the months and years that follow. To see how the rate of word learning changes over time, consider the following estimates of rate of vocabulary growth by children of different ages. The ones up to 30 months are from Fenson et al. (1994) based on parental reports of children's vocabulary sizes. The ones with six-, eight-, and 10-year-olds are from Anglin (1993), based on comprehension studies that use a representative sample of dictionary entries. (For the estimates below, Anglin included only those words whose meanings could not be figured out using "problem-solving" strategies

and hence must be learned.) Judging vocabulary size is tricky for several reasons (see Miller & Wakefield, 1993), so these numbers should be taken only as rough approximations. Still, the pattern is suggestive:

12 months to 16 months	0.3 words per day
16 months to 23 months	0.8 words per day
23 months to 30 months	1.6 words per day
30 months to 6 years	3.6 words per day
6 years to 8 years	6.6 words per day
8 years to 10 years	12.1 words per day

This increase in the rate of word learning has to stop sometime; adults are not learning dozens of words a day. This decline might start where Anglin leaves off. He calculates that the vocabulary size of a 10-year-old is about 40,000 words. If we take the 60,000 estimate as gospel, this leaves 20,000 words to learn in seven years—about eight words a day, though we know nothing about how the rate of word learning might change in the course of these years. All we can say with certainty is that word learning typically reaches its peak not at 18 months but somewhere between 10 and 17 years.

Explaining the Course of Word Learning

Several questions arise from the facts reviewed above, including the following:

- Why does word learning start at about the age of 12 months?
- Why does the rate of word learning gradually increase from the age of 12 months to sometime after the age of 10?
- Why does the rate of word learning slow down sometime before the age of 17?

"Why" questions are notoriously ambiguous, and it is worth being clear that strictly functional answers will not do for our purposes here. One might argue that there are excellent selective advantages to being able to learn words at such-and-so age and this explains why we have evolved to do so. And such a proposal might be right, but our concern here is the further question of precisely what happens at that age, for any individual child, that makes word learning possible. Explanations solely in terms of neural development are incomplete for the same reason. It might be that word learning starts because of, say, a dramatic increase in synaptic connectivity, but we would still need to know what higher-level capacity (phonological? conceptual? memory?) this neurological change gives rise to.

In the end, nobody knows why word learning starts at about 12 months and not at six months or three years. But we can reject certain hypotheses. Syntactic knowledge is often argued to facilitate word learning. But it is very unlikely that the onset of word learning can be explained in terms of the timing of the onset of syntactic knowledge. At least some words can be learned without the help of syntax, and very young children seem oblivious to the syntax of a word when learning its meaning (e.g., Waxman & Markow, 1995).

Another possibility that can be rejected is that the onset of word learning is explained by environmental factors, such as how parents speak to children of different ages. Some aspects of development are plainly explained this way. Questions such as why children stop breast feeding at one age or start learning to use a toilet at another, while constrained by psychological and physiological factors, plainly deserve an answer in cultural terms. But nothing special happens to children at about 12 months that makes them start learning words, and the individual variation that exists, at least within a culture, is not traceable to how parents interact with their children. In this regard, word learning is different from weaning and toilet training.

Also, the onset of word learning cannot be entirely explained in terms of the development of motor control capacities involved in speech. The onset of words—as well as other milestones of language development—is the same across spoken and signed languages (Petitto, 1992). Furthermore, appealing to motor control can't address the emergence of language comprehension, only production. So even if it were true that the point at which children begin to speak is determined by motor-control capacities, the question would still remain: Why do children start *understanding* words at the age that they do?

There are other, more plausible, hypotheses, none of which are mutually exclusive. The emergence of word learning could reflect the emergence of adequate phonological knowledge (where the notion of phonology extends to both speech and sign). Another possibility is memory; perhaps very young children cannot store arbitrary form-meaning correspondences for long enough to be of any use. Conceptual abilities are a third possibility. It may be that the onset of word learning occurs only once children can encode the notions that words map onto. Although some ability to perceptually distinguish between members of different categories, such as dogs and chairs, appears to be present quite early (e.g., Cohen & Strauss, 1979; Mandler & McDonough, 1993), the appropriate understanding of kinds and individuals (see chapters 5 and 6) might emerge only at about the age of 12 months, as argued by Xu and Carey (1996).

One further proposal seems to me plausible, though admittedly there is not much evidence for it. This is that word learning must wait for children to develop enough of an understanding of referential intent to figure out what people are talking about when they use words. More generally, it might be that the onset of word learning has to await the development of certain specific aspects of naive psychology, or theory of mind.

If this were the case, then you might expect some correlation between the development of theory of mind and the onset of word learning. To explore this, Morales, Mundy, and Rojas (1998) used a highly sensitive measure to test the ability of six-month-olds to follow their mother's gaze. A substantial number of children were able to do so, and a significant correlation was found between a six-month-old's ability to follow direction of gaze and his or her receptive vocabulary at 12 months, as measured by parental report. Gaze detection might be a precursor to the ability to appreciate a speaker's referential intent, and hence such a finding is consistent with the idea that the emergence of theory of mind abilities is related to the onset of word learning (see also chapter 3). This result is at best suggestive, since some more general factor might underlie the emergence of both gaze following and word learning, and so the two might have no direct relationship. But it is at least consistent with a theory-of-mind account of why word learning starts when it does.

Once children start to learn words, why do they start so slowly, and why does this rate gradually increase? The relevant factors here have to do with development and with experience.

Candidate developmental factors include the maturation of memory and attention, perhaps as the product of the quite radical brain changes that occur in the first few years of life. Children might also spend the first months of word learning getting better at figuring out the communicative intentions of other people. A parallel can be found with other complicated things that children come to do more quickly and efficiently as the result of practice, such as walking and counting. An independent developmental factor is children's increasing awareness of the different entities that can be named. As they learn about the world, more opportunities open up for word learning because they know more nameable things.

You can see what makes the above factors "developmental" with the following fanciful example. Imagine a normal adult who loses all memory of her first language. But (and this is the fanciful part) all the rest of her cognitive abilities are perfectly intact, including those involved in the learning of new words. Now she has to learn her language all over again. She would differ from children just starting to learn words in all of the ways above. She would have better memory and a longer attention span. She would already be perfectly good at figuring out the communicative intentions of other people. And she would be different from a child in that she knows a lot more about the world—that it contains rabbits and congressmen and genes, kissing and proofreading and logging on. She just wouldn't know what these things are *called*. For all these reasons, she would learn her first words much quicker than a child. And indeed, in those rare cases in which someone is exposed to a first language somewhat later in life, initial word learning tends to be quite rapid, as in the case of Ildefonso, which will be discussed in chapter 10.

Experiential factors must be considered as well. As you learn more of a language, you gain access to linguistic information relevant to word learning. Very young children start off with little or no syntactic knowledge to guide their interpretation of a new word. And before they have learned their first few words, they are obviously not going to be able to learn words from linguistic context. Slightly older children have more syntactic understanding and know a few more words. Later on, literacy exposes children to more words, and it is likely that the gargantuan vocabularies of some English speakers (well over 100,000 words) could not occur without the ability to read.

These experiential factors have nothing to do with age per se. Consider again the example of an otherwise normal person learning her first language as an adult. No matter how smart she is, her first words will have to be learned without the aid of linguistic cues. And only much later will she have enough linguistic knowledge to benefit from reading. In this way, certain factors involved in the changing rate of word learning are not themselves developmental; it just so happens that a large correlation exists between being a child and being a language novice.

Finally, the rate of word learning slows down. Most adults are not learning several new words a day. This is not because we are poor at word learning. Every word learning study that tests both children and adults finds either that no age difference exists or that adults do better (though this adult advantage could be due to extraneous reasons, such as the greater focus and cooperation of adult experimental participants). The reason that the rate slows down in adulthood is that adults have learned most of the words the immediate environment has to offer. Unless we learn a new language, our only opportunities for word learning are proper names, archaic or technical terms, or new words that enter the language.

Individual Differences

The story is told that Albert Einstein did not speak until the age of three. His first words were reportedly said one evening at dinner, when he suddenly put down his spoon and exclaimed, "The soup is too hot!" His parents were stunned to hear him talk and asked him why he had never done so before. "Well," he said, "up to now, everything has been fine."

Just as with any other type of development, cognitive or physical, variation exists in the development of word learning. I consider three types of variation—in the rate of word learning, in the sorts of words that are learned, and in the number of words a person ends up with—and for each, I review some candidate explanations for why such variation exists. This section concludes with some general comments about what individual differences tell us about word learning in general.

Rate

The most easily studied difference between children of the same age is how many words they know. Even if we restrict ourselves to the population of children who grow up to be normal language users, we still find a huge range. Some children have quite large productive vocabularies at the age of 16 months, and others barely speak at all until past their third birthday. This population of *late-talking children* is almost exclusively male, and some evidence suggests that these boys tend to have poor social skills and good abilities in math and music (Sowell, 1997). To put it in the language of pop psychology, late talkers seem to be very right-brained. But this generalization is anecdotal, and we actually know little about late-talking children (or early-talking children, for that matter).

The most thorough study of normal variation is that of Fenson et al. (1994), who explored the vocabularies of 1,803 babies and toddlers (see also Bates et al., 1994, for further analyses on the same dataset). The vocabulary range at different ages is summarized in table 2.5; this is based on parents' reports of their children's productive vocabularies.

The numbers for the top 10 percent at the ages of 24 and 30 months should not be taken seriously; there is a ceiling effect, since the word checklist has only 680 words in it. As a result, 24- and 30-month-olds in the top 10 percent may know many more words than 680, but if these words are not in the checklist, then they are less likely to be recorded.

What causes these differences in rate of word learning? Why does one two-year-old know seven words and another know 668? The extent to which parents talk to their children is related to the size of their vocabularies (Smolak & Weinraub, 1983; Tomasello, Mannle & Kruger,

Table 2.5
Estimates of children's productive vocabulary sizes

Age	Number of Words		
	Bottom 10 Percent	Median	Top 10 Percent
12 months	0	6	26–52
16 months	0–8	40	179–347
24 months	7–57	311	534–668
30 months	208–262	574	654–675

1986; Huttenlocher et al., 1991). And so is the number of words that the parents know: parental scores on vocabulary tests account for about 10 to 20 percent of the variation in children's scores (e.g., Scarr & Weisberg, 1978; see Huttenlocher et al., 1991, for review). This might not seem like a large effect, but it is at this point the best predictor of children's vocabulary size.

These correlations can be explained in many ways. Parental linguistic abilities might *directly* affect children's vocabulary size, either through environmental factors (hearing a lot of speech might cause children's vocabularies to grow more rapidly), genetic factors (variation in the ability to learn words might be hereditary), or both. Or there might be a more indirect relationship. Vocabulary size in adults is, after all, highly correlated with other intellectual and social capacities (Sternberg, 1987), and these capacities might be passed on from parents to children—again either through social interaction, genes, or both.

As usual with these issues, carefully designed twin studies and adoption studies might give us some insight. For instance, Ganger, Pinker, and Wallis (1997) find that the early vocabulary growth of monozygotic twins is more similar than that of same-sex dyzygotic twins, consistent with some genetic cause to this variability. At the same time, however, nobody doubts that some of the variation in vocabulary size is due to environmental factors. Words must be learned from exposure, after all, and the more words children hear, the more opportunity they have to learn them. It is reassuring to find that this intuition is correct: Huttenlocher et al. (1991) find that the more often parents use a given word, the more likely it is that children know its meaning.

Fenson et al. (1994) find other factors that relate to how much children know. Girls tend to know more words than boys of the same age, a finding that is consistent with other studies of language development (e.g., McCarthy, 1954; Nelson, 1973). Children of educated parents score higher than children of less educated parents (at least with regard to productive vocabulary), and first-borns do better than later-borns. But as Fenson et al. emphasize, these effects, while statistically significant due to the large sample, are nevertheless minuscule. For instance, despite the popular notion that girls are much more linguistically precocious than boys, less than 2 percent of the variance in vocabulary size can be accounted for in terms of whether the child is a boy or a girl.

Style
Another type of variation is in the "style" of vocabulary development. As Nelson (1973) discovered, only some children adopt a *referential* style—the textbook pattern of development in which children first learn single words, typically a lot of nouns, and later combine them in phrases and sentences. Other children are more *expressive;* they tend to be less caught up in naming and more into using memorized routines, often strings of words, for social or instrumental purposes, such as *thank you, go away, I want it, don't do it,* and the ubiquitous *no*. While extremes are reported in the literature—such as Julia, a very referential child (Bates, Bretherton & Snyder, 1988), and Maia, a very expressive child (Adamson, Tomasello & Benbisty, 1984)—most children fall somewhere in between.

Pine and Lieven (1990) note that children who know 100 words tend to have a higher proportion of nouns in their vocabulary than children who know 50 words (see also Bates et al., 1994; Nelson, 1973). Because of this, if two children of the same age differ only in rate of vocabulary growth, these children will nonetheless have a different proportion of nouns in their vocabulary, giving the false impression of variation in style. But there is evidence for variation in style independent of variation in rate; when vocabulary size is held constant, dramatic differences can still be found in the proportion of nouns used by children (Bates et al., 1994).

What causes variation in style? Girls show more tendency to a referential style than boys, as do children of parents with high socioeconomic status and levels of education. But, again, these correlations are small, and one wouldn't be able to find them in a sample that didn't have hundreds of children. Another possibility is that variation in style emerges from personality differences. As Steven Pinker (1994b, p. 267) puts it, "Babies are people, only smaller. Some are interested in objects, others like to shmooze."

Outcome
A third type of variation, apart from rate and style, is outcome—how many words a person ends up knowing. This is strongly related to measures of intelligence. Sternberg (1987) points out that if you want

to know how well someone will do on a standard psychometric IQ test, the best predictor is a vocabulary test. There are many ways to make sense of this relationship. A general learning capacity might affect both word learning and other capacities that are tested in IQ tests. Or the relationship could be less direct. People who do well on IQ tests may be the same people who read a lot and thereby are exposed to a lot of words.

All other things being equal, the more words you encounter, the more chances you have to learn them, and the bigger your vocabulary will be. Some variation in exposure to words is due to endogenous characteristics of a person, such as how much they choose to read, their interest in talking to new people, and so on. Other characteristics are out of the person's control. One consideration in determining one's vocabulary size is whether the person is born into a literate society. A son of a British university professor is likely to end up with more words than the son of a Yanomamö headsman, even if they have otherwise identical interests and inclinations. Even within a society, one can imagine a Dickens-like situation, in which one takes identical twins with equal abilities and personalities and puts one into a family without books and without access to adequate schooling and the other into an environment that encourages scholarship. Their adult vocabulary sizes would diverge in a predictable way.

All these points about determinants of outcome are obvious, but they do underscore a difference between word learning and other aspects of language learning. Children vary as to when they come to know different aspects of phonology, morphology, and syntax, and they vary in their ability to use these aspects of language. But, for the most part, no differences are apparent in how much they come to know. Normal adults know the same principles of grammar. But words are different. There is no ceiling on how many words one can learn; there are always new proper names to encounter, terminological and archaic terms, esoteric slang, and the like. New words are invented every day, and other languages can be learned. All normal children will learn some base vocabulary, but where they go from there is the result of a complex interweaving of different factors, such as temperament, opportunity, and motivation.

What Do Individual Differences Tell Us about Word Learning?

Studies of individual differences are important for many reasons. By seeing the normal range of variation, we can better understand what counts as abnormal development and perhaps become better able to predict the early signs of language disorder. And certain discoveries could not have been made without the study of individual variation. For instance, there is a strong correlation between vocabulary growth and syntactic development that is statistically independent of age (Fenson et al., 1994), and it would be hard to discover this without an eye toward how children differ. More ambitiously, if we could determine the different dimensions of variation and what causes them, it might help us develop a theory of word learning in general.

On the other hand, the mere existence of individual differences is uninteresting from a theoretical standpoint because it is consistent with all theories of word learning. Some people think otherwise. For instance, Bates et al. (1994) suggest that their data poses a challenge to universalist models of word learning. And Shore (1995) argues that the existence of individual differences poses a severe problem for any nativist theory of language acquisition and is more consistent with alternatives such as connectionism, ecological psychology, and chaos theory.

Putting aside the question of how well this argument holds for other aspects of language development, such as syntax, it is hard to see how it applies to word learning. All the nativist accounts of word learning that I am aware of—perhaps Lila Gleitman (1990) could serve as the prototypical word-learning nativist—are explicit that the course of word learning is determined by many factors, including the words children hear, their memory and attentional capacities, the concepts they possess, and their phonological, morphological, and syntactic knowledge. Individual differences in any of these factors, then, could lead to variation in how children learn the meanings of words, and individual differences in children's personalities could lead to variation in how they express this knowledge in their production and comprehension.[1]

Bates and her colleagues also see their data as arguing against the notion of the modal child, a "mythical creature" who passes through a predetermined sequence of stages at a standard rate that is highly constrained by maturational factors. But the modal child is alive and well. The very same studies that address issues of variation also find robust and interesting universals of vocabulary development, and Fenson et al. and Bates et al. report several generalizations about the developmental process, many of which hold in other languages as well (Caselli et al., 1995). These have to do with the sorts of words children learn first, developmental changes in the rate at which children learn nouns versus verbs versus determiners, and correlations between vocabulary growth and syntactic development.

In the end, the descriptive facts about variation are interesting enough, but they exist in a theoretical vacuum. We have little idea as to why young children differ in how they acquire language. It's not just that we can't explain this variation; we don't even know what correlates with it. The standard factors that psychologists look for—sex, birth order, social class, educational level of parents—tell us little about how any individual child will learn language. So although studying the variation that exists in word learning might conceivably tell us about how the normal process works, my hunch is that more progress will be made from the other direction. Individual differences will be best understood, and appreciated, through a theory of how word learning works in general. It is to this we now turn.

Notes

1. The strong correlation between syntactic development and vocabulary development is also not an embarrassment for nativist theories, contrary to what Shore (1995) suggests. In fact, in light of the intimate relationship between syntax and vocabulary in modern linguistic theories, many nativist theories have argued that exactly this sort of relationship should exist (e.g., Gleitman, 1990; Macnamara, 1982; Pinker, 1984).

Chapter 3

Word Learning and Theory of Mind

Learning a word is a social act. When children learn that rabbits eat carrots, they are learning something about the external world, but when they learn that *rabbit* refers to rabbits, they are learning an arbitrary convention shared by a community of speakers, an implicitly agreed-upon way of communicating. When children learn the meaning of a word, they are—whether they know it or not—learning something about the thoughts of other people.

What does this tell us about how words are learned? Maybe nothing. Just because the relationship between a word and its meaning is a social fact doesn't entail that one needs social competence or knowledge to learn this fact. After all, when dogs learn to obey the command "Sit!," they are also learning an arbitrary convention, one that exists in the minds of a community of English speakers. But dogs surely don't know this and can learn the command without ruminating about the thoughts of others. All they might do is associate the right behavior with the right sound, in the same way that they would learn other, nonsocial, facts. Maybe this is also true for how children learn words.

I argue here that it isn't. This chapter reviews evidence showing that children's word learning actually draws extensively on their understanding of the thoughts of others—on their theory of mind. Theory of mind underlies how children learn the entities to which words refer, intuit how words relate to one another, and understand how words can serve as communicative signs. I discuss certain alternatives, such as the view that word learning is done through general associative principles, aided by the careful naming practices of parents. I suggest that these fail to capture basic facts about language development.

This is a long chapter, but it is nowhere near long enough. It deals only with the most central ways in which theory of mind underlies word learning. But the role of theory of mind is something we return to several times in the chapters that follow, with regard to the learning of proper names and pronouns, the nature of artifact concepts, and the naming of representations. There is, however, much more to word learning than understanding the thoughts of other people, and this chapter concludes with a discussion of certain learning problems that must be solved in other ways.

The Associative Infant

A central aspect of word learning is figuring out which objects specific words refer to. This is far from all there is to word learning. Some words refer to nothing at all (words such as *of* and *the*), and others refer to things that are not objects (words such as *joke* and *number*). And even if we restrict ourselves to middle-sized objects such as rabbits and tables, we are stuck with Quine's problem, which is that children who hear a word and know that it refers to a rabbit are still faced with an indefinite number of possible meanings for this word: it could be a proper name, an adjective referring to the rabbit's color, and so on. But the ability to figure out which objects specific words refer to is nonetheless central to word learning; in its absence, some of these other issues don't even arise.

Associationism is a popular solution to this learning problem and has dominated psychological and philosophical thought for centuries. This is the view, defended in detail by empiricist philosophers such as John Stuart Mill, David Hume, and John Locke, that the mechanism for word learning is a sensitivity to covariation, one rooted in general principles of learning. If two thoughts occur at the same time, they become associated, and one gives rise to the other. Children learn the meaning of *rabbit*, then, because the word is used when they are observing or thinking about rabbits. As a result, the word and the thought become associated, and children could be said to have learned what the word means.

One version of this theory was adopted by B.F. Skinner (1957), who proposed that learning the meaning of a word is a matter of establishing—through reinforcement and punishment—a connection between a set of stimuli and a verbal response. Many computational models of word learning work in similar ways. Richards and Goldfarb (1986), for instance, propose that children come to know the meaning of the word *car* through repeatedly associating the verbal label ("car") with their experience at the time that the label is used. For those perceptual properties that repeatedly cooccur with the label, the association will strengthen, as with *four wheels*; for those that do not, as with *blue*, the association will weaken. As a result of this process, children come to associate the label "car" with those properties that only cars possess and could be said to have learned the meaning of the word.

Plunkett, Sinha, Møller, and Strandsby (1992) present a similar model, in which labels and images are fed through distinct "sensory" pathways into a network, and the network is trained to associate the two. Successful production occurs when the network generates the appropriate label in response to an image; successful comprehension occurs when the appropriate image is generated in response to a label. This is proposed as a theory of how young children learn words, and it is suggested that word learning—as well as language learning more generally (Plunkett, 1997)—is best explained through a connectionist architecture that is sensitive to statistical regularities in the environment.

Many facts about word learning are consistent with this perspective. Children's first words often refer to things they can see and touch, which is exactly what one would expect under an associationist learning procedure. And words are learned best in precisely the conditions in which an associative match would be easiest to make. If you want to teach someone *dog*, an excellent way to do so is to point to a dog, make sure the person is attending to it, and say "dog." If you wait until there are no dogs around and nobody is thinking about dogs, and then say "dog," the word will not be learned.

Lois Bloom summarizes one associationist theory of word learning as follows (1994, p. 221):

> Once the child learns something about objects and events, and about words *qua* words, word learning consists of good old-fashioned associative learning. In the beginning, the data for learning the meanings of language are in the circumstances of use in which children hear words and sentences. The meanings of early words like *cookie, gone, more,* and *mama,* or little sentences like "eat meat" or "throw ball" can be gotten from the words and their corresponding events. . . . Associative learning has now reappeared in contemporary theory as "connectionism." . . . Connectionism will continue to be debated in the realm of syntax for some time, but so far it offers a more parsimonious account of lexical learning than a theory based on a priori lexical principles.

This version of associationism posits more abilities on the part of children than the philosophical and computational versions discussed above, as Bloom implies that the input to the learning mechanism is already categorized in terms of objects and events, words and sentences. But what makes her view a bona fide associative theory is the proposal that the relationship between the words and what they refer to is established not through a process of reasoning and inference and not through specialized word-learning mechanisms, but through a sensitivity to covariation.

Because of this, Bloom's proposal retains one of the merits of associationism—parsimony. If she is right, word learning involves mental capacities that are present in the minds of other animals. Just as rats can come to associate a certain tone with a painful shock, children can learn to associate the word *cookie* with the sight and smell of cookies. Another virtue of this view is that it posits mechanisms that we know something about. There is no great mystery in how a brain could form associations between ideas or sensations that are present at the same time, and it is relatively straightforward to construct a computing device (either symbolic or connectionist) that does the same thing. Computational models of associative word learning (e.g., Gasser & Smith, 1998; Plunkett, Sinha, Møller & Strandsky, 1992; Richards & Goldfarb, 1986) are simple and elegant things.

But despite the merits of this proposal, it suffers from certain serious problems. One has to do with the input that children receive. Any associationist procedure requires that the right correlations are present in the environment. In the case of word learning, this entails that the words are presented at the same time that children are attending to what the words refer to. John Locke (1690/1964, p. 108) is clear about this: "For if we observe how children learn languages, we shall find that, to make them understand what the names of simple ideas or substances stand for, people ordinarily show them the thing whereof they would have them have the idea; and then repeat to them the name that stands for it: as *white, sweet, milk, sugar, cat, dog.*"

But Locke is wrong. Words are not ordinarily used at the same time that their referents are being perceived. The best case for Locke is the learning of object names. But even for these, and even if we focus only on parent-child interactions within a supportive family environment, about 30 percent to 50 percent of the time that a word is used, young children are *not* attending to the object that the adult is talking about (Collins, 1977; Harris, Jones & Grant, 1983). Some of the time, for instance, that children hear "Want a cookie?," they will be staring at someone's face. But *cookie* doesn't mean face, and no child has thought that it does.

Solutions to the problem of noisy input can be found. It may be that some of the time *cookie* is used, for instance, children are not attending to cookies, but, in the fullness of time, the percepts that are most associated with the word are those elicited by encounters with cookies. So children who start off associating *cookie* with faces might, after hearing the word used over and over again, weaken this association and strengthen the association with cookies. An associative procedure doesn't need a perfect correlation, after all—just a statistically reliable one.

But this proposal makes the wrong prediction. It predicts that before children have enough data to converge on the right hypothesis, they should make frequent mapping errors, such as thinking that *cookie* means face. But this never happens. To account for this error-free learning, one might imagine that children are inherently cautious and use a word only when they have adequate statistical evidence for its meaning, such as hearing the word with a consistent referent a dozen times, across suitably different situations. But this also doesn't happen. Children do not wait: they can learn a word after hearing it used a few times in a single situation (e.g., Markson & Bloom, 1997; see chapter 2). The fact that object-name acquisition is typically both fast and errorless suggests that it is not a form of statistical learning.

Furthermore, Locke was assuming the Western model of adult-child interaction in which parents carefully name objects for their children. But this is not universal. In some cultures, this sort of ostensive labeling does not occur, and if children waited for adults to name objects that they were attending to, they would wait forever. Object names must instead be learned by attending to overheard speech (Lieven, 1994; Schieffelin, 1985). Despite this sort of cultural variation, all normal children learn the meanings of words.

Things get worse for an associationist account when one considers the problems that arise with the learning of names for things that you cannot see or touch. These include imaginary things, such as fictional characters, as well as abstract entities like numbers, geometrical forms, ideas, and mistakes. This is a problem that Locke and his contemporaries were well aware of, but it has never been solved. One might perhaps restrict the domain of associative learning to children's early vocabularies. But even these words can be surprisingly abstract. Nelson, Hampson, and Shaw (1993) examined the speech of 45 20-month-olds and found that only about half of children's nominals referred to basic-level object kinds; the rest referred to members of other conceptual categories, such as locations (*beach, kitchen*), actions (*kiss, nap*), social roles (*doctor, brother*), natural phenomena (*sky, rain*), and temporal entities (*morning, day*). Furthermore, despite their impoverished perceptual experience, blind children learn words, often at the same rate as sighted children (Landau & Gleitman, 1985).

The case against associationist theories of word learning gets stronger when we consider certain experiments that find that a statistical covariation between word and percept is neither necessary nor sufficient for word learning. And consider finally the fact (discussed below) that nonhuman primates, who are excellent at associative learning and have rich perceptual and motor systems, are quite abysmal at word learning.

I think the evidence is actually quite strong that associationism is simply false as a theory of early word learning. But to avoid confusion on this point, note that the objections above apply to associationism only under a particular, somewhat technical sense of the term. Another sense is highly general: to say that children "associate" a word with its meaning simply means that they have learned the meaning of the word. This is a harmless use of the term, but it has nothing to do with the empirical and testable proposal that word learning is done through a mechanism sensitive to statistical covariation, as proposed by Locke and others.

Furthermore, nobody is arguing against the view that children attend to the situation when they are learning a word. That would be crazy. No child has ever learned *dog* by hearing someone whisper the word in his ear as he lay in bed with his eyes closed. It may well be that children will learn *dog* best when they are attending to a dog when the word is used and that the more often they hear the word, the more likely they are to learn it. The issue is over why this is the case.

Finally, a rejection of associative theories of word learning does not entail the rejection of connectionism. There is a difference between the claim that word learning is not done through a sensitivity to statistical covariation and the stronger claim that the mechanisms that underlie word learning, whatever they are, do not emerge from connectionist learning algorithms. I suggest below that children learn the meanings of words through theory of mind. If this is right, then a *direct* connectionist implementation of word learning, in which sounds are associated with percepts, is unfeasible. (And this does preclude all connectionist theories of word learning that I am aware of.) But it leaves open the possibility that the mechanisms underlying word learning, while themselves not associationist, are somehow the product of associationist learning mechanisms. In particular, if a connectionist theory can account for the origin and nature of the relevant theory of mind capacities, then connectionism is consistent with the facts of early word learning. If it can't, it isn't.

The Augustinian Infant

How do children make the connection between words and what they refer to? One promising theory is that they do so through their understanding of the referential intentions of others. Instead of Locke, consider Augustine (398/1961, p. 11):

When [my elders] named any thing, and as they spoke turned towards it, I saw and remembered that they called what they would point out by the name they uttered. And that they meant this thing and no other was plain from the motion of their body, the natural language, as it were, of all nations, expressed by the countenance, glances of the eye, gestures of the limbs, and tones of the voice, indicating the affections of the mind, as it pursues, possesses, rejects, or shuns. And thus by constantly hearing words, as they occurred in various sentences, I collected gradually for what they stood; and having broken in my mouth to these signs, I thereby gave utterance to my will.

To put this in more contemporary terms, children use their *naive psychology* or *theory of mind* to figure out what people are referring to when they use words. Word learning is a species of intentional inference or, as Simon Baron-Cohen (1995) has put it, mind reading.

This Augustinian perspective has not been popular in the last century. One of the central philosophical works of our time—Ludwig Wittgenstein's *Philosophical Investigations*—begins by ridiculing Augustine's assumption that children know about objects and people prior to language. His mistake, according to Wittgenstein, is the view that "the child could already *think,* only not yet speak." But Augustine's proposal is no longer seen as the goofy idea that it once was. Increasing evidence shows that some capacity to understand the minds of others may be present in babies before they begin to speak.

There are many names for this capacity, including *mind-reading, social cognition,* and *pragmatic understanding,* but in what follows, I use the term *theory of mind*. This is in part because I want to explore the implications that this proposal has for the study of language development in children with autism, which is often described as a deficit that particularly affects theory of mind (e.g., Baron-Cohen, Leslie & Frith, 1985). But two qualifications must be made about this usage. First, I'm using the term without any commitment to whether theory of mind is really a theory in any nontrivial sense (for different perspectives, see Baron-Cohen, 1995; Gopnik & Meltzoff, 1997; Leslie, 1994). And second, some researchers link the attainment of a theory of mind with the ability to pass the false-belief task (Wimmer & Perner, 1983), something that occurs at the age of three or four. There is considerable debate over why younger children do not pass this task and whether not passing it is really due to limitations in their understanding of the thoughts of others, but, in any case, I am using *theory of mind* in a broader sense that need not include the ability to reason about false beliefs.

What understanding do prelinguistic children have about the minds of others? Consider first sensitivity to what other people are attending to. By around nine months, a baby will naturally follow its mother's line of regard (Butterworth, 1991; Scaife & Bruner, 1975) and will also follow her pointing gestures (Murphy & Messer, 1977). At about the same age, babies can monitor their parents' emotional reactions to potentially dangerous situations and react accordingly. For instance, when seeing a spider, a baby will be less likely to approach it if its mother seems fearful than if she seems happy (Zarbatany & Lamb, 1985), and when babies are uncertain or hesitant, they check what their mother is looking at and how she is reacting (e.g., Bretherton, 1992).

These findings raise the question of what goes on when a baby follows the gaze of an adult. It might be that babies have an implicit assumption that the adult is attending to something and thinking about or reacting to that object. This would make gaze following a reflection of theory of mind (e.g., Baron-Cohen, 1995). Alternatively, gaze following might be the product of an automatic orienting procedure, either innate or learned, that is initiated by exposure to certain stimuli, such as eyes and faces, but has nothing to do with intentional attribution (e.g., Butterworth, 1991; Corkum & Moore, 1995; Perner, 1991).

One way to address this question is to ask what sort of stimuli elicit gaze following in babies. A study with 12-month-olds by Johnson, Slaughter, and Carey (in press) reports an intriguing finding. When exposed to a robot that interacts contingently with them, through beeping and light flashing, but that has no face, babies will nonetheless follow its "gaze" (the orientation of the front, reactive part of the robot), treating it as if it were a person. But they will not do so if a faceless robot fails to interact with them in a meaningful way. This suggests that gaze following is applied to entities that give some sign of having intentional states, regardless of their appearance, and supports the view that gaze following is related, at least for 12-months-olds, to intentional attribution.

Children are not merely passive observers of others. By about a year, they point on their own and then observe the adult's gaze, as if checking to see if they have succeeded in changing the adult's focus of attention (Bretherton, 1992). When they fail to capture an adult's attention in the right way, they often alternate between gazing at the object and at the adult and will modify their behavior until they succeed at getting the adult's attention (Golinkoff, 1986). Even at nine months, babies get adults to do things, such as open things, and play games—and they do so by first attracting the adult's attention and then making clear what they want, through gestures and vocalizations (Piaget, 1952). Finally, two-year-olds are sensitive to the knowledge of other people when they communicate. In one study, two-year-olds observed as an attractive toy was put on a high shelf. When later asking for help in retrieving the toy, they were more likely to name the toy and gesture to the location when their parent had not been present to witness the placement of toy, suggesting that even young children can take into account the knowledge and ignorance of other people (O'Neill, 1996).

All the examples so far involve children either trying to figure out the actions of an adult that they are interacting with or trying to manipulate the adult in some manner. But at least by their first birthday, children's abilities extend beyond this. They interpret abstract figures on a computer screen as goal-directed agents and expect them to behave in accord with canons of rational behavior (Gergely, Nádasdy, Csibra & Biró, 1995). They expect people to affect each other by action at a distance, but they have the opposite expectation about the behavior of inanimate objects (Spelke, Phillips & Woodward, 1995). They expect hands to move in goal-directed ways but do not have the same expectations about inanimate entities such as sticks (Woodward, 1998). One-year-olds can pretend that one object is another, as when pretending that a banana is a telephone, and by two—if not earlier—they can understand pretense by others. This appreciation of pretense shows up early in the words they use. If they know the word *telephone*, they have no hesitation, in the course of pretend play, in using this word to talk about a banana (Leslie, 1995).

These findings raise the possibility that children use these abilities to help them figure out what adults are intending to refer to when words are used. Again, this is not an alternative to the claim that children use perceptual information to learn words. After all, children are not telepathic: the only way they can infer the intentions of another person is by observing the properties of the situation, such as what the adult is looking or pointing at and what objects are present in the scene. The interesting question, then, is not whether children use such perceptual information (they plainly do) but what they do with it. Is it the basis for statistical reasoning, intentional inference, or both?

Both Locke and Augustine give the example of simple ostensive naming, in which an object is present and the child hears an adult name it. But what really goes on in this situation? In a fascinating series of studies, Dare Baldwin (1991, 1993b) tested babies in a context in which they were given one object to play with while another object was put into a bucket that was in front of the experimenter. When the baby was looking at the object in front of her, the experimenter looked at the object in the bucket and said a new word, such as "It's a modi!" This gives rise to a perfect Lockean correspondence between the new word and the object the baby was looking at. But 18-month-olds don't take *modi* as naming this object. Instead, they look at the experimenter and redirect their attention to what she is looking at, in this case, at the object in the bucket. And when later shown the two objects and asked to "find the modi," they assume that the word refers to the object the experimenter was looking at when she said the word—not the object that the child herself was looking at.

Similar results held even when the experiment was modified in the following way (Baldwin, 1993a). Two objects were hidden in different opaque containers. The experimenter opened one container, looked inside, said "It's a modi!," and then opened the other container, removed the toy, and gave it to the baby to look at and play with. After at least 10 seconds had passed, the experimenter removed the first object from the container and gave that to the baby as well. Again, when later tested, it was found that babies assumed that the word referred to the first object, the one that the experiment had named, despite the 10-second gap between hearing the name and seeing the object and despite the fact that they had interacted with another novel object in the meantime.

These studies show that a contiguity between word and percept is not necessary for word learning. Further work suggests that contiguity is also not sufficient. In another study, 15- to 20-month-olds were alone in a room with a novel object. When they looked at the object, they heard a disembodied voice (from a hidden adult outside the room) saying something such as "Dawnoo! There's a dawnoo!" Under this circumstances, they did not learn the word (Baldwin et al., 1996). That is, even with a perfect association between hearing a word and attending to an object, young children will make the connection only if they have some warrant to believe that it is an act of naming—and for this, the speaker has to be present. (Adults, of course, could learn the word in the above situation, presumably not because we are more associationist than children but because we would infer that the disembodied voice is actually an act of naming by a person who we can't see.)

Michael Tomasello and his colleagues have found that older children show a more subtle appreciation of intentional cues. In one study with 24-month-olds (Tomasello & Barton, 1994), the experimenter looked into the child's eyes and said, "Let's find the toma. Where's the toma?" Both the experimenter and the child then approached a row of five buckets, each of which contained a novel object. In the "without search" condition, the experimenter immediately withdrew an object from one of the buckets, held it up with an excited look, gasped "Ah!," and then handed it to the child. In the "with search" condition, the experimenter withdrew one object, scowled, and put it back; did the same with a second object; and then withdrew a third object, held it up, looked excited, gasped "Ah!," and handed it to the child. After both conditions, the experimenter then extracted the remaining objects from each of the buckets, saying each time, "Let's see what's in *here?*" When later shown the five objects and asked to find the toma, children performed equally well in both conditions, picking out the object that the experimenter seemed happy with, despite the fact that it was not the last object they saw and, in the "with search" condition, not the first.

Success in this task could not be due to any procedure based on direction of gaze. It instead had to result from children's sensitivity to what the adult's goal was and when it was satisfied, as indicated by cues such as the experimenter's expressions of happiness and the fact that the object was given to the child. Modified versions of these studies have found the same abilities with 18-month-olds (Tomasello, Strosberg & Akhtar, 1996).

Another set of studies explored the acquisition of verbs. The experimenter would introduce a new verb, saying, "I am going to plonk Big Bird!" Then she would perform an action and say "There!" and then perform another action and say "Whoops!" This was meant to give the impression that the first action was intentional and the second was accidental. (In another condition, the order of the intentional and accidental actions was reversed.) Two-year-olds were sensitive to this emotional cue of intent: When later asked "Can you go plonk Big Bird?," they tended to imitate the intentional action, not the accidental one (Tomasello & Barton, 1994).

Lexical Contrast

The Phenomena
Consider children who hear a new word in a situation in which intentional factors such as direction of gaze suggest that a certain object is the referent of the word. But the object already has a name. For instance, children might hear a word, note that the person is looking at several objects, including a rabbit—but already know the word *rabbit.* What do children do in such a situation?

Abundant evidence suggests they are biased to think that the word does not have the same meaning as *rabbit.* The original study to test this was done by Kagan (1981), as part of large-scale study of development in the second year. Children were shown three objects, two of them familiar (a doll and a dog) and one unfamiliar. Children were allowed to play with the three objects and were then asked to "Give me the zoob." By the age of about 22 months, both American and Fijian children tended to choose the novel object, suggesting that they believe that a novel word does not refer to objects that already have names.

A concern with this study, however, is that these children were repeatedly tested over several months, which might have helped train them into making the appropriate response. A later study by Markman and Wachtel (1988) is immune from this concern. Preschool children were shown two objects, one familiar and one novel, such as a banana and a whisk, and were presented with a new word, as in "Show me the fendle." They tend to interpret the new word as naming the whisk, not the banana. If only the banana is present, children are prone to take a novel name as referring to a part of the object, not the object itself. Markman and Wachtel (1988) explain this in terms of a mutual exclusivity principle, one that biases children to think that words should not have overlapping reference or, equivalently, that each object can have only one label.

These findings have been replicated and extended in many ways (e.g., Au & Glusman, 1990; Hall, 1991; Hutchinson, 1986; Merriman & Bowman, 1989). A similar effect shows up with verbs. Golinkoff, Shuff-Bailey, Olguin, and Ruan (1995) and Merriman, Marazita, and Jarvis (1995) found that if you show children two actions, one familiar and one unfamiliar, and produce a novel verb (as in "Where's gorping?"), they will tend to assume that this new verb refers to the action they do not already have a name for.

In a study by Markman and Wasow (reported in Woodward & Markman, 1997), even 15-months-olds appear to be sensitive to mutual exclusivity. When shown an object with an already known name, such as a spoon, and asked "Can you show me the modi? Where's the modi?," they tend to look around for a referent for the word. If there is a bucket present, they will look in the bucket, searching for the modi, reflecting a tacit expectation that the spoon is not likely to be the modi.

Mutual exclusivity can also explain certain facts about language development. A child who calls cats "dogs" might stop doing so once learning the word *cat,* and neologisms, such as *climber,* drop off once children learn the correct English word for the object, in this case, *ladder* (Clark, 1987). Or consider children's problems with superordinates. Macnamara (1982) reports that his two-year-old son Kieran rigorously refused to call a single dog "an animal," and the same phenomenon has been found experimentally (Callanan & Markman, 1982; Macnamara, 1982, 1986). Perhaps children are reluctant to use superordinates (such as *animal*) because they already have names (such as *dog*) for the objects that the superordinates refer to (Markman, 1989).

Mutual exclusivity applies only relative to a particular language. If a Spanish-English bilingual child knows the name of something in

English and then is given a second name for the same object in Spanish, she has no problem learning it (Au & Glusman, 1990). Furthermore, mutual exclusivity is a bias or default assumption, not an immutable restriction (Markman, 1992; see Behrend, 1990, and Nelson, 1988, for discussion). After all, languages frequently violate mutual exclusivity. Consider *dog, puppy, pet, animal,* and *Fido,* all of which could label the very same object. Words that have overlapping reference can be learned by children; it is just that they are harder to learn.

Mutual exclusivity is not a subtle phenomenon: you don't need to test dozens of children in careful laboratory conditions to see it at work. I often sit with my son Max and look at picture books with him, and like a typical Western parent, I point to pictures and say "What's that?" Sometimes he gets it wrong: when looking through a book about vehicles, for instance, he might call a dump truck "a tractor." Since I try to be supportive, I don't tell him he's wrong. Instead, I point to the same picture and say cheerfully "That's a dump truck!" This has the same effect, however, as a direct correction. By about 22 months he would look up at me and say, with considerable seriousness: "Dump truck. *Not* tractor. Dump truck."

Its Nature and Origin

This bias could be a specifically lexical phenomenon, a fact about how words work that is either innate or acquired in the course of language development (e.g., Mervis, Golinkoff & Bertrand, 1994). Or it could be a special case of a general principle of learning, one guiding children to prefer one-to-one mappings as part of a general tendency to exaggerate regularities (e.g., Markman, 1992). A third possibility, which I explore here, is that mutual exclusivity is a product of children's theory of mind.

This view has been defended by Eve Clark (1987, 1993, 1997; see also Gathercole, 1987). The main idea is that children's bias against lexical overlap can be explained in terms of a pragmatic principle—the principle of contrast—which states that every difference in form corresponds to some difference in meaning. There are no synonyms.

This is a controversial claim, and whether you find it convincing will depend on what you think meaning is. If you equate meaning with reference, for instance, then there certainly are synonyms, such as *cop* and *policeman,* that pick out the very same entities in the world. But Clark is endorsing a theory of meaning that includes a host of other factors as well, including considerations of register (*cop* versus *policeman*), emotive qualities (*statesman* versus *politician*), and dialect differences (*tap* versus *faucet*), and, under this very fine-grained notion of meaning, it is plausible that such a principle applies.

As Clark notes, the principle of contrast is an old idea and has been proposed, in slightly different variants, by Bloomfield, de Saussure, and von Humboldt. It is typically seen as resulting from the psychologies of individual people: speakers will not use terms interchangeably. Should synonymous terms somehow come to exist—through language contact, for instance—children would not learn them.

Why not? The answer might lie in children's inferences about the thoughts of others. Consider again the Markman and Wachtel (1988) study in which children were shown a banana and a whisk and asked to "Show me the fendle." A child might reason as follows (implicitly, of course):

1. I know that a banana is called *banana.*
2. If the speaker meant to refer to the banana, she would have asked me to show her the banana.
3. But she didn't; she used a strange word, *fendle.*
4. So she must intend to refer to something other than the banana.
5. A plausible candidate is the whisk.
6. *Fendle* must refer to the whisk.

Statements 1 and 2 capture what Clark calls the principle of conventionality—that words have fixed conventional meanings; 4 captures the principle of contrast; and 5 is the result of the child's assumption that new words presented in a neutral context such as "Show me the" are names for basic-level object kinds and not colors, parts, superordinate kinds, and so on (see chapters 4 and 6). If—contrary to how the mind actually works—children were prone to take a new noun used in a neutral context as a color term, then the color of the banana would be salient. But since children are biased to take a new word in this circumstance as describing a basic-level object kind, and since another object is present, then the principle of contrast explains why children are drawn to the whisk as the referent of *fendle.*

This pattern of reasoning applies to any communication system, not just words. To see this, imagine the following situation. A cube and a sphere are in front of you. An experimenter holds up a red card and motions to you to hand over the cube. You obey, and the experimenter thanks you. Game over. Now you play again. The experimenter holds up the red card, and you hand over the cube. (If you hand her the sphere, she shouts "Wrong!") And again and again.

All of a sudden she holds up an orange card. What do you do? It seems likely that you would go through the same reasoning as above:

1. I know that the red card means "hand over the cube."
2. If the experimenter had meant for me to hand over the cube, she would have held up the red card.

3. But she didn't; she used a different card, an orange one.
4. So she must intend me to do something other than hand over the cube.
5. A plausible candidate is to hand over the sphere.
6. The orange card must mean "hand over the sphere."

The idea here is that a mutual-exclusivity bias will arise in the learning of any conventional communicative system. It is not limited to language. But it is not entirely broad either; it does not apply to the learning of any system of mappings. Nothing should stop children, say, from assuming that a single object has many properties, so long as the properties are not inherently conflicting. To see this, consider children who see a banana and know two things about it: it is called *banana*, and it is yellow. They will be loath to accept that it could have another name but should not have the same unwillingness to learn that it could have another *property*, such as being tasty.

We can therefore distinguish these theories in terms of their scope. A strictly lexical theory predicts that contrast should apply only to words, a simplicity-of-mapping theory predicts that it should apply to all domains, and the theory-of-mind proposal predicts that it should apply only to communicative situations.

Little research is available on this topic. It would be nice to know, for instance, if mutual exclusivity applies when children learn new gestures or when they learn the sounds that different animals make. One set of studies, however, by Gil Diesendruck and Lori Markson (under review), does bear directly on this issue.

In one experiment, three-year-olds were presented with two unfamiliar objects and told a novel name for one of them ("This is a mep"). When exposed to both objects and asked about the meaning of a second different name ("Can you show me a jop?"), they tended to think that it referred to the other unnamed object, replicating previous studies. In another condition, a different group of children was shown two objects, told a novel *fact* about one of them ("My sister gave this to me"), and then asked to select the referent of a different fact ("Can you show me the one that dogs like to play with?"). The same result ensued as in the word study: children tended to choose the other object as the referent of the new information. This is presumably because they were reasoning that if the experimenter had intended to refer to the first object, she would have referred to it by using the original fact ("the one my sister gave me"); she would not have introduced a different fact.

Diesendruck and Markson went on to test a further prediction—that if children are using pragmatic reasoning about the adult's intentions in using the new fact, they should be less inclined to produce such a response in a two-speaker scenario, where the second speaker lacks mutual knowledge with the child. That is, if one speaker tells the child "My sister gave this to me" about one object, and then a different speaker, new to the discourse context, enters the room and asks "Can you give me the one that dogs like to play with?," the prediction is that children should now choose each of the objects with equal frequency. This is precisely what occurred.

Taken together, these findings support the notion that lexical contrast has its origin in children's expectations about the communicative behavior of others. It applies just as strongly when children are taught facts about objects as when they are taught words, and it does not apply when the pragmatic expectations are modified, as in the two-speaker condition. In sum, the reasoning that underlies the assumption of lexical contrast is not limited to words or to a general bias in favor of one-to-one mappings.

An important difference between words and facts, however, was discovered when Diesendruck and Markson did the two-speaker condition with novel words. In this condition, one speaker tells the child "This is a mep," and a different speaker enters the room and asks "Can you show me the jop?" Here children chose the object that wasn't originally labeled as the *mep*, the same as they did in the one-speaker condition with novel words—but different from their behavior in the two-speaker fact condition.

This suggests that children know something about words that isn't true about facts. Words have public meanings. If one person says of an object, "My sister gave this to me," there is no reason to expect this utterance to relate to the linguistic behavior of someone who later arrives on the scene. But if one person describes an object as a *mep*, it would be reasonable for a child to infer that other people know this word as well. Hence when a second person, new to the discourse content, asks for the jop, children could infer that if she meant to refer to the mep, she would have asked for it. Since she didn't, she must have meant to refer to the second object. This analysis raises the question of how children come to understand that words have this special property of having public meanings, something I return to later in the chapter.

Objections
One argument against this attempt to reduce lexical contrast to children's assumptions about the communicative goals of other people goes as follows. If lexical contrast applies even in cases where the speaker's intent to use the word to refer to a given object is entirely clear, this would suggest that the bias has a nonintentional origin.

Woodward and Markman (1997) report an experiment by Nowinsky and Markman that involves a familiar object, such as a shoe, and an unfamiliar one, such as a whisk. In one condition, children were asked "Please hand me the item," and they tended to hand over the whisk. Since *item* is an unfamiliar word, this replicates the standard mutual exclusivity finding. But in another condition, the experimenter would first point to the shoe and say "Look at the item," making her intent to refer to the shoe perfectly clear, *and then* would show the children both objects and ask "Please hand me the item." Children still treat *item* as referring to the whisk. This finding led Woodward and Markman to conclude that mutual exclusivity cannot reduce entirely to a pragmatic bias since, after all, there is abundant pragmatic evidence that *item* refers to the shoe.

Is this evidence against a pragmatic version of mutual exclusivity? The problem with this conclusion is that in the second condition, the referential intent *isn't* clear; it is conflicting (see Clark, 1997, pp. 35–36, for discussion of a similar case). On the one hand, the speaker has plainly just called the shoe "an item." On the other hand, the principle of contrast states that *item* cannot mean "shoe," since *shoe* means "shoe." If children possess the principle of contrast, they are in a difficult situation. They might choose to entirely ignore the fact that the shoe was called "the item." Or they might treat *item* as a superordinate term that could refer to either the shoe or the whisk (which is in fact the correct interpretation of the word). Either interpretation is consistent with the fact that children end up choosing the whisk as the item, and so this finding is not evidence against the theory of mind analysis.

A different sort of objection, raised by Dan Sperber (1997), applies to the more general program of explaining early word learning in terms of theory of mind. Complicated reasoning about the thoughts of other people is slow and difficult. Even if one accepts that children have the requisite background knowledge for these inferences, is it really reasonable to believe that they can carry them out in the course of word learning?

It is true that the sort of inferences involved in early word learning probably *are* slow and difficult for young children. But this is actually consistent with the developmental facts. For instance, 18-month-olds can cope with discrepant-looking situations, but younger children cannot. Baldwin (1991) finds that 16- to 17-month-olds succeed at learning words in a joint-attention condition—that is, when the child and adult are both looking at the same object—but do not learn the word in a discrepant condition, when the child and the adult are looking at different objects. This suggests that 16- to 17-month-olds understand the relevance of attentional focus (if they didn't, the children would have simply taken the new word as naming what they were looking at when they heard it), but that the processing demands of this task were too much for them. Similarly, while one- and two-year-olds show a bias against lexical overlap, it is initially quite weak; the strength of this bias grows in the years that follow (see Merriman, Marazita & Jarvis, 1995, for review). If one does something over and over again, a slow and effortful process can become fast and easy, and this might be what happens for mutual exclusivity in particular and (as argued in chapter 2) for word learning in general.

After all, the use of theory of mind is a ubiquitous part of communication. Understanding a sentence involves more than using lexical and syntactic knowledge to decode a message. It is an act of intentional interpretation, involving a mutual expectation of cooperation between speaker and listener (see Grice, 1975; Sperber & Wilson, 1986). This explains the resolution of ambiguity, as well our understanding of non-literal language such as metaphor, irony, humor, sarcasm, and politeness. If someone asks you "Would you mind telling me what time it is?," it would be perverse or rude to focus on the literal form of the question and answer "No, I wouldn't mind at all." Nonliteral language is processed very rapidly by adults (Gibbs, 1983) and comes naturally to young children, who find it easier to attend to the intended meaning of a sentence than to its literal form (Beal & Flavell, 1984). It is clear, then, that at some point, relatively early in development, such inferences do become second nature.

Its Function

What is the assumption of lexical contrast good for? What would happen to a child who was normal in every way except that she had no bias to assume that people use different words to convey different meanings? While a normal child who hears words such as *Fido, dog, white, animal, pet,* and *tail* applied to a dog would assume that these words all have different meanings, our imaginary child will make no such assumption and could take them all as mutually synonymous. It is not obvious that this child will be at any long-term disadvantage. Since these words really do refer to different things, sooner or later the child will converge on their right meanings. She will notice, for instance, that cats are also called "animals" and infer that *animal* and *dog* are not synonymous. Syntactic cues could aid in distinguishing proper names, common nouns, and adjectives, and pragmatic and contextual cues could distinguish names for parts and wholes.

But this child will face a subtler problem (pointed out to me by Gregory Murphy), which does require a mutual exclusivity bias. Many of the words that children learn are going to refer to categories whose boundaries are arbitrary, at least from the child's standpoint. A bat is not a bird, a bean-bag chair is not a pillow, boots are not shoes, and so on. An avoidance of lexical overlap might be essential to learning about the status of entities that lie on these boundaries and hence could rescue children from overextensions.

Consider the plight of the child who comes to the reasonable, but wrong, view that *ring* refers to any piece of jewelry that encompasses the hand or wrist and so includes bracelets. What can correct this impression? If children call a bracelet "a ring," they might be corrected. But it is implausible that this sort of error and subsequent correction are necessary and that if they never occurred, the misinterpretation would never go away. (If error and correction were necessary, then a significant number of people reading this will be surprised to hear that a bracelet is not a ring.) Instead, children who possess the assumption of lexical contrast can learn that bracelets are not rings just by hearing them called "bracelets." And the same for learning that bats are not birds and bean-bag chairs are not pillows. The precise boundaries of categories can be acquired though noting how words contrast with another.

Note, however, that it is not *just* the fact that the bracelet is called "bracelet" that leads children to figure out that it cannot be a ring. After all, when a child hears a poodle described as "an animal," "a pet," or "a poodle," she does not conclude that poodles actually aren't dogs. As Clark (1998) puts it, children appreciate that people can take multiple perspectives when describing an entity; only when two words are understood as involving the same perspective does the principle of contrast (rooted in theory of mind) kick in, and the child infers that one of the words has to go. In this case, children know that both *bracelet* and *ring* are basic-level object names (see chapters 4 and 6), and this leads them to the insight that they have overextended *ring*—that rings are one kind of thing and bracelets are another.

This sort of account can be taken too far. Ferdinand de Saussure (1916/ 1959) thought names were entirely acquired and understood through this sensitivity to opposition. But this cannot be right. Children start off generalizing words in a constrained way, and even their earliest words tend to be used in a roughly appropriate manner. Although children might think that a bracelet could be called "a ring," they will not extend *ring* to refer to an aardvark, regardless of whether they know the word *aardvark*. This pragmatic understanding of how words relate to one another is instrumental in fine-tuning children's understanding of words; it is not necessary for word learning in general.

The Origin of Words

The discussion above assumes that children already have some implicit notion of what a word is. To see why, consider a child who sees her father point to a dog and say "dog." Suppose the child can infer that her father is referring to a dog. Still, all she could really be said to know is that he intended to refer to the dog and produced a sound as he did so. More is required for the child to know that *dog* is a word that refers to dogs. She has to infer that this sound is related to the act of reference. And she has to realize that anyone, including herself, can refer to dogs by making the same sound. In other words, the child has to make the inferential leap from hearing someone say "dog" when referring to something to the conclusion that *dog* is a word, a Saussurian sign.

Words have unusual properties. Saussure famously stressed their arbitrary nature, the fact that it is an accident of history that a particular form gets mapped onto a particular meaning. But he also noted that words are bidirectional with regard to comprehension and production. James Hurford (1989) points out that this fact is not a logical necessity; there are other ways a communication system could work and other expectations children might have. They could infer that the sound is a symbol in an asymmetric communication system.

A lot of communication is asymmetric. Suppose a child observes her father react to a wasp by gasping. It would be mistaken for her to assume that if on another occasion *she* gasped, her father would think there was a wasp present. Some dogs come to their owner when they are called, but no dogs make the inference that if they were to produce the same sound, their owner will obediently run to them. My computer sometimes asks me questions ("Are you sure you want to permanently remove these items?"), but if I were to type in the same questions, no communication would take place. These are all non-Saussurian systems.

Hurford notes that humans could conceivably have evolved to use non-Saussurian languages. Here is how such a language could work. Imagine two speakers (A and B) and two things to talk about (dogs and cats). If Speaker A wants Speaker B to think about dogs, she says "dog," and if she wants him to think about cats, she says "cat." In contrast, if Speaker B wants Speaker A to think about dogs, he says "chien," and if he wants her to think about cats, he says "chat."

This system is non-Saussurian: while speaker A produces "dog" to communicate about dogs, she might not understand the word "dog" if she heard it. Such systems are sometimes used in the real world. Two bilinguals could converse, each of them speaking in his or her preferred language. And a blind person and a deaf person could communicate this way: the blind person could transmit in a sign language such as ASL and receive in a spoken language such as English, and the deaf person could transmit in English and receive in ASL. So why haven't such systems evolved?

Hurford argues that while non-Saussurian systems might be usable, they are almost impossible to learn. With two speakers, it is bad enough; each has to generate a language and teach it to the other. As the number of speakers increases, the burden increases exponentially. A child who is born into a community of 10 speakers has to not only learn 10 languages but also teach her own language to each of the 10 other speakers. Using a computer simulation, Hurford found that an animal that adopts a Saussurian strategy (and learns words as bidirectional symbols) communicates better than an animal who use a non-Saussurian communication system (see Skyrms, 1996, for a similar analysis).

Under this view, the Saussurian nature of words has evolved through natural selection as part of the evolution of language. But there are reasons to favor an alternative, which is that children's assumption that words will be Saussurian signs is a natural consequence of their theory of mind (see Lewis, 1969). This fact about words is not something that has evolved once in the history of our species; it is discovered anew by every child.

One argument for this alternative is that this Saussurian assumption of bidirectionality is not limited to language. A similar phenomenon shows up in other domains. In an experiment by Mcltzoff (1988), for instance, 14-month-olds are shown an unusual act that achieves a goal, as when an adult bends at the waist to touch a panel with her forehead, causing a light to go on. When shown this, babies will often spontaneously imitate the act. And when 18-month-olds are shown an action that an adult tries to do and fails, such as attempting to hang a loop on a metal prong, they will often imitate the entire successful action, even though they had never seen it before (Meltzoff, 1995).

Actions are not symbols, but what goes on in Meltzoff's experiments might be very similar to what happens when children learn a new word. To see this, consider the inference that babies made in the first study:

Scene: An adult touches a panel with his or her forehead, and a light goes on.
Goal: Turning on the light
Action: Touching the panel with the forehead
Inference: The light can be turned on by touching the panel with one's forehead.

The second study suggests that the same sort of inference can be made when the action and the goal are themselves inferred and not actually witnessed:

Scene: An adult tries to hang a flexible loop on a metal prong and fails.

Goal: Hanging the loop on the prong

Action: Moving the loop to the appropriate location

Inference: The loop can be hung on the prong by moving it to the appropriate location.

Evidence suggests that children's understanding of the goal in the above studies is based on inference about the intentions of the actor and not on observation of the physical motions. When a separate group of babies in the Meltzoff (1995) study saw the same physical motions performed by a mechanical handlike device, they did *not* imitate the attempted actions; they do so only if they see an intentional agent do it. Similarly, when habituated to a hand reaching toward and grasping one of two objects, six-month-olds looked longer when the hand subsequently made the same reaching motion to grasp the second object than when the hand made a physically different reaching motion to grasp the original object. But they showed the reverse pattern of results when habituated to an inanimate rod that repeatedly reached out and contacted one of the objects (Woodward, 1998). Again, only the actions of intentional agents are treated as goal oriented.

Consider now the case in which a child hears an adult use the word *dog* and infers that the adult intends to refer to a dog. For the child to figure out that she can also use the word in the same way (that it is a Saussurian sign), perhaps precisely the same sort of inference as above is needed:

Scene: An adult says "dog" while looking at a dog.

Goal: Referring to the dog

Action: Saying "dog"

Inference: A reference to dogs can be established by saying "dog."

Once a child believes that the adult's use of the word *dog* was used with the intent to refer to a dog, she can infer that if she herself has the same intent (to refer to a dog), then she could use the same means (saying "dog") to satisfy this goal. Just like touching a switch with your forehead turns on a light, saying the word "dog" refers to dogs.

From this perspective, it should be the asymmetrical cases that are hard for children to learn, since something has to block this inference from action to goal. Nobody has ever tried, but it should be terribly difficult to teach children a communicative system that is not Saussurian. (By the same token, it should be just as hard to teach children a noncommunicative asymmetric mapping, in which they observe someone perform an action that achieves a desirable goal but somehow infer that they themselves cannot achieve the same goal by doing the same action.) Note that the examples of asymmetric communication systems that do exist either will involve creatures who do not have a full-blown theory of mind—such as dogs and computers—or are cases that are not actually intentional. If Dad gasps when he sees a wasp, this is properly viewed *not* as a goal-directed action but as an involuntary reaction, and so children do not make the inference that this is an appropriate action to take on encountering wasps.

This theory of mind analysis makes a prediction, which is that children should start off treating *any* communicative act as a potential word. This is in contrast to the prediction that comes from the Hurford view that children's initial assumption about words is part of a special language capacity and hence that only those symbols that are linguistic units (with phonology, morphology, and syntax) should be treated this way.

Some recent studies bear on this issue. Namy and Waxman (1998) taught babies (who were learning English and not a sign language) novel gestures as object labels. For instance, the researcher would show a baby a toy apple, say "We call this," and then produce a novel gesture with her hand. In the test phase, the experimenter would then show the baby another toy apple and a different object, such as a toy pig, and ask "Can you get [the gesture]?" Woodward and Hoyne (1999) used a noisemaker that makes a squeak. The experimenter would show the baby a novel object and say something like "Look at this. [squeak]. Yeah, see it? [squeak]. Wow, look! [squeak]." In the test phase, a second experimenter would show the baby both the original object and a different object and ask "Can you get one of these? [squeak]."

Both studies found that the youngest children who were tested (18-month-olds in the gesture study and 13-month-olds in the noisemaker study) remembered the novel mapping. But the older children who were tested (26-month-olds in the gesture study; 20-month-olds in the noisemaker study) did not. A third study, by Baldwin, Bill, and Ontai (1996), used a gaze-following paradigm and found that neither 12-month-olds nor 18-month-olds treated an adult's sigh in the same way that they treated a word that the adult uttered ("dax").

These findings suggest that an understanding of words develops along two tracks. One is a notion of word that corresponds to a phonological unit, such that *dog* is a word but a squeak or gesture (for children learning a spoken language) is not. Innate language-specific expectations may be held about words in this sense that concern their phonological, morphological, and syntactic properties. Another notion of word corresponds to a Saussurian sign. This emerges from theory of mind, and hence, initially, any intentional communicative act is treated as a Saussurian sign (a phonological string, a gesture, or a sound made by a noisemaker—but not an accidental sound such as a sigh).

The results from the above studies suggest that not until some time after 18 months do these two notions come together and that children realize that only the phonological word is typically used as a Saussurian sign. They learn that people name things with phonological words, not with gestures or squeaks, and only then is their understanding of communication fully integrated into their understanding of language.

Word Learning with and without Theory of Mind

A focus on theory of mind makes some strong predictions about how certain disorders should affect the course of word learning. One central case is that of autism, a developmental disorder that affects about one in a thousand children. It is characterized by a range of deficits, including impairments of socialization, communication, and imagination. One theory is that this cluster of deficits is the product of a delayed, impaired, or nonexistent theory of mind (Baron-Cohen, Leslie & Frith, 1985). This elegantly explains the range of specific problems that autistic children have, including difficulties with understanding false belief, deception, and ignorance, while at the same time accounting for preserved abilities in other domains. (It should be noted, however, that certain other facts about autistic individuals, such as their excellent rote memories and preoccupation with parts of objects, cannot be explained in terms of this theory of mind deficit; see Happé, 1996.)

One proposal, defended in detail by Uta Frith and Francesca Happé (1994), is that the linguistic impairments of autistic individuals are not due to an additional deficit that is special to language, but exists because autistic children are impaired in the theory-of-mind abilities necessary for normal language learning.

Autistic individuals differ profoundly in their linguistic abilities. On one extreme are those with no language. About 30 percent of the individuals who are labeled autistic fall into this class. They might first appear to be deaf, since they often fail to orient to speech, and they sometimes produce odd vocalizations that do not resemble speech or babbling. On the other extreme are those who come to talk, as Asperger (1944) put it, like "little professors." They might have perfect syntax, but their prosody is bizarre (often either monotone or sing-song), and so is their pragmatics. Their language is highly literal. When asked

"Can you pass the salt?," for instance, such individuals might answer yes but do nothing. Most relevant for our purposes here, their vocabularies are said to be normal. Some of them have Asperger's syndrome, which includes only those autistic individuals who show normal language development.[1]

Falling between these two extremes are the majority of autistic individuals, who have some limited language skills. They might echo back words and phrases, either immediately or after a delay. They will show pronominal reversal, using "I" for "you" and vice-versa, and might use entire phrases in such a parroted way—for instance, saying "Do you want a biscuit?" to mean "I want a biscuit." Words and phrases are used in a "simple associative way" (Frith & Happé, 1994), so that "Apple" might always mean "Give me an apple."

Some of this odd linguistic behavior can be readily explained in terms of associative learning mechanisms. In an often cited anecdote, Kanner (1943) reported an autistic boy who used the phrase "Peter eater" to talk about saucepans. His mother explained this by recounting that when he was two years old, she was reciting the rhyme "Peter, Peter, Pumpkin Eater" to him when she dropped a saucepan with a loud clatter. Baron-Cohen, Baldwin, and Crowson (1997) discuss an autistic toddler who would call a toy truck "a sausage," apparently because his mother had said "Tommy, come and eat your sausage" as the boy was looking at his truck. These examples may indicate the hazards of learning language through a strictly associationist learning mechanism.

To explore this issue, Baron-Cohen, Baldwin, and Crowson (1997) studied autistic children using the discrepant-looking paradigm of Baldwin (1991), in which an experimenter looks at one object and utters its name while a child is attending to another object. A purely associative mechanism would lead children to map the word onto what they are attending to, while learning based on theory of mind would lead them to map the word onto what the experimenter is looking at. Autistic children made associatively based mapping errors, while both normal children and mentally handicapped children, matched to the autistic group in mental age, did not. This supports the view that these autistic children's difficulties in word learning are due to their deficit in theory of mind; they lack the inferential capacities that come naturally to normal children who are younger than two.

But so far we have explained only a subset of the autistic population, the middle group, those who have some limited success at learning language but who make unusual errors. But what about the children on the extremes? Some learn no language at all, and, more puzzling for the account here, some show surprising success at language. There are even autobiographies written by autistic individuals such as Temple Grandin. How can this be explained?

One possibility is to appeal to factors independent of theory of mind. Autism is often associated with severe mental retardation and other deficits, perhaps including specifically linguistic problems. It is plausible that these problems—in addition to a deficit in theory of mind— explain those autistic children who remain entirely mute. Harder to explain is the existence of autistic individuals who are almost normal in their language. One proposal is that a continuum of theory-of-mind abilities runs from a severely autistic individual to a normal unimpaired person. This is the approach taken by Frith and Happé (1994), who observe that those individuals who have relatively preserved language skills are the same individuals who tend to perform well on tasks designed to tap their understanding of the thoughts of other people.

In general, then, the extent of the language deficit found in autistic children may be a direct function of the severity of the theory-of-mind deficit. A severe theory-of-mind deficit might leave children without the ability to orient preferentially to speech, share attention, or follow eye gaze, and they might never be able to grasp the notion of an arbitrary sign, leading to no word learning at all. A less severe impairment might make word learning possible but limited and idiosyncratic. And in some cases, the theory-of-mind impairment might be sufficiently mild so as to leave word learning fairly unimpaired, although such individuals might still have problems with aspects of language such as irony and metaphor.

The autism research bears on an alternative perspective on the role of theory of mind in word learning, proposed by Sperber (1997) and others. Suppose that children's ability to understand the communicative intentions of other people really is essential for word learning. Still, it might be that this ability does not arise from a more general capacity to reason about mental states but instead comes from a specialized system that is part of language itself—not a theory of mind, but a *theory of communication*. This would be consistent with the view that word learning is dependent on modular systems that are special to language learning.

The weakness with this theory is that the same inferential capacities relevant to communication apply as well to noncommunicative situations. As discussed above, the same capacity required to appreciate the bidirectional nature of language (Saussure, 1916/1959) underlies the understanding of goal-directed action in general (Meltzoff, 1988). The same direction of gaze cues that children use when figuring out what object someone is labeling (Baldwin, 1991) are used to figure out which object an adult is disgusted by (Baldwin & Moses, 1994). The same ability to distinguish accidental versus purposeful action that is involved in word learning (Tomasello & Barton, 1994) extends to children's choices about which actions to imitate (Meltzoff, 1995). It is highly suggestive that these noncommunicative aspects of theory of mind emerge in normal children at roughly the same age as the communicative aspects of theory of mind, which is also the point at which children begin to learn words.

And consider autism. If a theory of communication were distinct from theory of mind, then we would expect to find autistic children with severe problems understanding the *non*communicative actions of other people but with nonetheless normal language and communication skills. But such cases do not exist.

Williams syndrome (WS) provides an interesting contrast with autism. Like autism, it is a severe disorder of genetic origin. It is rare, affecting about 1 in 20,000 to 50,000 live births, and involves severe deficits in cognitive skills, including number, problem solving, and spatial cognition. Interestingly, language (along with face processing) is relatively spared (e.g., Bellugi, Marks, Bihrle & Sabo, 1988). Despite their low IQs, the vocabulary size of individuals with WS is typically closer to their chronological age than their mental age. While developmental differences do appear in word learning between WS children and normal children (Thal, Bates & Bellugi, 1989; Stevens & Karmiloff-Smith, 1997), the outcomes are quite similar—and very different from most autistic children.

The relevant point here is that people with Williams syndrome are highly social and appear to possess a fully functioning theory of mind (Karmiloff-Smith et al., 1995). Because of their retardation, WS individuals have difficulties in domains that autistic children often succeed at, such as learning to read. But the reverse pattern shows up for language. Because of their social capacities, language is relatively spared in WS—just as it is impaired in autism. If many autistic individuals show how damaging it can be to word learning to have an impaired theory of mind, many people with WS show how a preserved theory of mind can sustain language development in the presence of other problems.

The Adult's Theory of Mind

The starting point for countless discussions of word learning is Quine's "gavagai" example: a child hears a novel word and must figure out, from an infinity of possibilities, the correct meaning. The moral that is typically drawn from this is that constraints or biases must exist. The scope, nature, and origin of such constraints is a matter of debate, but their necessity cannot be in doubt.

Katherine Nelson (1988, p. 240) suggests that this is all wrong: "The typical way children acquire words in their first language is almost completely the reverse of the Quinean paradigm. Children do not try to guess what it is that the adult intends to; rather they have certain conceptions of these aspects of the world they find interesting and, in successful cases of word acquisition it is the adult [at least in Western middle-class societies] who guesses what the child is focused on and applies an appropriate word."

This is an intriguing perspective, and it shows that alternatives do exist to viewing word learning as an inductive process. Parents could notice what a child is observing, such as a dog, and then produce the word for it, "dog." Given that children can form associations, this could be the foundation of word learning. Similarly, Lois Bloom (1993) has suggested, as part of her principle of relevance, "Words are learned when they are relevant to what the child has in mind."

There is still an emphasis on theory of mind here, but it is the *adult's*, not the child's. There is some appeal to this view. After all, one can question how good one- and two-year-olds really are at successfully inferring the thoughts of others. But nobody doubts that adults can, at least some of the time, figure out their child's thoughts and that they are motivated to help their children learn words.

Furthermore, abundant evidence exists that Western parents tailor their use of words to accord with their children's mental states. When interacting with young children, they tend to talk in the here and now, adjusting their conversational patterns to fit the current situation. They engage in "follow-in" labeling, in which they notice what their babies are looking at and name it (e.g., Collins, 1977; Golinkoff, 1986). They even seem to have an implicit understanding that children assume that new words referring to objects will be basic-level names, such as *dog* or *shoe*, and so when adults present children with words that are not basic-level names, they use linguistic cues to make it clear that the words have a different status. For instance, when adults present part names to children, they hardly ever simply point and say "Look at the ears." Instead, they typically begin by talking about the whole object ("This is a rabbit") and then introduce the part name with a possessive construction ("and these are his *ears*") (Masur, 1997; Ninio, 1980; Shipley, Kuhn & Madden, 1983). Similar linguistic support occurs for subordinates ("A *pug* is a kind of dog") and superordinates ("These are *animals*. Dogs and cats are kinds of *animals*") (Adams & Bullock, 1985; Blewitt, 1983; Callanan, 1985; Poulin-Dubois, Graham & Sippola, 1995; Shipley, Kuhn & Madden, 1983).

What role does this sort of support play in word learning? Under a strong version of the parent-centered view, children wouldn't be able to cope without it. But this is unlikely. All the experimental evidence reviewed above shows that children can learn words when the condition of preexisting joint attention is not met. Furthermore, neglected and abused children, raised in situations in which nobody is trying to teach them language, nevertheless come to know the meanings of words. And even in the happiest of families, words are not always used to refer to what children are attending to, and yet serious mapping errors are nonexistent. Finally—as Nelson herself parenthetically notes in the quotation above—these naming practices are not universal; in some societies adults make no effort to teach the meanings of words to their young children.

On the other hand, it is unlikely that all of this careful behavior on the part of adults is an utter waste of time. The argument so far has been that children are remarkably good at figuring out the thoughts of adults; this is the engine that drives the word-learning process. Is it really plausible, then, that *adults* are so inept at figuring out the thoughts of their children that they go through elaborate efforts that have no effect at all? It is more likely that parents know what they are doing and hence these strategies really do help children learn words.

This assumption has considerable support. One does not need to do a controlled study to learn that the best way to teach children a new object name is to make sure they are paying attention to the object when the word is used. Verbs are different; children actually find it harder to learn a novel verb when it is used to comment on an already ongoing event; they do better when the verb is used immediately before the event (Tomasello & Kruger, 1992)—which is exactly when parents tend to use novel verbs (Tomasello, 1992). Studies with novel categories find that children's natural assumption when exposed to a novel object label is to interpret it as referring to a basic-level object kind, which is again exactly in accord with how adults use such words (Horton & Markman, 1980; Markman & Wachtel, 1988; Mervis & Crisafi, 1982).

All of this suggests that these naming patterns on the part of adults are useful but that they just aren't necessary. The important thing to realize here is that nothing about adult naming behavior is special to dealing with children. Imagine that a college student from another country is living with you and speaks no English but wants to learn. You might slow down your rate of speech, talk about the here and now, point to objects and name them, and so on, just as you would do for a young child. If you wanted to teach the student the word *handle*, you would not pick up a cup and say "Handle"; you would more likely say something like "This is a cup, and [touching the handle] this is the handle." If you wanted to teach the word *animal*, you would not point to the dog and say, "This is an animal"; instead you would say something like "This is a dog. A dog is a kind of animal," or you would wait to find a heterogeneous group of animals and say "These are animals."

Most children raised in Western societies are in the situation of the student: they are surrounded by people who want to teach them words and who are pretty good at doing so. Children in other cultures are in the position of a student who is surrounded by people who love him, find him adorable, but have no interest in teaching him how to speak. Adults can learn words even in this more impoverished environment—and so can children.

This leads to the prediction that children raised in environments in which this support is present should learn words *faster* than those raised in other environments. If not, then most Western parents really would be wasting their time. In fact, there is a correlation between the extent to which parents engage their children in joint attention interactions and their rate of word learning (Akhtar, Dunham & Dunham, 1991; Harris, Jones & Grant, 1983; Tomasello & Todd, 1983), which is consistent with the view that parental naming behavior affects vocabulary growth, though (as discussed in chapter 2) there are other explanations for such correlations. Furthermore, anecdotal evidence shows that children raised in societies without object labeling do learn words somewhat slower than those raised in most Western societies (Lieven, 1994), though as yet no systematic research has been done into this issue.

In sum, adults' attempts to teach children words might help speed up the word-learning process. But they are not necessary for word learning and, even when they are present, do not substitute for the child's own ability to infer the referential intentions of others.

Word Learning in Chimpanzees

Another reason to believe that adult naming practices cannot entirely explain word learning has to do with species differences. This issue of precisely what nonhuman primates can and cannot learn is a controversial one, but some facts are clear. The signal systems of primates in the wild, such as vervet monkeys, are based on a small, fixed number of signs with determinate meanings; individuals do not create new words and do not teach words to their offspring (e.g., Cheney & Seyfarth, 1990). And no matter how supportive an environment they are placed in, nonhuman primates do not learn words in the same way that human children do. Even by the most enthusiastic claims, chimpanzees who are trained in the use of sign language come to use about 200 to 300 signs after years of extensive interaction (e.g., Savage-Rambaugh et al., 1993). As Lila Gleitman once remarked, if a child ever learned language the way that an ape does, the child's parents would run screaming to the nearest neurologist.

Why are chimpanzees so bad at word learning? Under a theory that sees the capacity for word learning as part of a dedicated language faculty, there is a ready answer: chimps have not evolved this language faculty, and so they do not learn words for the same reason that they do not learn phonology, morphology, and syntax. But I have suggested here that there is no special faculty for word learning, that it emerges from a host of other capacities that humans possess. So why are chimps—who are smart and capable animals, superior to one- and two-year-olds in many ways—so much worse at word learning?

One possibility is that despite their quite rich social abilities, they lack relevant aspects of theory of mind. In particular, they lack an instinctive understanding of referential intent. This is the position taken by Tomasello (1998). He notes that chimpanzees in the wild never show, offer, or point to objects for other chimpanzees. And while you can train them to point to direct their trainers to food, they never quite get the hang of it; when they see someone else point, they are mystified (Call & Tomasello, 1994; Povinelli et al., 1997). In a nice turn of phrase, Tomasello summarizes the species difference: "children use symbols, whereas other primates use signals." Under this view, a chimpanzee is in the position of the most autistic of autistic children, never understanding how words work.

Just as with babies, it is always risky making claims about what nonhuman primates cannot do; if you wait long enough, some clever researcher will prove you wrong. Moreover, chimpanzees plainly *do* have certain capacities related to theory of mind, such as the capacity to categorize certain social relationships and to conceive of conspecifics as animate and goal-directed entities. But Tomasello's hypothesis is appealing in a couple of ways.

First, it is not obvious what *other* capacity chimpanzees lack that could explain their failure to learn words. They have fine perceptual and motor skills, they are excellent at associative learning, and they seem to have the right sort of conceptual understanding of the external world. Theory of mind is the only area, other than language itself, in which they are manifestly inferior to human children.

Second, this proposal captures an insight about the behavior of nonhuman primates in the wild. As Tomasello notes, chimpanzees communicate to regulate dyadic interactions such as play and sex, but they don't communicate about other entities; they don't *refer*. This limitation in theory of mind extends to noncommunicative contexts as well, as they do not spontaneously imitate the goal-directed behavior of others. In all of these ways, a chimpanzee is profoundly different from a human without language, such as a baby or an aphasic adult. This could explain why they can never fully engage in the process of word learning.

Limitations of Theory of Mind

Could theory of mind be the whole story of word learning? Perhaps learning the meaning of a word just reduces to intentional inference; once we know how children divine the intentions of others, there is nothing left to explain.

But a lot more is needed. No matter how good they are at understanding the minds of others, children cannot learn a word without the ability to grasp the associated concept. Suppose, for the sake of argument, that two-year-olds have the same theory of mind as adults. Still, two-year-olds will not be able to learn words such as *modem* and *stockbroker* (even though these refer to observable middle-sized objects) because they don't yet know what such categories are. What theory of mind does for children is enable them to establish the mapping between a word and a concept. But this presupposes the availability of the concept.[2]

And there is still Quine's problem. Putting aside exotic possibilities such as undetached rabbit parts, how do children know whether the adult is describing the individual rabbit (as in "This is Flopsy") versus describing the rabbit as a member of a category (as in "This is a rabbit")? Pointing and eye gaze are useless here, as the overt behavior of someone using a proper name is indistinguishable from the behavior of someone using a common noun (Baldwin, 1995). So unless children are *literally* mind-readers, they have to use some other cue to tell the difference. Candidate proposals as to how this is done include a sensitivity to syntactic cues, an understanding of what sorts of things get proper names, and information gained by hearing a word used on multiple occasions (see chapter 5).

Consider also children's default expectations as to what words mean. When shown a new object and given a word for it, children are prone to think that the new word is a name for the whole object, as in *rabbit*. It is conceivable that this bias is product of theory of mind; children favor the object interpretation because they think that objects are what adults are most likely to refer to. This is a reasonable hypothesis, but in the next chapter, I present evidence suggesting that it is mistaken. For one thing, it turns out that the "object bias" is relatively impervious to pragmatic factors. It is very hard to teach a solid substance name like *wood*, for instance; regardless of what an adult says or does, young children tend to think the word is an object name. For another, the same whole object bias shows up in noncommunicative domains such as tracking and enumeration.

What is the proper place, then, of theory of mind in an account of early word learning? One way to look at it is that children use inferences about the referential intentions of others to create arrows, or pointers, from words to the world. A child hears the word "rabbit" and uses a speaker's direction of gaze to figure out what he or she is referring to. In the child's mind, an arrow is now going from *rabbit* to a rabbit. This understanding is necessary to learn the word. But the point of the arrow does not touch a concept or meaning; it touches an object in the world, a rabbit. It is up to the child to figure out from this what the word means. Does it refer to the kind (*rabbit*), a specific individual (*Flopsy*), or a property (*white*)? If the word refers to the kind, what other objects belong to the same kind—that is, what other objects are rabbits? Even with a full-blown theory of mind, the child's problems have just begun.

Notes

1. Though the criteria for "normal" here are quite liberal. For instance, Francesca Happé has pointed out to me that if a child produces only one word at the age of 24 months, this would likely count as normal development for the purposes of diagnosis. Little is known about the early language development of children who are later diagnosed with Asperger's syndrome.
2. It also presupposes the availability of the *form* of a word, which requires the ability to segment the speech stream—also a separate capacity from theory of mind.

Chapter 4

Object Names and Other Common Nouns

The first words of a child of Harvard graduate students in the 1960s
are much the same as those of a child learning French in the Paris of
the 1920s or one currently learning Kaluli in the highlands of Papua
New Guinea. Many early words refer to middle-sized objects—things
that can move and be moved. These include names for specific people
(*Mama, Dada*), animals (*dog, cat*), toys (*ball, block*), articles of clothing
(*sock, shirt*), and other artifacts (*fork, chair*). There are names for substances (*juice, milk*), names for parts, typically body parts (*nose, foot*),
modifiers (*hot, more*), words that refer to actions or changes (*up, allgone*),
and routines that are linked to certain social interactions (*bye-bye,
peek-a-boo*) (see Clark, 1993, for review). Soon afterward, verbs appear
(*go, make*), as do prepositions (*in, on*) and more abstract terms (*kitchen,
nap*).

This chapter addresses the question of why children's early vocabularies are the way they are. The initial focus is on object names, but it
also discusses nominals in general, including those that refer to substances, actions, parts, and collections. The chapter concludes by shifting attention away from meaning and toward form, asking how
children figure out which words in an utterance are the relevant ones
to attend to. This problem is largely ignored in discussions of word
learning, but it is a serious one, and its solution leads to some rather
surprising conclusions about the sort of experience necessary for
successful word learning.

Explaining the Words People Know

Learning a word involves mapping a form, such as the sound "dog,"
onto a meaning or concept, such as the concept of dogs. This perspective leads to three considerations underlying why children and adults
know the words they do.

Access to the Form

People cannot learn words unless they are exposed to them. We can explain much of the character of children's vocabularies in terms of this banal fact, without positing any differences between the minds of children and adults. No matter how smart babies are, their first words are more likely to include *milk* and *spoon* than *weed* and *gene*. These are the words they hear.

Note, however, that there is more to figuring the accessibility of a form than simply determining its frequency in speech to children. It is not how often the adult says the word that matters; it is how often the child processes it. (This distinction is sometimes expressed as *input* versus *intake*). For instance, in English-speaking mothers' speech to one-year-olds, names for things are loudest and most likely to be in final position (Goldfield, 1993; Messer, 1981); such factors make it relatively easy for children to extract these words from the speech stream. In contrast, closed-class morphemes like *a* and *the* are very frequent, far more so than any particular object name, but they are harder for children to process.

Access to the Concept

To learn what a word means, one needs to possess the relevant concept. A two-year-old child of parents who are buying a house might often hear the word *mortgage,* but the word will not be learned because two-year-olds don't have the concept of mortgages.

In some cases, the relative ease with which words are acquired can be explained in terms of conceptual access. For instance, children learn *dog* before *animal* and *car* before *vehicle.* Not only are basic-level terms more frequent in the input (e.g., Brown, 1958a), but children also find it more natural to categorize a novel object as an instance of a basic-level kind than as an instance of a superordinate kind. As a result, children (and adults) find it easier to learn novel basic-level names than novel superordinates, even when the words are used equally often (e.g., Horton & Markman, 1980; see chapter 6).

Access to the Mapping

Form X and form Y could be equally accessible to the child, and so could concept X and concept Y, but word X might still be learned earlier than word Y. It might be easier for children to figure out that form X maps onto concept X than to figure out that form Y maps onto concept Y. To learn a word, after all, you not only need to hear the form and possess the relevant concept; you have to put the two together.

Lila Gleitman and Henry Gleitman (1997) suggest that mapping difficulties are one reason why mental-state verbs such as *thinking* take so long to learn. They report a study by Gillette et al. in which they exposed adults to videotaped mother-child interactions with the sound turned off; the adult heard beeps whenever the mothers used a noun or a verb. The subjects were asked to guess which English words the beeps corresponded to. Under these circumstances, adults found it fairly easy to recognize when the mother was using an object name like *chair* but quite difficult to figure out when she was using a mental-state verb like *thinking*. Since the words were presented an equal number of times, and since adults already have the concepts of chairs and thinking, it is likely that the relative difficulty has to do with establishing the mapping. Under the circumstances in which these words are typically used, it is easier to figure out that *chair* refers to chairs than it is to figure out that *thinking* refers to thinking.

With these three factors in mind, we can go back to children's first words. It has long been observed that names for objects have a special place in child language. This point is often overstated. Not all or even most of children's words are object names. (Typically, fewer than half of children's first 50 words are object names.) In fact, not all of children's *nouns* refer to objects; before their second birthday, children produce nouns referring to substances, parts, actions, and locations (e.g., L. Bloom, Tinker & Margulis, 1993; P. Bloom, 1990; Gordon, 1992; Nelson, Hampson & Shaw, 1993).

Nonetheless, object names really are special. They constitute a much larger proportion of children's early vocabularies than they do of the vocabularies of older children and adults (Brown, 1957; Macnamara, 1982; Pinker, 1984). This is true for every language that has been studied, including English, Italian, Japanese, Kaluli, Mandarin Chinese, Navajo, Turkish, and Tzeltal (see Gentner & Boroditsky, in press, for review). Korean has been argued to be an exception to this generalization. It is a verb-final language and allows for nominal ellipsis, both factors that lead to more emphasis on verbs in the input. Choi and Gopnik (1995) present evidence suggesting that the noun bias is not as prevalent in the vocabularies of young Korean children. This is a controversial claim, as other investigators *have* found a strong noun bias in children learning Korean (Au, Dapretto & Song, 1994) as well as in children learning Japanese, which is also verb-final with nominal ellipsis (Fernald & Morikawa, 1993). But in any case, as Gentner and Boroditsky (in press) point out, even in the Choi and Gopnik (1995) study there does exist a noun bias in children's first 50 words (44 percent nouns versus 31 percent verbs)—despite the fact that verbs are more salient than nouns in the speech that these children hear.

Children are biased to interpret new words as object names. John Macnamara (1972, p. 4) was one of the first to note that this is children's default assumption when learning a new word: "It is obvious that an infant has the capacity to distinguish from the rest of the physical environment an object which his mother draws to his attention and names. It seems clear too that in such circumstances he adopts the strategy of taking the word he hears as a name for the object as a whole rather than as a subset of its properties, or for its position, or weight, or worth, or anything else."

I've said before that children almost never make mapping errors, but those that do occur can be captured in terms of this bias. Macnamara (1972) describes a 17-month-old who would refer to the kitchen stove as *hot*. Assuming that she really thought *hot* was the name for the stove (and was not using the word appropriately to comment on its most interesting property, as an adult might), this could be because she heard someone talk about the stove as being hot and mistakenly viewed the term as naming not a property but the object itself.

Considerable experimental evidence supports the existence of an object bias. When shown an object (such as a rabbit) and given a name for it, children will assume that the word refers to that object and not to a part of the object (the tail), a property (white), the action that the object is doing (hopping), or the stuff that the object is made of (rabbit meat) (e.g., Baldwin, 1989; Dockrell & Campbell, 1986; Golinkoff, Mervis & Hirsh-Pasek, 1994; Hall, Waxman & Hurwitz, 1993; Landau, Smith & Jones, 1988; Markman & Hutchinson, 1984; Markman & Wachtel, 1988; Soja, Carey & Spelke, 1991; Waxman & Markow, 1995). This is often described as a finding about children, but it is actually a fact about people in general. When shown a novel object and given a word that refers to it, adults do exactly the same thing: we take the word as an object name.

What is the nature of this whole-object bias? There are many possibilities. It could be a conceptual bias: we might naturally see the world as containing objects, and so, when we hear new words and have to figure out what they refer to, objects are natural candidates. It could be a mapping bias, based on theory of mind: we might believe that other people, when they use words, typically wish to draw our attention to objects. Or it might be an assumption about language, about how words work. Under all of these accounts, the further question arises as to whether the relevant biases or expectations are learned, perhaps through experience with language, or innate, perhaps evolved to facilitate the process of word learning.

Before addressing these alternatives, it is first necessary to consider more precisely what we mean by *object*. This inquiry bears on a certain class of theories about the origin and nature of the object bias, and it also is relevant for the question of how children learn names for entities other than objects.

Objects

What is an object? Put like that, the question is vague; the word *object* is used in many ways in both colloquial English and within psychology and philosophy. A better question is: When we conclude that children are biased to treat words as object names—because, for instance, they assume that a new word that is used in the presence of a rabbit means *rabbit* and not *white, jumping,* or *tail*—exactly which notion of "object" are we appealing to? Which criteria are children using when choosing *rabbit* over all of these alternatives?

We can quickly reject some proposals. When Simone de Beauvoir says that a woman stands before a man "as an object," she is describing a lamentable state of affairs; it degrades a person to be viewed in this manner. This is plainly not the notion of object we are interested in here. Logicians sometimes use the word *object* to describe anything that one can quantify over and, under this reading, literally anything can be a single object, including, say, my shoe and the top half of the Eiffel Tower. This also won't do. Similarly, when Gottlob Frege (1892) says that every proper name has an associated object, this would include not only individual people but also places (*London*), events (*World War II*), corporations (*Burger King*), and groups (*Spice Girls*). Again, this might be a perfectly good way to use the word for other purposes, but it is not relevant for our purposes.

More promising notions come from perceptual psychology, where similar questions arise. The relationship between parts and wholes poses a particularly important problem. David Marr (1982, p. 270) discusses this and presents a skeptical solution: "Is a nose an object? Is a head one? Is it still one if it is attached to a body? What about a man on horseback? . . . There is really no answer to [these questions]—all these things can be an object if you want to think of them that way, or they can be part of a larger object."

What we are looking for is a notion of object that best comports with children's word learning biases, one consistent with the finding that names for such entities are easy to learn. From this perspective, we can answer Marr's questions: a man on horseback is not an object in our sense because no child could ever learn a word that refers to such an entity. A nose and a head are not objects either; they are parts of objects.

In my view, the notion of object that best corresponds to the findings from language acquisition has been elaborated by Elizabeth Spelke on the basis of her infant research (e.g., Spelke, 1994; Spelke, Phillips & Woodward, 1995). We can call these entities *Spelke-objects*, though most of the time, when there is no danger of confusion, I'll just call them *objects*. To anticipate an argument I make below, it is not an accident that a notion of object developed from studies of how babies see the world so elegantly captures the word-learning biases we find in children and adults. Instead, humans are naturally predisposed to see the world as composed of Spelke-objects—and this explains the object bias present in early word learning.

What is a Spelke-object? Such entities follow principles, the most central one being the *principle of cohesion*. To be an object is to be a connected and bounded region of matter that maintains its connectedness and boundaries when it is in motion. With objects of the right size, this suggests a crude test of objecthood: grab some portion of stuff and *pull*; all the stuff that comes with you belongs to the same object; the stuff that remains behind does not (Pinker, 1997). By this criteria, heads are not typically objects; if you tug on a person's head, the rest of their body follows. When a head is severed, however, it is an object. A man on horseback is two objects, not one, because the man can move and be moved independently from the horse and vice-versa.

The principle of cohesion is a claim about our understanding of what it is to be an object, not a claim about the perceptual cues necessary for online object parsing. You don't have to actually see cohesive and bounded movement to realize something is an object; it is enough that you can infer that there *could* be such movement. Hence adults can parse stationary scenes into distinct objects because the gaps between entities imply that they will not move together (as when we see two shoes next to each other but not touching), because we recognize entities we know from prior experience exist as independently moving objects (as when we see a man on a horse), or because Gestalt cues such as good continuity and sameness of color and texture suggest that different entities have the potential for independent movement (as when we see a shiny red sphere resting on a flat green surface). Such inferences from stationary scenes can be mistaken, however. The man on horseback might be a statue, for instance, carved from a single piece of marble, in which case it would be one object, not two.

Babies are sensitive to shared patterns of movement when reasoning about objects. Kellman and Spelke (1983) showed three-month-olds a wide screen with one stick poking out at the top and another stick poking out at the bottom. If the sticks move back and forth in tandem, undergoing common motion, three-month-olds assume that they are part of a single object—and are surprised if the screen is removed and they are not connected. And eight-month-olds, though perhaps not younger babies, show some ability to use Gestalt cues such as good continuation to parse stationary scenes into multiple objects even if the objects are touching (Needham & Baillargeon, 1997).

There is evidence for an early grasp of other object principles proposed by Spelke. Babies expect objects to follow a continuous pathway through space; they do not disappear from one point and reappear at another (the *principle of continuity*), and they know that objects do not pass through each other (the *principle of solidity*). One finding that demonstrates both principles is that when an object is placed immediately behind a screen and the screen rotates backward, four-month-olds expect the screen to hit the object and stop; when it goes through the space that should be occupied by the hidden object, they are surprised (Baillargeon, Spelke & Wasserman, 1985). This suggests that they expect the object to (1) continue to exist behind the screen and (2) be solid and stop the screen from dropping. A final principle—*the principle of contact*—applies only to inanimate Spelke-objects: babies expect inanimate objects to move if and only if they touch (e.g., Leslie, 1982), though they do not have this expectation about people (Spelke, Phillips & Woodward, 1995).

These principles (cohesion, continuity, solidity, and contact) are said by Spelke to constitute *core knowledge* on the part of children and are likely to be innate. Other facts about objects, such as the fact that they will fall if unsupported, do not seem to be present in young babies and are possibly learned through experience.

How are these principles related? Spelke (e.g., 1994; Carey & Spelke, 1994) treats them as similar in nature and equally important. Certain considerations, however, suggest that the principle of cohesion has a special status. Consider how we deal with violations of the other principles. Violations of the contact principle are frequent; they occur when wind blows papers off my desk, for instance. Even when we have no idea why the principle is violated (as would be the case if my computer was to suddenly slide forward without anyone touching it), we are surprised, but the violation doesn't make us doubt that we are dealing with objects. Science fiction involves frequent violations of the continuity and solidity principles, as when people and machines are instantaneously teleported from one place to another or when an alien has the power to walk through walls. But, again, such violations do not lead us to doubt whether these entities really are objects. When Captain Kirk is teleported onto a planet (violating the continuity principle), you still expect him to be cohesive, solid, and so on. If he subsequently walks into a wall, you expect him to stop, not go through it.

But now consider violations of the cohesion principle. Imagine seeing someone reach for what looks to be a solid pyramid resting on a table, grabbing the top, and lifting . . . and then just the top half rises, the base of the pyramid remains on the table. You would be surprised to see this, just as three-month-olds are (Spelke, Breinlinger, Jacobson & Phillips, 1993). But it is a different sort of surprise than you get with violations of the other principles. With the other violations, you are surprised because they violate expectations of what objects should do: objects should not disappear and reappear elsewhere, go through walls, or move spontaneously. But in the pyramid case, the surprise isn't because violating cohesion is a strange thing for an object to do. It is because the action reveals that, contrary to your expectation, it isn't a single object at all: it is two objects. The principles of solidity, continuity, and contact describe our understanding about *how objects should behave*; the principle of cohesion describes our understanding of *what it is to be an object*.

In fact, this distinction between the cohesion principle and the other principles is implicit in the design of the studies described above. A typical study involves showing babies an object and having it act in some unusual way, such as move by itself, go through a barrier, teleport, defy gravity, and so on. If the babies are surprised, as shown by their pattern of looking, this suggests that they have certain expectations about how objects should behave. But such studies make sense only if one assumes that the babies have some antecedent way of knowing that the object in question actually *is* an object. Babies do know this, and this is because they are first shown that the entity obeys the principle of cohesion: it moves as a single unit. This tells them that it is an object and sets the stage for the experimenter to explore how much they know about the properties that objects do and do not have.

Versions of the principle of cohesion have been around for a long time. Consider Aristotle's (330 B.C. / 1941, 1015b36–1016a9) proposal in his *Metaphysics* that a "continuous thing" "has by its own nature one movement and cannot have any other; and the movement is one when it is indivisible, and indivisible in time. Those things are continuous by their own nature which are not one merely by contact; *for if you put pieces of wood touching one another, you will not say that these are one piece of wood or one body or one continuum of any sort*."

Aristotle raises an important consideration here, which is that our understanding of what an object is rests in part on our intuitions about its "nature" (see also Cohen, 1996). Suppose I firmly hold a block of wood between my thumb and fingers. Under an overly literal interpretation of the Spelke principles, the block and I constitute a single object: we are solid, bounded, and continuous and move as a single unit. But this is not, of course, the sort of interpretation that people would naturally make. This sort of cohesiveness is seen as *accidental*. It is a different sort of cohesiveness that holds between, say, my head and the rest of my body. Or consider a large desk. It might take a lot of force to move such a desk separately from the rug it is on—more force than it would take to break off a small branch from a tree. Nevertheless, we see the desk as an object and the branch as an object part (and we would do so even if we had never before seen a desk or a tree).

The point here, following Aristotle, is that when we parse the world into objects, we do not merely use a simple algorithm about what moves together and what does not; we use a more sophisticated understanding of whether this common motion is by "nature."

It might be that an understanding of cohesion becomes increasingly more abstract with age. A baby might start off with a simple idea: "Something is a single object if and only if it moves as a bounded and cohesive region." By the time babies are 12 months old, however, their understanding of Spelke-objects is sufficiently subtle that they do not have to actually witness this movement. They can infer it—as when they parse a stationary scene into a cup and a spoon—because they've previously seen these objects in independent motion. Further development would involve an appreciation of more subtle cases, as when something that cannot easily move independently, such as a block of wood that someone is holding, is nonetheless treated as an object.

The importance of cohesion is obvious when we think of what object knowledge is most likely for, which is to parse the world into ecologically relevant units. The other principles don't segment the world in the right way. The principles of solidity and continuity are too broad: they apply to all portions of solid substance. A patch of ground is solid and continuous, and so is the top half of a rabbit. And the principle of contact is too narrow; it applies only to middle-sized inanimate entities, such as sticks and stones, and not to people, birds, or rabbits. But the principle of cohesion is just right. Armed only with this principle, an animal would succeed in identifying entities that *move*, and this includes the most important entities of all—other animals. Initially parsing the world on the basis of cohesion establishes a foundation that underlies the application of the other object principles.

The Bias toward Object Names

The analysis so far motivates an explanation for the object bias in word learning, one originally proposed by Dedre Gentner (1982). It is that we are predisposed to view words as describing whole objects because we are predisposed to think about the world as containing whole objects. Once children know that words are used to refer, objects are the natural candidates for what they are referring to (see also Macnamara, 1982; Maratsos, 1991).

This is not to say that babies are insensitive to properties and entities other than objects. Babies are sensitive to size and color, to movement, and to numerosity. But the objects are seen as the important entities; everything else is secondary. In other words, babies see the world as adults do.

Some of the merits of this approach become clear when we look at the alternatives. One theory is that the whole object bias is primarily an assumption about *words*. Such an assumption might emerge from innate properties of language or thought (e.g., Markman, 1989; Waxman, 1994; Waxman & Markow, 1995; Woodward & Markman, 1997), in which case it would apply to children's first words and should be universal. Or it could be learned through experience with words (Choi & Gopnik, 1995; Golinkoff, Mervis & Hirsh-Pasek, 1994; Gopnik & Choi, 1995; Nelson, 1988), in which case it should apply somewhat later in development, after children have had sufficient experience with language, and it might not be universal.

Another possibility is that the whole-object bias has a syntactic basis. For instance, children know that count nouns correspond to kinds of individuals, and objects are salient individuals; so when children hear a count noun, they are prone to assume that it refers to an object kind (P. Bloom, 1994b). Under this view, the bias should apply only after children are able to identify count nouns and mass nouns in English utterances, which is long after they have started to learn and use words (e.g., Gordon, 1988; Soja, Carey & Spelke, 1991).

A final proposal is based on theory of mind. Children's object bias might emerge from a sensitivity to the referential intentions of others. Children might be biased to assume that when adults use words in certain contexts, they are intending to refer to objects (e.g., Tomasello & Akhtar, 1995). Under this view, the whole-object bias does not reflect how children think about the world, about words, or about nouns: it reflects how they think about the minds of other people.

When you look at an older child or adult, all these factors might apply. It might be that when four-year-olds see someone point to a strange animal and say, "This is a lemur," they see the object as a distinct and salient entity in the world *and* they know that a novel word is likely to be an object name *and* they know that count noun syntax is indicative of reference to an object category *and* they can figure out that the situation is typical of an adult intending to refer to an object.

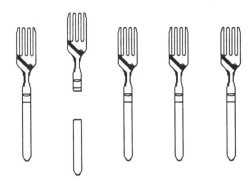

Figure 4.1
"Can you count the forks?" (from Shipley & Shepperson, 1990)

For four-year-olds, the whole object bias could be overdetermined. The debate is over which of these factors is primary.

Two facts about the whole-object bias strongly constrain how we can explain it. The first is that the whole-object bias is precocious. As noted above, object terms—either common nouns that refer to kinds of objects or proper names that refer to individual objects—are frequent among children's first words. Hearing a new word draws even 12-month-olds' attention to an object category (Waxman & Markow, 1995). This precludes certain accounts of where the bias comes from. For instance, it is unlikely to be the product of experience with words. It is also unlikely to exist through a sensitivity to the semantics of words belonging to the syntactic category of count nouns or lexical NPs, since 12-month-olds cannot yet distinguish members of these categories from other parts of speech.

The second fact is that the bias in favor of objects is not limited to word learning. I have already discussed a body of research showing that babies are biased to think of the world in terms of whole objects. Other research has found the same sort of bias in another domain, that of number. A particularly clever study was done by Elizabeth Shipley and Barbara Shepperson (1990). They showed preschool children pictures of objects, such as the picture in figure 4.1.

If you were shown this picture and asked to "Count the forks," you would say either "four" or "five" (depending on how open-minded you are about the broken fork). Shipley and Shepperson find that preschool children tend to answer "six." That is, even when told to count the *forks*, they count each of the *objects*. Similarly, when shown two red apples and three yellow bananas and asked to count the colors or the kinds of fruit, the preschooler's answer is dictated by the number of objects that are present, and so they tend to answer "five." It is not that these children don't know what forks, colors, or kinds are. It is that, in these circumstances, they focus on the objects.

What's the best way to make sense of this result? Stanislaus Dehaene (1997, p. 61) reviews this research, along with several other studies showing that babies can enumerate small sets of objects, and he draws the following conclusion: "the maxim 'Number is a property of sets of discrete physical objects' is deeply embedded in their brains."

This might well be true, but babies' numerical understanding extends beyond objects. After all, they can also enumerate sounds and actions (Starkey, Spelke & Gelman, 1990; Wynn, 1996). And young children have no problem counting entities such as sounds (Wynn, 1990). This suggests that the counting errors do not arise because children can count only objects. A more likely explanation is provided by Shipley and Shepperson (1990), who suggest that children have a strong bias to parse the world into discrete physical objects. As a result, when objects are present in the scene, children are strongly biased to count them. But in the absence of objects in the scene, children have no problem counting other entities.

It would be missing an important generalization to posit three independent object biases—one that underlies how babies track and individuate entities in the world (as found by Spelke), another guiding how they interpret the meanings of words (as found by Macnamara), and a third underlying their counting preferences (as found by Shipley and Shepperson). It makes more sense to use the first fact to explain the other two. Children think about the world as containing Spelke-objects. Hence, when figuring out what people are referring to when they use a new word, and when figuring out which entities to count, objects are natural candidates.

As a final example of the object bias at work, Geoff Hall (1996a) showed four-year-olds and adults entities that were presented in familiar geometrical forms. Some were Spelke-objects, such as a square made of wood; others were substances, such as a square made out of peanut butter. When simply asked "What is that?," subjects would talk about the objects with words that referred to the entire individual such as *square* (even though they knew the word *wood*), and the substances with substance names such as *peanut butter* (even though they knew the word *square*). That is, when shown a Spelke-object, children and adults are drawn to focus on it (and not the material that it is made from) even in a situation that does not involve the learning of words.

Simple Objects and Complex Objects

Gentner (1982) was one of the first proponents of the view that the whole-object bias has its origin in how children experience the world. More recently, in collaboration with Mutsumi Imai, she has proposed an intriguing modification to this view. Imai and Gentner (1997) suggest that all Spelke-objects are not created equal, at least not for the purpose of word learning. Instead, across different languages, complex objects are always perceived as distinct individuals, nonsolid substances are never thought of in this way, and simple objects fall in between. Depending on the language they are exposed to, children can come to think of simple objects as distinct nameable entities or as undifferentiated stuff.

The empirical basis for this claim is an experiment with American and Japanese children and adults, one that was a modified replication of Soja, Carey, and Spelke (1991). The subjects were shown substances (such as sand in an S-shape), simple objects (such as a kidney-shaped piece of paraffin), and complex objects (such as a wood whisk). These entities were named with neutral syntax, as in "Look at the dax" (and the equivalent neutral form in Japanese). Subjects were given a forced-choice task to see how they would generalize the words. They were shown another entity of the same shape made from a different material (consistent with an object interpretation) and another entity of a different shape but made from the same material (consistent with a substance interpretation) and were asked to "Point to the tray that also has the dax on it."

The subjects were young two-year-olds (mean age: two years, one month), older two-year-olds (mean age: two years, eight months), four-year-olds, and adults. The responses of the youngest children are the basis for Imai and Gentner's proposal. Replicating Soja, Carey, and Spelke (1991), they found that children learning English tended to extend the names for both simple objects and complex objects on the basis of shape but did not tend to do so for the names for substances. This is consistent with the view that the Spelke-principles underlie the whole-object bias. But the Japanese children behaved differently. Although they tended to generalize names for complex objects on the basis of shape and names for substances on the basis of material, they responded differently for the simple objects. Here they showed no generalization on the basis of shape; they responded at chance.

Imai and Gentner explain this difference between American and Japanese children as the consequence of the syntax of these languages. English has a grammatical count-mass distinction, in which count nouns (nouns that occur with determiners such as *another* and *many*) differ in their semantics from mass nouns (nouns that occur with determiners such as *much*) (P. Bloom, 1994b; Jackendoff, 1990). Spelke-objects are named by count nouns, as in "a dog" and "many bricks," while material entities that are not Spelke-objects are named with mass nouns, as in "some water" and "much sand." But Japanese has no grammatical count-mass distinction; the words *dog* and *water* fall into the same syntactic class. Imai and Gentner (1997, p. 193) propose that the syntax that children learn affects how they construe simple objects and suggest that the original object proposal of Gentner should be modified accordingly: "Gentner's (1982) natural-partitions hypothesis asserts that object names are learned earlier than relational terms because objects are . . . more easily individuated and parsed out from the perceptual context than other kinds of referents. Our results suggest adding the assumption of graded individuability: for example, that complex objects are more readily individuated (and thus mapped onto language) than simple objects."[1]

Sandeep Prasada (1999) presents a related proposal. He suggests that the psychologically relevant notion of object is strongly linked to intuitions as to how an entity is created (what Aristotle called its *formal cause*). Most important here is whether the entity is seen as having non-accidental structure. Under this view, a wood whisk is an object, but an irregularly shaped chunk of wood is not and is merely a portion of solid stuff. This raises an interesting prediction (1999, pp. 124–125): "A spatiotemporally contiguous amount of matter is distinguished from an object by the presence of the formal cause in the object. Given this understanding of the nature of things and stuff, we predict that subjects should be more likely to construe a solid entity as an object if they are presented with evidence that the entity has a definite form that is the product of a process directed at creating that structure and that it possesses functional properties that depend on that structure."

To test this, Prasada showed different entities to English-speaking adults and asked them if they would prefer to describe them as objects, with a count noun ("There is a blicket in the tray") or as substances, with a mass noun ("There is blicket in the tray"). He found that the object label was preferred when people were shown regularly shaped entities or entities that perform a structure-dependent function, and a substance label was preferred for jagged entities or entities that do not perform a structure-dependent function.

Such findings make a convincing case that a psychological difference exists between simple objects and complex objects. But I doubt that the reason for this difference is that children conceive of simple objects as clumps of solid substance and not as objects at all. After all, abundant evidence from infant research shows that babies individuate, count, and track simple objects, such as ping-pong balls, just as well as they do complex objects, such as Mickey Mouse dolls. There is every reason to believe that babies, like adults, think that a chunk of wood is just as much of an individual object as is a wooden whisk.

Consider a different way to capture the essence of the simple-object versus complex-object distinction, one suggested to me by Susan Carey. Count nouns, words such as *dog* and *whisk*, refer to psychologically interesting kinds of individuals. Their members share relevant and distinctive properties: once you know that an object is a whisk, for instance, you know that it was designed to fulfill a particular function, and this distinguishes it in a useful way from other objects. Chunks of wood, on the other hand, were not created with a specific intent, do not have a common function, and do not share internal properties. They are neither artifacts nor natural kinds, and so we are not predisposed to learn a count noun that refers to chunks of wood as members of a distinct kind.

Simple objects and complex objects, then, are all individuals. But complex objects are more likely to be thought of as members of distinct kinds, and therefore adults prefer to use a novel count noun to describe a complex object than to describe a simple one. All of the Aristotelian considerations raised by Prasada (involving form, structure, and non-random causation) still apply—but to the question of what makes a psychologically natural *kind* and not to what makes a psychologically natural individual (see chapter 6 for discussion).

What about the cross-linguistic differences? As discussed above, Imai and Gentner (1997) found that their youngest group of American and Japanese children differed only with regard to simple objects: the Americans generalized them on the basis of shape, and the Japanese performed randomly. But when you look at the other three age groups, you see a more general difference between the Americans and the Japanese. The results are shown in figure 4.2.

The American responses in the substance condition might seem crazy. Why would they generalize the substance name on the basis of shape about half of the time? The answer probably lies in the distinctive shapes in which these substances were originally presented. If you see an S-shaped array of sand, hear it given a name, and then see an S-shaped array of glass pieces, the temptation is to assume that the two go together. It couldn't be an accident, after all, that they have the same shape, so this might be the "right answer." (An even more killjoy argument is that the Americans thought that the new word actually meant "the letter S"—but the other substance stimuli did not correspond to English letters.) The Japanese subjects were less prone to do this.

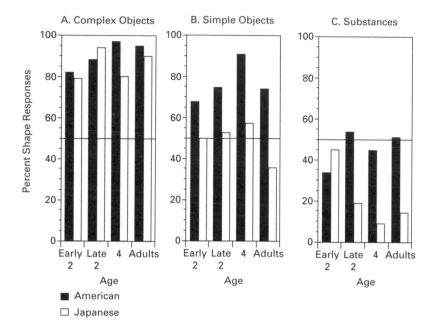

Figure 4.2
Generalization of novel words on the basis of shape by American and Japanese subjects (from Imai & Gentner, 1997)

They almost never generalized on the basis of shape, tending instead to extend the name for S-shaped sand array to the sand piles.

Whatever the precise explanation for this difference in shape generalization, it is clear that for the older two-year-olds, the four-year-olds, and the adults, an effect of equal magnitude exists in both the simple object condition *and the substance condition:* in both conditions, Americans focus more on shape than the Japanese. Such results are inconsistent with the claim that the two populations differ solely in how they think about simple objects. Instead, it may be that the Americans are more eager than the Japanese to construe words as referring to kinds of individuals, even if the words refer to nonsolid substances that are arrayed in a certain nonaccidental form, such as a S-shaped pile of sand.

In sum, the difference between simple objects and complex objects is an intriguing one, but there are reasons to doubt that it exists because only complex objects are thought of as distinct individuals. Instead, complex objects are more readily construed as members of distinct kinds than simple objects and hence are more naturally described with count nouns, explaining the findings of Prasada. And the American and Japanese difference found by Imai and Gentner is consistent with the theory that, for whatever reason, American subjects are more willing than Japanese subjects to assume that a new word (for a simple object or for a substance in a nonrandom shape) refers to a kind of individual.

Overcoming the Object Bias

Consider a child who sees a rabbit, hears the word *rabbit,* and has to figure out what the word refers to. Children who assume that words refer to whole objects can solve this problem: they infer that the word refers to the rabbit and not to its tail, its top half, and so on. The original motivation for constraints on word learning is to solve such problems of induction, and this approach works well for this example.

But the limits of the whole-object bias as a solution to Quine's problem are embarrassingly clear. A whole-object bias is wonderful for explaining how children learn words that refer to whole objects. It is less wonderful for explaining how they learn words that don't. Children learn substance names, part names, verbs, and adjectives, words such as *water, tail, hopping,* and *white.* What tells children that a new word is not an object name?

One consideration has to do with the nonlinguistic situation in which the word is presented. Children are predisposed to parse the world into objects, but if they have no available objects, other candidates rise to the top. This can be clearly seen in the domain of counting. As pointed out above, it is not particularly hard to get children to count entities that are not objects. The trick is to ask them to do so when there are no salient objects in sight. Under this circumstance, young children have no problem counting nonobject entities, such as sounds.

Similarly, it is not surprising that some of the earliest nonobject words learned are names for substances, such as *water* and *milk.* Such words are learned easily. In an experiment by Soja, Carey, and Spelke (1991), two-year-olds were presented with novel words either in neutral syntax ("This is my blicket"), count syntax ("This is a/another blicket"), or mass syntax ("This is some/some more blicket"). The words were used to refer to objects (e.g., a T-shaped plumbing fixture) or substances (e.g., Nivea cream). Soja et al. found that children extended words referring to solid objects to objects of the same shape, ignoring substance, but extended words referring to nonsolid substances to portions of the same substance, ignoring shape. For the youngest children, syntax had no effect on children's responses. Even before they have learned the syntax of count and mass nouns, children find it just as easy to learn a word like *water* as a word like *spoon*.

The ease with which children learn nonsolid substance names is in sharp contrast to the difficulty they have with solid-substance names such as *wood* and *metal* (Dickinson, 1988; Prasada, 1993). Such names are hard to learn for two related reasons. First, it is considerably easier to construe water as a substance category than it is to think of a solid entity such as wood that way (Bloom, 1994b). And second, children can learn *water* without the distraction of a salient object, but learning *wood* requires that children actively focus on a bounded object and think of it not just as an object but as a portion of solid stuff. This is analogous to a counting task in which they must attend to a set of objects and think of them not as objects but as forks, colors, or kinds (Shipley & Shepperson, 1990).

A second consideration relevant to learning words that are not object names is the pragmatics of the situation. The object bias will be suppressed if children are given good reason to believe that an adult is not intending to refer to an object. This will occur in cases of lexical contrast (discussed in detail in the last chapter). If an object already has a name, then another word used to label it is taken by children as likely to have some other meaning, such as referring to a part or property (e.g., Markman & Wachtel, 1988).

In some cases, speakers explicitly make clear their intent to refer to something other than an object. Consider the naming of body parts. Young children learn words such as *nose* and *eye* and typically do so even before they have a common noun such as *body* or *person*, but they never misinterpret these part names as referring to their whole body. Why not? The answer is that no parent has ever pointed at their child and said "Nose!" Instead, in at least some cultures, part names are presented with linguistic support ("This is *your nose*"), with the addition of other nonlinguistic cues (such as outlining the boundaries of the child's nose with a finger). When naming parts, then, adults take great pains to make it clear to children that they are not referring to the whole object, and apparently even one-year-olds are savvy enough to appreciate these pragmatic cues (see chapter 3).

Cues from discourse context can apply in more subtle ways as well. Tomasello and Akhtar (1995) presented two-year-olds with a new word in isolation—"Modi!"—that described a scene in which a novel object was engaged in a novel action. What children thought the word meant depended on which aspect of the scene, the object or the action, was new to the discourse situation. If, prior to hearing the word, children observed several different actions done on the same object, they tended to interpret *modi* as an action name, but if they had instead previously observed the same action done to several other objects, they tended to interpret it as an object name.

A third consideration is syntax. For instance, if children hear a word used as a verb, as in "he's glipping the table," they can readily infer that it does not refer to an object but instead to an action, and if they hear it used an adjective, as in "that is a glippy thing," they can infer that it refers to a property. Once children have some command of the syntax of their language, syntax can play an important role in leading them away from inappropriate object interpretations.

It is sometimes said that syntax is a weak cue to word meaning, at least early in development. For young children, the argument runs, the bias to treat words as object labels is stronger than their sensitivity to syntax, and hence children will make the object interpretation even in the face of conflicting grammatical cues (e.g., Waxman & Markow, 1995; Woodward & Markman, 1997). One study that is said to support this was done by Hall, Waxman, and Hurwitz (1993). They showed two-year-olds an unfamiliar object, such as glass tongs, and presented the children with a novel adjective, as in "That's a fep one." Children were then shown an object that was different in kind but shared a salient property with the target object, such as a glass napkin ring, and an object that belonged to the same kind but lacked the property, such as red plastic tongs, and they were asked, "Can you find another one that is fep?" Children tended to choose the object of the same kind, treating *fep* as an object name despite the fact that it was used as an adjective. Other studies find that when children are presented with mass nouns that are used to refer to whole objects, as in "This is some blicket," they interpret them as object names, not solid substance names (Dickinson, 1988; Markman & Wachtel, 1988).

These results are usually taken as showing that the object bias is stronger than syntax. But there is a another interpretation. All of the studies that show limits of syntax are based on the failures of younger children to use syntactic cues to learn a word as either a solid substance name or as an adjective denoting the substance an object is made of. Maybe their problem doesn't lie with syntax at all. It is instead that words that refer to solid substances are hard to learn, for reasons discussed earlier.

It is easy enough to test which interpretation is right. Just consider what children do in a situation where they have to use syntax to figure out that a word is not an object name but where the word also doesn't refer to a solid substance. If their problem really does have to do with syntax, then they should find it equally hard to learn adjectives such as *big* or verbs such as *hit*. But if their problem has to do with solid substance names, such words should pose no special problem. In fact, young children do learn adjectives and verbs, and plenty of experimental evidence (reviewed in chapter 8) shows that syntax helps them do so.

Individuals That Are Not Objects

Proper names and count nouns correspond to entities we think of as individuals—entities that can be individuated, counted, and tracked over space and time. Proper names such as *Fido* correspond to specific individuals, while count nouns such as *dog* correspond to kinds of individuals. It makes sense to talk of two dogs or 10 dogs, to say that a certain dog is the same one that I saw yesterday, or to ask what happened to Fido. Not all parts of speech refer to individuals; adjectives like *big*, verbs like *give*, and mass nouns like *water* do not correspond to entities that are thought of in this way.

What sorts of entities are naturally thought of as individuals? We individuate, count, and track dogs: they are psychologically natural individuals. As a result, words that refer to this kind (*dog*) and words that refer to individual members of this kind (*Fido*) are learned by children. But not every possible individual is acceptable from the standpoint of human psychology. For instance, construing the spatially discontinuous entity composed of my dog and his favorite bone as a single individual is conceptually unnatural. We could not easily learn a proper name (*Fidobone,* say) for this entity, nor can we easily track it over space and time. Why is it that Fido is a psychologically possible individual, but Fidobone is not?

It might seem that we have already solved this problem. Fido is a possible object because Fido is a Spelke-object; it satisfies the object principles. Fidobone does not; it does not satisfy the principle of cohesion. Because of this, children see the world as containing Fido and not Fidobone.

This is fine as far as it goes, but children also learn many names that refer to individuals that are not Spelke-objects. Two-year-olds know words for parts such as *finger* and *eye*. They know names for actions such as *sneeze, cough, laugh, kiss, smile, hug,* and *bite.* (Max understood *somersault* at about 18 months; when he was asked to "do a somersault," he would attempt the appropriate motion, and he would appropriately identify the somersaults of others.) They know words for periods of time, such as *minute* and *hour;* for "negative spaces" such as *hole;* for sounds, such as *sound* and *noise;* and for collections, such as *family, forest,* and *bunch.* So while being a Spelke-object may be a sufficient condition for being a nameable individual, it is plainly not a necessary one.

What about these nonobject individuals makes them acceptable candidates for being named? How is it that children parse the world into certain parts, actions, collections, and the like, and hence have these notions available as possible word meanings?

The Generalization Hypothesis
One intriguing possibility is that the principles underlying these individuals are related to those that apply to objects. It has often been argued that abstract language and thought involves the metaphorical extension of spatial notions (e.g., Jackendoff, 1990; Lakoff, 1987; Pinker, 1989, 1997). For instance, we talk about a shoe *in* a box (spatial), as well as a week *in* a semester (temporal), and a character *in* a play (more abstract). Perhaps humans have evolved patterns of thought for physical objects, including the Spelke-principles. These constrain our reasoning about nonmaterial entities, such as sounds, events, and collections. And certain other entities, such as parts, shadows, and negative spaces, may be construed as individuals because they satisfy a subset of the principles; they aren't objects, but they are close enough.

Consider object parts. Parts do not obey the principle of cohesion and do not exhibit independent motion; this is why they are parts and not whole objects. But cohesion may nevertheless be relevant to our understanding of what a natural part is because the cohesion principle involves two conditions—boundedness and connectedness (Spelke, Phillips & Woodward, 1995). A psychologically natural part, while not bounded, will nonetheless move as an internally connected region. Hence fingers are natural parts and so are toes, but it is profoundly unnatural to think of the ring finger and the kneecap as a single body part (a fingerknee) because fingers and knees are unconnected.

But connectedness isn't enough. A one-inch wide ribbon of skin running from the left hand, up the arm, over the shoulder, and ending up at the middle of the lower back is connected (and also conforms to the principles of solidity and continuity), but it is not naturally seen as a body part. Something more is required. It might be that a psychologically natural part is a part that could readily be turned into an object. This is related to the observation by perception psychologists that objects are parsed into natural parts through a sensitivity to discontinuities in surface contour (Hoffman & Richards, 1984; Leyton, 1992). A finger, for instance, is an excellent part because—unpleasant as it is to think about—it is seen as having a potential separateness from the rest of the body, in that it can be cleanly severed. The possibility of a certain amount of independent movement is also relevant; you can wiggle your fingers while the rest of your body stays still. (Though not all parts move independently; consider teeth in a mouth or the handle of a cup.) Parts are likely to fall into a continuum in terms of how natural they are. All languages have a word corresponding to *finger* because it is very natural to parse the body into fingers; other English body part names, such as *chest* and *shin*, correspond to parts that are less intuitively natural and so are not as frequent in other languages (see Andersen, 1978).

Negative spaces are a particularly fascinating domain of study (Casati & Varzi, 1994). We naturally parse the world into negative spaces (holes, cavities, gaps, tunnels, caves, and so on), and even three-year-olds have no problem identifying and counting holes (Giralt & Bloom, in press). A psychologically natural negative space is a mirror image of a Spelke-object: instead of being a connected portion of matter moving through empty space, it is a connected portion of empty space nestled into matter. And some negative spaces even move, as when an air bubble rises to the top of a swimming pool or a whirlpool makes its way across an ocean.

Karen Wynn has suggested to me that a temporal analog to the principle of cohesion is relevant for some sounds and actions. To be counted as a single sound, a noise must be bounded and connected in space and time; if one hears a beep from the right side and a simultaneous beep from the left side, this is two sounds, not one. And if one hears, from a single location, a beep, a pause, then another beep, this is again two sounds (Bregman, 1990). By the same token, motion is parsed into distinct action if separated either in space (two people each jumping at the same time) or time (one person jumping twice with a pause in between). When motion is connected in time and space, it is naturally thought of as a single action.

Consider finally collections, such as families, flocks, armies, bikinis, and bunches. A noun such as *flock* is not itself an object name; instead it refers to a collection that is composed of objects. Hence learning such a word requires that children somehow override the bias to focus on whole objects and instead focus on the group. Two-year-olds typically know some collective nouns, such as *family*, and evidence suggests that such nouns are easier to learn than superordinates such as *animal* and *furniture* (Callanan & Markman, 1982; Markman, Horton & McLanahan, 1980). My students and I have been interested in what makes some groups of objects, and not others, natural individuals (e.g., P. Bloom, 1994a, 1996b; Bloom & Kelemen, 1995; Bloom, Kelemen, Fountain & Courtney, 1995).

It is not trivial to teach someone a new collective noun. If you simply show children or adults a display of three groups of stationary objects (as in figure 4.3A) and describe the display with a plural count noun, as in "These are fendles," the tendency is to view *fendle* as an object

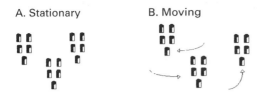

Figure 4.3
Stationary (A) and moving (B) collections

name, not as a collective noun. The display is seen as containing 15 fendles, not three fendles.

What can drive people to view such groups as individuals? One factor is motion. In one study, adults were shown three groups of five objects each on a computer screen, each object moving independently within its collection while also following the trajectory traced by the collection as a whole (see figure 4.3B). The groups behaved in an animate manner, like three swarms of bees, tracing paths along the screen and moving past each other. Under these circumstances, the groups are seen as individuals, and *fendle* is interpreted as a collective noun: subjects view the display as containing three fendles, not 15.

To test whether this effect is due to experience with real-world collections like flocks of birds or schools of fish, Karen Wynn, Wen-Chi Chiang, and I conducted a modified replication of this study with five-month-olds. We showed half the babies two collections of three objects each and the other half four collections of three objects each. Each collection traced a vertical path up and down on a computer screen. Once babies were habituated to this display, they were presented alternately with two collections of four objects and four collections of two objects, each moving horizontally back and forth on the screen. Babies looked reliably longer at the new number of collections, showing that they treated each of the collections as an individual for the purposes of enumeration (Wynn, Bloom & Chiang, under review).

Why does movement have this effect? It might make the collections objectlike, as if each collection were a surrogate object with unattached parts. This would be the inverse case of parts: parts satisfy connectedness but not boundedness; moving collections satisfy boundedness but not connectedness.

Limits of the Generalization Hypothesis
Unfortunately, the generalization hypothesis fails to account for many of the names we learn. Many refer to individuals that are *not* plausibly seen as objects, potential objects, or surrogate objects. They instead

refer to entities that emerge through our intuitions about the goals, intentions, and desires of others.

For instance, event nouns such as *conference, fight,* and *party* refer to individuals that are bounded on the basis of subtle intentional and social factors, not psychophysical ones. An ability to parse motionful scenes on the basis of such factors emerges quite early. Eighteen-month-olds who watch an adult attempt to perform an action and fail will often imitate the entire action that was intended, even though they never witnessed it (Meltzoff, 1995). Much younger babies—six-month-olds—can count the jumps of a continually moving puppet, one that wags back and forth between jumps (Wynn, 1996). This shows, at minimum, that they are not limited to individuating actions that are bounded by stillness. This ability to parse the scene into jumps might be the result of their sensitivity to systematic patterns of motion, or it might be the result of their construing of jumping, and not wagging, as an intentional act, which motivates them to extract it from the motionful scene.

Other nonobject individuals exist because they are seen as the objects of intentional regard by other people. Chapters, stories, and jokes are individuals just because they are created and thought of by others as singular entities. There is no independent motivation for treating them as such. A bikini can be viewed as a single individual because it is created and used for a singular purpose; and the world is divided into distinct countries (many of them, such as the United States, physically discontinuous) through social and historical factors, not solely physical ones. And while it is true that many parts can be identified on the basis of discontinuity of contour and the potential for independent movement, this might be because such factors are cues to the presence of deeper causal processes. In the case of body parts such as fingers, such processes have to do with growth and adaptation; in the case of artifact parts such as pedals, they have to do with design and function.

With this in mind, let's return to the question of what people see as a natural collection. As discussed above, if subjects are simply shown three groups of objects and given a name for them, the tendency is to treat the word as an object name (see figure 4.4A). But a collective interpretation can be induced if the subjects are convinced that each of the collections is thought of as a single individual in the mind of the experimenter. One way to do this is through syntax and discourse cues. If you point to each of the groups in turn, and say "This is a fendle, and this is a fendle, and this is a fendle," adults and five-year-olds tend to interpret *fendle* as a collective noun (Bloom & Kelemen,

A. Interacting

B. Moving in Plates

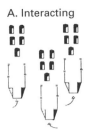
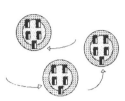

Figure 4.4
Machines interacting with collections (A) and moving collections on plates (B)

1995). But one can get the same effect in a more subtle way. In another study, an experimenter carefully arranged three groups of objects in front of the subjects, placing a picture frame around each group, giving the impression that each group was an independent artistic creation. The frames were then removed, and the entire display was described as "These are fendles." Under these circumstances, even four-year-olds tended to interpret the word as a collective noun (P. Bloom, 1996b).

In another study, subjects were shown a display in which three "machines" came into view, each surrounding one of the groups (figure 4.4A), with colored balloons popping out of each machine when it made contact. The machines then gradually retreated from the screen, leaving the screen empty except for the original, still stationary, groups. Subjects again tended to interpret *fendle* as a collective noun, either referring to each group (the target of an action) or to each group and its corresponding machine (all of the participants in an action). This supports the above finding that something can be seen as a collection if it is treated as a single individual by someone or something else (Bloom, Kelemen, Fountain & Courtney, 1995).

This brings us back to the question of why movement induces a collective interpretation. In another study with adults, each moving group was surrounded by a circle, and subjects were told "These are fendles on plates" to make it clear that we were defining the circles as plates (figure 4.4B). Placing the groups on "plates" explains the common movement of the objects within a group without appeal to any deeper shared properties of the objects. Without such a motivation to treat the groups as distinct causal entities, subjects abandoned the collective interpretation and treated *fendle* as an object name (15 fendles), despite the fact that the groups were moving. This suggests that, at least for adults, common movement is a cue to individuation only to the extent that it indicates some underlying causal property of the moving group. It is an open question whether this is also the case for children.

A different domain, studied by Nancy Soja and Tracy Burns (Soja, 1994; Burns & Soja, 1995) is that of *NP-type nouns*. Words such as *church* and *school* can refer to physical entities, as in "There is a church on the corner." But they can also be abstract proper names that do not refer to Spelke-objects, as when one says "John goes to church regularly," where the lack of a determiner indicates that the word is a noun phrase, or NP. Not all common nouns work that way; one can say "There is a bookstore on the corner," but it is unacceptable to say "John goes to bookstore regularly." Preschoolers use NP-type nouns correctly in their own speech and are sensitive to the subtle semantic criteria that determine whether a word falls into this category. If they are given a novel word that refers to an enduring cultural institution, something that people participate in at predictable times, children will treat the word as an NP-type noun, as a proper name for an abstract individual, but will not do so if these semantic criteria are not met. Such criteria are rooted in social considerations and have nothing to do with the Spelke-principles.

I am not denying here that once we think of something as a distinct individual, we tend to view it as objectlike in certain respects (e.g., Lakoff, 1987; Langacker, 1987). After all, we talk about individuals like jokes and chapters as if they are moveable sizable entities, as in "He shortened the joke and moved it out of the first chapter and into the second." But there is a big difference between claiming that once we think of an abstract entity as an individual, we then see it as having objectlike properties (something that is probably true) and the much stronger claim that we think of an abstract entity as an individual just *because* we see it as objectlike (something that is probably false in many instances).

The considerations reviewed above are consistent with the view that many of the candidate referents for common nouns and proper names emerge through one of two distinct cognitive systems. The first is an object system with an eye toward portions of matter that satisfy the Spelke-principles, particularly cohesion. This gives us dogs and bricks, whisks and chunks of wood. It might also provide us with—as a result of the extension of these principles—individuals such as fingers, toes, holes, shadows, and jumps. The second system is theory of mind, which parses motion and matter through an understanding of goal, function, and intent, giving rise to individuals such as games, parties, chapters, families, and church.

Finding the Right Words

Up to now we have viewed the problem of word learning as that of hearing a word and trying to discover its meaning. But another problem, raised by Landau and Gleitman (1985), is how children find the relevant words in the sentences they hear. Imagine a child who sees a dog, notices that the adult is also looking at the dog, and hears "Look at the dog." Suppose that the child can parse such an utterance into distinct words (see Jusczyk, 1997). How does she figure out which of the words, if any, correspond to the dog?

It is true that some Western parents are considerate enough to simply point and say "Dog!" But this is not a universal human behavior. Furthermore, some words are never used in isolation. Nobody ever points and says "The!" or "Of!" The problem of finding the right words has to be solvable by all children, for at least some of the words they learn.

As a starting point, we have to rethink certain assumptions about words and reference. The problem of word learning can be framed, as I have done up to now, in terms of how children figure out what words refer to, how they come to know that *dog* refers to dogs, *cup* refers to cups, *eating* refers to eating, and so on. This suffices for most circumstances, but it is not precisely right. Nouns do *not* refer to objects, and verbs do *not* refer to actions. Noun phrases refer to objects, and verb phrases refer to actions. As children attempt to make sense of what they hear, these NPs and VPs stand out as the referential elements and are used to refer to objects and actions in the world.

Consider how someone might draw your attention to a dog. She might say "Look at the dog" or "That's a dog" or "There's that big dog again." The part of the sentence that refers is not the noun *dog;* it is the NP *the dog* or *a dog* or *that big dog.* The noun contributes to the meaning of these phrases, but it does not, by itself, refer to any particular thing in the world. If common nouns refer at all, they refer to the kind or category of dogs (e.g., Macnamara, 1986). Pronouns and proper names are different; they stand alone to refer to specific individuals ("Look at him. Look at Fred") and hence are lexical NPs, not nouns.

In theories of formal semantics, nouns are viewed as predicates, which must combine with determiners to establish reference (e.g., Barwise & Cooper, 1981). More generally, it is often said that nouns are semantically incomplete (or "unsaturated"; see Higginbotham, 1983); only NPs are semantically complete. As such, only NPs can participate in certain forms of semantic interaction, such as being able to refer to entities in the world (as in "Look at the big dog"), having thematic roles (in the sentence "The big dog bit the ugly cat," the NPs, not the nouns *dog* and *cat*, are the agents and patients), and participating in coreference relations (in the sentence "The big dog likes himself," the NP "the big dog," not the noun *dog*, corefers with the reflexive *himself*).

The way children learn what nouns and verbs mean, then, is through their contribution to the meaning of the phrases in which they are used. It is easy to ignore this when discussing English because English noun and verb stems often appear in isolation. In other languages, such as Quechua, verb roots cannot stand as independent morphemes, and hence their meanings can *only* be determined through their contribution to the larger syntactic constituent that they belong to (Courtney, 1994; Lefebvre & Muysken, 1988).

Because of this, in an important sense the learning of nouns and verbs is similar to the learning of determiners. Children obviously don't learn the meaning of *the* by hearing this word used in isolation and figuring out what it refers to. They instead attend to NPs such as "the dog" and "the cups" and figure out the semantic role of the determiner across all of these phrases (Pinker, 1984, 1989). The suggestion here is that much the same holds for nouns and verbs.

This might seem somewhat baroque. Is it really true that to learn names for things (words like *dog* and *cup*) children have to figure out the contribution that these words make toward the meaning of the phrase, in the same way that they figure out how words such as *the* and *another* contribute? If so, why do children find it so much easier to learn the meanings of nouns than the meanings of determiners?

The thing to keep in mind here is that it is not difficult to find the noun inside the NP. In some cultures, parents might solve the problem for children by omitting the determiner: they might point to a dog and simply say "dog." Even if they are uttered, determiners are not phonologically salient, and so young children may not perceive them (Gleitman & Wanner, 1982). Parents might say "the dog," but children might hear just "Dog." Finally, children might have certain expectations about phonological and semantic differences between closed-class words and open-class words, allowing them to categorize these parts of speech (Gerken, Landau & Remez, 1989) and guiding them to expect that it is the open-class term that refers to the kind of entity, not the closed-class one (Pinker, 1984, 1989).

To see how this would work, imagine learning a new language. You are capable of parsing phrases into words and of figuring out what the phrases refer to, but you don't yet know what any words mean. You hear the following phrases in the following contexts:

Phrase	Used to Refer to . . .
za loob	a dog
te murpet	a chair
he murpet	two chairs
he loob	several dogs
wo murpet	a chair

If you don't hear the determiners *za*, *te*, *he*, and *wo*, there is no problem at all in finding the word that corresponds to the relevant entity or entities. Based on what you *perceive*, the mappings are straightforward:

Phrase	Used to Refer to . . .
loob	a dog
murpet	a chair
murpet	two chairs
loob	several dogs
murpet	a chair

But even if you do hear the determiners, it is not difficult to extract the nouns and infer that *loob* means dog and *murpet* means chair. This is because the most phonologically salient part of the phrase is the noun and the most semantically salient part of the context is the object.

These factors explain why it is harder to learn determiners than nouns. Not only are determiners less phonologically salient, but they also correspond to contrasts that are less semantically salient. The difference between dogs and chairs is more striking than the differences between one chair versus multiple chairs. Some of the semantic notions encoded by determiners are subtle indeed, requiring a sophisticated analysis of the scene and multiple exposures to narrow down the hypothesis space. What does *wo* mean? Based on the data above, it is impossible to tell. It could have a meaning akin to *the*, *this*, *that*, *a*, or *my*, to give only a few examples. To make matters worse, determiners often encode nonsemantic contrasts, as in the French contrast between *le* and *la*. These require a different sort of learning procedure altogether, one that is again based on multiple trials (see Levy, 1988).

Not all phrasal decompositions are equally easy. Finding the verb in a VP might be considerably harder than finding the noun in an NP. For one thing, a VP typically contains at least one NP, and hence many content words must be sifted through. Finding the verb might have to wait until the child either already knows the meanings of the nouns or has enough linguistic knowledge to use morphological and syntactic cues to parse the sentence. Furthermore, the referent of the verb might not "jump out" of the scene in the same way as the referent of a noun. For these reasons, among others, it should be harder to learn verbs than to learn nouns—and it is. We return to this issue in chapter 8.

Even if children have a procedure for extracting nouns from NPs, this might not entirely solve the problem posed by Landau and Gleitman (1985). Children still have to find the NPs. To see the problem this raises, imagine seeing a bird in the sky and hearing, in a language you wish to learn, "Zav bo goop wicket mep!"

By hypothesis, you know no words at this point, no inflections, and nothing about the syntax. (And we might be simplifying here by assuming that the sentence is parsed into strings of words; if not, the input is "Zavbogoopwicketmep!") So how can you determine which word or strings of words (if any) refer to the bird?

There are two possible solutions. The first is that learning a language requires a constrained distributional analysis; children store sentence-situation pairs in memory and then look for correlations between specific words or phrases and discrete aspects of meaning. For instance, if children later hear "blub mendle wicket mep" to refer to another bird, they might infer that "wicket mep" (which was present in both sentences) is used to refer to birds and is an NP. The analysis might be simplified if children store only strings of stressed phrases (instead of whole sentences) and representations of relevant individuals (instead of entire situations).

Such a distributional analysis might conceivably lead to problems. Imagine a child who sees one bird, hears the equivalent of "Isn't that pretty?," sees another bird, and hears the equivalent of "That's also pretty." Such a child, using the procedure above, would infer that "pretty" is an NP referring to the bird. Then again, some such confusions, such as using "hot" to refer to a stove, might actually occur in child language.

The alternative is that the input to children might be more congenial to word learning than we first assumed. The problem above might never arise. Perhaps all children are exposed to *some* NPs in isolation, and this can serve as a starting point for word learning. For instance, proper names have a special role in language acquisition. They appear among the very first words of children learning a range of different languages (Gentner, 1982), and they might be the one class of words that all children are guaranteed to have been exposed to in isolation or at least in some special stressed context.

Even in cultures in which adults do not usually label objects for children, proper names might be taught to children. Looking at Kaluli children, Bambi Schieffelin (1985, p. 534) notes:

> There are no labeling games to facilitate or encourage the learning of object names. This is primarily due to the linguistic ideology of the culture. It is only in families who are acquiring literacy that

one sees any attention paid to saying the names of objects, and this activity is initiated by the child when the mother is looking at books. When extended by the child to other contexts, the mother's response is disinterest.

In contrast, because of the cultural importance placed on learning the proper names and kinterms of the individuals with whom they interact, Kaluli children are consistently encouraged to master a large number of proper names, kinterms, and other relationship terms.

Perhaps every culture has some class of nominals that are special with regard to interaction with children. In Western societies, this is a very broad class, while for the Kaluli it is much more narrow, restricted to proper names and relationship terms. Another candidate for privileged nominals is the class of deictic pronouns, like *this* and *that*. These are also universal, show up early in child language, and draw children's attention to objects and other individuals in the environment.

In sum, it might be that all cultures will use some NPs that refer to individuals in isolation, allowing children to learn their first object names. If not, then children must be capable of somehow learning the meanings of words that are embedded in sentences, by extracting the referential NPs from such sentences through a constrained distributional analysis. An adequate theory of word learning must assume either strong extrinsic constraints (all cultures use some nominals in isolation) or a powerful learning mechanism (one that can learn words not presented in isolation).

Going beyond the Mapping Problem

Much of the previous chapter addressed the mapping problem: Given that children have access to both words and the sorts of things that words refer to, how do they bring them together? It was proposed that they use their theory of mind and figure out the referential intentions of other people. The present chapter asked where this prior access to meaning and form comes from. How do children parse the world into the right sorts of entities, and how do they parse the language to find the names for these entities? Candidate proposals again make reference to theory of mind, but the emphasis was on other cognitive mechanisms, such as a grasp of the object principles and the capacity to perform a distributional analysis on the linguistic input.

Solving the mapping problem is just the first step. It is one thing for a child to learn that a word is used to talk about a particular dog and quite another to know what the word means. The next two chapters address the question of how children figure out whether a word refers to an individual (as with *that* or *Fido*) or to a kind (as with *dog*) and how such words are extended to novel instances.

Note

1. It is not entirely clear what Imai and Gentner (1997) mean by *simple* and *complex* here. Elsewhere, Gentner and Boroditsky (in press) suggest that complex objects have "perceptual coherence," which entails a large number of internal links between the components (such as geons or parts) of an object. Complex objects are also said to possess "well-formed structure," which involves symmetry and regularity. But this gets confusing because Imai and Gentner (1997, p. 193) give *spheres* as an example of simple objects, even though spheres are perfectly symmetrical and regular and so should have well-formed structure and hence be complex. This is not a criticism of their study, since the contrast between simple objects versus complex objects is intuitively clear for the materials that they used (and this was confirmed by the ratings of naive adult subjects), but it is an area that would benefit from some clarification.

Chapter 5
Pronouns and Proper Names

A central question in cognitive psychology is how humans and other animals determine the category or kind a novel entity belongs to—how we categorize something as an apple or a table, a face or some water. And most research in word learning addresses how we learn names for these kinds—*apple, table, face,* and *water.*

But we also think about and name individuals. If someone tosses you an apple, it is not enough to know the kind it belongs to; you need to follow that specific apple, tracking its movement through space. Our emotions are tied to specific people and things. Original artwork and autographs can be worth fortunes, while perfect duplicates might be worthless. You might love your own newborn baby and be indifferent toward somebody else's—even if you are unable to tell them apart. In fact, without the ability to individuate, you couldn't tell the difference between one baby and two, except that two usually make more noise and take up more space. Although the understanding of individuals is much less studied than the understanding of kinds, it is every bit as central to our mental life.

The following three sections address how children learn names for individuals—pronouns and proper names—distinguishing them from common nouns that refer to kinds. The rest of the chapter addresses the broader question of the relationship between our understanding of individuals and our understanding of kinds.

Pronouns

Preliminaries
Pronouns belong to a class of linguistic expressions known as deictics or indexicals. These are words whose interpretation changes radically as a result of the contexts in which they are used. If you hear "Dogs like to chase cats," you can safely assume that the person is talking about the same types of entities (dogs and cats) and the same activities (liking and chasing) that anybody else would be talking about when

saying the same sentence. But understanding "Bring me the cup on the left now" and interpreting the words *me, left,* and *now* require knowing who is saying the sentence, where that person is, and when it is being said.

Pronouns are the first deictic expressions learned, and the demonstrative pronouns *this* and *that* are typically found among children's first words (Nelson, 1973). Some children are so impatient that they coin their own demonstrative pronoun. For instance, at the age of about 12 months, Max would point to different objects and say "doh?," sometimes with the intent that we do something with the objects, such as bring them to him, and sometimes just wanting us to appreciate their existence. Once children combine words into two-word strings, pronouns are used extensively, showing up in utterances such as "Want this" and "That nice." The early usage of pronouns is not restricted in English; it holds as well for Chinese, Danish, Finnish, French, German, Italian, Japanese, Korean, modern Hebrew, Quechua, Samoan, and Swedish (Wales, 1979).

Demonstrative pronouns are not restricted to referring to physical objects (Jackendoff, 1990). You can say "I like that," and *that* could refer to some soup, a song, a dance step, a poem, or a grant proposal. Even children's first word combinations contain many utterances in which pronouns refer to entities other than objects (P. Bloom, 1990).

The personal pronouns *I, me,* and *you* are understood by children some time after they have learned the deictic pronouns, by about the age of 18 months (Clark, 1978; Macnamara, 1982; Oshima-Takane, 1988, 1999; Shipley & Shipley, 1969). The order in which these words are learned is unclear, and some children behave strangely when tested: in comprehension tasks, they do better with *you* than with *I;* in production tasks, they do better with *I* than with *you.* The most plausible explanation of this comes from John Macnamara (1982), who suggests that children are most comfortable dealing with pronouns when they refer to themselves (*you* when they are listening, *I* when they are speaking). These are the situations they have had the most experience with, as well as the ones they find the most interesting.

Cues to Learning Pronouns

When children hear a word, how do they know it is a pronoun? One potential cue is its syntax. Pronouns, like proper names, are not nouns. They are lexical noun phrases (NPs) and hence cannot be modified by adjectives, determiners, or quantifiers. In one study, the early word combinations of several one- and two-year-olds were studied, and their use of pronouns, proper names, and common nouns was analyzed (P. Bloom, 1990). The children honored the restriction that adjectives cannot appear before pronouns and proper names; they almost never produced phrases like "big he" or "nice Fred." But they had no such prohibition against using adjectives before common nouns, as in "big dog" and "nice drink." This is just what one would expect if the children know that pronouns and proper names are lexical NPs and thereby cannot appear with prenominal adjectives. In sum, even one- and two-year-olds know the syntactic difference between nouns such as *dog* and NPs such as *he* and *Fred*.

This opens up the possibility that young children can use syntax to learn which words are pronouns. They might know that if a word is an NP, as in "Look at fep," it can be a pronoun but that if it is a noun, as in "Look at the fep," it cannot.

Syntax is a useful cue, but it can play at best a limited role in pronoun learning. First, while pronouns are lexical NPs, so are proper names. No strictly syntactic context distinguishes them. Second, the cues that identify NP contexts in English are ambiguous, as they also signal the presence of adjectives and mass nouns. The word *fep* in "Look at the fep" can be a proper name, as in "This is Fido," but it could also be a mass noun, as in "Look at the water." Third, the syntactic cue is not universal. In German, for instance, articles may precede proper nouns ("the Hans"), and it has been argued that Japanese common nouns have the same syntax as Japanese pronouns and proper names (Fukui, 1987).

The fourth reason that syntax is of limited importance has to do with how syntactic cues to word meaning are learned in the first place. Since such cues vary across languages, they cannot be innate. For instance, children exposed to English have to somehow figure out that *fep* can be a pronoun or proper name when used in the context "Look at fep" but not when used in the context "Look at the fep." But this learning can take place only if children can use *non*syntactic information to learn the meanings of some pronouns and proper names. More generally, children's use of syntactic cues to help to learn words that belong to a certain class requires them to be able to learn the meanings of at least some words that belong to that class *without* syntactic support (see chapter 8 for discussion). For instance, a child might learn that *him* refers to an individual. Once the child knows this, hearing a sentence such as "Look at him" can give rise to the understanding that novel words that appear in the context "Look at ____" also refer to individuals.

So while syntax might help identify pronouns in some languages, it falls short of a complete solution. What other cues exist?

The most obvious cue that a word is a pronoun is the range of entities that it is used to refer to. A child could learn that *this* and *that* are deictic pronouns by noting that they refer to a diverse set of entities in the environment—to the dog, the cereal, the child's mother, the marks on the wall, and so on. The specific meanings of these pronouns (roughly, *this* refers to closer objects than *that*) can be learned by observing the conditions in which they are used and by attending to utterances in which they are explicitly contrasted, as in "Don't eat that. Eat this instead."

But the learning of personal pronouns is considerably more complicated. Consider a child, Margaret, who is learning the pronoun *I*. Suppose she talks only with her mother. Margaret might reasonably draw the conclusion that *I* is her mother's name. Her mother uses this word only to refer to herself, after all, and the word has the same syntax as *Margaret* and *Mommy*. It would help rescue Margaret from this semantic dead-end if she hears another person use *I*. But other wrong hypotheses remain. After all, Margaret hears the word *I* used to refer to everyone but Margaret herself (Margaret is always called either *Margaret* or *you*), and so it would be sensible—but wrong—for her to conclude that this word can refer to everyone but her. For whatever reason, this is not the sort of generalization that children make. Maybe, as Macnamara (1982, p. 43) suggests, Margaret knows that she "is a person just as much as any others who take part in conversations, and so has as much right as any of them to be an I sometimes."

The second-person pronoun, *you*, poses a learning problem that cannot be resolved in the same way. Since the child is addressed as *you*, why doesn't she infer that *you* is her name? After all, the way Margaret learned her name is *Margaret* was presumably by hearing herself, and nobody else, called *Margaret*. So why doesn't the same reasoning apply when she hears herself called *you*?

One might be tempted to appeal to some lexical contrast principle; perhaps Margaret thinks *you* cannot be a proper name because she already has a name, *Margaret*, and she is loath to assume she has two. (Though this raises the question of how she figures out which of the words—*Margaret* and *you*—is the proper name and which is the pronoun.) The question of whether such a bias against multiple names exists is discussed below, but note that sooner or later children must be capable of learning that they have many names. Since Margaret will come to know that she is *Margaret*, *Maggie*, *Peggy*, and *Peg*, what stops her from adding *you* to this list?

Yuriko Oshima-Takane (1988, 1999) has proposed the following theory: children learn the meaning of the personal pronouns by attending to the conversations of other people. They learn *I* by hearing it used by different participants in a dialogue and observing that it is used by people to refer to themselves, not to other people. And they learn *you* by hearing other people use it to refer to those who they are talking to. Oshima-Takane suggests that overheard speech might be *essential* here, particularly for the second-person pronoun. Only when a child hears other people called *you* can she can reasonably infer that it is not her name.

This is a radical proposal, as it flies in the face of the assumption that, at least for children in Western societies, word meanings are learned from child-directed speech. If this proposal is correct, then children's success at learning the personal pronouns has to be in part by attending to, and understanding, people who are talking to each other. If these people are adults, which would be the usual situation for a first-born child, this would require that children can cope with utterances that are faster, longer, and more complex than those typically directed at them. This reinforces the position, defended in chapter 3, that while child-directed speech might facilitate word learning, it is not necessary.

One source of support for Oshima-Takane's theory has to do with the errors children make. Although consistent reversal errors with pronouns are infrequent in normally developing children (Shipley & Shipley, 1969; Girouard, Ricard & Decarie, 1997), they do sometimes exist. Oshima-Takane reports an 18-month-old who used *you* to refer to himself and *me* to refer to his mother. Laura Petitto (1987) reports a similar error in a child learning American Sign Language, which is particularly striking given the potentially iconic nature of the pronouns in that language: the sign for *you* is a point away from the speaker, the sign for *me* is a point toward the speaker.

Oshima-Takane (1988) hypothesized that the main determinant of children's errors is the extent of exposure to overheard speech. In a training study, she found that 19-month-olds can improve their understanding of the personal pronouns by being exposed to their parents using them not with the child but with each other. And Oshima-Takane, Goodz, and Derevensky (1996) found that second-born children produced correct pronouns earlier than first-borns, even though the two groups did not otherwise differ in measures such as mean length of utterance and vocabulary size. Such findings support the claim that exposure to overheard speech is important in learning the meanings of these words.

Autistic children often have problems with the personal pronouns, going for a long period in which they reverse them. If learning these pronouns requires attending to and understanding the conversations of others, it is no surprise that autistic children find this particularly difficult; it follows in a clear way from their theory of mind deficit.

It is not as obvious, however, why blind children have similar problems (Andersen, Dunlea & Kekelis, 1983). One possibility, raised by Hobson (1994), is that visual coorientation might be an important precursor to the development of theory of mind; hence, like autistic children, blind children's problems with pronouns are due to a deficit in theory of mind. An alternative is that blind children find it harder to make sense of dialogues that they are not part of for the simple reason that it is harder to tell who is speaking to whom if you cannot see. As Landau and Gleitman (1985) note, being blind is like taking part in a conversation where everyone else is present together and you are connected to them by telephone. In either case, the special problems that autistic and blind children have with the personal pronouns is consistent with the view that learning these words involves attending to the conversations of other people.

Proper Names

Preliminaries
Pronouns are fickle; proper names are loyal. A proper name sticks faithfully to the same individual across all situations. One can use the name to talk about an individual in the past, present, and future and in hypothetical situations. These facts were first pointed out by philosophers in support of specific theories of reference (Donnellan, 1977; Kripke, 1980; Putnam, 1975), but there is nothing arcane about them. For instance, when presented with a scenario in which Dan Quayle changes his name and appearance to those of John F. Kennedy, even philosophically innocent college undergraduates are quite comfortable with the idea that this character is still Dan Quayle (Sternberg, Chawarski & Allbritton, 1998).

The intuition here is that a proper name picks out a particular individual. Unlike a common noun, which has an indefinite number of possible referents, a proper name has just one. If the dog in the corner is *Fido* and another animal walks through the door, the other animal can be a dog but cannot be *Fido*, regardless of how similar they are.

There is a subtlety here: *Fido* is such a popular dog's name that it is possible that this other dog *could* actually be named *Fido*. But *Fido* is still a proper name, referring to just one individual even though more than one *Fido* may exist. The multiple *Fidos* should be thought of in the same way that we think of the multiple words *bug*. It isn't that a single word refers to both winged insects and listening devices. Instead, there are two words: one *bug* refers to winged insects, the other *bug* refers to listening devices, and these happen to sound the same.

Cues to Learning Proper Names

When children hear a word, how do they know it is a proper name?

Katz, Baker, and Macnamara (1974) explored the role of syntax. They presented children with a novel word occurring either with or without a determiner (e.g., "This is zav" versus "This is a/the zav"). In a sentence like "This is zav," *zav* can be a lexical NP, while in a sentence like "This is a/the zav," *zav* must be a common noun. The word was applied either to a doll or to a block. After being taught the word, children were tested to see whether they would extend it to another doll or block (consistent with the kind interpretation) or whether they would restrict it to the original item (consistent with the individual interpretation).

Seventeen-month-old girls (but only 27-month-old boys) were sensitive to syntactic cues when learning the name for the doll, construing *zav* in "This is zav" as a proper name and *zav* in "This is a/the zav" as a name for the kind. In contrast, all the children applied the kind interpretation for words referring to the block regardless of the syntactic context in which they were used.

Gelman and Taylor (1984) replicated this study with slightly older children, changing the methodology and stimuli in certain regards. One change involved using unfamiliar kinds of objects; another involved adding a distracter item to the forced choice during testing to control for the possibility of guessing. They found much the same as Katz, Baker, and Macnamara (1974): two-and-a-half year olds were sensitive to the syntax when words named the animate entities. They also found that when a lexical NP was used to refer to an inanimate object, children often chose the distracter item, which is consistent with the view that they were confused by the use of the NP to refer to this sort of object (why would an inanimate thing get its own name?) and were searching for another referent to apply it to.

Liittschwager and Markman (1993) explored the possibility that children in the above studies might have been taking the new word within the "This is zav" sentences as an *adjective* (and thus denoting a subkind or property, as in "This is red"). If so, then their choice of the original item during testing would not be because they were picking out the same individual originally named as *zav*, but because they were picking out the object that has the same perceptual properties as this individual. To test this, Liittschwager and Markman showed three-year-olds an object (such as a bear or shoe), named it ("This is zav" or "This is a zav"), and then moved it to another location and removed a salient property, so that it looked different. Then they took out a second item, also without this property, and placed it next to the first, so that children were faced with two objects that looked identical. Children were then asked "Where's zav?" or "Where's a zav?" If they were learning the lexical NP as a name for the individual, they should point to the moved object, tracking it over space and time, while if they thought the word named a property, they should show no preference in its usage, since the items looked identical. Liittschwager and Markman found that when given sentences such as "This is zav" (but not when given sentences such as "This is a zav"), children chose the same individual they were first shown, consistent with the view that they took the lexical NP as naming an individual, not a property (see also Sorrentino, 1999, for a similar finding).

These studies suggest that syntax can help children learn proper names. Nevertheless, the limitations of syntax discussed above with regard to pronouns apply to proper names as well. First, proper names and pronouns are syntactically indistinguishable. Second, the same cues that suggest that a word is an NP are also cues that it is an adjective or mass noun. Third, the syntactic status of proper names is not universal. And fourth, to learn about the syntactic cues in the first place, children need to be able to identity some words as proper names without the support of syntax.

What are the alternatives to syntax? Four nonsyntactic sources of information have been proposed by Geoff Hall and his colleagues (see Hall, 1999), and I discuss them in turn.

The first is that an object gets only one proper name. Hall and Graham (1997) presented four-year-olds with an object, such as a stuffed dog. For half the children, it was explicitly given a proper name ("This dog is named Zavy"); for the other children, it was described with a novel adjective ("This dog is very zavy"). An identical animal was then brought out and children were asked, "Show me the dog that is named Daxy." In the condition in which the first dog had a proper name of Zavy, children chose the second dog as being named Daxy but had no such preference when the first dog was said to have the property of being "very zavy."

This suggests that if something already has a proper name, children believe that another proper name cannot describe the same object. But there are reasons to doubt the generality of this cue. After all, as Hall (1999) notes, people actually have many names. Even ignoring middle names, last names, titles, and pseudonyms, the same person can be William, Will, Bill, and Billy; James, Jim, Jimmy, and Jimbo; and Margaret, Maggie, Peggy, and Peg. Young children, who are cute and helpless, also suffer the indignity of being addressed as Half-pint, Pumpkin, Sailor, Silly Girl, Spanky, Stinkbug, Stinky, Sweetie-Slug, Turtle, and Twinky-Winky. There are no systematic data on multiple names, but an informal poll of a dozen friends revealed that all use multiple terms to refer to their children (see the examples above), and that their children have never been confused by this.

Admittedly, such nicknames aren't actually proper names for a specific child (anybody can be called *Pumpkin*), but it is not clear whether children know this. And in any case, some examples don't involve nicknames, as with one boy who knew both his English name and his Chinese name before his first birthday. Even in a single language there are pet names that are limited to specific children. Steve Lewis (1997, pp. 71–72) presents some exotic examples of this:

> And of course, Clover is not the only one with unusual tags. Cael is Bubba, but he was Ralph Barca for years. Nancy has evolved to The Turtle from previous incarnations as Puppy Turtle, Turkey Puddle, The Scooper, and "Woopy Woop for a Full year till She's Full Grown" (which I later shortened to Wooper). Addie has worn, among several other monikers, Aderlwyn Yacht, Yetso Yurt, YD, The Bulldozer, and most recently Al-Edward, or Edward for short. Danny, who was Graybadge and E-man (Encyclopedia Man) and Danzek and Dansak and most recently Dazulu or Zule, is now Donald.

If children can cope with this multiple dubbing, why do they refuse to accept overlap in the Hall and Graham study? The answer has to do with the pragmatics of the situation. While a single individual can have many names, such names typically differ in nonreferential ways, such as in formality, and it would be odd to switch names in the middle of a conversation for no apparent reason (Clark, 1997). Imagine that someone says "I was talking to Mary yesterday" and then asks "Have you seen Molly recently?" You might well assume that the speaker was now referring to a different person. Similarly, even if children have no particular problem with multiple proper names, when they hear "This dog is named Zavy" and then are asked "Can you show me the dog named Daxy?," it would be reasonable for them to infer that the person is intending to talk about a different dog. This isn't an objection to Hall and Graham's proposal, but it does suggest that the bias against multiple proper names might be restricted to situations in which the multiple names are used in the very same discourse context.

A second cue also involves lexical contrast. Hall (1991) found that four-year-olds were more willing to treat a word as a proper name if it was used to refer to a familiar kind of stuffed animal (a cat) than to an unfamiliar kind (a monster). This is presumably because children know *cat* but have no basic-level name for the monster. A new word that refers to a cat is unlikely to be another basic-level name, which makes it more likely, though not necessary, that it is a proper name.

Summing up so far, if children know a proper name for an object, a different word referring to the same object is less likely to be a proper name, and if they know a common noun for an object, then a different word referring to the same object is more likely to be a proper name. These cues are important, but they are not essential: people *do* have more than one name, and objects *are* described by multiple common nouns. Further, such cues cannot apply at the very onset of word learning. Plainly, a bias against believing an object has two proper names is not going to be of any help to children who haven't yet learned their first proper names. And since children learn their first proper names for people long before they learn any common noun that refers to these individuals (such as *person* or *parent*), the second constraint cannot help either.

The third cue discussed by Hall is that only some entities get proper names. Humans and some animals are natural candidates for having names; most other things, such as bricks, are not. This fact about proper names is not the result of a limitation in what our conceptual systems can individuate. After all, bricks are conceptually just as much individuals as people: one can count bricks, point to them, throw them, follow their movement, and so on. Bricks don't receive proper names because they are seen as interchangeable. There is no value in giving a particular brick its own name, as opposed to describing it just as a member of a kind, as "a brick."

Any individual entity can conceivably receive a proper name if people come to find it interestingly distinct from other members of the same kind. John Locke (1690/1964, p. 16) notes that

> Besides persons, countries also, cities, rivers, mountains . . . have usually found peculiar names, and that for the same reason; they being such as men have often an occasion to make particularly, and, as it were, set before others in their discourses with them. And I doubt not but, if we had reason to mention particular horses as often as we have to mention particular men, we should have proper names for the one, as familiar as for the other. . . . And therefore we see that, amongst jockeys, horses have their proper names to be known and distinguished by, as commonly as their servants: because, amongst them, there is often occasion to mention this or that particular horse when he is out of sight.

This is a claim about why proper names come to exist, not how they are learned and understood. Do young children appreciate that only some things receive proper names?

There is some evidence they do. When given a novel word in a context such as "This is Daxy," two- and three-year-olds will treat the word as a proper name if it refers to a doll but not a block (Katz, Baker & Macnamara, 1974), a monster but not a toy (Gelman & Taylor, 1984), and a bear but not a shoe (Hall, 1994; Liittschwager & Markman, 1993; Sorrentino, 1999). One possibility is that these children have observed that proper names refer only to living things and representations of living things and restrict their own inferences accordingly. But this is too simple, since even two-year-olds will accept a proper name for an inanimate entity (such as a foam rectangle with a cube on top of it) if it is described as possessing mental states (Sorrentino, 1997, 1999). This could mean either that it is not animacy that is relevant but intentionality, or that such an entity is thought of as a "surrogate animal" in the way that children think of a stuffed bear.

Older children's intuitions concerning what entities can get a proper name are quite sophisticated. Four-year-olds, like adults, are typically unwilling to give a proper name to an animal such as a bee, snake, or spider. But if they are told that such an animal is owned by the experimenter—he says "This is my bee"—this reluctance goes away (Hall, 1994). Also, as discussed in the last chapter, four-year-olds learn proper names for cultural institutions, such as *church* and *school*, and they appreciate that such names apply only to those individuals that have a certain social importance (Soja, 1994).

Several questions remain about children's understanding of what can get named. At some point, children must be able to learn proper names for artifacts (*Big Ben*, the *Titanic*), as well as names for events, groups, books, plays, and so on. No evidence has shown that young children can learn proper names for such nonintentional entities, but so far children have been tested only on entities that have no special value (a truck, a shoe). It would be interesting to see what children would do if exposed to a name for something they are especially attached to, such as a favorite blanket. There is also the question of the precise nature of their intuitions in the Hall and Soja studies. For instance, are the children reasoning that the pet bee is likely to have its own name simply because it is a pet? Or because being a pet makes it more salient and interesting in its own right? Or do they reason as Locke does: the bee is likely to have its own name because it is important in the eyes of other person, the person who owns it? These are open questions.

Hall's fourth cue is the most important. While a common noun is used to describe many entities (as is an adjective), a proper name is used to describe only one. This is the opposite cue that applies for the acquisition of pronouns: there the *diversity* of reference across multiple trials tells the child their semantic class; here *fidelity* of reference does so.

If children expect proper names to pick out unique individuals, then they should have problems coping with the fact that multiple individuals can have the same name. And they do. Macnamara (1982, p. 28) tells of his son Kieran, at 16 months, who "had a cousin of his, Lisa. He was then introduced to a girl of about the same age as Lisa also called Lisa. They played for half an hour, yet, most unusual for him, he refused to say her name, no matter how often anyone said it or urged him."

Hall (1999, p. 350) gives the anecdote from the mother of a 20-month-old named Matthew who "has a friend Rebecca at the sitters' that he loves to play with very much. He calls her Becca because it's easier for him to say. I have a friend who has a three-month-old daughter named Rebecca and Matthew will not call her by her name. I introduced him to her saying that her name was Rebecca, and he said 'No Becca!' He has since been calling her 'baby.'"

Hall (1996b) explored this experimentally, by presenting two groups of four-year-olds with a word in a context such as "This is zavy," in which the word could be either a proper name or an adjective. One group heard the label applied to one object, such as a striped dog; the other group heard it used first for one striped dog and then for another identical dog. The first group interpreted *zavy* as a proper name, using it only with the named dog, while the second group interpreted it as an adjective, extending it to both the original dog and to other striped objects as well. This supports Hall's conclusion that if a word refers to more than one object, children do not expect it to be a proper name.

How then do children come to make their way through a world of Johns, Marys, Lisas, and Rebeccas? In part, this is because they are sensitive to other cues that something is a proper name. If a child named John is explicitly told of another child "His name is John. He is also called John, just like you are," the child finds it sufficiently clear that *John* must be a proper name and will learn the name. In fact, Hall (1996b) found that you can prod children into accepting two identical proper names if, instead of the ambiguous and subtle "This dog is Zavy" for both dogs, you say "The name of this dog is Zavy. This dog is called Zavy. This dog's name is Zavy," and same for the other dog. Under these conditions, children treat *Zavy* as two proper names, one for each dog.

Finally, children learn certain conventions as to how proper names work. In some parts of the world, they learn that *John, Fred,* and *Paul* are boy's names and that *Mary, Jane,* and *Susan* are girl's names; that siblings tend to share last names but not first names; that a short form of *David* is *Dave*; and so on. They will come to use names as a signal for nationality and ethnic origin, social class, and age and will come to appreciate the range of conventions underlying names for entities as diverse as cities, boats, rock groups, artwork, action movies, superheros, novels, and more.

Naming is a creative act, and at a certain point children move from being passive consumers of names and start to create their own. A skilled namer can choose to draw on connotations and conventions. David Lodge (1994) discusses trying to choose evocative names for the two main characters of his novel *Nice Work*—a coarse engineer and a cultured literature professor. He decided on *Vic Wilcox* and *Robyn Penrose*—and it is not hard to figure out who is who. Early on, children come to learn about the conventions underlying names; it would be a rare four-year-old indeed who named her imaginary friends *Daxy*, *Blicket*, *Fendle*, and *Wug*.

Names for Kinds and Individuals

Suppose a two-year-old hears a word that refers to an object. What can tell this child whether this word is a pronoun, a proper name, or a common noun?

We have discussed four considerations above. There is syntax: if a word is used as a common noun (as in "This is a fep"), it cannot be a pronoun or proper name; if it is used with NP syntax (as in "This is fep"), it can be. If a language marks this distinction, as English does, this can be a powerful cue. There is lexical contrast: if an object already has a common noun associated with it, another word that refers to the object is more likely to be a pronoun or proper name, while if an object already has a proper name, another word that refers to the object is *less* likely to be a proper name and so could be a pronoun or common noun. A third cue is the type of entity the word refers to: common nouns and deictic pronouns can refer to anything. Personal pronouns, obviously enough, refer only to people and certain animals. And proper names pick out individuals that are in some sense *special*, including, but not limited to, people.

Even with all this information available, more is sometimes needed. Suppose the two-year-old hears "This is fep" used to refer to a rabbit, and suppose the child already knows a common noun (*rabbit*) that would otherwise refer to this individual. All the cues are in place here—syntactic, contrast, and entity type—but still the child can't yet know whether *fep* is a pronoun or proper name.

This brings us to the most important cue—the word's range of reference. Even if no other information is present, this alone could tell children whether a word is a pronoun or a proper name. After all, being a pronoun is to refer to different individuals depending on the discourse context; being a proper name is to refer to a unique individual. If a word refers to different individuals depending on the discourse context, then it is a pronoun; if a word consistently refers to a single individual, it is the proper name.

This raises a question. Since children can tell for certain whether a word referring to a person is a pronoun or a proper name only by observing its usage over multiple occasions, then any single usage is ambiguous. What is the default hypothesis? Children might start big and assume that a word describing a person is a pronoun (as with *her*). If this is wrong and the word is a proper name, they could change this interpretation by observing that adults do not use the word to refer to anyone other than that person. Or children could start small and assume that a word describing an individual is a proper name (as with *Sally*). If this is wrong and the word is a pronoun, they could change this interpretation by observing that adults use the word in a more general way to refer to other people. Which do children do?

They start small. If they started big, we would expect errors in which children used proper names with inappropriately broad reference. For instance, a child named Harry might go through a brief phase where he calls everything and everyone "Harry." Such errors do not occur. Macnamara notes of his son Kieran, at 14 months, "It was uncanny how accurately he used proper names for particular individuals. His only mistakes were mistakes of identity owing to similarity of appearance" (1982, p. 28). Some putative exceptions to this are *Mommy* and *Daddy*, which are often overextended. But as Macnamara (1986) observes, such words are also used as kinship terms, as in "your Daddy" and "Joe's Mommy," and so it is quite legitimate for children to use them to refer to people other than their own parents.

The early understanding of proper names is an old observation. Locke (1690/1964, p. 17) says that for children, "the ideas of the nurse and the mother are well framed in their minds. . . . The names they first gave to them are confined to these individuals; and the names of *nurse* and *mamma*, the child uses, determine themselves to these persons."

Locke goes on to insist that at this early stage, children know only proper names. But this isn't correct; as soon as children are using proper names (and pronouns) to refer to individuals, they are also using common nouns to refer to kinds. This brings us to the question of how their understanding of kinds and individuals is related.

Thinking about Kinds and Individuals

Before they utter their first words, human babies think about the world in terms of both kinds and individuals. They categorize objects as falling into basic-level and superordinate categories (Mandler & McDonough, 1993; Xu & Carey; 1996). And they can track and enumerate specific individuals. For instance, in one set of studies, a Mickey Mouse doll is placed in front of a baby, a screen rises to hide it, and then a hand places another Mickey Mouse doll behind the screen. Babies expect to see two Mickey Mouse dolls and are surprised if the screen drops to reveal one or three (Wynn, 1992a). This result entails that each of the different dolls is thought of as a distinct individual, even though they are perceptually identical and most likely belong to the same kind. When tested the same way, macaque monkeys show precisely the same understanding (Hauser, MacNeilage & Ware, 1995).

It is easy to see why humans and other animals would have an understanding of kinds; as discussed in the following chapter, even the lowliest creature benefits from being able to make inferences based on whether something belongs to categories such as food, predator, and prey. But what are the benefits of an understanding of individuals?

One benefit is numerical. Gallistel (1990) reviews evidence that animals can determine rate of food return during foraging (calculated as number of food encounters per unit of time multiplied by average amount of food observed or obtained per encounter), and he notes that "the adaptive value of being able to estimate rate of return is obvious." Numerical cognition requires some ability to conceptualize each of the to-be-counted entities as distinct and hence requires some capacity for individuation.

A second benefit has to do with tracking. Predators and prey have the troublesome property of moving and disappearing behind other objects. Tracking might involve numerical reasoning, particularly when dealing with multiple objects that look alike (Wynn & Bloom, 1992). For instance, imagine being chased by three dogs who are shifting in position, moving behind trees, and so on. The knowledge that there are three of them governs one's expectations in obvious ways. In a moment when only two can be seen, you know that the third exists temporarily out of sight.

In some contexts a sensitivity to spatiotemporal continuity is essential for tracking, even for a single individual. Predators of herding animals will pick a single animal from the group and chase that specific animal, trying to wear it down. If predators were to switch quarries, they would get exhausted, and their prey would not (Pinker, 1997). To choose a gentler example, newly hatched ducklings will follow whatever moving object they first see and form an attachment to that object. This tracking behavior is adaptive since that *specific* object, but not other objects that look the same, is typically the birds' mother and has an interest in its welfare.

A third benefit of individuation is social. It is adaptive for certain animals to keep track of their past histories with other animals, using what Pinker (1994b) calls "a mental Rolodex." Who are your children, your siblings, your parents? Whom have you mated with in the past, and whom have you fought with? Who owes you, and whom do you owe? The ability to engage in reciprocal relationships over a sustained period of time is a central part of the social abilities of humans and some other primates (Cosmides & Tooby, 1992).

A fourth benefit concerns the understanding of object kinds. It is hard to see how people could learn about dogs, for instance, without the ability to parse the world into individual dogs. This is particularly so given the importance of object shape in our understanding of such kinds.

Susan Carey (1994), however, suggests that *conceptual* individuation is not necessary for this understanding. After all, we distinguish between spaghetti and macaroni based on the shape of the pieces, but we think of these kinds as stuff, not individuals. One does not count spaghetti and macaroni, and they are named in English with mass nouns, not count nouns. Carey suggests that babies might think of all object categories in this manner, even though "the child's *perceptual* system must pick out individuals in order to represent shape" (p. 146, my emphasis).

This is plausible, but only insofar as an appreciation of objects as individuals is not relevant to how babies reason about them. The reason that saying we don't individuate spaghetti makes sense is that our inferences about that kind (what it tastes like, how to cook it, how much to prepare) involves its properties as *stuff*. The shape of spaghetti pieces might be relevant for perceptual recognition but nothing else. At least for adults, the shape of objects such as dogs and chairs is used not only for recognition but also for inferences about their behavior, function, and so on, and therefore our representation of their shapes must be more than perceptual. But as Carey notes, this is more of an open question with regard to babies.

Individuation and Identity

It is often said that one needs to have prior knowledge of kinds or even of *sortals* (nouns that denote kinds) to understand reference to individuals. This view was first defended by philosophers (e.g., Geach,

1962; Gupta, 1980; Wiggins, 1980), but its implications for linguistic and conceptual development were elaborated by Macnamara (1986) and extended by Carey (1994), Hall (1994, 1996b, 1999), Macnamara and Reyes (1994), Oshima-Takane (1999), Xu (1997), and Xu and Carey (1996), among others. This issue is an important one, worth considering in some detail.

Macnamara (1986) has two main arguments for the importance of kinds. The first has to do with individuation. Macnamara (1986, p. 51) suggests that "there is no individuation of entities that is not sortal dependent. . . . individuals cannot be counted without the guidance of a sortal." It makes little sense to demand that someone simply count. You have to tell the person *what* to count (the people, the shoes, and so on).

Even referring to a single individual might be dependent on an understanding of a kind. To understand a sentence such as "That is Fred," one needs to know whether the pronoun *That* and the proper name *Fred* refer to the entire body, the visible surface, the clothes, the set of molecules, or the person himself. Macnamara argues that it is knowledge of the kind that specifies the relevant individual in such a case and thereby underlies the learning and use of pronouns and proper names.

The second argument concerns identity. Macnamara notes that a person (Margaret Thatcher, say) can over her life change all her inessential properties—her size, weight, shape, complexion, number of limbs, and so on. But we think of her as the same person and continue to call her *Margaret Thatcher*. And we do this because, according to Macnamara (1986, p. 51), "we have access to the substance sortal PERSON, which traces 'the identity of an individual over its whole existence and across all possible circumstances in which it might be. . . . Clearly, a PN [proper name] requires the support of a . . . sortal.'" The idea here is that we intuit that the proper name sticks to Thatcher through all these transformations because we recognize that she remains a person throughout.

Macnamara is surely right that to understand the reference of a pronoun or proper name we need some way to determine the scope of its reference, to pick out the right individual. And we also need to have some ability to track that individual: to realize, for instance, that a proper name continues to refer to someone when they get a haircut—but perhaps not if they are decapitated. It is clear that *something* must govern our intuitions about individuation and identity. What is less obvious is whether these intuitions are best explained in terms of our knowledge of the kinds that these individuals belong to.

There are three reasons to doubt that this is so. First, we individuate and track entities that belong to unknown or unfamiliar kinds. When someone points to a dot in the sky and says "It's a bird. It's a plane.

It's Superman!," they are demonstrating that one doesn't need to know what something is to talk about it and follow it through space and time (Kahneman, Treisman & Gibbs, 1992). Second, we individuate and track the referents of many object names (shoes, tables, cups, and so on) in precisely the same way—by attending to principles of spatiotemporal contiguity. It misses a generalization, then, to say that each kind imposes its own particular principles of identity and individuation. Third, we can track objects that change kind. With saw, hammer, and nails, one can turn a wooden table into a wooden chair, changing its kind. Proponents of the sortal theory (e.g., Wiggins, 1980) point out that it is no longer "the same table," which is true enough. (If it isn't a table, then it can't be the same table.) But there is a clear sense in which we think of it as *the same individual* that was once a table, otherwise a sentence like "This chair used to be a table" would make no sense at all (see also Xu, 1997).

These three considerations refute the claim that basic-level kinds underlie our understanding of individuals. This is not to say that kind membership is irrelevant. Suppose you see a toy truck move behind a screen, there is a pause, and then a toy duck emerges from the other side of the screen. The duck then moves back behind the screen and a truck emerges from the other side. Then the truck returns behind the screen. The screen then drops to reveal either one object or two objects. Adults—and 12-month-olds—expect to see two objects, not one, even though only one object was visible at any time (Xu & Carey, 1996). This finding suggests that 12-month-olds have the concepts of duck and truck (Xu & Carey, 1996), and it is consistent with the view that kind membership can affect individuation: if you see a toy duck at one moment and a toy truck a couple of seconds later, it's likely that they aren't the same individual. After all, a duck does not typically turn into a truck.

But there's nothing special about kinds here; all sorts of factors can affect our intuitions about sameness. If you see a tiny red truck at one moment and a large green truck a couple of seconds later, you are also likely to view these as distinct individuals, since small red trucks are unlikely to change into large green trucks—even though they belong to the same kind. Or suppose I leave my coffee cup in the mailroom on Monday. On Tuesday, I turn on the TV and see a politician in Russia drinking from a coffee cup that looks exactly like mine (same kind, same properties). But I won't infer that the politician's cup is the same individual cup as mine because it would be wildly implausible that my cup could have made its way to Russia. My inference would be different if on Tuesday I were to see a graduate student in the mailroom drinking from such a cup; this *could* be my cup because the student would have had easy access to it.

These examples suggest that what is really essential for something being the same individual is spatiotemporal continuity: something is the same object if and only if it tracks a continuous path through space. Other factors are relevant *only insofar as they are cues to spatiotemporal continuity*. Trucks don't typically morph into ducks, nor do they suddenly change size and color, and so kind membership and property information are relevant for individuation. I don't think that my cup is in Russia simply because it is unlikely that my cup could have traveled across the ocean to get there, and so location information is relevant as well. The spatiotemporal continuity requirement is central. Facts about kind (duck or truck?), property (small and red or large and green?), and location (in the psychology department or in Russia?) are important only because they bear on how likely it is that this condition has been met.

One response to these concerns is to shift the focus away from basic-level kinds and toward more general ones. Macnamara himself (1986, p. 60) raises the possibility that babies might possess only the kind *maximally-connected physical object*, an idea that he attributes to Ray Jackendoff. Fei Xu (1997) expands on this idea, arguing that the notion of *object* that has emerged from Spelke's work (what I have called earlier a *Spelke-object*) will do the trick.

I think this is half right. It works well for individuation. As discussed in the last chapter, considerable evidence shows that children and adults are biased to parse the world into Spelke-objects. If someone points and says "Look at that," the default assumption is that the speaker is referring to an object. And if someone shows you an array of different things and demands "Count!," you would likely count the objects. Other entities, such as parts, collections, and actions, are individuated according to different principles, but these might correspond to other superordinate kinds.

But a shift to Spelke-objects cannot entirely explain our intuitions about identity. Xu (1997, p. 385) focuses on the crucial issue here when she suggests that "in virtually all metamorphoses, the transformations do not violate the criteria for object-hood such as spatio-temporal continuity or the constraint that one object cannot be at two places at the same time." But this isn't true for our beliefs about personal identity. Some people believe in reincarnation, and I am told that if I misbehave in this life, I risk returning to the next world as a cockroach. That is, a cockroach scuttling around will be *me*, the very same individual I am now, even though my body will reside in a grave.

One might respond by observing that the individual in such transformation stories, though no longer the same object, is always a person, which is a distinct kind from Spelke-object. After all, it is likely that we intuitively conceptualize people as immaterial entities: we are not our bodies; we just occupy them. As Jon Stephen Fink (1997, p. 76) puts it: "It is human essence: this is what we are at heart and in fact, individual spirit not sagging meat and calcifying bones, not chemicals but consciousness—a life-hungry soul fills each body to the fingertips and shapes a single lifetime." Even if you don't believe this is so, and even if you reject the notions of life after death, reincarnation, astral projection, and the like, these ideas are psychologically natural: everyone can understand them, if only as fiction.

But it is not the case that *person* tracks an individual over its history. That is, it is not true that someone is the same individual if and only if he or she remains a person through all transformations. It is conceivable that someone can cease to be a thinking and feeling entity and then be "revived." Joe might be frozen for several years and then, through science-fiction technology, warmed up until he is conscious and in good health. (If you like your examples gruesome, you can imagine that his frozen body was chopped up and then reassembled immediately prior to warming.) When he awakes, it is still Joe. But during the period of freezing he was not a sentient being, which suggests that our intuitions about the personal identity of Joe do not entail that he remain a member of the kind person through his existence.

One could respond here that even when frozen (and dismantled) Joe is still a person. Some people might have this intuition, but consider: Why do you think the frozen lump (or lumps) is a person? It does not satisfy properties that people possess: it doesn't think, feel, experience pain. Instead, you believe that the lump (or lumps) *was once Joe* and that, since it has the potential to become Joe again, it should be counted as a person. There is nothing unreasonable about this sort of intuition, but note that your intuition about kind membership does not underlie your judgment about identity. Rather, your intuition about identity (that the lump is still Joe) underlies your judgment about kind membership (that the lump is a person).

It is fair to focus on people when discussing proper names, since these are the most nameable individuals. But what about inanimate entities? Xu is correct that transformations of objects do not violate the condition of spatiotemporal continuity. They do, however, violate other principles that characterize Spelke-objects. You can take something apart and put it back together again, and it can still be the same individual. To modify an example from Hirsch (1982), suppose I want to send a friend a gift. I buy a bicycle, dismantle it, put the pieces in separate boxes, and send them by mail. At this point, many distinct Spelke-objects are separated in space; no single object exists that could be called a bicycle—just sticks of metal, gears, and wheels. When my friend receives the boxes, she reassembles the parts, ending up with the original bicycle. If you share the intuition that she now owns the *same* bicycle that I originally bought (and this is in fact the intuition of U.S. Customs), then you cannot believe that the identity of this individual has to do with the kind Spelke-object.

It is true that we need an account of individuation and an account of identity. But they are not the same accounts. Individuation is likely to be done, at least in part, though the Spelke-principles, as suggested by Macnamara (1986) and Xu (1997). But identity is a different story. People can retain their identity even if there is a period in which they are no longer people; objects can retain their identity even if there is a period in which they are no longer objects. Hence our identity intuitions are not entirely explained by appealing to kinds.

How then can we explain these intuitions? I have nothing to say here about questions of personal identity, except to note that this is a notoriously messy area and that our naive intuitions about the conditions under which someone remains the same person are often fuzzy and sometimes incoherent (see Dennett, 1987; Parfit, 1994). But an account of object identity may be more within our grasp. One hypothesis is that we are sensitive to the spatiotemporal continuity of the *stuff* that makes up the object. The tracking of stuff does not require appealing to the notion of Spelke-object. The bicycle that my friend reassembles is the same one I sent to her because it is made out of the same stuff. And since it was once a bicycle and is now a bicycle, it is the same bicycle.

We know little about the conceptual and perceptual capacities involved in the tracking of stuff. Nevertheless, we know that such capacities exist. After all, we can track entities that are not individuals, such as sand, whiskey, and spaghetti. Perhaps there is no substantive difference between how we track a bicycle and how we track a lump of spaghetti. And the simple fact that an object can be taken apart and put back together again, and still be the same object, suggests that some proposal of this nature is likely to be correct, at least for adults.

How does an understanding of identity develop? It is possible that the initial appreciation of identity really is limited to the tracking of Spelke-objects, as maintained by Xu (1997) and Xu and Carey (1996). Babies have problems reasoning about nonsolid substances (Huntley-Fenner & Carey, 1995), and, perhaps, unlike adults, they will not believe that something retains its identity if it is disassembled and reassembled. This specific question has never been addressed, though the few studies that have been done on children's identity judgments (Gutheil & Rosengren, in press; Hall, 1998) suggest that their understanding of object identity does not differ substantively from that of adults.

Consider finally the famous ship of Theseus (Hobbes, 1672/1913). The story goes as follows. Over years of sailing, the parts of Theseus' ship wore out and were discarded and replaced, one part at a time. Eventually, the ship was made of entirely new parts. Is it the same ship? Under some circumstances, people agree that it is, even though it contains none of the stuff that the original ship was composed of (Hall, 1998; Hirsch, 1982; Wiggins, 1980).

But this is not a counterexample to the theory of object identity outlined above. Imagine that there are 20 instances in which a part is replaced: S1 (the original ship), S2, S3, . . . S21 (the final ship). S1 shares no common substance with S21, and so if one looks only at the endpoints, they are not the same ship. But note that each individual transformation preserves sameness of stuff: S2 has most of the same stuff as S1, S3 has most of the same stuff as S2, and so on. Since intuitions of identity are transitive (if S3 is the same ship as S2, and S2 is the same as S1, then S3 is the same ship as S1), it follows that S21 is the same ship as S1, even if sameness of stuff is all that is involved in identity judgments. In support of this analysis, our belief that S21 is the same ship as S1 increases if our attention is drawn to the series of individual transitions, as when there are many parts that are discarded and replaced, and when the change takes place over a long period of time (Hirsch, 1982; Hume, 1739/1978; see Hall, 1998 for review).

The discussion so far has focused on objects and people, but we track—and name—other sorts of individuals. Noam Chomsky (1995, p. 21) gives some examples:

> A city is both concrete and abstract, both animate and inanimate. Los Angeles may be pondering its fate grimly, fearing its destruction by another earthquake or administrative decision. . . . London could be destroyed and rebuilt, perhaps after millennia, still being London. . . . We have no problems understanding a report in the daily press about the unfortunate town of Chelsea, which is "preparing to move" (viewed as animate), with some residents opposed because "by moving the town, it will take the spirit out of it," while others counter that "unless Chelsea moves, floods will eventually kill it."

The principles that work to track the identity of cups clearly will not suffice for entities such as cities. It might be that our intuitions about the identity conditions of each distinct type of entity (artifacts, animals, foods, companies, cities, and so on) are based on its own special principles.

But there is another possibility. In the previous chapter, it was suggested that individuation is done mainly through two cognitive systems—one that deals with the domain of objects, another that deals with the domain of people. These same systems may underlie our judgments about identity. That is, any entity is tracked as either an inanimate body or an animate being, and such modes of tracking are distinct, for babies and perhaps for other animals as well. When faced with an individual that is neither a body or a person, we nonetheless shoehorn it into one of these categories. In some cases, we put it into *both*; so, as Chomsky notes, a city can be thought of as either animate or inanimate, and a shift in how one thinks about the city leads to an accompanying shift in identity intuitions.

To put this proposal in its strongest terms, we have evolved to think of the world as containing bodies and souls. These we individuate, count, and track and refer to with pronouns and proper names.

Chapter 6
Concepts and Categories

Imagine a language with only proper names. A new word that names a dog must refer to that particular dog and nothing else. Learning this language would require the ability to track individuals over time, but it wouldn't require any ability to generalize, to recognize how collies are different from terriers or how dogs are different from tables.

Such languages don't exist, of course. Children who hear a word that refers to a dog have to cope with the possibility that it can also refer to other individuals that belong to the same category or kind. It could be a common noun, such as *dog*. To learn such words, they need some grasp of the conditions underlying category membership, some understanding of what is and is not a dog. Within psychology, this understanding is usually described as a concept (the concept of dog), and the concept that is associated with a word is usually described as the word's meaning (the meaning of *dog*).

This chapter discusses the concepts expressed by common nouns. It begins by asking why such concepts exist at all and goes on to defend an essentialist theory of their nature, contrasting this with the view that children's words are generalized solely on the basis of perceptual properties. It concludes with a discussion of the relationship between essentialized concepts and naive theories.

What Are Concepts For?

Why do we have concepts at all? What is the value of treating dogs as members of a category, instead of seeing them just as distinct individuals? John Locke (1690/1964, bk. 2) has an insightful discussion of this issue, in the course of asking why *general terms* (what we would call *common nouns*) exist in natural language.

He has three proposals. The first is often found in the contemporary psychological literature. This is the idea that thinking about the world only in terms of individuals is just too hard for us (p. 14): "it is beyond the power of human capacity to frame and retain distinct ideas of all the particular things we meet with: every bird and beast men saw; every tree and plant that affected the senses, could not find a place in the most capacious understanding."

But this is a weak argument for several reasons. First, even if Locke is right about our capacity limitations (and he might not be; Pinker, 1997), it doesn't actually explain what concepts are good for. It is like answering the question "Why is that person carrying a duck?" by saying: "Well, he isn't strong enough to carry a *car!*" You cannot explain the existence of X (carrying a duck, having concepts) just by stating the impossibility of Y (carrying a car, storing all individual instances).

Second, in some cases we form concepts even though we also store the individual instances, and so categorization is not necessarily an alternative to individuation. For instance, I know all the members of my immediate family, but I also recognize that they fall into different categories (males, females, siblings, parents, and so on). For reasons that we get to below, even if an animal had a perfect memory and lived in a world with a small number of objects, it would still benefit from categorizing these objects.

Finally, categorization is not always useful. Consider the following categorization: all objects bigger than a bread box fall into one category; everything else falls into another. This would lead to great savings in memory—but presumably it isn't what Locke had in mind. Perhaps it isn't merely possessing concepts that is advantageous; it is possessing the *right* concepts.

Here is Locke's second proposal (p. 15): "If it were possible [to name all individual instances], it would be useless; because it would not serve to the chief end of language. . . . Men learn names, and use them in talk with others, only that they may be understood. . . . This cannot be done by names applied to particular things; whereof I alone having the ideas in my mind, the names of them could not be significant or intelligible to another, who was not acquainted with all those very particular things which had fallen under my notice."

This is reasonable. In a language with only proper names, I couldn't tell you about anything unless you were also directly acquainted with it, and this would severely limit the language's efficacy as a communication system. But this explanation applies specifically to words; it does not extend to concepts more generally (nor was it intended to). Since at least some concepts exist independently of words (see chapter 10), the fact that general terms are necessary for communication about novel entities does not explain the function of concepts more generally.

I think Locke's third proposal, however, is exactly right, and applies to both words and concepts (p. 15): "a distinct name for every particular thing would not be of any great use for the improvement of knowledge: which, though founded in particular things, enlarges itself by general views; to which things reduced into sorts, under general names, are properly subservient."

In other words, we need general terms—and the concepts that underlie them—for the purpose of generalization. Generalization is essential for inductive learning, and successful induction is the stuff of life.

You drink orange juice, and you like it. You drink oil, and you don't. A chair supports you when you sit on it; when you sit on a cardboard box, the box collapses, and you fall to the floor. If you pat the cat, it rubs against you and purrs; if you pat the dog, it snarls. These events provide valuable lessons—about the joys of drinking juice and the hazards of drinking oil, about what you can and cannot sit on, and what creatures it pays to interact with. But you can learn from these events only if you have some mental representation of the relevant kinds. To learn from the juice episode, it is not enough to know that *this* liquid at *this* time is tasty; you have to be able to generalize to other liquids. A creature without concepts would be unable to learn and would be at a severe disadvantage relative to creatures that did have these sorts of mental representations.

Not all potential concepts are of equal value. Objects in the world are not randomly distributed with regard to the properties they possess. Instead, there is what Tolman and Brunswik (1935) call "the causal texture of the environment." Objects fall into categories because they are the products of physical law, biological evolution, and intentional design. And concepts might be useful only insofar as they correspond to categories that have many relevant properties in common.

This is an old idea. For instance, John Stuart Mill (1843, p. 153) notes that "some classes have little or nothing to characterize them by, except precisely what is connoted by the name." As an example of this, he says that all that white things have in common is that they are white, nothing else, and hence *white things* would be a poor category for inductive purposes. (And this might be why no language has a noun that refers only to white things; Markman, 1989.) Similarly, Jorge Luis Borges imagines a dictionary that divides animals into different categories, one of which is "those that have just broken a flower vase," and a children's joke goes as follows:

Question: What do a donkey and a refrigerator have in common?

Answer: Neither one of them is an elephant.

It is not a thigh-slapper, but it counts as a joke because of the manifest unfairness of the answer. The category "not an elephant" is profoundly unnatural from a psychological standpoint because there is nothing that nonelephants have in common that distinguishes them from elephants—other than the fact that they are not elephants, of course. Real categories—such as dogs, chairs, and water—have members that tend to share certain properties; once you know that something belongs to such a category, you know further facts about it that are not true of things that don't belong to that category.

Considerations of inductive utility help explain the privileged status of certain concepts. Roger Brown (1958a) noted that some names are more frequently used than others when talking about objects. For instance, we usually call Fido "a dog," not "an animal" or "a terrier." Eleanor Rosch and her colleagues (e.g., Rosch & Mervis, 1975; Rosch et al., 1976) have confirmed the importance of such basic-level concepts. They found that the basic level is the most inclusive level in which objects are judged to have many features in common, that people tend to interact with categories at the basic level using the same bodily movements, and that members of a basic-level category tend to share a common shape. And names for such categories are among the first common nouns learned by children.

What makes them so special? Brown speculated that we describe things at the basic level "so as to categorize them in a maximally useful way" (p. 20). Subsequent work has led to more explicit formulations of this insight. Murphy and Lassaline (1997) propose that the basic level is an optimal compromise between informativeness and distinctiveness: you can infer many unobserved properties once you know which basic-level category something belongs to (informativeness), and it is also relatively easy to make this categorization (distinctiveness). For instance, if you know something is a dog, you can infer a lot about it (it barks, eats meat, is a pet), much more than if you just know that it belongs to a superordinate category such as animal. And it is fairly easy to distinguish dogs from members of other basic-level kinds, such as horses, much more so than distinguishing members of contrasting subordinate categories such as collies versus terriers. For these reasons, we are most prone to think about and name Fido as a dog than as an animal or terrier.

This analysis gets us only so far. To say that good concepts divide the world into categories that are informative and distinctive is a bit like saying that good investment strategies make a lot of money: it might be true, but it is a poor guide to practical action. Humans have no direct access to the causal texture of the environment. So although we have an answer to the question of *why* we have concepts—having the right concepts underlies adaptive generalization—we are left with another, harder question: *How* is it that we come to possess these useful concepts?

Perception, Properties, and Essences

Regardless of how smart babies are, all they have access to when categorizing novel entities is the perceptual properties of these entities—what they look like, what sounds they make, and so on. Under one view, humans possess an "animal similarity space" that guides our initial learning about the world (Quine, 1960). We have evolved to see one dog as looking more like another dog than like a tree, and this perceptual similarity serves as the basis for early concept formation (see Keil, 1989, for discussion).

But a single invariant similarity space runs afoul of the fact that different properties are relevant for the adaptive categorization of different entities. For rigid objects, for instance, shape is highly relevant; this is how we typically distinguish tables and chairs. But for substances, color and texture are what matter: a circle of white paste is likely to have the same unobservable properties (such as taste) as a square of white paste, not a circle of red foam. Some animals undergo radical shape transformations, such as snakes; others don't, such as starfish. And the same entity might be categorized in different ways depending on the sort of induction one needs to make. For instance, different properties are relevant for determining whether something is poisonous versus whether it floats.

Young children are appropriately flexible in their categorization; the properties they attend to when categorizing a novel entity depend on whether it is an object versus a nonsolid substance (Soja, Carey & Spelke, 1991), a plant versus a rock (Keil, 1994), a real monkey versus a toy monkey (Carey, 1985), or an animal versus a tool (Becker & Ward, 1991). A shift in the properties that underlie categorization can be caused by quite subtle cues, as when eyes are added to simple geometrical shapes, giving them the appearance of being snakelike animals (Jones, Smith & Landau, 1991), and can also be motivated simply by changes in how an entity is described (e.g., Keil, 1994). Even babies show different patterns of generalization depending on the nature of what they are observing: the movements of objects are categorized on the basis of their trajectories, while the movements of animate beings are categorized on the basis of inferred goals (Spelke, Phillips & Woodward, 1995; Woodward, 1998).

Perhaps multiple innate similarity spaces are triggered by different stimuli, such as rigid objects, substances, and animate beings. In addition to this, similarity is a flexible notion (Jones & Smith, 1993). People can learn to categorize objects as falling into distinct categories on the basis of arbitrary contrasts along one or more dimensions, and such learning affects their subsequent intuitions of object similarity

(Goldstone, 1994). If you view objects as points in a multidimensional similarity space, and categories as clusters of objects, this modification can be viewed as the shrinking or stretching of different dimensions, bringing objects closer together or pulling them apart (Nosofsky, 1988).

If we were to stop here, we would have a minimalist proposal about the nature of human concepts. People are born with one or more perceptual similarity spaces that can be modified through experience with specific domains. Objects are seen as belonging to the same category to the extent that they cluster together in that space, and a concept is a representation of that clustering, as captured by exemplar (Nosofsky, 1988) or prototype (Hampton, 1995) models.

There are two reasons, however, to believe that this proposal is too minimal, even for young children. The first has to do with novel properties; the second concerns intuitions about essences.

Properties

Consider more abstract categories. We categorize people as, among other things, *stockbrokers* and *atheists,* objects as *dollars* and *menus,* actions as *swearing* and *weaning.* Under the theory that entities are categorized on the basis of the properties they possess (encoded either as features in a prototype representation or dimensions in a similarity space), the questions arise: What are the relevant properties in these cases, and where does our knowledge of them come from?

It is not a serious proposal that they emerge directly from our perceptual systems; we do not categorize people as stockbrokers solely on the basis of what they look like. It is also unlikely that these properties are abstract innate primitives. The existence of stockbrokers is unlikely to have been anticipated by biological evolution. And if stockbroker is an innate concept (or equivalently if stockbrokerhood is an innate property), then some way is needed for it to make contact with the external world, to connect (however indirectly) to our perceptual and motoric systems. This problem of "embodiment" arises for all putatively innate categories, and for many of them—such as *noun, cause, object,* and *person*—there exist plausible theories as to how the problem can be solved (e.g., Carey & Spelke, 1994; Pinker, 1984). There are no such proposals for stockbroker.

The traditional solution to the problem of abstract properties is empiricist. Humans start off with a perceptually based similarity space, but somehow—through perceptual and linguistic experience—this space comes to respond to increasingly more abstract notions. It starts off being able to categorize on the basis of features such as color and shape, and, through a sensitivity to the statistical properties of the environment, it becomes sensitive to the presence of stockbrokers and menus. Abstract notions are built up from perceptual ones. Explaining precisely how this occurs has long been a central project in empiricist philosophy, but the extent of progress has not been impressive. As Fodor (1981) points out, despite thousands of years of trying, *no* cases can be found in which any natural concept has been shown to emerge from a perceptually based similarity space.

There might be a principled reason for this failure. Perhaps concepts are not statistical abstractions from perceptual experience. Instead, they might be constituted, at least in part, in terms of their role in naive theories of the world (e.g., Carey, 1985, 1988; Gopnik & Meltzoff, 1997; Keil, 1989; Murphy & Medin, 1985). Our concept of stockbroker isn't a vector in some multidimensional perceptual state-space, then; it is instead rooted in our implicit understanding of society, money, jobs, and so on.

This proposal—sometimes called the *theory theory*—comes in different strengths. In its mildest form, the role of theories guides the choice of which of a set of available features will be relevant in any given situation—color for food, shape for artifacts, and so on. Under a stronger version, theories actually lead to the creation of new features (e.g., Wisniewski & Medin, 1994). The most radical version rejects the very idea that category membership is computed on the basis of similarity of features. Murphy and Medin (1985) give the example of seeing someone at a party jump fully dressed into a swimming pool and categorizing him as being drunk. This categorization isn't made because the person is perceptually similar to other drunks; it is made because categorizing him this way provides the most plausible explanation for his behavior. The proposal that causal and explanatory considerations underlie categorization is something that I return to at the end of this chapter.

Essences
A related issue concerns the relationship between the superficial properties of an object and how it is categorized. This relationship might be direct. That is, if objects resemble one another to a sufficient extent, they fall into the same category.

Many creatures might categorize objects this way, but humans do not. We see commonalities that transcend appearance. We categorize a caterpillar and the butterfly it later becomes, and a squalling infant and a grown man, as the same individuals, despite the radical changes in appearance. A hummingbird, ostrich, and falcon belong to the same category (birds) and are distinct from other perceptually similar animals such as bats. Whales are not fish, fool's gold is not gold, marsupial mice are closely related to kangaroos, and glass is actually a liquid. At least for educated adults, the category that a thing belongs to is not merely a matter of what it resembles.

The term for what is maintained through the transformation from caterpillar to chrysalis to butterfly, and for what hummingbirds, ostriches, and falcons share, is *essence*. Locke (1690/1964, p. 26) defines this as follows: "Essences may be taken for the very being of anything, whereby it is what it is. And thus the real internal, but generally . . . unknown constitution of things, whereon their discoverable qualities depend, may be called their essence."

People's naive intuition that certain categories have essences is called *naive essentialism* or *psychological essentialism* (Medin & Ortony, 1989). This proposal does not entail that people actually know what the essences are. For instance, to be an essentialist about water does not require that you know the internal properties that make something water (presumably being H_2O), just that you believe some such properties exist. Hence an essentialist should be able to entertain the possibility that something might resemble water but not actually be water (because it lacks the essence) or not resemble water but be water nonetheless (because it has the essence). It is possible that people were essentialists about water before the development of modern science; in fact, the belief that certain entities have essences might be what motivates scientific inquiry in the first place.

There is a difference, of course, between the claim that people believe that categories have essences and the claim that such essences actually exist. In an important review, Susan Gelman and Larry Hirschfeld (1999, p. 405) suggest that although naive essentialism might be innate and universal, it nonetheless "may yield little insight about the nature of the world." In particular, as Gelman and Hirschfeld point out, contemporary biologists are adamant that species actually have no essences. This is nicely summed up in the title of a classic article by David Hull (1965): "The Effect of Essentialism on Taxonomy: Two Thousand Years of Stasis."

But I don't think the human propensity toward essentialism is actually a mistake (see also Pinker, 1997). In modern biology, species are viewed as populations that evolve, with no sharp boundaries in space or time, and so biologists reject the Aristotelian notion that species are unchangeable ideal types with no intermediate forms; something either is a bird or isn't; there's nothing in between (e.g., Mayr, 1982). It is *this* sort of "essentialism" that is mistaken. But this is much stronger than Lockean essentialism, under which the superficial features of entities are the result of deeper causal properties. Essentialism in this more general form is simply a belief that reasons exist as to why things fall into certain categories: birds are not merely objects that resemble each other but instead have deeper properties in common. This sort of essentialism is rampant in current biological thought, both in the sciences and in the folk theories of different cultures (Atran, 1998).

Essentialism is an adaptive way of looking at the world; it is adaptive because it is true. In biology, animals are hierarchically grouped into species, families, classes, and so on because of their evolutionary history. One can usually classify an animal on the basis of its appearance, but when there is doubt, the most reliable indicators of an animal's category are properties such as embryonic features and genetic structure. (This is how we know, for instance, that chimpanzees are more related to humans than they are to any other primate). The scientific notion that a hummingbird, ostrich, and falcon all belong to a different category than a bat or that a peacock and a peahen belong to the same species are biological insights that emerge from an essentialist world view (see Pinker, 1997, for discussion).[1]

The idea that essentialism is an adaptive stance toward the material and biological world raises the possibility that it is unlearned. This is a controversial proposal. Many scholars would argue instead that essentialism is a cultural construct. Jerry Fodor (1998, p. 155), for instance, suggests that it emerged only with the modern rise of science, and so "*of course* Homer had no notion that water has a hidden essence, or a characteristic microstructure (or that anything else does); a fortiori, he had no notion that the hidden essence of water is causally responsible for its phenomenal properties."

Fodor notes that we have to be cautious with regard to what counts as evidence that children, or adults from other cultures, are naive essentialists. It is not enough to show that they have categories that are not purely perceptual (surely Homer knew about jokes), or that they distinguish between appearance and reality, or even that they believe that things have hidden properties. To be an essentialist in the Lockean sense, you must believe that these hidden properties are causally responsible for the superficial properties of an entity and determine the category that it belongs to.

Fodor is right that there is no proof that essentialism is either innate or universal. But quite a bit of evidence is highly suggestive. Some of this comes from cross-cultural research (e.g., Atran, 1998), but I want to focus here on studies of young children.

Preschoolers use category membership to infer deeper properties that animals have. For instance, in one set of experiments (Gelman & Markman, 1986, 1987), children were told that a brontosaurus has one property (cold blood) and rhinoceros has another (warm blood) and were then asked which property a triceratops had. A triceratops looks more like a rhinoceros than a brontosaurus, and so if children's inductions are solely based on perception, they should guess that the triceratops has warm blood like the rhinoceros. But when both the triceratops and the brontosaurus are described as "dinosaurs," children infer that the triceratops has cold blood. Such a finding can be explained by children's use of the sameness of label as a cue that the triceratops and the brontosaurus fall into the same category and their belief that members of the same category share the same deep properties, even if they don't look alike (see also chapter 10).

Young children also know that membership in a category is not solely determined by appearance. A porcupine that has been transformed so that it looks like a cactus is still a porcupine; a tiger that is put into a lion suit is still a tiger (Keil, 1989). Four-year-olds know that if you remove the insides of a dog (its blood and bones), it is no longer a dog and cannot do typical dog things such as bark and eat dog food, but if you remove the outside of a dog (its fur), it remains a dog, retaining these dog properties (Gelman & Wellman, 1991). They believe that the skin color of a human child is determined by the biological parents, not the people who raised the child (Hirschfeld, 1996).

Finally, four-year-olds are more likely to accept a common label for animals described as sharing internal properties ("the same sort of stuff inside, the same kind of bones, blood, muscles, and brain") than superficial properties ("lives in the same kind of zoo and the same kind of cage"). This holds for both middle-class children raised in Western societies (Diesendruck, Gelman & Lebowitz, 1998) and Brazilian children from shanty-towns, with little formal education, and with limited access to books and television programs (Diesendruck, under review).

Early emergence of essentialist ideas does not entail their innateness, of course. It is conceivable that children somehow pick up this perspective from the adults around them, but there is little support for this view. Even highly educated parents in university towns rarely talk to their children about insides and essences (Gelman et al., in press a), and working-class parents are considerably less likely to do so (Heath, 1986).

The Importance of Shape

Even if children do have an understanding of essences, this might play little role in their learning and use of words (e.g., Malt, 1991, 1994). It is sometimes suggested that children's naming is done entirely on the basis of superficial properties that entities possess. The strongest and most interesting version of this claim has been defended by Linda Smith, Susan Jones, and Barbara Landau (1992, pp. 145–146):

In learning language, children repeatedly experience specific linguistic contexts (e.g., "This is a _____" or "This is some _____") with attention to specific object properties and clusters of properties (e.g., shape or color plus texture). Thus, by this view, these linguistic contexts come to serve as cues that automatically command attention. The evidence on children's novel word interpretations also suggests that the momentary salience of object properties interacts with contextual cues and influences children's generalization of a novel word (e.g., Smith et al., 1992). All in all, the data from artificial word-learning experiments are consistent with the idea that dumb forces on selective attentions—that is, associative connections and direct stimulus pulls—underlie the seeming smartness of children's novel word interpretations.

As they discuss, evidence suggests that children rely on perceptual properties—and specifically shape—when generalizing words. In particular, when given a new count noun that refers to a rigid object, children will typically extend that noun to other rigid objects of the same shape, not to those of the same size, color, or texture (e.g., Baldwin, 1989; Jones, Smith & Landau, 1991; Landau, Smith & Jones, 1988, 1998; Smith, Jones & Landau, 1992, 1996). Following Landau, Smith, and Jones (1988), we can call this the *shape bias*.

There are two theories about the nature of this bias. One is outlined in the quote above: shape is important because children observe that words used in the context "This is a _____" that refer to rigid objects are generalized on the basis of shape. Because of this, when children first hear "This is a dog" used to refer to a dog, they know that it should be extended to other similarly shaped objects. We can call this the *brute-shape theory*.

An alternative, which is more consistent with an essentialist perspective on concepts, is that shape is important because it is seen as a cue to category membership. Children know that count nouns can refer to kinds of objects, and they believe that an object's shape is highly related to the kind it belongs to (e.g., Bloom, 1996a; Gelman & Diesendruck, in press; Keil, 1994). We can call this the *shape-as-cue theory*.

Where would this belief about the importance of shape come from? There are several possibilities. It could be that the importance of shape for object categories is unlearned (e.g., Biederman, 1987; Landau & Jackendoff, 1993). It could be that shape is important because it is seen as highly nonrandom (see Leyton, 1992), and therefore if two objects are of the same shape, children infer that they most likely share deeper properties. Or it could be that children learn through experience that entities of the same kind tend to share the same shape. Under this view, the shape bias is learned, just as in the brute-shape view.

These two theories differ in a couple of substantial ways. First, brute shape predicts that the shape bias should be limited to words, while shape-as-cue predicts that it should apply to categorization more generally (see Ward, Becker, Hass & Vela, 1991, for discussion). Second, brute shape implies that shape *determines* naming, while shape-as-cue predicts that shape is a *cue* to naming. This raises a clear prediction: If brute shape is right, then children should sometimes generalize object names on the basis of shape, using them to refer to entities that belong to different kinds, while if shape-as-cue is right, children should sometimes generalize object names on the basis of kind, using them to refer to entities that have different shapes.

Familiar Categories
One way to address this issue is by studying how children learn new words that refer to familiar categories. Some researchers have used a procedure in which they show children a target object, give it a novel name (such as "This is a dax"), and test whether children extend the word to either a same-shaped item that belongs to a different-kind, or to a different-shaped item that belongs to the same kind (e.g., Baldwin, 1992; Golinkoff et al., 1995; Imai, Gentner & Uchida, 1994). An example of this, from Baldwin's study, is shown in figure 6.1.

Such studies typically find that children are biased to extend the word to the same-shape item, despite the difference in kind. For instance, preschool children who are told that the egg is "a dax" think that the football, and not the loaf of bread, is also a dax. This is said to support the view that young children assume words refer to categories that share a common shape, not a common kind, in support of brute shape.

But there is something worrying about the design of these experiments. As mentioned above, if two objects are the same shape, they are likely to belong to the same basic-level kind (Rosch et al., 1976),

Egg   Nest   Football   Bread

Figure 6.1
Stimuli from generalization study (from Baldwin, 1992)

and so, to contrast shape and kind, the stimuli are designed so that the sameness of kind is at the *superordinate* level. For instance, in the example above, the egg and the loaf of bread are both foods.

This makes generalization on the basis of kind particularly difficult for children. For one thing, if an object is simply labeled "This is an X," X is typically a basic-level term. It would be odd to point to an egg and say "That is food" (e.g., Brown, 1957; Horton & Markman, 1980; Mervis & Crisafi, 1982; see chapter 2). In addition, categorizing on the basis of a superordinate kind is harder than categorizing on the basis of a basic-level kind (e.g., Rosch & Mervis, 1975; Markman, 1989). For these reasons, children might fail to consider the superordinate kind when it comes to extending the name and instead might fall back on choosing the more perceptually similar item (Gelman & Diesendruck, in press).

If this is so, then one would expect quite another result if the different-shaped item belonged to the same *basic-level* kind. Golinkoff et al. (1995) contrasted a target item (such as a banana) with another object of the same shape but a different kind (the moon) as well as an object of the same basic-level kind (another banana). This shift to a basic-level kind made a dramatic difference: when children were given a name for the target object, they tended to generalize this word to the object of the same kind, not the one of the same shape.

This result could be taken as supporting shape-as-cue. But unfortunately the Golinkoff et al. study has another problem, one that bedevils all experiments that use familiar categories. Children may interpret the words they hear as synonyms for existing category labels. There are no pragmatic cues to the contrary and no other plausible meanings the words could have. In the example above, then, they might have construed the word as *banana*, and then, when asked to extend the word, they simply looked for the other banana.

Even if this is the case, this study still tells us something interesting: it shows that children know some object names that they do not extend solely on the basis of shape. That is, for three- and four-year-olds, *banana* does *not* merely mean "an object that has such-and-so shape." What does this understanding tell us about the nature of the shape bias?

Familiar Words

Consider a child who uses the word *clock* to refer to both a grandfather clock and a digital clock. A proponent of shape-as-cue might say that this reflects the child's understanding that these different-shape objects belong to the same kind. But there is a reasonable brute-shape reply: since the grandfather clock and the digital clock really are both clocks, the child might have heard other people name each of them this way and is simply parroting back this usage. A similar response could be made about the non-shape-based responses in the Golinkoff et al. study.

A more revealing source of information may be children's errors. Suppose, for instance, that the child calls a sandal "a boot." Since adults do not use the word in this manner, this sort of error should give us some insight into how children make sense of the meanings of words.[2]

Many of children's errors are uninformative, given that perceptual similarity and sameness of kind are highly correlated in real-world object categories. If a child calls a cat "a dog," this could be because she thinks that the cat belongs to the same kind as other dogs she has seen (in accord with shape-as-cue), or it could be because it is similar in shape to other dogs she has seen (in accord with brute shape).

There are potentially more telling errors, but these are also difficult to interpret. For instance, as mentioned in chapter 2, at 20 months, Max put a piece of yellow pepper on his head at dinnertime and said "hat." It is tempting to view this as evidence against brute shape, since the pepper was not shaped like a typical hat. On the other hand, at 21 months, he called a penis-shape ice cream cone "pee-pee"—which seems like a serious problem for shape-as-cue. But it is hard to know what to make of either case; perhaps Max might have been trying to express his opinions that these items *were similar to* a hat and a penis, not that they actually were members of these categories. (Or he could have been goofing around.)

Experimental studies have problems as well (Gelman et al., in press b). Suppose, for instance, that two-year-olds are shown a picture of a collie and a picture of a horse and are asked to "Point to the dog." They are likely to choose the collie. But this doesn't show that they have an adult understanding of *dog*, since the children might actually believe that both of the pictures denote dogs. It is just that the collie is a more typical dog, and so it is a better choice. On the other hand, if you were to show the children a display without a dog, such as a picture of a book and a picture of a horse, and ask the same question, they might choose the horse. But this would not necessarily show that they believe that a horse is a dog, it might be because the horse most resembles a dog and the children felt pressured to choose *something*. Preferential-looking tasks (e.g., Naigles & Gelman, 1995) suffer from the related problem that direction of gaze does not necessarily reflect intuitions about word meanings. If I am shown a picture of a horse and a picture of a book and hear the word *dog*, I might again look at the horse, not because I believe it is a dog but because it looks most like a dog.

Dromi (1987) points out that a robust test of children's understanding is a procedure that allows children to refuse to choose a picture if no correct referent is available. This is precisely what Gelman et al. (in press b) devised, based on a methodology originally used by Hutchinson and Herman (1991). They presented children with two pictures. One was visible, and the other was hidden behind a cardboard screen. The children were asked questions such as "Where's the dog?"

In one condition, the visible picture shows a dog, and children who know the word should point to this picture; they should not choose the hidden one. In another condition, the visible picture shows a cow. If children know that a cow is not a dog, then they should choose the hidden picture when asked for "the dog." If they do pick the cow (and if they show other indications of being able to understand the task), this suggests that they really do think that the word *dog* extends to cows.

Gelman et al. tested children on two nouns—*apple* and *dog*. Even two-year-olds were usually correct (they did not tend to confuse apples and oranges, for instance). On the occasions that overgeneralizations did occur, the children were just as likely to generalize to other objects of the same (superordinate) kind but of a different shape (picking a banana as "an apple") as they were to choose objects of a different kind but the same shape (picking a baseball as "an apple"). Gelman et al. concluded from this that shape has no privileged status in children's errors.

Gelman et al. went on to discuss why other investigators so often find shape-based errors in production and comprehension. Such errors tend to be most frequent with items that are unfamiliar for children, which follows from shape-as-cue. If you know little or nothing about an object, it is a reasonable assumption that shape is relevant to kind membership—particularly in an experiment where all that is available is a line drawing. Also, some overgeneralizations on the basis of shape might occur because the same-shape object is seen as a *representation* of the item being named. For instance, Gelman et al. found that even four-year-olds often selected a pink spherical candle as "an apple," perhaps because the children, not knowing that the item was a candle, thought it was a representation of an apple, such as a toy apple. The naming of representations is an issue we return to in the next chapter.

New Words for New Categories
When learning a new word for a novel category, how do children generalize this word? It depends. One consideration is the word's syntactic category. For instance, nouns are treated differently from adjectives. If children hear an unfamiliar object named as "a zav," they will tend to generalize the word on the basis of shape, but if they hear it described as "a zavish one," they are more prone to generalize on the basis of color or texture (e.g., Hall, Waxman & Hurwitz, 1993; Smith, Jones & Landau, 1992; Taylor & Gelman, 1988; see chapter 8).

It also depends on the kind of entity. While names for rigid objects are typically generalized on the basis of shape, even two-year-olds generalize names for nonsolid substances, such as jelly, paste, or instant coffee, on the basis of texture and color (Macario, 1991; Soja, Carey & Spelke, 1991). If a named object looks like an animal that can undergo postural change, the shape bias again goes away (Becker & Ward, 1991; Jones, Smith & Landau, 1991).

Finally, a word's interpretation can depend on how the entity is described. Keil (1994) finds that three- and four-year-olds tend to generalize names for objects described as animals on the basis of shape ("This is my hydrax. It's a kind of animal"), but if the same objects are described as nonliving natural kinds ("This is my malachite. It's a kind of rock"), they ignore shape and focus on color. There is the same effect of being told that something is a kind of animal versus a kind of food (Becker & Ward, 1991).

These studies tell us that children are not limited to generalizing words—even count nouns that refer to rigid objects—on the basis of shape. They are appropriately sensitive to other considerations, such as color and texture, which accords with the results of Gelman et al.'s study of children's overgeneralizations.

This is all consistent with shape-as-cue, but it is hardly decisive evidence for it, let alone for naive essentialism more generally. The results reviewed in this section are easily accounted for by the theory that perceptual properties directly underlie categorization, so long as one makes the reasonable assumption that the relevant features (or weights of the relevant dimensions) can change as a function of experience (e.g., Jones & Smith, 1993). Under such a view, for instance, it is *not* that the presence of eyes on an object tells children that the object is a snakelike animal (one that can bend and twist), and this is why they extend a name for this object to other objects of different shapes. Instead, children have simply observed that words that refer to objects with eyes are generalized on the basis of texture and color, not shape. None of these studies, then, resolves the question of whether children's naming of objects is based on an essentialist understanding of categories.

Artifacts

One domain of considerable interest is the learning of names for artifact categories—for human-made entities such as chairs and clocks.

What is the nature of adults' understanding of such categories? Chairs and clocks come in a range of shapes and sizes: there are bean-bag chairs, basket chairs, deck chairs, chairs for dolls, chairs shaped like hands, and chairs suspended from ceilings on chains; there are grandfather clocks, digital clocks, clocks shaped like coke bottles, and clocks for the blind that tell the time at the press of a button. In the course of your life, you will be exposed to an extraordinary array of chairs and clocks, some emerging through technological advance, others that extend the boundaries of fashion or aesthetics, still others that exist in fiction, either historical, fantasy, or futuristic. What makes these things chairs and clocks plainly does not reduce to facts about their appearance.

What about function? Perhaps chairs are things we sit on; clocks are things that tell time. But this is also a nonstarter. One can sit on the floor, but this doesn't make it a chair. And a fragile chair that would break if you tried to sit on it is nonetheless still a chair. I can tell the time by looking at the shadow of a tree, but a shadow is not a clock, and if Big Ben stopped working—if it could no longer fulfill the function of telling time—it would not cease being a clock.

What about *intended* function? This is more promising. Perhaps a chair is something that was built with the intention that people sit on it; a clock is something that was built with the intention that it tell time. This is a better cue to artifact-kind membership than current function; in studies in which intended function and current function are pitted against each other, intended function wins out (Hall, 1995; Keil, 1989; Rips, 1989). A theory based on intended function also accounts for our intuitions that the floor isn't a chair and a shadow isn't a clock, but a broken chair and broken clock remain a chair and a clock.

But such a theory doesn't fully capture our intuitions about artifact category membership. Barbara Malt and Eric Johnson (1992) found that adults will often agree that something that looks very much like a boat *is* a boat, even if they are explicitly told that it wasn't created with the intent to serve the sorts of functions that boats typically perform. Similarly, it is true that chairs are usually designed for people to sit on—but benches, stools, and sofas are also designed for this purpose, and no unique function seems to distinguish chairs from these other categories. Finally, there is nothing incoherent about someone creating a chair without any desire that people sit on it. For instance, someone might build a chair as a prop in a play; it gets shattered with a sledgehammer in the first act. Still, it is a chair and everyone would call it one.

An alternative theory is that the categorization of artifacts is rooted in our intuitions about creator's intent and how it relates to the design of an object (Bloom, 1996a, 1998; Dennett, 1990; Keil, 1989; see also Malt & Johnson, 1998, for a critical discussion). We categorize something as being a member of an artifact kind if its current appearance and use are best explained in terms of the intent to create something that falls into that kind. Under this view, when we judge that something is a chair, we are not judging that it looks and functions like other chairs we have encountered; we are instead judging that it looks and functions as if it was created with the same intent as other chairs we have encountered.

Much of the time the relationship between appearance and intent is transparent. If something resembles a typical chair, for instance, then it is highly likely that it was created with the intent to be a chair. As Daniel Dennett (1990) notes, "There can be little doubt what an axe is, or what a telephone is for; we hardly need to consult Alexander Graham Bell's biography for clues about what he had in mind."

Categorization becomes more complicated, however, when dealing with atypical exemplars, and here the merits of an intention-based theory emerge. Malt and Johnson (1992) found that if an object was described as looking very different from typical members of a category, it was usually not judged to be a member of the category, regardless of its function. For instance, a rubber sphere hitched to a team of dolphins is not called *a boat*, even if it is described as being created for the function of carrying people across water. But there were a few exceptions to this finding. For instance, a small cube with an extendible rod and a digital display was categorized as a *ruler*, and a large disk suspended from the ceiling by cables, with a fold-down seat attached, was categorized as a *desk*.

What distinguishes the atypical entities that were judged as being category members from those that weren't? Malt and Johnson (1992) point out that for the atypical objects, "the unusual physical features ... may be construed as more advanced or effective than the current features, and the descriptions may be interpreted as plausible futuristic versions of the articles" (p. 209). In other words, we can envision someone creating the cube and the disk with the intent to make a (more advanced, more effective) ruler and desk, while it is implausible that someone who intended to build an object belonging to the class of boats would make the sphere.

This is an essentialist account of artifacts. Applying essentialism to this domain is controversial. Philosophers such as Locke and Mill have proposed essentialism as a doctrine exclusively about categories in the natural world—about natural kinds—and many psychologists would argue that this holds as well for psychological essentialism: humans are naive essentialists about entities such as birds and water, but not about chairs and clocks. As Steven Schwartz (1978, p. 572) puts it, "The big difference between artifact kinds and [natural kinds] is that we do not propose that there is any underlying nature that makes something the kind of artifact that it is."

It is true that we don't think of artifacts as having internal essences in the sense of natural kinds. But this doesn't refute the view that artifacts are seen as having essences in the sense of having deeper causal properties that explain their superficial features and determine the categories they belong to. Instead of being biological and chemical, the essences of artifacts are social and psychological (see Keil, 1989; Putnam, 1975). In fact, the same essentialist intuitions we find for natural kinds apply to artifacts as well. Just as the superficial parts and properties of animals can be explained in part by their internal essence, the superficial parts and properties of artifacts can be explained in part by the intentions underlying their creation. Most of the time, we can categorize animals by their superficial properties, but in hard cases, experts might look at their internal structure. Most of the time we can categorize artifacts by their superficial properties, but in hard cases, experts—such as archaeologists, anthropologists, and historians—will attempt to figure out what they were intended to be. (Consider the debates over whether certain carved stones left by Neanderthals are tools, religious artifacts, or artwork.) This sort of *artifact hermeneutics,* to use Dennett's (1990) term, is rooted in essentialist assumptions about the nature of artifacts.

Naming by Children

Do children have this same essentialist understanding of artifacts? Few people have explored this issue. Most studies that have explored this domain have asked instead whether children extend these names on the basis of shape or on the basis of function. Implicit in this question is the notion that function determines how adults categorize artifact kinds (e.g., Miller & Johnson-Laird, 1976). Hence if children attend to function, they are being adultlike; if they attend to shape, they are more perception-bound.

Some evidence suggests an early understanding of function by children. Using a dishabituation paradigm, Kolstad and Baillargeon (1990) found that 10-month-olds are sensitive to a functional property—the ability to serve as a container—when categorizing objects and that this can override perceptual similarity. Similarly, Brown (1990) found that two-year-olds, having learned to retrieve an object with a rake, would attempt the same action with other objects of dissimilar shape but not with same-shape objects that lacked the length and rigidity to do this action—a finding that Hauser (1997) replicated with cotton-top tamarins. Other studies have found that two-year-olds are sensitive to correlations between the form of an animal and the "functions" that it can fulfill (McCarrell & Callanan, 1995).

But is function the basis for their generalization of novel artifact names? In a classic study, Dedre Gentner (1978) showed children and adults two novel objects. The "jiggy" was a square box with a cartoon face; operating a lever on the box made the face change expression. The "zimbo" was a modified gumball machine; operating a lever caused jellybeans to drop. Subjects were then shown a hybrid object that looked like a jiggy but dispensed jellybeans like a zimbo and were asked whether it was a jiggy or a zimbo. Two- to five-year-olds generalized the word on the basis of appearance (saying that it was a jiggy), while five- to 15-year-olds generalized on the basis of function (saying that it was a zimbo). Surprisingly, however, adults acted just like the younger children; they said it was a jiggy, generalizing on the basis of appearance.

Two recent studies that pit shape against function are those of Deborah Kemler-Nelson et al. (1995) and Landau, Smith, and Jones (1998).[3] Kemler-Nelson et al. showed three-, four-, and five-year-olds a novel artifact, such as a T-shaped metal object with attached brushes. They were told that the object was "a stennet." The experimenter modeled its function, such as dipping the stennet into paint and making a design, and the children were then encouraged to use the stennet to make their own designs. They were then shown other objects: some had the same overall shape, others had a different shape; some could do the same function, others could not. For each, they were asked, "Do you think this is a stennet or that this is not a stennet?" Children in all age groups tended to extend the word on the basis of function, not shape. In a recent set of studies with similar stimuli, Kemler-Nelson (in press) found that even two-year-olds generalized new artifact names on the basis of function.

Landau, Smith, and Jones (1998) used a similar design. Two-, three-, and five-year-olds and adults were shown a simple object and told, for instance, that it was "a rif." Then they were told "Rifs are made by a special company so they can do this," and a function, such as wiping up water, was demonstrated. Then the subjects were shown different objects and asked for each one: "Is this a rif?" Landau et al. obtained the opposite result from Kemler-Nelson. The word tended to be extended by children on the basis of shape, not function. Adults, in contrast, did extend the word on the basis of function.

How can one explain these different results? Both Kemler-Nelson et al. (1995) and Landau, Smith, and Jones (1998) have some suggestions, including the fact that the stimuli in the Kemler-Nelson et al. study were more complicated and realistic than those in the Landau et al. study and contained familiar object parts. Also, the subjects in the

Kemler-Nelson et al. study had more experience with the objects' functions, perhaps making function more salient.

As I noted earlier, one concern with these studies is that, at least for adults, artifacts aren't categorized exclusively on the basis of shape or function. It may be that these considerations are relevant only to the extent that they are cues to the intent underlying the creation of the object. From this perspective, we are in a position to speculate—in what is admittedly a post hoc fashion—as to why the two studies got such different results.

In the Kemler-Nelson et al. study, the functions were highly specific and reflected intentional design: being able to paint parallel lines isn't the sort of thing that an artifact can do by accident. This should motivate categorization on the basis of function; children (as well as adults) might reason that other objects would be able to do the same thing only if they were intended to fall into the same category.

In the Landau et al. study, the functions—such as wiping up water—were simple and dependent only on the substances that the artifacts were made of. There was no motivation to believe, then, that the objects were created with the express intent that they fulfill that function. This might motivate categorization on the basis of shape. After all, in the absence of any other reliable cue, shape is highly diagnostic as to creator's intent.

As I said, this is post hoc, but it does lead to a prediction. One can have a situation in which two objects have the same shape, there is some explanation for why they are that shape, but the explanation doesn't entail that they have been intended to belong to the same kind. If this hypothesis is right, the shape bias should go away.

To test this hypothesis, Lori Markson, Gil Diesendruck, and I exposed children to a situation like the one shown in figure 6.2, using stimuli based on those used by Landau et al. (Bloom, Markson & Diesendruck, 1998). We used a target object and two test objects—one of the same shape and a different material from the target, the other of a different shape and the same material.

We tested adults and four-year-olds. There were two conditions. In one, we simply put down the target object and named it, as in "This is a fendle." We then presented the other two objects and asked, "Which one of these is a fendle?" Not surprisingly, we got a shape bias, replicating Landau et al. (children: 83 percent, adults: 90 percent).

The second condition was identical, except that the same-shape object was used as a tight-fitting container for the target object—and, at the start of the study, the target object was removed from this container. We reasoned that this manipulation would indicate to our

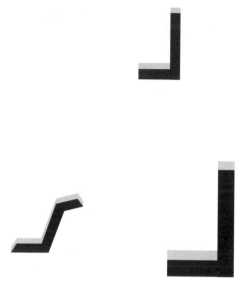

Figure 6.2
Stimuli from container study

subjects that the two same-shape objects were created for different purposes, while at the same time giving some intuitive rationale for why
they were the same shape.[4] In this condition, the shape bias goes away
(children: 55 percent, adults: 50 percent). This is exactly as predicted by
shape-as-cue and, more generally, by an essentialist theory of artifact
categories.

Several facts about children's generalizations still need to be explained: Why did the adults in the Gentner study behave differently
from the older children and adolescents? Why did Landau et al. find
a developmental shift while Kemler-Nelson did not? But I think that a
change in perspective—moving away from pitting shape and function
against each other and instead exploring the extent to which they serve
as cues to underlying intent—might give us insight into some of these
puzzles (see also Bloom, Markson & Diesendruck, 1998).

The debate over whether children are essentialists in their language
and thought has focused almost exclusively on the domain of animals.
Biological species have long been the paradigm case of essentialized
categories within philosophy, and psychologists have followed suit.
But by many accounts, young children's understanding of biology is
quite limited (e.g., Carey, 1985; Keil, 1989), particularly in contrast with
their rich understanding of, and interest in, goals and desires. If chil-

dren really are essentialists, then, this might show up most clearly in a domain in which the essences have to do with these very mental states—the domain of artifacts.

The Structure of Concepts

If an essentialist perspective on concepts is correct, it would entail that many words correspond to concepts that do not exhaustively decompose into simpler notions. Although concepts might be associated with prototypes or sets of exemplars, they do not reduce to them.

I have focused here on common nouns, but the same considerations apply to the meanings of proper names. When we first meet someone and learn that he is named *Bob,* we form a representation of that person and associate it with that proper name. This representation might include Bob's appearance and the tone of his voice. But we nonetheless assume that the proper name corresponds to *that individual,* tracking him over space and time; we encode this other information as contingent facts about the individual. Because of this, it is possible for us to question whether Gödel was the man who did a certain mathematical proof (even if the only thing we know about Gödel was that he did this proof), whether Shakespeare wrote *Hamlet, Macbeth,* etc. (even if all we know about Shakespeare is that he wrote *Hamlet, Macbeth,* etc.), whether Moses really crossed the Red Sea, and so on (Kripke, 1980).

This is a plausible way for the human mind to have evolved: we would want the capacity to think about, recognize, and track people, not merely properties that are associated with people. Similarly, we would want the capacity to refer to members of categories that occur in the physical and social world (things like birds and chairs), to reason about them, to have desires that implicate them, and so on—but to also understand that things can be members of these kinds even if they appear different from typical members and that they might not be members of these kinds even if they appear similar to typical members.

Essentialism Lite

It is sometimes argued that humans have innate knowledge of space, time, causality, and number. A set of innate naive theories or stances includes intuitive physics, theory of mind, and naive biology. Long before they start to speak, babies think about people as intentional agents, about rabbits as biological entities, about chairs as intentionally created entities. The abstract understanding of the world that educated adult scientists possess is not a radical departure from this initial innate understanding; it is merely an extension of it.

This is one perspective on the structure of the mind (see Pinker, 1997), one I am sympathetic to. But suppose it is wrong, every word of it. Psychological essentialism could still be right. Imagine, following Quine, that humans start with nothing more than an animal similarity space: entities are thought about as similar and hence are thought more likely to fall into the same kind, depending on their relative locations in that space. To give rise to essentialism, all one needs to add is the notion that a distinction exists between, roughly, *looking* the same and *being* the same.

In particular, it is not the case that to have an essentialized concept you need to have a theory encompassing the domain that the category belongs to. And so the essentialism proposal does not entail the theory theory—the view that concepts are characterized by the role they play within naive theories. The theory theory works well for many concepts, particularly those that are part of bona fide scientific theories—concepts such as electricity and heat. Block (1986) notes that many such concepts are acquired not through ostensive naming but instead in the course of acquiring the relevant theories. And in some cases, a set of concepts might be learned all at once (force, mass, acceleration; gene, codon, chromosome), just by being connected to one another within a larger explanatory system.

But this approach does not naturally apply to all concepts. Laboratory studies have found that people can acquire concepts that correspond to arbitrary correlations of features (e.g., Nosofsky, 1988; Posner & Keele, 1968). While top-down expectations do affect the sorts of properties people attend to in these studies (Kelemen & Bloom, 1994), the *specific* concepts that they come to learn are defined entirely in terms of statistical information. And it is implausible that two-year-olds who know the meanings of the words *milk* and *juice* distinguish the two in terms of their explanatory roles within naive theories. More likely, they do so on the basis of color and taste.

Fodor (1998) makes a similar point using the example of water. He notes that we know the properties of water—that it is liquid, transparent, drinkable—and we know that these properties are correlated. But even most adults don't know *why* they are correlated. More generally, the notion that a concept is held together by an understanding of why it has the properties it does "set[s] the conditions for concept possession impossibly high" (p. 118).

The essentialist view doesn't have problems with such cases. It simply entails that children will have the implicit assumption that some deeper fact relates to the matter—that these properties of water are the result of some deeper essence. In such cases, children aren't like scientists who have theories; they are like scientists *before* they have theories, trying to make sense of some domain they know little about. More generally, before developing a theory as to why there is a correlation between certain features, you have to first notice that this correlation exists, and hence there is a symbiotic relationship between statistical learning and theory-based inference (Keil, 1994).

The studies reviewed in this chapter support the view that, early in development, children do possess intuitive theories of natural kinds and artifacts. A word that names a novel animal, such as an aardvark, will be extended in a different way than a word that names a novel artifact, such as a modem. But children also possess a more general intuition—one that can apply in the absence of intuitive theories. This is the intuition that concepts—and hence words—correspond to how things really are and not just how they appear to be.

Notes

1. This isn't to say that essentialism is always correct. Humans can *over*essentialize and infer causes when none exist. We are, at heart, conspiracy theorists. The most pernicious example of this is race. Human groups differ in properties such as skin color and facial morphology, and to a biologist these are literally skin deep—typically superficial adaptations to climate differences. But even young children tend to think of races as deep and immutable categories (Hirschfeld, 1996).

2. Underextension, in which a child has a narrower extension of the word than the adult does—refusing to call a pelican "a bird," for instance—could provide similar insights, but underextensions are harder to observe in spontaneous speech and harder to study experimentally.

3. Another study using a similar design was reported in Tomikawa and Dodd (1980), but those stimuli were described to the children as characters "who have various exciting adventures," and not as artifacts, and so the results from this study do not bear directly on the question of how children treat artifact names.

4. For some real-world examples of this, consider a glove (hand-shaped), a sheath (knife-shaped), and a violin case (violin-shaped). We do *not* call these "hands," "knives," or "violins," presumably because we know that there is another explanation for the sameness of shape, one that does not entail that they were intended to be—or represent—hands, knives, or violins.

Chapter 7

Naming Representations

Modern humans live in a world of visual representations. William Ittelson (1996, p. 171) gives some examples of this:

> As I sit here at my breakfast table, my morning newspaper has printing on it; it has a graph telling me how the national budget will be spent, a map trying to tell me something about the weather; a table of baseball statistics, an engineering drawing with which I can build a garden chair, photographs of distant places and people, a caricature expressing what the editor thinks of a political figure, and an artist's rendition of what the city will look like 20 years from now. . . . On the wall in front of me hangs an abstract painting. Next to that, there is a calendar. Above the calendar is a clock. All this and more, and I haven't even turned on the TV or the computer.

Children live in the same world. While young ones do not read, they often look at picture books. They draw, paint, sculpt, and observe the artistic endeavors of others. In many homes, they watch cartoons, videos, documentaries, and other television programs. Much of what children—and adults—know about the world is the result of exposure to visual representations. In some instances, children's appreciation of pictures is parasitic on an understanding of the external world (as when a child looks at a photograph of his mother and knows who it represents), but often it is the other way around: the understanding of the representation comes first. Most children will see a picture of a gorilla before seeing an actual gorilla, and much of the mature understanding of everything from planets to popes comes not from experience with the actual entities but through experience with visual representations.

We talk about these representations using the same words we use for talking about real things. (The terminology I am using here is informal, since, of course, pictures are also real things.) We might point to a painting of a chair and say "Look at the chair" or to a drawing of a dog and say "That's an ugly dog." The focus of this chapter is the nature and development of the naming of visual representations.

This might seem like a perverse topic to include in a book on word learning. In most studies of word learning, objects and representations of objects are thought of as interchangeable, so much so that experiments designed to see how children interpret new object names typically teach children names for pictures of objects, not objects themselves. For instance, studies looking at how children learn names for natural-kind categories rarely show children actual members of natural-kind categories, just drawings or photographs of them. The equivalence of objects and representations is so natural that it is usually never mentioned. A paper on word learning (e.g., Bloom & Kelemen, 1995) will typically begin with some claims of how children learn names for objects, the description of the methods will note that drawings of objects were used, and the paper will end with some conclusions about how children learn names for objects, without any mention that these weren't what they were actually tested on.

Developmental psychologists are in good company; the same assumption about the interchangeability of pictures and what they depict is held by perception psychologists. Ittelson (1996) points out that in their classic study "Mental Rotation of Three-Dimensional Objects," Shepard and Metzler (1971) used no three-dimensional objects; that the extensive literature on face recognition has almost no studies that involve the recognition of faces; and that when the journal *Perception* devoted two special issues in 1994 to "Perceptual Organization and Object Recognition," none of the papers reported a single experiment using objects. These researchers, while plainly knowing that a perceptual difference exists between looking at a picture and looking at an object (because people can tell which is which just by looking), see this as having no theoretical import: if you have a theory of how people recognize dogs, it is perfectly reasonable to test the theory with a study of how people recognize pictures of dogs.

But there is good reason to believe that this equivalence assumption is mistaken, at least for word learning. The naming of pictures is very different from the naming of real-world objects. When you call a dog "a dog," you are naming a member of a natural kind, a flesh-and-blood creature. But when you call a picture of a dog "a dog," you are naming an artifact, a marked-up piece of paper.

I argue below that this makes a big difference. The developing understanding of visual representations is an interesting topic in its own right, but the motivation for discussing it here is to explore and extend certain proposals that were made in the previous chapter concerning the naming and categorization of artifacts. Studies of how children

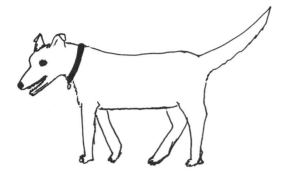

Figure 7.1
A dog

name and categorize visual representations show that they have a surprisingly sophisticated understanding of these types of artifacts, one
that is intimately linked to their theory of mind.

Adult Naming of Visual Representations

How do adults name pictures? Consider the picture in figure 7.1. If
asked "What's this?," you might say "A dog." But you would not confuse it for an actual dog. It will not bark, bite, or piddle on the page;
it has no color, depth, mass, texture, or smell.

The word *dog* can name both a real object and a visual representation
of an object. In general, words describe both reality and depictions of
reality (Jackendoff, 1992). No words refer to dogs but not representations of dogs or refer to representations of dogs but not the real things.
(Even the word *picture* can refer to either a picture or a picture of a
picture.) This is a curious fact about language. After all, it is not as if
we call *anything* dog-related "a dog." Statues, photographs, and drawings of dogs are called "dogs," but stories, descriptions, jokes, and
thoughts of dogs are not. If you enjoy my pictures of dogs, you can
ask me to "draw a dog," but if you enjoy my jokes about dogs, it would
be bizarre to ask me to "tell a dog."

What is the relationship between the drawing and an actual dog?
What licenses the use of the noun *dog* to describe the markings on the
page? One proposal sees picture naming as the product of cultural conventions that are learned by experience (Gombrich, 1960; Goodman,
1968). Under this view, the psychological account of why one describes
the above drawing as "a dog" will be similar to an account of why
one describes a skull-and-crossbones as "poison": it is a learned

convention. This account is supported by anecdotes in which people from societies with no visual representations are shown pictures and cannot recognize or name them, presumably because they haven't learned the arbitrary code underlying the relationship between pictures and what they depict. They will not name the drawing in figure 7.1 as a dog for the same reason that they won't spontaneously name the skull-and-crossbones as poison.

This cannot be entirely right, however. There is evidence for an unlearned appreciation of the correspondence between some pictures and what they depict. In one case, a boy was raised in a situation in which pictures were kept from his general vicinity. When at the age of 19 months he was exposed to several photographs and line drawings, he was highly successful at naming them, even though he had never before seen a picture being named (Hochberg & Brooks, 1962). Even infants appreciate the correspondence between pictures and reality. DeLoache, Strauss, and Maynard (1979) let five-month-olds play with a doll and then showed them two pictures—one of the doll they had played with and the other of a different doll. They tended to look longer at the picture of the new doll, suggesting that they recognized the other picture as being somehow familiar. Finally, the anthropological anecdotes shouldn't be trusted: more careful studies have found that adults with no experience with pictures can nonetheless recognize—and name—the object depicted on first viewing (e.g., Ekman & Friesen, 1975).

Such findings support a more commonsense view about the relationship between pictures and objects. The obvious answer to the question of why the above drawing is called "a dog" is that it looks like a dog. More generally, some pictures resemble what they depict and can be recognized without any other information. One recognizes an unfamiliar picture of a dog as a dog in much the same way that one recognizes an unfamiliar animal as a dog: it looks like previously encountered dogs. In fact, both Euclid and Leonardo Da Vinci claimed that the visual information obtained from a painting and from the world is, under ideal circumstances, identical. And for some artwork (*trompe l'oeil*), the painting is cleverly created and displayed so that the pattern of light that the observer sees is the very same pattern that would exist if an actual scene were visible, and so the painting fools the eye: it is taken for real. Animals can also be fooled; dogs will sniff at the hindquarters of life-size pictures of real dogs (Cabe, 1980).

This is all consistent with a simple theory of how we name pictures. We call a picture of a dog "dog" because the picture resembles a real dog (or more formally, because it accesses the same structural description as a real dog). The fact that we recognize and name line drawings shows that color, size, and texture are not criterial, but shape is: the drawing in figure 7.1 looks like a dog because it has the same shape as a real dog.

More generally, these facts about the naming of representations can be taken as support for the brute-shape theory discussed in the previous chapter, which posits that, at least for children, artifact names refer to objects that share the same shape but not deeper properties. As Landau, Smith, and Jones (1988, p. 317) point out, "A mechanical monkey and a real monkey are both called monkey. A 60-foot sculpture of a clothespin gracing downtown Philadelphia is universally recognized and labeled as a clothespin, albeit a 60-foot metallic clothespin. In these cases, qualifiers capture the differences, whereas the head noun captures the shape similarity."

This account seems to capture certain facts about the naming of representations. But it cannot be a complete theory of how we name representations (Bloom, 1996a; Gelman & Diesendruck, in press; Soja, Carey & Spelke, 1992).

For one thing, representations are inherently ambiguous. Any picture looks like an indefinite number of things and could be named in many different ways. Depending on the context, an oval can be an egg or a football; a triangle can be a rocket ship or a mountain; a rectangle can be a computer or a landing strip. Imagine that my dog Fido has run away and I put the drawing in figure 7.1 on lampposts with the caption "Lost dog named Fido. Reward." With this information, it would be taken as a picture of Fido. No doubt there exists some other dog (Bingo, who lives in Brazil, say) that the picture resembles more than it does Fido. But this doesn't make the drawing a picture of Bingo.

Or suppose that I saw a robot dog in a science museum and I was so amazed that I drew a picture of it to show my friends. Then it is a drawing of a robot, not of a dog, though we might add that it sure does look like a real dog. Similarly, a rendition by a courtroom artist of the defendant in a murder trial might look like me, but if someone points to the picture and asks "Who is that?," it would be strange indeed for me to answer "It's me!" (but perfectly natural to say "Somebody who looks just like me"). In general, there is a psychological difference between what a picture *is* and what a picture *looks like*.

This holds as well for extremely precise depictions. You might not be able to tell by looking whether a snowswept landscape is a drawing of the Canadian prairies or of the Arctic circle—until you hear it was drawn in Saskatchewan. If a skilled artist draws a portrait of Sam, it may look just like his identical twin brother Moe, but it will nonetheless still be a portrait of Sam—and will remain so even if Sam subsequently cuts his hair and shaves his beard so that the picture actually ends up looking more like Moe. And, once again, one might point to the picture and say "This is Sam—even though it looks more like Moe."

Finally, we can name visual representations that bear no resemblance at all to what they depict. An X on a pirate's map can be described as buried treasure, an O in an organizational chart as the vice-provost, and the juxtaposition of geometrical forms in a painting by Picasso as one of his lovers.

What underlies the naming in all these examples is the understood intent of the creator. What makes us call an oval "an egg" in one context and "a football" in another is our assumption about what the oval was intended to represent, and the same for whether a picture is described as a generic dog, Fido, Bingo, or a robot, or as a murderer, or as me. The naming of the representation draws on our understanding of the context in which it was created—what it was *intended* to be.

Two other facts support this proposal. First, if we see someone draw a picture and we do not know who or what it is a picture of, we are likely to ask the artist: we assume that he or she should know. If intentionality wasn't relevant to picture naming, why would we care? And second, we accept the possibility of inept or sloppy representations. My picture of a dog might look more like a cat, but this makes it a bad picture of a dog, not a good picture of a cat.

We do not have psychic access to the intentions of others, however; we can't read their minds and tell what they intend the picture to be. Instead we must infer this intent. There are many ways this could take place. The artist could tell us what the picture is in a sincere fashion, as in "Look at my drawing of a dog." The picture could be titled appropriately, as in "My Dog." We could see the artist staring intently at a dog while creating the picture, or we might know that the artist is obsessed with dogs and draws nothing else. But in the simplest case, we infer that the picture was intended to represent a dog—and is therefore a picture of a dog—by virtue of what it looks like. It is a reasonable inference that something is a picture of a dog if it looks like a dog because we believe that someone who intends to represent a dog will try to create something that will be recognized as one.

This is a useful generalization, but there are exceptions to it. Modern art is the most philosophically examined (e.g., Danto, 1981, 1992; Davies, 1991). Some artists will intend to create something that represents X but do not wish others to infer, or at least not easily, that it is a representation of X. In fact, they might choose to purposefully flaunt the convention associated with the above generalization, so as to make a statement about art itself, as when Magritte drew a picture that looked exactly like a pipe, writing below it, "Ceci n'est pas une pipe." Other artists do wish to inform others that the picture represents X but choose other ways to do so; they might have a helpful title or include the name of X within the picture itself (political satirists often use this technique, and it is useful for cases when viewers cannot be assumed to know what the represented people actually look like).

And again there is bad art. Bad artists sometimes wish others to believe that something is a representation of X and wish to do so by making it look like X—but fail due to incompetence. Someone might look at my picture (a clumsy line drawing that looks something like a cat) and assume that I intended to draw a cat—but this would be wrong. I intended to draw a dog; I just did a poor job at it. In this example, the ineptness of the picture makes it easy to attribute a variety of different intentions to the artist, as it gives the impression that he is the sort who suffers a lot of slippage between intent and result.

The story up to now, which was defended in Bloom (1996a), is a purely intentionalist one: We name pictures on the basis of what we think they were intended to depict. But intention cannot be the sole route to picture naming. For one thing, autistic people have no special problem naming and creating realistic pictures, despite their deficit in understanding the intentions of others. For another, one-year-olds can name pictures, and evidence (discussed below) suggests that they lack an intentionalist understanding of visual representations. Finally, adults can name representations that were not created through intentional processes, as when looking at a closed-circuit television in a department store. You can identify people you see on television ("Hey, look at Sam on the TV"), even if you know that no one had any intent to depict that particular person.

Different routes, then, can be taken to picture naming. Without the right understanding of pictures and how they are made, one is limited to naming on the basis of appearance, and this may be what very young children and some autistic individuals do. But I would maintain that this is never the case for normal adults. Even for the television example above, it is not appearance per se that drives our naming; it is our causal intuitions as to what caused the image. Sam and Moe look identical, but we name the image on the television "Sam" because we believe it was Sam who was actually in front of the camera, not Moe.

Consider finally the naming of entities that resemble certain objects but were created through a random process, as in the recent discovery in Nashville, Tennessee, of a bun shaped like Mother Teresa   the Nun Bun. Are these exceptions to the claim that the adult naming of representations is never based solely on appearance? Not necessarily. People are prone to see such entities as the product of some intentional process. The reason that people have flocked to see the Nun Bun isn't because the bun itself is so special (if I purposely carved a muffin into the shape of Mother Teresa, nobody would care), but because its remarkable resemblance seems to reflect the handiwork of a divine creator.

In sum, the adult naming of representational pictures is driven by factors that run deeper than appearance. This is the only way to explain our appreciation of ambiguous drawings, drawings that do not look like what they depict, and bad art, and it explains as well our interest in artist's intent. But what about young children?

Children's Understanding of Visual Representations

Some ability to understand pictures is unlearned. As discussed above, children can spontaneously name pictures without prior experience (Hochberg & Brooks, 1962), and infants are less interested in a picture of a familiar doll than in a picture of an unfamiliar one, showing that they have some tacit appreciation of a relationship between the doll and the picture (DeLoache, Strauss & Maynard, 1979). They can also distinguish between a picture and the real thing; when shown a doll and a picture of the doll, they prefer to look at the actual doll (DeLoache, Strauss & Maynard, 1979).

It is unlikely that babies are thinking about pictures in terms of representational intent. They most likely do not see pictures (or photographs or statues) as representations at all. Instead, they show certain signs of being confused about their status. One-year-olds will often grab at pictures, trying to pick up the depicted object (DeLoache, Miller & Rosengren, 1997; Ninio & Bruner, 1978; Werner & Kaplan, 1963). Perner (1991) describes a 16-month-old who tried to put on a picture of a shoe.

Could these be instances of pretend play? If so, one would expect them to continue in the years that follow. But such behavior is rare past the age of two. It looks instead like genuine befuddlement, as if these children cannot make sense of the dual nature of their perceptions—that they are seeing something that is a shoe and, at the same time, something that is a flat surface. So even though they can detect the similarity between an object and a picture of the object (same shape) as well as the difference (one is flat; one is not), they are at a loss as to what pictures actually are.

The tendency to confuse pictures with the things they depict is sometimes called *childhood realism* (Piaget, 1929) or *iconic realism* (Beilin & Pearlman, 1991), and this is a fair description of children before the age of two. What I want to argue, however, is that before children reach their third birthday, they are thinking about pictures, and representations in general, in the same intentionalist way as adults.

This might seem to be an untenable view given all the research in the developmental literature that has been taken to show that iconic realism drags on until the school years. But I show, first, that the evidence for this view is actually not very strong and, second, that positive evidence exists for early intentionalist understanding.

Consider the motivation for the claim that three- and four-year-olds are confused about the relationship between pictures and their referents. Beilin and Pearlman (1991) asked children questions about both real objects, such as a baby's rattle, and actual-size color photographs of the same objects. They found that three-year-olds would often say yes when asked questions such as "If you shook this picture, would you hear the rattle?" or "Can you eat this picture of an ice cream cone?" The children also sometimes agreed that if you get close to a picture of a rose, you can smell it. They even, though quite rarely, agreed that if you modify a picture, the depicted object will also be modified and vice versa. For instance, some children agreed that if you cut a picture of a rattle in half, something would happen to the real rattle. Another study found that when asked to "point to things you can really eat," children pointed not only to real foods but also to pictures of food—even if they had previously agreed that the pictures are "just pictures" (Thomas, Nye & Robinson, 1994).

How do we best explain this? Adults do not respond this way. Most of us would deny that you would hear a sound if you shook a picture of a rattle. But this developmental difference could occur because we are more savvy to the ways of psychologists and careful to focus on the precise wording of the question ("a picture of a rattle"). Adults can also ignore the pragmatics of being shown a picture and asked about it, a situation in which one would normally focus on what is depicted. If I showed you a photograph of a car and asked, "How old do you think it is?," it would be unusual for you to think I was asking about the photograph. Similarly, if shown a picture of an apple and asked if you could eat it, an acceptable answer is yes—referring to the depicted entity, of course, not to the picture itself (and if asked if you can *really* eat it, or even *really really* eat it, the answer is still yes). Finally, there is nothing wrong with sniffing a picture of a rose. It is like throwing darts at a photograph of an enemy or gently kissing a photograph of a distant loved one. It might be silly or sentimental, but it does not necessarily reflect a confusion between appearance and reality.

Pretend play has its limits, of course. It is one thing to lean over to sniff a picture of a rose; it is quite another to try to take a bite out of a picture of an ice cream cone. But children show appropriate restraint. Three-year-olds might say that a picture of an ice cream cone will feel cold and wet and that you could eat it—but if you ask them to actually try to eat it, they decline (Beilin & Pearlman, 1991). And although a few children say that if you destroy a picture of a rose, the rose itself would be destroyed, this also seems more like a willingness to partake in fantasy than an honest belief, and, again, it has its limits. As Freeman (1991) points out, it is unlikely that a three-year-old would be struck with mortal terror if told that a picture of her was about to be torn up.

Instead of confusing the properties of the pictures with what they refer to, it is more likely that the children in the above studies are playing along with the experimenter and responding as if the depicted objects are real. As suggested above, adults and older children are less prone to behave this way because they are aware—through attention to the precise wording of the questions and an understanding of what goes in this sort of experimental situation—that they are being tested on their understanding of the difference between pictures and objects and hence are careful not to engage in pretense. Note finally that two- and three-year-olds, outside of psychology experiments, do not show confusion between pictures and what they depict. They do not grab at pictures of rattles; they do not try to put on pictures of clothing. The experiment has never been done, but it is unlikely that hungry three-year-olds would be pleased if you handed them pictures of chocolate pudding.

This isn't to deny that differences exist between how children and adults think about pictures. First, several studies, relatively free of the methodological concerns above, suggest that children have problems recognizing that representations can conflict with reality. In one study, preschool children watched as a picture was taken of Rubber Duckie sitting on the bed. Then Rubber Duckie was moved into the bathtub, and children were asked, "In the picture, where is Rubber Duckie?" Three- and four-year-olds often failed this task, failing to realize that the picture corresponds to the situation in the past, not the current situation (Zaitchik, 1990; see also Leslie & Thaiss, 1992; Robinson, Nye & Thomas, 1994). This may be because children don't understand the precise relationship between representations and what they depict or because they sometimes confuse reality and representation in memory.

Second, children have problems coping with the dual nature of representations—the fact that they are both concrete entities and abstract symbolic ones. A color photograph of a dog is at once a piece of paper with colored markings on it and a symbol representing an external object. Judy DeLoache (1995) argues that children find it hard to appreciate the representational nature of a symbol to the extent that they are focused on its physical properties. The same holds for adults;

DeLoache cites Susanne Langer (1942), who remarks that a peach would make a poor symbol because "we are too much interested in peaches themselves."

The child's difficulty leads to an almost paradoxical result. Two-and-a-half-year-olds can use a picture of a room to recover the location of a hidden toy, but they find it much harder to use a three-dimensional scale model of the room to do the same thing, even though this scale model is more informative. DeLoache argues that the result obtains because the model is so salient and interesting that children focus on it as a thing-in-itself, and this distracts them from its representational properties. To them, it is a peach. In accord with this hypothesis, when the model is made less salient and interesting (for instance, when children are prevented from touching it), they become better able to use it to find the hidden toy (DeLoache, 1995). In another study, the model was presented to the children not as a representation but as the actual room itself, reduced in size by a "shrinking machine." In this situation, two-and-a-half-year-olds had no problem using the model to later find the toy (DeLoache, Miller & Rosengren, 1997).

Third, even older children have odd beliefs about art and pictures. Their naive theory of art is incomplete and confused. In an interview study, Gardner, Winner, and Kircher (1975) found that some four-year-olds say that animals can paint and write and that anyone, or at least any adult, can hang their paintings in a museum. They have strict realist beliefs about pictures, stating, for instance, that you can draw a picture of someone only if that person is present at the time and that pictures should look like what they depict. (This is an odd finding given the nature of children's own drawings.) And there is evidence that even older children do not understand that a picture of a beautiful thing is not necessarily a beautiful picture and that a picture of an ugly thing is not necessarily an ugly picture (Freeman, 1991).

So far we have discussed children's problems with representations. What are they good at? As noted above, children under two can name pictures, at least realistic ones, and by the time they are two they will not grab at them or show any signs of believing that they are real objects. Most impressively, 30-month-olds shown a picture that depicts the location of a toy in a room are able to use the picture to find the toy (DeLoache & Burns, 1994). Using the example of a picture that depicts a Big Bird toy behind a chair, DeLoache and Burns note that success at this task requires several things. Children must recognize that the depictions in the picture are of Big Bird and a chair and that the depicted relationship is of Big Bird being behind the chair. Children must appreciate the relationship between this depiction and the real world, knowing that it represents the actual current situation and is not, for

Figure 7.2
A three-year-old's drawing of his parents (from Cox, 1992)

instance, a picture of how the situation used to be or how it should be in the future. (In this task, children are led to this interpretation by the experimenter, who explicitly tells them that the picture shows them where the toy is right now.) And children must be able to use the picture as a guide to action, helping them find where the toy actually is.

The fact that two-and-a-half-year-olds can succeed at such a task suggests they are able to reason in a quite sophisticated way about representations. This raises the question of how they name them.

The Intentional Basis of Children's Picture Naming

Young children produce drawings, but they are not skilled artists. An example is shown in figure 7.2 (from Cox, 1992).

The interesting thing is that children *name* their drawings, using the same names as the real-world objects that capture their interest. For instance, the drawing in figure 7.2 is, according to Simon, the three-year-old who drew it, "Mommy and Daddy." Plainly, Simon is not naming the components of his picture on the basis of what they look like. This is entirely typical. Refrigerator doors are covered with drawings and paintings by children that could just as well be imitations of artists like Klee and Pollock. But children name these artworks not with abstract names such as "Untitled" and "Spirits in decline"—but as "cow," "truck," and "Grandma."

Such picture naming might reflect children's taking an intentional perspective toward the categorization and naming of artwork. Like adults, young children name pictures on the basis of what they see as the intention of the artist, and this intention is most obvious for pictures that they themselves create. Since Simon intended to depict his mother and father, he calls the scribbles "Mommy" and "Daddy."

Nobody ever told Simon that this is how pictures should be named. This naming is instead the product of his more general understanding that artifacts are categorized in terms of creator's intent (see chapter 6). For pictures created by other people, there are myriad cues to this intent (typically, what they look like), but for those drawn by the child himself, the intent is plain on introspection. This explains Simon's naming of a picture that nobody else can recognize.

This analysis might seem overly complicated, attributing far too much to the child, and there are admittedly simpler alternatives. Howard Gardner (1980), for instance, calls the child's naming "romancing," and he notes that it is hard to tell whether a child who names a picture "birdie" is actually viewing the picture as a representation of a bird or is merely making a random comment to please inquisitive adults. Other researchers show similar caution about taking these early scribbles as representations in any real sense, arguing that a representational appreciation of drawings emerges only much later in development (e.g., Cox, 1992; Freeman, 1991; Golomb, 1993).

A series of recent studies bears on this issue. In one study with four- and five-year-olds, two objects, such as a fork and a spoon, were placed in front of the child, one to the left and one to the right (Bloom & Markson, 1997). The experimenter looked intently at one of the objects (such as the fork) and appeared to draw a picture of it. The picture was actually predrawn to look equally like both of the objects, and in a control condition, when simply shown the picture and asked whether it was a fork or a spoon, children responded randomly. The picture was then placed between the two objects, and the child was asked what it was a picture of. Over 90 percent of the time, the answer depended on what they thought the experimenter was intending to draw: if she had been looking at the spoon while "drawing" it, they called it "a spoon"; if she was looking at the fork, they called it "a fork."

In another study, Gelman and Ebeling (1998) showed two- and three-year-olds simple line drawings of various shapes, such as in the shape of a man. Half of the children were told that these depicted intentional creations—for instance, "When John was painting in art class, he used some paint to make something for his teacher. This is what it looked like." Half of them were told these were accidental creations—for instance, "When John's dad was painting the house, John accidentally spilled some paint on the floor. This is what it looked like." The children were then asked, "What is it?"

Only the children in the intentional condition showed a tendency to name the entity that the drawing resembled ("a man"), while only children in the accidental condition tended to name the material that the entity was made of ("paint"). This suggests that even two-year-olds have some idea that artist's intent is relevant to how a picture should be named.

Both of the above studies suggest that children can be swayed by intentional cues. But both involve depictions that bear some resemblance to what they depict. The drawing in the Bloom and Markson

A. Size

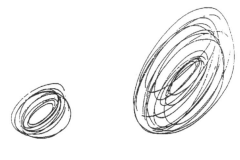

B. Oddity

Figure 7.3
Size (A) and oddity (B) tasks (from Bloom & Markson, 1998)

(1997) study resembled both a fork and a spoon, and the drawing in the Gelman and Ebeling (1998) study resembled a man. Can children name pictures that do not look like what they depict?

To explore this, Lori Markson and I asked children to name pictures that represent objects without resembling them (Bloom & Markson, 1998). In one study, we explored children's ability to use analogical relations to name pictures. Children were told that they were going to be shown some pictures drawn by a boy or girl (same sex as the child) their own age who had a broken arm. They were informed that the boy or girl tried *really* hard to draw good pictures but, because of the broken arm, the pictures did not always come out looking like what the boy or girl wanted.

In one condition (the size task), the children were shown a drawing that depicted two shapes of unequal size and told, for example, "She drew a picture of a spider and a tree" (see figure 7.3a). In another condition (the oddity task), they were shown a drawing of four ovals, one with a different orientation than the rest, and told, for example, "She drew three pigs and one chicken" (see figure 7.3b). During testing, the experimenter pointed to each figure in the picture and asked the children to describe it.

These are easy tasks for adults. For the size task, we take the relative sizes of the markings to correspond to the relative sizes of the objects in the world and name the smaller object as the spider and the larger one as the tree. For the oddity task, we assume that the markings that look the same correspond to objects of the same kind (the pigs) and the one that looks different corresponds to the object of a different kind (the chicken). Such reasoning might be based on assumptions about the artist's representational intent (for instance, even if she lacked precise motor control, a person who was trying to depict the pigs as distinct from the chicken would reasonably use the same symbol for all of the pigs and a different one for the chicken). Or it could be based on nonintentional analogical reasoning, such as by noting the formal parallel between the numbers of ovals of different orientations and the number of pigs and chickens (Gentner, 1983). In either case, it could not be done solely by attending to appearance.

Four-year-olds did better than three-year-olds, and, not surprisingly, the oddity task was harder than the size task. Nevertheless, children of both age groups performed considerably better than chance on both tasks. They can name pictures on the basis of cues other than appearance: the small mark does not look like a spider; the large one does not look like a tree.

Related to this, Kagan (1981) reports a study in which children were handed two identical yellow ping-pong balls, one much heavier than the other, and were told "I have a daddy and a baby." On some trials they were asked to give "the daddy" to the researcher; on others they were asked to give "the baby." By the age of about two-and-a-half, children succeeded at this task.

This understanding of analogical relations suggests that naming does not require sameness of appearance. But it does not show an appreciation of creator's intent. To explore this, we did a further experiment in which children were asked to draw pictures and later to name them. Preschool children are notoriously unskilled artists, and by having them draw different pictures of entities similar in appearance, we reasoned that their subsequent naming of these pictures could not be based on appearance but would have to be determined, at least in part, by their memory of their own representational intent.

Children were requested to draw four pictures on separate sheets of paper, each with a different colored crayon. These were (1) a balloon, (2) a lollipop, (3) the child himself or herself, and (4) the experimenter.

After a several-minute pause during which the child and the experimenter engaged in another activity, the experimenter "rediscovered" the drawings and asked the child to describe them.

It is important to note that the drawings often did not look anything like balloons, lollipops, or people, and even when they did—mostly for the four-year-olds—one could not tell from its appearance whether a given drawing represented a lollipop versus a balloon or the experimenter versus the child. An example of one four-year-olds' drawings is shown in figure 7.4; these are, starting at the upper left and going clockwise, a lollipop, a balloon, the experimenter, and the child.

When later asked to name the drawings, both the three-year-olds and four-year-olds showed a strong tendency to do so on the basis of what they had intended them to represent. Children's responses were usually not subtle, both in the experiment itself and in informal discussion after the experiment. A child might insist, for instance, that one of his pictures was "a balloon" and rigorously correct the experimenter if she describes it as a lollipop—even though it looked equally like either object. This is in accord with anecdotes of what happens with children's own drawings; a good way to upset a child is to take a picture that is described as "Mommy" and call it a car, pointing out, after all, that it looks just as much like a car than it does anything else.

Intention-based naming is not unique to pictures; it shows up as well in pretend play. If two-year-olds are pretending that their father is a dog, they will call him "a dog"; if they are pretending that a banana is a telephone, they will call it "a telephone" (e.g., Leslie, 1995). Plainly, what makes the objects "dog" and "telephone" isn't their appearance but the particular way the child chooses to think about them.

Are picture naming and pretense the same thing? When children name a picture, are they engaging in pretend play? There is a subtle distinction between picture naming and pretense. If a child draws a picture of a telephone and someone later says "Oh, what a nice sword!," the child will object. This fits the adult intuition: if I draw something with the intention to depict something, it remains a representation of that thing no matter what someone else wishes it to be. But at least for adults, pretense is different. If I spend a few minutes pretending a banana is a telephone, this pretense does not *stick*; you are free to later pick up the banana and pretend it is a sword, and— if I feel like participating in this new game—now the banana can be a sword. It is an open question, however, whether the same flexibility in pretense exists for young children.

But there is a less subtle difference as well, one that definitely does hold for children. When a child pretends that a banana is a telephone, she treats it like a telephone—picks it up, talks into it, and so on. But

Figure 7.4
Drawings by a four-year-old (from Bloom & Markson, 1998)

a child who draws a picture of a telephone will do none of these things; she will just look at it, show it to others, and name it. Children do not try to frolic with pictures of dogs; they do not hug pictures of their mothers. So while naming representations and naming in the course of pretend play have much in common (in both cases, the names are based not on what something is or what it looks like but instead on what it is intended to represent), they are nonetheless distinct.

The Development of Picture Naming

Based on the evidence reviewed above, one proposal for how picture naming develops is that babies start off with no understanding of what pictures are. Their visual systems can detect what a picture and an object have in common, giving them the ability to match pictures with objects. When a child, such as the boy studied by Hochberg and Brooks (1962), names a picture, this naming is governed solely by the sameness of appearance. A picture of a dog is called "dog" because it resembles other dogs. Children might think it is a bizarre flat dog, or they might know that it isn't really a dog, but in any case, they do not know that it is a representation.

By the time children reach their second birthday, they no longer show any sign of confusing pictures with the real things they depict; they no longer grab at pictures. Thirty-month-olds show a richer understanding of representations, using them in a productive way in the DeLoache studies. There is experimental evidence that three-year-olds (Bloom & Markson, 1998) and even two-year-olds (Gelman & Ebeling, 1998) can name pictures on the basis of the artist's intent.

What brings them to this knowledge? One possibility is that it emerges from an awareness that pictures are artifacts. Children realize, for instance, that a drawing of a dog is something made by a person, something that was intended to depict a dog. Once this knowledge is in place, children should be able to name pictures (their own and others) that do not resemble what they depict.

The naming and understanding of representations develops considerably in the years that follow. Young two-year-olds have a difficult time using models as representations, many three-year-olds were unable to name the scribbles in our oddity tasks (Bloom & Markson, 1998), and even some four-year-olds fail on a task requiring an appreciation that a photograph of a scene doesn't change when the scene itself is changed (Zaitchik, 1990). Some of these difficulties might be due to factors extraneous to an understanding of representations, such as memory and attentional demands. But linguistic and conceptual development must also occur. Children have to learn, for instance, that there is a difference between naming a representation and naming the artwork that contains that representation. If a painting includes a representation of a dog, children and adults would normally describe that representation as "a dog." But of course, the painting itself might not be called "A Dog"; its name is entirely up to the whim of the artist. Children also have to learn about different sorts of representations. In fact, even adults vary considerably in their understanding of written words, musical notation, maps, graphs, wiring diagrams, and modern art (Ittelson, 1996).

How children name pictures has implications for a theory of naming more generally. The findings discussed above are inconsistent with the brute-shape proposal that children are limited to extending nouns on the basis of shape. As with artifacts in general, shape is an excellent cue to what a visual representation should be called because it is an excellent cue to the intent of the artifact's creator. Just as it is extremely unlikely that a functional artifact would be shaped like a clothespin if it was not made with the intent to be a clothespin, it is extremely unlikely that a drawing or statue would be shaped like a clothespin if it was not made with the intent to represent a clothespin. But just as with nonrepresentational artifacts, sameness of shape is neither necessary nor sufficient to determine children's naming preferences. Something can be shaped like a lollipop but not called "a lollipop"; something can be called "a pig" even if it isn't shaped like a pig. Shape is relevant—but only insofar as it is a cue to the intent of the artifact's creator.

Finally, children's naming of pictures also tells us something about how they think about individuals. Many scholars have argued that our thoughts about objects are partially determined by historical factors, such as the intent underlying their creation. This claim was defended in the previous chapter with regard to naming and categorization, but it applies as well to individuation and valuation (e.g., Gelman & Hirschfeld, 1999). For instance, a gold watch given by a deceased friend may be irreplaceable in the sense that if it were lost, nothing else would be of the same value, regardless of how similar it was to the original. At an auction, John F. Kennedy's golf clubs are immensely more valuable than identical golf clubs previously owned by someone else, and if it were discovered that Rembrandt's *The Night Watch* is actually a forgery, it could, according to Dutch law, be promptly destroyed. The very notion of a fake or forgery rests on the intuition that there is more to an artwork than its material nature (Dutton, 1979), and it is interesting to find some glimmer of the same metaphysical commitment in three-year-olds. When shown two of their own pictures that are virtually identical in form, children believe that they should be treated differently and should get different names, much the same way as we distinguish Warhol's *Brillo Box* and Duchamp's *Fountain* from ordinary Brillo Boxes and urinals (e.g., Danto, 1981; Levinson, 1993)

The world of pictures that we live in is a modern development in human history; it is not even a human universal. And young children are not explicitly taught about pictures and how to name them. Because of this, children's naming of pictures is relatively untainted by either specific evolved biases or cultural expectations. It instead reflects their creative use of language and thought; their own intuitions about artifacts and how they should be named. And so even something as mundane as a two-year-old's naming a scribble as "Mommy" can give us surprising insights as to how the mind works.

Chapter 8

Learning Words through Linguistic Context

Suppose you had no language at all and were about to learn your first word. What could it be? It might be a name for a specific person, such as *Fred*, or a name for an object kind such as *dog*. It could refer to a property, as with *hot*, or an action, as with *hitting*. You would be able to learn these words because they correspond to entities, properties, and actions that are accessible through observation of the material world and attention to the intentional acts of the people around you.

But this first word couldn't be a determiner, quantifier, modal, conjunction, or preposition. It couldn't be a verb such as *dreaming*, an adjective such as *former*, or a noun such as *mortgage*. These words—in fact, most words—do not refer to entities that can be learned by someone without language because their meanings are not accessible in the same way.

How then are these words learned? The answer, in general terms, is obvious enough: we hear them in the context of sentences and use this linguistic context to figure out what they mean. This chapter discusses how such learning takes place.

Learning Words through Nonsyntactic Context

A few months ago, I learned the word *hobbledehoy*. It wasn't in the same way I learned the words *dog* and *foot*; nobody referred to a hobbledehoy in my presence and uttered the word aloud. Instead, I came across the word by reading a passage of a book in which a disapproving father in the 1930s explains to his son why he is forbidden to meet a schoolmate (Amis, 1994, p. 28): "Anyway, to me at least, in one way and another he looks a bit of a hobbledehoy. Also, to me just now over the telephone, he sounded a good deal of a hobbledehoy. Do I make myself clear?"

Syntactically, *hobbledehoy* is a garden-variety count noun, and so—from a solely grammatical standpoint—it could refer to anything from pickles to phonemes. The precise understanding of the word's meaning emerges instead through a sensitivity to the meaning of the passage as a whole. One can tell, for instance, that *hobbledehoy* refers to a kind of person and that it is a bad thing to be.

This is enough to get a good idea about the meaning of the word, and it gets better with the next passage, which provides a definition of sorts (Amis, 1994, p. 28): "You do, thought Robin. . . . Even bloody clearer than you thought. To you at least Wade is a rough, a rowdy, a hooligan, a johnny whose mother sews him up for the winter, who habitually makes rude noises in front of people and shouts at them from up or downstairs or in the next room instead of going where they are and speaking politely, who picks his nose and eats it and never learnt to talk proper."

This is not the best way to learn words. Children tend to learn better from both ostensive naming and from carefully designed age-appropriate sets of examples (Miller & Gildea, 1987). But once you are no longer a toddler, you don't encounter much ostensive naming, with the exception of learning proper names by being introduced to new people. Explicit sets of examples are useful, but not all children receive this sort of teaching, and even those who do learn at most a few words a week from it (Nagy & Herman, 1987). When it comes to explaining how children end up learning thousands of words each year, the only possibility is that they learn most of them through linguistic context (Sternberg, 1987).

The best way to learn a word through context is by hearing it used in a conversation with another person (Nagy & Herman, 1987). This method has several advantages. There might be a rich extralinguistic context to the conversation, the speaker will often have some sensitivity to the extent of the listener's knowledge, and the listener can ask questions. It is likely that many words are learned this way, particularly by preliterate children and by older children and adults in nonliterate societies.

A less efficient source is through written context, but this is nonetheless how literate people learn most of their words. Under one estimate, even students who read relatively little, and only during the school year, will read about half a million words a year and be exposed to about 10,000 words a year that they do not know (Nagy & Herman, 1987). This is many more words than they would be exposed to through conversation, particularly since most conversation takes place between children of the same age who have roughly the same vocabularies. The only way to explain how adults can acquire very large vocabularies—over 100,000 words, in some cases (Miller, 1996)—is through reading.

How does learning from context take place? Robert Sternberg (1987) discusses three processes. *Selective encoding* is distinguishing between the relevant and the irrelevant information when learning the word. Focusing on just the first passage in which *hobbledehoy* was used, it is relevant for the meaning of the word that the father is disapproving but irrelevant that he spoke to the boy over a telephone. *Selective combination* has to do with combining the cues into a workable meaning of a word. And *selective comparison* relates new information to background knowledge. For instance, the meaning of *hobbledehoy* can be learned from the passage above only if you have some idea of the sorts of qualities that parents tend to disapprove of. In the absence of such knowledge, one might just as well think that *hobbledehoy* could refer to someone who was overly polite or who was injured in a war.

Word learning through attention to nonsyntactic information is an instance of a quite general learning process. In fact, the processes that people use to infer the meaning of *hobbledehoy* in the passages above are the same that psychometric intelligence tests assess, and a strong correlation exists between IQ and vocabulary size. Sternberg (1987) suggests that this correlation exists because the number of words a person knows is related to their ability to learn words from context and that this is the same general learning ability tested on standard IQ tests.

While a large educational literature exists on how to best teach children to learn words from context, little research has been conducted on how this process actually works. An exception to this is a study by Diane Beals (1998; see also Beals & Tabors, 1995). She finds that children are often exposed to rare words in the course of casual conversations at home, such as during mealtime, and that most of the time there is contextual information relevant to the meanings of these words. Two examples follow, the first involving an explicit definition and the second involving more implicit cues:

Mother: You have to wait a little while so you don't get *cramps.*

George (age 4):   What's *cramps?*

Mother: *Cramps* are when your stomach feels tight, and it hurts 'cause you have food in it.

Doug (age 4):   Can I have an ice cream sandwich please, Mom? Mama, please can I have an ice cream?

Susan: Just a minute! Someone scarfed the last ice cream sandwich, right?

Doug: Oh.

Susan: How about cookies?

Doug: Tammy, can I please have one of your twisters?

Tammy: That's the only one. Gary had two.

Mother: What's the matter? Is this the great ice cream *debate?*

We do not know how, or even if, children learn the meanings of words in these situations. Beals finds a significant positive correlation between the extent of exposure to rare words and children's later vocabulary, but, as she notes, this could occur for many reasons, and it is possible that there is no direct causal relationship between the two factors (see chapter 2). Nevertheless, nobody would deny that children can learn at least some words from hearing them used in conversation, without the referent being present, since they come to know words such as *vacation* and *dreaming,* which couldn't be learned any other way. But the precise nature of this learning process is a mystery.

I think it will remain a mystery for a long time. The right explanation of how people learn word meanings from nonsyntactic context will not emerge from an analysis of capacities such as theory of mind, the ability to form concepts, and an understanding of syntax—although such capacities have to be there for these inferences to be made. It will instead emerge from a theory of problem solving in general—what philosophers call *nondemonstrative inference* (Fodor, 1983). Perhaps for this reason the research focus of many developmental psychologists has instead been on a far more encapsulated (and tractable) issue—the role of syntactic cues in word learning.

Syntactic Cues to Word Meaning

If David Hume were to rise from the dead, walk to the nearest university library, and pick up any state-of-the-art review on the topic of word learning, little of what is written would be entirely unfamiliar to him. This is not to deny that progress has been made in this area of study; it is just that most of this progress has been the development and extension of theories proposed long ago. Debates over the role of perception in the understanding of names for artifacts and natural kinds, for instance, have been going on since antiquity. And Hume would have found arguments over the merits of associative learning in learning common nouns reassuringly familiar.

One exception to this continuity in theory in the study of word learning is a proposal first made by Roger Brown in a paper published in 1957 entitled "Linguistic Determinism and the Part of Speech." In the study reported in that paper, Brown showed three- and four-year-olds a picture of a strange action performed on a novel substance with a novel object. One group of children was told, "Do you know what it means to sib? In this picture, you can see sibbing" (verb syntax). Another group was told, "Do you know what a sib is? In this picture, you can see a sib" (count noun syntax). A third group was told, "Have you seen any sib? In this picture, you can see sib" (mass noun syntax). The children were then shown three pictures—one depicting the same action, another depicting the same object, and a third depicting the same substance. They were asked, according to what they were initially told, "Show me another picture of sibbing" (verb syntax), "another picture of a sib" (count noun syntax), or "another picture of sib" (mass noun syntax). Brown found that the preschoolers tended to construe the verb as referring to the action, the count noun as referring to the object, and the mass noun as referring to the substance.

It is a simple study, but it supports a profound idea, which is that "the part-of-speech membership of [a] new word could operate as a filter selecting for attention probably relevant features of the nonlinguistic world" (Brown, 1957, p. 21). More generally, "young English-speaking children take the part-of-speech membership of a new word as a clue to the meaning of a new word" (p. 26).

This is a radical claim. It shifts the emphasis from the *content* of the situation toward the *form* of the linguistic expression, raising the possibility that word learning succeeds, at least in part, because children attend to the grammatical contexts in which words are used.

Evidence for Syntactic Cues to Word Meaning

This is an intriguing idea, but is it true? Before reviewing the specific studies that address the role of syntactic cues in the acquisition of word meaning, it is worth discussing what counts (and doesn't count) as evidence for Brown's proposal.

First, a distinction must be made between information conveyed by syntax versus information conveyed by sentence meaning, as in the *hobbledehoy* example above. To take a simple example, hearing the sentence "John learned to drive a zoop" can tell you a lot about what *zoop* refers to. It is unlikely to be a nightmare, for instance, or a spoon, but it could be a car or a truck. This inference is based on our understanding of the sorts of things people drive, not the syntactic context in which the word *zoop* appears.

The distinction between syntactic context and semantics context might seem clear enough in principle, but the two contexts are often difficult to distinguish in practice. This is particularly the case when it comes to the role of closed-class words, such as prepositions and determiners, which fall between the cracks of syntax and semantics. For instance, Fisher, Hall, Rakowitz, and Gleitman (1994) describe three- and four-year-olds' understanding of the semantic implications of the contrast between "The bunny is zorking the ball to the elephant" versus "The bunny is zorking the ball from the elephant" as evidence for sensitivity to syntax, while Pinker (1994a) argues that children are drawing inferences from the semantic properties of the prepositions, not from their syntax.

Second, there is a difference between showing that children understand mappings between syntax and semantics and showing that this understanding guides inferences about word meaning. Gathercole (1986) points out, for instance, that the Brown experiment described above does not actually demonstrate that children can use syntax to *learn* aspects of word meaning, since they could have succeeded at his task without attending to the new word; all they had to attend to was the syntactic frame of the questions: "Show me another picture of ____ ing/of a ____ / of ____." A similar point applies to other studies, such as those reported by P. Bloom (1994a) and Hirsh-Pasek et al. (1988). These show that children are sensitive to the semantic implications of syntactic structure, which is consistent with, but not the same as, the stronger finding that they can use this understanding to learn words.

A final concern is that in some experiments children might be guessing the meaning of a word by using syntactic cues to identify an already known English word it corresponds to. Pinker (1994a) notes that children can use syntax as a *retrieval cue* even if they have no ability to use syntax to actually learn new words—in fact, even if there is no relationship between a word's syntax and its meaning. To make this point, he gives the example of an experimenter showing children a scene ambiguous between pushing and falling and saying either "The puppet calls this p . . ." or "The puppet calls this f . . . ." In such a task, children would presumably say "pushing" and "falling" appropriately, by using the sound as a retrieval cue to the relevant English word. But this surely does not show that children can use universal sound-meaning mappings to learn word meanings or even that such mappings exist. By the same token, then, studies in which children can use syntax to match up a novel word with a preexisting lexical item do not entail that syntax-semantics mappings play any role in the acquisition of a first language.

In sum, when evaluating studies of the role of syntax on word meaning we have to bear in mind certain considerations, including (1) the distinction between syntactic versus nonsyntactic linguistic information, (2) the distinction between using syntax to learn a new word versus being sensitive to the relationship between syntax and meaning, and (3) the distinction between using syntax to learn a new word versus using syntax to find an existing word that a new word is closely related to.

For the purposes of review, we move through parts of speech—first nominals, then verbs, then adjectives, and finally prepositions. (This is an expanded version of an earlier review in P. Bloom, 1996c). A further domain, number words, is the topic of the next chapter.

Syntax and the Acquisition of Nominals

Every language has a distinct grammatical class of nominals. These words serve as names and refer to entities in the world (Bloomfield, 1933; Schacter, 1985). In English, nominals fall into three main classes— count nouns, mass nouns, and lexical noun phrases (lexical NPs). Count nouns are words like *dog* and *nightmare*, which can follow determiners such as *a, many*, and *several* and which can be counted and pluralized. Mass nouns are words like *sand* and *advice*, which can follow determiners such as *much* and (in the singular form) *some* and *any* and which cannot be counted or pluralized. Lexical NPs are words like *Fred* and *she*, which are identical syntactically to phrasal noun phrases, such as *the dog* or *my cat* and cannot be modified or quantified at all.

I introduced the term *lexical NP* in the chapter on pronouns and proper names but without much elaboration. It is admittedly an awkward term, but it is the only one that is accurate. The usual alternative is to call words like *Fred* "proper names" and words like *she* "pronouns," but these terms pick out semantic classes, not syntactic ones. It is an interesting empirical claim that children can use the fact that *Fred* is an NP as a cue that it refers to a specific individual (see chapter 5). But it is nothing more than a tautology to say that children can use the fact that *Fred* is a proper name as a cue that Fred refers to a specific individual—since to be a proper name is to refer to an individual. If one is going to explore the possibility that children use syntax to learn about meaning, it is important to characterize the syntactic categories distinct from the semantic ones.

When it comes to learning at least some nominals, one can do fine without syntax. If I pointed to a strange object and said "gloppel," you would take the word as a name for that kind of object; if I pointed to a strange substance and said "gloppel," you would take it as a name for that kind of substance; and if I pointed to a person and said "gloppel," you would take it as a name for that particular person. The same is true for children. Two-year-olds treat words that refer to objects differently from words that refer to substances even if the words are presented in syntactically neutral form (Soja, Carey & Spelke, 1991; see chapter 4). And names for specific individuals, such as pronouns and proper names, are learned by children long before they can attend to syntactic information; some such expressions appear among their very first words (Nelson, 1973).

So syntax is not necessary for at least some nominal learning. But evidence suggests that children are sensitive to nominal syntax and can use it to modify their assumptions about word meanings. I focus below on the count-mass distinction; the role of the noun-NP contrast in learning pronouns and proper names was discussed in chapter 5.

Objects, Substances, and Individuals

Nancy Soja (1992) found that once two-year-olds have productive command of the count-mass distinction, they can use count-mass syntax to infer aspects of word meaning. When taught a mass noun that describes a pile of stuff, they tend to construe it as referring to that kind of stuff (as having a similar meaning to a word like *clay*), but when taught a count noun that describes the same pile of stuff, many construe it as referring not to the stuff itself but to the bounded pile (as having a similar meaning to words like *puddle* or *pile*).

This effect of syntax was limited to the stuff condition. When children were taught count nouns and mass nouns describing a novel object, their interpretation was not affected by the mass-noun syntax: they did *not* construe the mass noun as having the same meaning as words like *wood* or *metal*. This is an interesting asymmetry; count-noun syntax can guide children away from construing a word referring to a substance as naming the kind of substance, but mass-noun syntax cannot override the tendency to treat a word referring to an object as naming a kind of object. This is consistent with other research on the acquisition of solid-substance names that is discussed below.

A study by Leslie McPherson (1991) explored two- and three-year-olds' sensitivity to syntax in a different way, exploiting the ambiguity of the phrase *a little*, which can be a quantifier indicating a small amount when used with a mass noun (*a little water*) or a determiner and adjective indicating a small object when used with a count noun (*a little cup*). Children were taught a word with either count or mass syntax ("These are vaxes. Have you ever seen so many vaxes?" versus "This is vax. Have you ever seen so much vax?") and shown either objects (small yellow pom-poms of two different sizes with faces on them) or stuff (tapioca pearls of two different sizes). They then were asked to "Give me a little vax."

McPherson found that children were more likely to choose a small pom-pom when presented with a count noun than with a mass noun and more likely to scoop up a small amount of tapioca when presented with a mass noun than with a count noun. This suggests that the count-noun syntax biased them toward treating "a little vax" as referring to a small object, while mass-noun syntax favored treating the phrase as referring to a small amount, providing further evidence that children are sensitive to the relation between count-mass syntax and aspects of word meaning.

These studies, along with the findings of Brown (1957), suggest that count-noun syntax can inform young children that a word refers to an object kind. But there are reasons to believe that the semantic import of being a count noun is not limited to objects but extends to individuals more generally (see also chapter 4).

First, count nouns that refer to nonobject individuals show up in the spontaneous speech of young children. For instance, Nelson, Hampson, and Shaw (1993) analyzed the speech of 45 20-month-olds and found that only about half of their nominals referred to basic-level object kinds; many referred to entities such as locations (*beach*), periods of time (*minute*), and events (*party*). And once children start to use count-mass syntax in their productive speech, names for these nonobject individuals are marked appropriately as count nouns, just as words like *dog* are (Gordon, 1992).

Second, there is evidence that children can use count noun syntax to acquire the meanings of words that refer to kinds of nonobject individuals. One such study was mentioned above; recall that Soja (1992) found that when a substance was named with a count noun, many two-year-olds inferred that the noun extended to other bounded individuals of the same kind; they did not infer that it was a name for the kind of stuff. In other words, they treated it as having a meaning like *puddle*, referring to a bounded portion of stuff. In another study (P. Bloom, 1994a), three- and four-year-olds were taught names for a string of bell sounds from a tape-recorder, presented in rapid sequence so that they could be construed either as a set of discrete sounds or as undifferentiated noise. They were told either "These are feps. There really are a lot of feps here" (count-noun condition) or "This is fep. There really is a lot of fep here" (mass-noun condition). Then children were given a stick and a bell; those who were taught the word as a count noun were asked to "make a fep," while those taught the word as a mass noun were told to "make fep." Even the three-year-olds tended to make a single sound when asked to make "a fep" and to make a lot of sounds when asked to make "fep," suggesting that they can map count-noun syntax onto discrete sounds or actions and mass-noun syntax onto continuous sounds or actions.

Bloom and Kelemen (1995) attempted to teach four-year-olds, five-year-olds, and adults novel collective nouns. Subjects were shown an array of unfamiliar objects described either as "These are fendles" or as "This is a fendle." The prediction was that subjects would interpret the plural count noun as an object name, while singular count-noun syntax would focus them on the collection as a single individual, on a par with nouns like *army* and *family*.

The results were mixed. Adults and five-year-olds were sensitive to the syntactic manipulation; as predicted, they treated the plural count noun as an object name and the singular count noun as a collective noun. The four-year-olds showed the same trend, but the effect was not significant. This was not due to a bias toward construing the word as an object name: errors tended to be evenly divided, with many of the children mistakenly treating the plural count noun as naming the collection. The failure of the four-year-olds to learn the collective noun is instead consistent with the view that their understanding of what sorts of entities can be individuals differs from that of adults in interesting ways (see Bloom & Kelemen, 1995, for discussion).

Solid Substances

Mass syntax can direct a child toward interpreting a new word as referring to an amorphous substance such as water or sand (P. Bloom, 1994b; Brown, 1957, Soja, 1992). But what about words for solid substances, such as *wood*? From a quantificational standpoint these are also nonindividuated entities: one cannot count wood; one must count *pieces* of wood. Wood also passes the *universal grinder* test for stuff (Pelletier, 1979); if you grind up wood, you still get wood (compare this with what happens when you grind up a desk).

Solid substances differ in significant ways from nonsolid substances, however. For one thing, they are not malleable or fluid; they retain their shapes as they move through space. Moreover, any chunk of solid substance is also, by necessity, a discrete physical object, and so it might require some conceptual work on the part of the child to think about the chunk as a portion of stuff rather than thinking about it as an individual countable entity, as a whole object (see chapter 4 for discussion). Do these considerations make such words harder to learn?

Explorations of children's production (Soja, 1991) and comprehension (Dickinson, 1988; Prasada, 1993) suggest that two- and three-year-olds' understanding of English solid-substance names is relatively limited. On the other hand, Soja (1991) found that adults rarely use such names when speaking to children, so children's ignorance could be due to the input they receive and not to limitations in their own capacities.

Dickinson (1988) attempted to teach preschoolers new substance names in a set of experiments in which he showed children objects or chunks of objects made of novel solid substances. Children were presented with words in neutral syntax ("This is the blicket"), count syntax ("This is a blicket"), mass syntax ("This is some blicket"), or an informative mass-noun condition ("This is made of blicket"). When the items were objects, the preschoolers rarely interpreted the words as solid-substance names, regardless of the linguistic context (see also Markman & Wachtel, 1988). Five-year-olds, on the other hand, showed more sensitivity to the linguistic manipulation, giving the substance interpretation over half of the time in the "made of" condition as compared to less than one-fifth of the time in the neutral condition. Dickinson concluded that young children find solid-substance names hard to learn, regardless of the linguistic context.

In contrast, Prasada (1993) found that even two- and three-year-olds were capable of learning solid-substance names when they were presented with mass syntax in "made of" constructions, so long as they referred to familiar objects that already had names. Similarly, Markman and Wachtel (1988) found that three- and four-year-olds could interpret the word *pewter* in the sentence "This is pewter" as a substance name (or as an adjective referring to a substancelike property) when the object that it referred to already had a name.

Why do children find it so difficult to learn solid-substance names for unfamiliar objects? It can't merely be due to a bias to treat words for unfamiliar objects as describing object kinds because even two-year-olds are capable of learning proper names that refer to unfamiliar objects (Gelman & Taylor, 1984) and slightly older children can learn adjectives for such objects (see below). Why isn't this also true for solid-substance names?

One suggestion was raised above. Children's problems with solid-substance names may be due in part to their strong bias to treat whole objects as individuals. Such a bias would not get in the way of learning proper names (which refer to specific individuals) or many adjectives (which refer to attributes of individuals). But it would interfere with the learning of solid-substance names, since construing an entity as a portion of stuff is plainly inconsistent with construing it as a single individual.

Syntax and the Acquisition of Verbs

The role of syntax in verb learning has generated considerable controversy. While investigators such as Brown were content to argue that syntax can facilitate the acquisition of nominal meanings, some scholars have made the stronger claim that syntax is essential for the acquisition of at least some verb meanings. This is a claim we return to below.

Letitia Naigles (1990) conducted one of the first studies on the role of syntactic cues in verb learning. She showed 25-month-olds videotaped scenes showing two events—a causal event with two participants and a noncausal event with a single participant. For instance, a duck would repeatedly push a rabbit into a bending position at the same time that both the rabbit and duck were waving their free arms. Children saw the video as they heard a novel verb either in a transitive context ("The duck is gorping the bunny") or an intransitive context ("The duck and the bunny are gorping"). Then children were shown two new videos simultaneously—one containing just the causal scene (a duck pushing a rabbit, with no arm waving), the other containing just the noncausal scene (the duck and rabbit arm waving, with no pushing)—and were told "Find gorping." The two-year-olds looked longer at the causal scene when they had heard the transitive verb and longer at the noncausal scene when they had heard the intransitive verb.

Naigles and Kako (1993) conducted further experiments suggesting that, while causation is associated with transitive verb frames, it is not an essential semantic correlate. Two-year-olds who were exposed to a verb in a transitive frame tended to associate the verb to actions of *contact without causation* (as when a frog repeatedly touches the duck, without any effect) more so than those children who were just exposed to the verb in a neutral frame ("Look! Gorping!"). This suggests that hearing a verb used in a transitive frame might inform the child that the verb refers to an action with some property more general than causation, such as *object affectedness* (see also Gropen, Pinker, Hollander & Goldberg, 1991; Pinker, 1989).

A different methodology was used by Cynthia Fisher and her colleagues (1994). Three-year-olds, four-year-olds, and adults were shown a video depicting an event and given sentences with novel verbs to describe it, such as "The bunny is nading the elephant" versus "The elephant is daking." The scenes were chosen so that actions in them could be described with existing English words. When participants were asked what these verbs meant, they tended to give correct translations or paraphrases. For instance, when presented with a video in which the bunny was giving food to the elephant, children would tend to say that *nading* meant "feeding" and *daking* meant "eating," suggesting that their interpretations of the meaning of the words were guided by syntactic cues.

The precise interpretation of the Fisher et al. results are a matter of some disagreement: Pinker (1994a) has suggested that they show children can *access* existing lexical items via syntactic structure but do not support the stronger claim that they can use syntax to *learn* new words. In response to this concern, Fisher et al. (1994) conducted a further analysis of just those instances where children responded with phrasal descriptions instead of existing English words (for instance, if they said "licking it off the spoon" instead of "eating"). An analysis of the three- and four-year-olds taken together found the same effect of syntax, suggesting that while prior lexical knowledge might play some role in children's responses (since they might have accessed these phrasal descriptions only via their knowledge of existing English words), these results cannot be entirely due to direct lexical retrieval.

Other research by Fisher (1996) explored the role of linguistic cues with three- and five-year-olds in a different fashion. Children were shown videos depicting novel events and were presented with sentences differing in number of arguments ("She's pilking" versus "She's pilking her") and in the type of preposition ("She's pilking the ball to her" versus "She's pilking the ball from her"). The subjects were then asked to point to the person performing the action ("Who's pilking the ball to her?"). Fisher found that both age groups responded to these linguistic manipulations (syntactic in the case of transitive versus intransitive; lexical in the case of *in* versus *from*) when identifying the agent of the new verb.

Other considerations support some of the premises behind the proposal that syntactic cues are relevant to verb learning. It has long been noted that correspondences exist between verb syntax and verb semantics, some of which are universal (e.g., Jackendoff 1990; Levin, 1993; Pinker, 1989). Studies of parental speech find that syntactic cues to verb meaning are present in the sentences that children hear (e.g., Fisher, Gleitman & Gleitman, 1991; Naigles & Hoff-Ginsberg, 1995, 1998) and that the extent of syntactic cues partially predicts the order in which verbs are acquired (Naigles & Hoff-Ginsberg, 1998).

The Role of Syntax in the Acquisition of Adjectives and Prepositions

Adjectives draw children's attention toward properties or subkinds. For instance, Taylor and Gelman (1988) presented two- and three-year-olds with either a novel noun ("a zav") or a novel adjective ("a zav one") describing an object. Children who heard the word as a noun extended the word to objects of the same kind more often than they extended the word to objects that share the same superficial properties, while children who heard the word as an adjective gave the opposite response—focusing more on properties, like color, pattern, and texture, and less on object kind (see also Gelman & Markman, 1985; Hall, Waxman & Hurwitz, 1993). Smith et al. (1992) obtained a similar finding, noting that the same shape bias that exists for count nouns does not apply to adjectives. Using a similar design, Waxman and Kosowski

(1990) found that nouns focused two- to five-year-olds on taxonomic categories (following Markman & Hutchinson, 1984) but that adjectives did not.

Other research explores the effect of the noun-adjective contrast on children's hierarchical classification. In a task involving classifying animals and foods, for instance, Waxman (1990) found that nouns facilitated categorization at the superordinate level but not at the subordinate level (see also Waxman & Gelman, 1986), while adjectives provided the opposite effect, drawing attention to subordinate kinds.

Some puzzles arise here, as the relationship between the two putative semantic roles of adjectives—adjectives as denoting properties (as viewed by Taylor & Gelman, 1988, for instance) versus adjectives as denoting subkinds (as viewed by Waxman, 1990, for instance)—is unclear. A typical adjective, such as *good*, does not pick out a meaningful subordinate category within a psychologically natural taxonomy. Conversely, poodles and collies are perfectly good subkinds, but this contrast is marked by nouns, not by adjectives.

It may be that the syntactic category *adjective* is too rough-grained to capture the sorts of semantic implications children and adults are sensitive to. Bolinger (1967) distinguishes between predication (as in "The dog is fep") and modification (as in "the fep dog"). Roughly, predication attributes a property to the entity denoted by an NP (the specific dog), while modification is *restrictive*; it picks out a subclass of the category referred to by a noun (the category of dogs). It may be that the results from the property studies are tapping children's sensitivity to adjectives as predicates while those from the subkind studies are tapping children's sensitivity to adjectives-as-modifiers. In support of this, Prasada (1997) finds that two- and three-year-olds are more likely to give an adjective a "restrictive" interpretation when it appears prenominally, as a modifier, than when it appears as a predicate.

Landau and Stecker (1990) explored whether the syntactic contrast between nouns and prepositions can cue young children toward the distinction between words referring to objects versus words referring to spatial relations. Children were shown a novel object placed on a box and were either told "This is a corp" (count noun syntax) or "This is acorp the box" (preposition syntax). In the count noun condition, both three-year-olds and adults generalized the application of the word to objects of the same shape regardless of location, while in the preposition condition, they generalized the word to objects in the same location (or class of locations), regardless of object shape. More recently, Landau (1996) found that English-speaking three-year-olds are sensitive to prepositional syntax when learning words that map onto spatial notions not present in English—such as the Tzeltal relational marker *lechtel,* which is used to denote a wide flat object that is lying flat (P. Brown, 1993).

Such results can be taken to support the proposal by Landau and Jackendoff (1993) that there is a universal distinction between the semantics of count nouns, which denote objects and other individuals, and prepositions, which denote only certain limited classes of spatial relationships. In contrast, Bowerman (1996) suggests that the constrained inferences that Landau and her colleagues find are not rooted in innate universals; they instead result from children's prior learning of the semantics of English nouns and prepositions. This issue is a matter of current debate, possibly to be resolved by research with much younger children.

How Do Children Learn about Syntactic Cues to Word Meaning?

The studies above suggest that preschool children can use the following cues to word meaning (see table 8.1). Where does this understanding come from? It is sometimes said to be acquired through observation of contingencies between the meanings of words and the syntactic categories they belong to. For instance, Brown (1957, p. 26) suggests that "Human beings are generally adept at picking up imperfect probabilistic implications, and so it may be the case that native speakers detect the semantic nature of the parts of speech of their language." And Katz, Baker, and Macnamara (1974, p. 472) state that "we can effectively eliminate the possibility that [the children] are determined by nature to notice definite and indefinite articles on the grounds that many languages, like Latin, do not have them." They propose that children notice the correlation between words without determiners and words that refer to animate beings.

Table 8.1
Syntactic cues to word meaning

Syntactic Cue	Usual Type of Meaning	Examples
"This is a *fep* / the *fep.*"	Individual member of a category	*cat, forest*
"These are *feps.*"	Multiple members of a category	*cats, forests*
"This is *fep.*"	Specific individual	*Fido, John*
"This is some *fep.*"	Nonindividuated stuff	*water, sand*
"John *feps.*"	Action with one participant	*sleeps, stands*
"John *feps* Bill."	Action with two participants	*hits, kisses*
"This thing is *feppy.*"	Property	*big, good*
"The dog is *fep* the table."	Spatial relationship	*on, near*

Cross-linguistic differences clearly exist. Some languages do not have a distinct class of adjectives, for instance; others lack a count-mass distinction. Furthermore, the surface realization of syntactic categories cannot be innate; it is an arbitrary fact about English that determiners precede nouns or that verbs are sometimes marked with -*ing*. So some learning must be going on (see Levy, 1988; Maratsos & Chalkley, 1981).

But what sort of learning? There are reasons to doubt that children relate meaning and form through a sensitivity to statistical correlations, observing that certain forms and certain meanings just happen to go together. Correlational learning is a fine way to learn arbitrary relationships, such as shapes of English letters and the sounds they correspond to. But the relationship between syntax and semantics is not an arbitrary one.

Consider a couple of examples. First, the number of NP arguments that a verb takes is related to the number of entities involved in the action that it refers to, in the following way:

V with 1 NP argument:	V = action with one entity, as in "John sleeps"
V with 2 NP arguments:	V = action with two entities, as in "John kissed the dog"
V with 3 NP arguments:	V = action with three entities, as in "John gave Fred the book"

Is it really reasonable that this one-to-one mapping between the number of NP arguments and the number of entities encoded in the meaning of the verb is learned through a sensitivity to correlations? That is, children just happen to notice that verbs with one NP argument have meanings like *sleep* and verbs with three NP arguments have meanings like *give*? This would suggest that children could have just as well learned the mapping the other way around and that the pattern is an accident of English; some languages should use one NP argument for *give* and three with *sleep*.

But this never happens. Instead the generalization appears to reflect a linguistic universal: an isomorphism between the conceptual structure of a predicate and its syntactic structure (Chomsky, 1981). It is striking support for the existence of this universal that the same relationship is also found in the spontaneous communication systems created by deaf children (home-sign; Goldin-Meadow & Mylander, 1984). For instance, one boy, David, used his invented sign for *give* (hand outstretched, palm upward) with three arguments but his sign for *sleep* with only one. As Lila Gleitman and Henry Gleitman put it (1997, p. 33): "Nobody has to learn from the external linguistic environment that the notion of giving requires three arguments and sleeping only one, or that these elements of conceptual structure map regularly onto the number of NP positions in the clause. At least some of this mapping comes for free."

Or consider the count-mass distinction. Children come to know the following:

a/another N: N = kind of individual

much N: N = kind of stuff

Clearly something must be learned here, since the specific English words that cue the count-mass distinction are not innate, and some languages have no count-mass distinction at all. But it is not that children note, over the fullness of time, that some kinds of words go with *a* and *another* and other kinds of words go with *much*. Such learning would be superfluous because the knowledge follows from what the determiners mean. Part of knowing *a* and *another* is knowing that they interact with nouns that refer to kinds of individuals to form NPs that refer to specific individuals. Part of knowing what *much* means is knowing that it interacts with nouns that refer to kinds of stuff to form NPs that refer to portions of that stuff. Once children have learned the meaning of these determiners (see chapter 4 for some discussion of how they do so), nothing more needs to be learned.

In general, then, the knowledge necessary to use syntactic cues to word meaning can be explained either in terms of other properties of language, such as universal relationships between meaning and form (as in the verb example) or the meanings of specific closed-class items (as in the count-mass example).

One issue remains. The ability to use syntax as a cue to word meaning presupposes the ability to syntactically categorize new words. This categorization is easy enough once the structure of a language, and some of its closed-class terms, have been learned. As someone who knows English, you can use your understanding of the grammar of English to parse the novel words in Lewis Carroll's sentence:

> And, as in uffish thought he stood,
> The Jabberwock, with eyes of flame,
> Came whiffling through the tulgey wood
> And burbled as it came.

It is easy to infer that *uffish* is an adjective and *whiffling* is a verb (see Pinker, 1984). And based on this syntactic categorization, you can infer that *uffish* refers to a property and *whiffling* to an action. But what if you don't know any English? How can a child who is new to the language figure out the syntactic category a word belongs to?

One proposal—sometimes called *semantic bootstrapping* (Pinker, 1984)—is that children use the mappings between syntax and semantics not to infer the meanings of words from their syntax as discussed throughout this chapter but the other way around—to infer their syntactic category from their meanings (Bloom, 1999; Grimshaw, 1981; Pinker, 1984). For instance, given that *dog* refers to an object and *big* refers to a property, children can infer that *dog* is a noun and *big* is an adjective and, hence, on hearing "big dog" can infer that adjectives precede nouns within the NP. Once children know this, they can use this grammatical knowledge to infer the syntactic category of words whose meaning they do not already know; for instance, when they hears "big idea," they can infer that *idea is* a noun.

Early in development, children appreciate the relationship between syntactic categories and semantic categories and can use this relationship both to bootstrap their way into the syntax of natural language and to infer aspects of the meanings of words. One obvious objection is that this account is circular. It cannot be the case, for instance, *both* that children know that *chair* refers to an object kind because it is a count noun *and* that they know that *chair* is a count noun because it refers to an object kind. But this isn't a serious concern, since under any account children can learn some word meanings (such as the meanings of words like *chair*) without the help of syntax. Once they do so, they can learn syntactic rules and use these rules to infer the syntactic categories of unfamiliar words, as in the Jabberwocky example above.

The Importance of Syntax

The experiments reviewed above show that children can use syntax to learn aspects of the meanings of words. But just how important is syntax?

A sensitivity to syntax clearly is not sufficient to learn the entire meaning of a word; at best it can help children learn aspects of the meaning of a word. For one thing, the relationship between the syntax of a word and its meaning is not entirely predictable: there is limited variation both within and across languages. Certain words that are count nouns in French are mass nouns in English and vice-versa; some verbs that appear in the double-object dative structure in English do not do so in Dutch, and so on. And near synonyms within a language (such as *clothing,* a mass noun, and *garments,* a plural count noun) can belong to different syntactic categories. This arbitrariness is quite constrained, but it does exist (Bloom, 1994a; Pinker, 1989).

Furthermore, grammar draws relatively crude distinctions, picking out ontological kinds (such as individuals versus stuff) and subtypes of events (such as events with one participant versus events with two participants). Word meanings are much more fine-grained. Children have to learn the difference between *cup* and *saucer* (both count nouns), *good* and *evil* (both adjectives), *five* and *six* (both quantifiers of precise numerosity), and *loving* and *hating* (both verbs with identical argument structures). No word meaning can be learned entirely through syntactic cues.

Is syntax ever necessary? As discussed above, children and adults can learn object names, substance names, and proper names without the aid of linguistic cues. But what about other parts of speech? Lila Gleitman and her colleagues (e.g., Fisher, Hall, Rakowitz & Gleitman, 1994; Gleitman, 1990) have argued that syntax plays a significant role for the acquisition of many verbs.

Why verbs? There are certain ways in which learning verbs might be harder than learning other words, such as object names, and therefore might require the helping hand of syntax.

First, object nouns can be taught through ostensive naming: parents can point at a dog and say "dog," and in at least some societies they tend to do just that. But parents almost never use verbs to name actions (Gleitman, 1990; Tomasello, 1992). A study mentioned earlier by Gillette et al., reported in Gleitman and Gleitman (1997), suggests that this might make verbs harder to learn. Adults were shown videos of interactions between mothers and one-year-olds. There was no audio, but when the mothers used a word, either a noun or a verb, subjects heard a beep. Their task was to guess which English word the beep corresponded to. When exposed to beeps that corresponded to nouns (and told to expect nouns), subjects got it right about 45 percent of the time, and they did much better over multiple trials. But when exposed to beeps that corresponded to verbs (and told to expect verbs), they got it right only about 15 percent of the time and didn't get better over multiple trials. Gleitman and Gleitman (1997) suggest that this is in part because of the poor temporal correspondence between verbs and what they refer to.

A second reason that verbs might have been more difficult to learn in the Gillette et al. study—and in real life—is that many verbs name events or activities that are not directly observable, such as *thinks*. Object names, of course, typically do refer to entities that one can see and touch.

Third, object nouns correspond to entities that humans universally see as distinct individuals (see chapter 4), but this is not necessarily so for verbs. Across languages, there are differences in how verbs typically "package" events. In languages such as English, verbs typically encode the manner of an event, as in *run, jump, skip, hop, dance, leap,* and *somersault*. The path of the motion is expressed as a prepositional phrase, as in this sentence: "He is running down the stairs."

In Romance languages such as French and Spanish, however, verbs typically encode the path of the motion. The manner is expressed through an adverb (Talmy, 1985; Naigles, Fowler & Helm, 1995): "Il descend l'escalier en courant" (literal translation: He goes down the stairs in running).

Even within a language, there is flexibility as to how events can be described. If Fred is handing something to Mary and a verb is used to describe the scene, it could (among other things) mean *giving*, but it could also mean *receiving*. Its meaning depends crucially on the perspective one takes. In general, then, events are cognitively ambiguous in a way that objects are not. Lila Gleitman (1990, p. 17) puts it as follows: "Verbs seem to describe specific perspectives taken on . . . events by the speakers, perspectives that are not 'in the events' in any direct way . . . since verbs represent not only events but the intent, beliefs, and perspectives of the speakers on these events, the meanings of the verbs can't be extracted solely by observing the events."

Syntax might help solve these special problems of verb learning. Consider the perspective problem raised above: How can children figure out whether a given verb means *giving* or *receiving?* One solution is syntactic. If Fred is handing something to Mary and the child hears "Fred is ＿＿＿＿ the thing to Mary" then the verb is likely to mean *giving;* if the child hears "Mary is ＿＿＿＿ the thing from Fred," the verb is likely to mean *receiving*. Or consider the problem of acquiring more abstract verbs such as *thinking*. If a verb is followed by a sentence, as in "John ＿＿＿＿ that Bill is upset," then its meaning is consistent with an action that has a proposition as its object, which entails that it is a verb of perception or cognition.

When one considers that reliable cues to word meaning exist and that young children can exploit these cues, and when we note as well the strong correlation between the growth of vocabulary size and the development of syntactic knowledge in young children (Caselli et al., 1995; Fenson et al., 1994), the evidence for the claim that syntax is central to verb learning seems quite decisive.

But syntax might not be necessary. Verbs are plainly distinct from object names, but they are not that different from other more abstract nouns. Consider a noun such as *nightmare*. It is just as hard to teach the noun through ostensive naming as it would be to teach a verb like *dreaming*. And just as there is flexibility in how verbs package events, there is also flexibility, both within and across languages, in how nouns encode more abstract nonobject individuals.

These considerations undermine the claim that syntax is necessary for learning the meanings of verbs. Children are supposed to need syntax to learn at least some verbs because such verbs are too difficult to learn otherwise. But abstract nouns are equally hard, and yet children learn them without syntactic support. And if they can do this for nouns, why can't they also do it for verbs? In other words, perhaps children learn a verb such as *dreaming* in the same (nonsyntactic) way that they learn a noun such as *nightmare*.

How then is a noun such as *nightmare* learned? It happens through the same sort of general inferential abilities that worked for the noun *hobbledehoy*. A child could wake up after a nightmare and be told that she just had a nightmare. She could hear the word used to refer to a scene in a story, in which the mental life of a sleeping character is described. Or the word might even be explicitly defined for her. Some such account has to be right because there is no alternative: syntax cannot do the trick. And again, since one of these proposals must work for the noun *nightmare*, it might apply as well to a verb like *dreaming*.

Although children might not need syntactic cues to learn *dreaming*, there is little doubt that they need *linguistic* cues—that is, children can learn the verb only by hearing it in the context of sentences. I agree, then, with the thrust of Gleitman's argument: simply "observing the events" does not suffice for the learning of most verbs. What is less clear is whether it is syntax that fills the gap, as opposed to the other information that sentences convey.

The Role of Syntax in a Theory of Word Learning

What role does syntax play in word learning? There are three possibilities, but only one of these fits with the evidence reviewed above.

The first is that syntax does very little. It is icing on the cake. This is the right position to take for object labels; the advantage that the child obtains knowing that *dog* is a count noun is negligible. But it is not right for most other words. If children hear that someone is "a nasty person," the fact that *nasty* is an adjective is an excellent cue that it refers to a type of person. It would be difficult to learn *wood* without knowing that it is a mass noun or *thinking* without knowing that it is a verb that takes a sentential complement. While syntax might not be necessary for learning the meanings of such words, it nonetheless plays an important role.

Another conception of the role of syntax is as a *filter* (Brown, 1957) or *zoom lens* (Gleitman, 1990; Pinker, 1994b). It draws the child's attention to relevant aspects of a scene, determining, for instance, whether an event should be construed as giving or receiving, thinking or standing, walking or moving.

But in certain regards, this is also an unrealistic perspective. The notion of a filter or zoom lens implies that children start off with all the candidate meanings in mind and then syntax helps them to filter out the irrelevant ones and zoom in on the right one. But in fact much of the time that words are used, the events or entities that they denote are not present in the environment. If syntax is going to play a role in actual word learning outside the laboratory, it has to be able to affect children's construals of scenes that are not being attended to.

A third perspective is that syntax is an important informational source as to the meanings of words, one that works in concert with information obtained from other inferential mechanisms of the sort discussed in previous chapters. The child's task in word learning, then, is to integrate these different sources of information and from them to infer the most plausible candidate for the word's meaning (see P. Bloom, 1996c; Gleitman & Gleitman, 1997).

The relative importance of syntactic information—and linguistic information, more generally—depends on a host of factors. The meanings of words such as the noun *dog*, the adjective *red*, and the verb *break* might be relatively easy to learn without linguistic support. These are learned first and provide the foundation for the learning of other words, such as the noun *mortgage*, the adjective *former*, and the verb *dreaming*, whose meanings can only be conveyed through the vehicle of language.

Chapter 9
Number Words

Children's emerging ability to think about and talk about numbers poses some fascinating puzzles for developmental psychologists. Numbers are unlike objects such as cats and shoes. They have no material existence—no color, shape, size, or mass. And they are unlike properties such as redness and sadness because they do not correspond to properties that any individual can possess. Instead, numbers correspond to properties of sets of individuals (Frege, 1893). When you say that three cats are outside, the *three* does not refer to any of the individual cats or any property that a cat might have. It instead refers to a property of the set of cats: it is of a certain numerosity; the set has three members.

Sets are notoriously abstract entities. One can see and hear cats, but nobody has ever been wakened in the middle of the night by the yowling of a set. The apprehension of sets might therefore require some cognitive capacity above and beyond the normal apprehension of entities in the world (Maddy, 1990). Then there is the question of the ontological status of numerical properties. Some philosophers and mathematicians take a so-called Platonist position, arguing that numbers are real entities, existing independently of human thought. This argument gains force from the utility that mathematical thought has for explaining and manipulating the natural world. If numbers don't exist, why is it so beneficial to use them in science? But this approach raises the mystery of how our material minds could make contact with such immaterial entities in the course of learning and evolution. Other scholars have proposed that numbers exist as constructions of the mind or that they are parts of a formal system that humans have invented, akin to the elements of chess. Some have even argued that numbers are fictional entities, like leprechauns—that no such things as numbers really exist.

Whatever, precisely, numbers are (or are not), children learn their names—words like *two* and *seven* and *one hundred and eight*. I first discuss what babies know about number and then review different theories about how number words are learned. Much of the rest of this chapter is taken up with discussing a proposal developed in collaboration with Karen Wynn, which is that children's sensitivity to linguistic cues guides them to an initial stage of number word understanding and then the rest of their knowledge emerges through an understanding of counting. I conclude with a discussion of certain proposals about the relationship between numerical language and numerical thought, both in human evolution and cognitive development.

Number in the Minds of Animals and Babies

Could numerical knowledge be a cultural product, developed over history, and learned by children the same way they learn about baseball or geology? This must be true for certain aspects of mathematical understanding (such as calculus), which have emerged only recently in human history and are not universal. But there is evidence that at least some understanding of number is universal and exists not only in humans but in other species (see Dehaene, 1997, for review).

Many animals can enumerate sets of items that are presented sequentially. One can train a rat or a pigeon to press a bar a minimum number of times (20, for instance) to obtain a reward, and studies of error patterns show that this response really is due to a sensitivity to number, not to related properties such as the amount of time that the animal has been pressing (e.g., Mechner & Guevrekian, 1962). Rats can count sounds and light flashes and can be trained to press one lever if they are presented with two sounds or two flashes and another lever if presented with four sounds or four flashes (Church & Meck, 1984).

Nonhumans can also enumerate items that are presented simultaneously. Raccoons can learn to choose a box containing a certain number of items (such as the box with three items) even when nonnumerical factors such as size and density are controlled for (Davis, 1984). Irene Pepperberg (1987) reports that Alex, an African grey parrot, can be presented with arrays of up to five items and when asked "How many?" will usually squawk the correct number word in reply. A chimpanzee who was taught to read Arabic numerals was able to determine the sum of two sets of oranges and pick out the numeral it corresponded to (Boysen & Berntson, 1989). It is likely that such abilities have evolved through natural selection as adaptations for tasks such as foraging and tracking (Gallistel, 1990; Wynn & Bloom, 1992).

Human babies have similar capacities. Seven-month-olds who are repeatedly presented with pictures containing three items will show increased interest when shown a new picture with two items, and vice-versa (Starkey & Cooper, 1980). Six-month-olds can distinguish two jumps of a puppet from three jumps of a puppet (Wynn 1996), two sounds from three sounds (Starkey, Spelke & Gelman 1990), and two moving black-and-white grids from three moving grids (von Loosbroek & Smitsman, 1990). Babies also have some understanding of the relative ordering of the numbers. If five-month-olds are shown one object added to another identical object, or one object removed from a collection of two identical objects, they will look longer, indicating surprise, when the number of objects revealed as the result of this operation is numerically incorrect than when the result is correct. This suggests that they expect one and one to equal two and one removed from two to equal one (Wynn, 1992a).

Considerable debate has occurred over the precise nature of babies' numerical abilities, particularly with regard to their performance in the addition and subtraction situations (for different perspectives, see Simon, 1997; Uller, Carey, Huntley Fenner & Klatt, in press; Wynn, 1998). But for the purposes here, the essential point is uncontroversial. Just like other animals, human babies can discriminate small numbers and have an implicit grasp of the relationships between these numbers. Long before language learning, then, they have the main prerequisite for learning the smaller number words: they have the concepts of oneness, twoness, and threeness. Their problem is simply figuring out the names that go with these concepts.

The Problem of Number Word Learning

How do children hear a number word and figure out that it refers to a number, and not to an object or property of an object? Much of what they hear is useless from a learning standpoint. Children in Western societies typically experience number words as they are used within the routine of linguistic counting, but frequently this counting is done without any objects present, as in rhymes and routines such as "one, two, three, go" (Durkin et al., 1986). There is no information here suggesting that these words refer to numbers, as opposed to being strings of nonsense words such as "eeny, meeny, miny" or the letters of the alphabet "A, B, C."

Some of the time, however, children observe the counting of entities, in which each number word is assigned to an individual item in a one-to-one correspondence, so that one item is described as "one," another as "two," and so on (Gelman & Gallistel, 1978). If children have some prior knowledge of the nature and function of counting, these situations might make it possible for them to learn the number words. They could map their numerical concepts directly onto the words of the counting sequence; the first word in the sequence corresponds to oneness, the second to twoness, and so on. Such children would be in the same situation as adults learning the number words of a new language, something that is a trivial exercise of memory. Once you hear someone produce an ordered series of words that correspond in a one-to-one fashion with a set of different items, you know that these are the number words and can easily infer which words correspond to which numbers.

Without some prior knowledge of what counting is, however, the situation is harder to figure out. The entities that are counted are often objects, and given children's propensity to treat words as object names, it might be especially difficult for them to learn that the number words do *not* describe the individual items being counted. Another possibility is that children might think of such words as demonstrative pronouns, akin to *this* and *that:* now *two* refers to the cup; an hour ago it was the dog, and yesterday it was one of my fingers. This would be a natural mistake, but it is one that, somehow, children never make.

Children learn to count early. Two-year-olds can usually count up to three or more (Gelman & Gallistel, 1978), and once children can count objects, they can also count actions and sounds (Wynn, 1990). By the time children are about four years of age, they begin to appreciate some of the generative rules underlying the language of numbers (Fuson, Richards & Briars, 1982; Siegler & Robinson, 1982). Amusing errors sometimes occur as the orderly minds of children clash with the occasionally arbitrary nature of this system. Ginsberg (1977) describes one child who thought that the number after "99" was "tenny."

What is the development of children's understanding of number words outside the context of counting? The most complete analysis available is from a longitudinal study (Wynn, 1992b). Since the findings of this study are the impetus for the theory of number word acquisition outlined below, it is worth discussing them in some detail.

The logic of this study required that children know the precise meaning of the word *one*—that it applies to only a single item and not to several items. Two-and-a-half- to three-and-a-half-year-olds were tested for this knowledge, and those who passed this pretest (almost all did so) were then presented with a series of tasks over a seven-month period. To test whether children know that the number words refer to numbers and not other properties, children were shown pairs of pictures. In each pair, one picture depicted a single item of a given kind of object, and the other depicted several (between two and six) items of the same kind but of a different color. For each pair, children were asked to identify the picture that showed a particular number of objects—for example, "Can you show me the four fish? / Can you show me the one fish?" (the items' names always had the same plural as singular forms, so that the only cue to numerosity was the number word). They were also asked questions with nonsense words—for example, "Can you show me the zoop fish?"—and, as predicted, they responded to these questions randomly.

If children know that a number word—other than *one*—refers to a specific number, they should infer that it does not refer to the same number as the word *one*. In the questions contrasting one object with multiple objects, then, they should choose the correct picture by a process of elimination. For instance, imagine a child who is shown a picture of one fish and a picture of four fish and is asked to point to the four fish. If she knows that *four* refers to a number and also knows that different number words within a language must refer to different numbers (in accord with principles of lexical contrast; see chapter 3), then, even if she does not know the precise meaning of *four*, she should be able to identify the correct picture. But if she does not know that a given number word picks out a specific number, she will have no basis for contrasting it with *one* and should respond randomly, as when asked a question with a nonsense word.

To test if children know the precise number that a given word picks out, they were shown pairs of pictures—one containing the number of items corresponding to the word in question and the other containing that number plus one. For example, to test whether children know the precise meaning of the word *four*, they would be shown a picture of four fish and one of five fish, and asked "Can you show me the four fish?" on some trials and "Can you show me the five fish?" on others. Here, knowing the meaning of *one* cannot help; to give the right answer, children have to know the precise meanings of at least one of these larger number words.

The results were surprising: even the youngest children succeeded when one of the pictures in the pair contained a single item. They correctly pointed out the number asked for almost all the time. They thus showed an understanding that the number words pick out numbers— that they belong to the same semantic class as the word *one*. This finding also shows, incidentally, that some version of the contrast principle discussed by Clark (1987) and Markman (1989) applies to number words as well: young children have an implicit understanding that there is only one number word per number.

Despite this early knowledge, however, it took children nearly a full additional year to learn which words refer to which numbers. For instance, a two-year-old who knows that *two* is a number word (as shown by the fact that she would never point to the single fish when asked "Can you show me the two fish?") might go for a year not knowing that *two* refers to two and not to three. When presented with a picture of two fish and a picture of three fish, she will treat the question "Can you show me the two fish?" in the same random fashion as she treats "Can you show me the zoop fish?"

In other words, children go through a lengthy developmental stage in which they know that words like *two* and *three* refer to numbers but do not know *which* numbers. This fact about the stages of number-word knowledge puts us in a position to assess different proposals about how these words are learned.

Theories of Number-Word Learning

Consider first the traditional empiricist view of how number words are learned, advanced by John Stuart Mill (1843), among others. Children see a scene, perceive its numerosity (such as twoness), hear a word used to refer to the set (such as *two*), and come to link this perception with the word that they hear.

One problem with this view was raised by Gottlob Frege (1893). Unlike properties such as color and temperature, the attribution of numerical properties makes sense only in the context of prior individuation. One cannot point to a scene, for instance, and ask "How many?" The natural response to such a question would be "How many *what*?" Any scene presented through ostension can have an indefinite number of numerosities applied to it. The perception of Watson and Wolfgang can be understood as corresponding to two cats—but also to four eyes, eight paws, several thousand cat hairs, and several million cat molecules. Because of this, an adequate theory of number-word learning cannot assume a direct mapping from the word to a scene; at best, it can be a mapping from a word to our *construal* of the scene as constituted in a particular way—for instance, as construed as discrete physical objects.

Second, Mill's proposal could work only for small numbers. We might perceive twoness without conscious counting, but we surely do not perceive one-hundred-twoness in this manner. The names for larger numerosities need to be acquired in some other way. Mill (1843, p. 400) himself was aware of this point, though he insisted that in the end, some sensory factors must always be involved, if only to explain why the number word exists in the first place: "And although a hundred and two horses are not so easily distinguished from a hundred and three, as two horses are from three—though in most positions the senses do not perceive any difference—yet they may be so placed that a difference will be perceptible, or else we should never have distinguished them, or given them different names."

The final objection to Mill's theory is that, even for small numbers, and even given some prior conception of the entities to be counted, it cannot explain the developmental sequence discussed above. The theory posits that children directly map words onto the perceptions that arise when they are exposed to different sets of objects and thereby fails to account for a lengthy stage in which children can clearly *distinguish* between two and three entities (recall that even babies can do this), know that *two* and *three* are number words—but do not yet know precisely what *two* and *three* mean.

A more promising theory involves counting. Rochel Gelman and her colleagues (e.g., Gelman & Gallistel, 1978; Gelman, Meck & Merkin, 1986) have suggested that children possess an innate set of principles that underlie their knowledge of counting. These include the *one-to-one correspondence principle*, which states that items to be counted must be in one-to-one correspondence with the counting words; the *stable-order principle*, which is that the counting words are consistently used in fixed order; and the *cardinality principle*, which states that the last counting word represents the cardinality (number) of the items counted.

All that has to happen for children to learn the number words of their language is for them to identify counting sequences—that is, situations in which strings of words are used in accord with the counting principles—and map the words in these sequences onto an innately given list of mental number tags. *Three* refers to threeness, for instance, because it is the final word in a count of three items.

One reason that the counting theory is so plausible is that the number words used in adjectival or predicative contexts, as in *three cats*, are the very same words used in counting. This is partially true across languages; the number words greater than three are either identical to the words used in the counting sequence or are predictable phonological variants of them (Hurford, in press). But this is not always the case for the smaller number words. Some cultures lack counting systems but nevertheless have some number words, such as Warlpiri speakers, who have words corresponding to *one*, *two*, and *a lot*. And some languages, such as Maltese and Chinese, use different words for counting one, two, or three items than they use for describing them (Hurford, in press).

Even for English-speaking children, one can dissociate knowledge of counting from knowledge of the number words. While the first two of the Gelman and Gallistel (1978) counting principles—one-to-one correspondence and stable-order—show up remarkably early in children's counting, the cardinality principle lags behind. Children go for a long period before they understand that counting determines the numerosity of a set. For instance, when asked to give a puppet some number of objects (Wynn, 1990) or to put some objects into a pile (Sophian, 1987), younger children do poorly, showing little understanding that they can use their counting skills to perform these tasks (see also Fuson, 1988). An example from Wynn (1995, p. 54) illustrates the child's confusion about the role of counting:

Experimenter: Can you give Big Bird five animals?

(The child grabs a handful that contains three animals and puts them in front of the puppet.)

Experimenter: Can you count and make sure there's five?

Child: *(Counting the three items perfectly)* One, two, three—that's five!

Experimenter: No, I really don't think that's five. How can we fix it so there's five?

Child: *(Pauses and then very carefully switches the positions of the three items)* There. Now there's five.

While these children do not know the cardinality principle and therefore do not know that counting is a procedure that tells one about the numerosity of a set, some of them do know the meanings of the smaller number words *one, two,* and *three.* Instead of the cardinality principle helping children learn the precise meanings of the smaller words, the opposite might be the case: children might first learn the meanings of the smaller words and then use this knowledge to figure out the cardinality principle (see also Klahr & Wallace, 1976).

Finally, if children did learn number words through mapping them onto the ordered counting sequence, one would expect them to understand early on that, for example, the word *three* can be applied only to sets of three and that *three* picks out larger sets than the word *two* and smaller sets than the word *four.* This knowledge should derive from an appreciation of counting: *three* is the third word in the English counting series, following *two* and preceding *four.* The fact that children go for a sustained period during which they know these facts about the counting sequence but do not know the meanings of these specific number words is a puzzle under this account.

A third perspective emerges from the work of Karen Fuson and her colleagues (e.g., Fuson 1988; Fuson, Richards & Briars, 1982). They propose that number words have different meanings in the distinct contexts in which they are used. Children first learn each number word as several distinct context-dependent words, which gradually become interrelated. For example, *sequence* meanings occur in contexts in which the number words are recited in sequence without reference to actual entities, *counting* meanings occur when number words are used to count groups of items, and *cardinal* meanings occur when number words are used to describe the cardinality, or numerosity, of sets of discrete objects or events.

One merit of this view is that it underscores the diverse contexts in which number words can be used. It would be a mistake to assume that children who can count to two ("one, two") can therefore understand the quantificational use of two ("two dogs"), the nominal use ("two is bigger than one"), or the arbitrary use of the word as a name ("the number two bus"). But this theory suffers from the same limitation as the previous proposals because it cannot account for a stage in which young children know that a number word picks out a specific number but do not know the precise number that the word maps onto.

Linguistic Cues to the Acquisition of Number Words

An alternative theory is that linguistic cues play a significant role in children's acquisition of number-word meaning (Bloom & Wynn, 1998; Wynn, 1992b). In particular, children's earliest knowledge of number-word meaning—that such words correspond to precise numbers—comes through attention to cues such as the words' ordering relative to other words in a sentence, the closed-class morphemes they co-occur with, and the count-mass status of the nouns they modify. These cues are diverse in nature: the information provided by relative order within the NP is best viewed as syntactic, but other cues—in particular, those provided by closed-class morphology—are better construed as semantic.

If this hypothesis is correct, three things must hold. First, such cues must exist. Second, they must be present in the input that children receive. Third, children must appreciate the import of these cues. It would support this third claim if, in children's own spontaneous speech, only number words appear in certain contexts, those same contexts that, by this theory, inform children about their meanings.

Consider first the question of whether these linguistic cues actually exist. Number words often appear in some of the same surface positions as adjectives and other, semantically distinct, quantifiers. In sentences such as "The two dogs waited," "The little dogs waited," and "The many dogs waited," the words behave identically. But other linguistic properties of number words differentiate them from adjectives and these quantifiers (see table 9.1):

1. Number words can be used only with count nouns, not with mass nouns, and thereby fall into the same category as certain quantifiers, such as *a, another,* and *many.* They are distinct from other quantifiers, such as *much* (which can cooccur only with mass nouns) and *all* (which can cooccur with both count nouns and mass nouns). They are distinct from most adjectives, which

Table 9.1
Potential linguistic cues to the meanings of number words

Cue	Information
Appears only with count nouns	Modifies or quantifies sets of individuals
Does not appear with modifiers	Is an absolute property
Precedes adjectives within the NP	Modifies or quantifies sets of individuals but not specific individuals
Occurs in the partitive construction	Is a quantifier

can appear with both count nouns and mass nouns (though some, such as *big* and *long*, typically appear only with count nouns because their meanings require that they cooccur with nouns referring to entities with spatial or temporal extent and these are typically denoted by count nouns).

Number words have this property because they are quantifiers of sets of individuals and count nouns describe individuals. (Note that a set could have only a single member, as in the phrase *one dog*.) Some understanding of this contrast between count nouns and mass nouns shows up early in language development, by about the age of two (P. Bloom, 1994b; Gordon, 1988, 1992; Soja, 1992).

2. Number words cannot appear with modifiers. The majority of adjectives are modifiable; one can specify the extent to which an adjective applies in a given instance by preceding it with a modifier, such as *very, too, somewhat*, and so on (*very tired, too happy*). Similarly, some quantifiers can be modified (*very few, too much*). Number words, however, pick out discrete, absolute properties and so cannot occur with modifiers; *very five* and *too three* are unacceptable.

3. Number words precede adjectives within the noun phrase (NP); they cannot follow them. In this respect, number words are similar to all other quantifiers. Just as saying "two big dogs" is acceptable and "big two dogs" is not, "many big dogs" is acceptable, and "big many dogs" is not.

Some semantic implications follow from this. Prenominal expressions within the English NP are analyzed in a linear order, so that each is a predicate of everything that follows. So the first adjective in "the big brown dogs" is about the brown dogs, and the second is about the dogs. In this regard, the fact that number words (and other quantifiers) must precede adjectives within the NP is informative as to what they mean. Adjectives describe properties of individuals; number words (and quantifiers) describe properties of *sets* of individuals. In a situation in which three dogs are brown, the *set* of (brown) dogs, not each individual dog, is three, and the dogs themselves, not the set, are brown. Because of this, "the three brown dogs" is acceptable, and "the brown three dogs" is not.[1]

4. Number words can occur in the partitive construction. The partitive construction in English is of the form ＿＿＿ of the Xs" (Jackendoff, 1977) and has the semantic role of expressing quantification, in which the first element "extracts" either some group of individuals from the reference set denoted by the noun ("some of the boys") or some portion of the nonindividuated entity that is denoted ("most of the water"). Most quantifiers, with the exception of *only*, can appear in this context, and all number words can ("two of the boys"). Adjectives, as they lack the semantic capacity to quantify, cannot appear in the partitive construction.

A learning problem arises here, however, with regard to how children could use the first two cues. Children are not given negative evidence; they are not explicitly told that "two water" or "very two" is ungrammatical, nor is it reasonable to assume that all children produce errors like "two water" and "very two" and receive corrective feedback a significant proportion of the time that they do so (see Marcus, 1993). How then could children know that number words *cannot* appear with mass nouns and modifiers—as opposed to inferring that they simply haven't yet *heard* them appear in these contexts?

One possibility involves what is sometimes called *indirect negative evidence* (Chomsky, 1981; for discussion, see Pinker, 1989; Valian, 1990). If children hear a word frequently enough but never in a certain context, they might infer it cannot be used in that context. This may explain how children come to know that number words are restricted to count nouns. Given the high frequency of mass-noun usage, it is reasonable to infer from the fact that number words are never used with mass nouns that they *cannot* be used with them. But this inference is less plausible with regard to modifiers, given their relatively low frequency. It wouldn't be reasonable for children to infer that because a given number word has not yet been used with a modifier, such a usage is unacceptable.

There is another option. Children might start off with the assumption that, in the absence of any syntactic and semantic evidence to the contrary, predicates cannot be used with modifiers; they denote absolute properties. If this is the case, then the presence of modifiers can serve as a cue to a word's meaning—that the word refers to a nonabsolute property.

An Analysis of the Linguistic Contexts in Which Number Words Are Used

Are these cues present in the input that children receive? And do children know about them? Do they treat number words differently from other parts of speech in the ways discussed above? While there has been extensive research on the social and pragmatic conditions under which adults use number words in their speech to children (e.g., Durkin et al. 1986; Saxe, Guberman & Gearhart, 1987), we know little about the syntax of number words in adults' speech to children and in children's own speech.

Karen Wynn and I used a database called CHILDES to carry out analyses of transcripts of the spontaneous speech of three children and their parents (MacWhinney & Snow, 1990). Our sample was chosen according to the following criteria. We wanted to study children before the age of three to capture the developmental period found by Wynn (1992b). We needed an adult caretaker in the samples to explore the question of whether linguistic cues are in the input. And we needed enough data to do statistical analyses. We found three mother-child dyads that met these criteria—Eve (1;6–2;3; from Brown 1973), Peter (1;9–3;1; from Bloom, Hood & Lightbown, 1974), and Naomi (1;2–2;11; from Sachs, 1983).

We searched for the number words from *two* to *ten*. (Note that our hypothesis does not apply to *one*, since there is no evidence that children go through a stage in which they know that *one* is a number word but do not know the precise number it corresponds to.) We also searched for a set of 12 adjectives, chosen to be highly frequent in the speech of children and adults, as found by Nelson (1976) and Valian (1986). And we chose 12 quantifiers to represent a good diversity of semantic categories; the different subtypes of quantifiers are discussed below.

The analyses and results are as follows. Unless explicitly noted otherwise, any differences that are discussed are statistically significant; the interested reader is referred to Bloom and Wynn (1998) for methodological and statistical details.

First, are number words used exclusively with count nouns? We expected number words to behave the same as other quantifiers that also cannot appear with mass nouns (the nonmassable quantifiers *few*, *many*, *both*, *several*, and *another*) but to behave differently from those quantifiers that can (the massable quantifiers *more*, *some*, *most*, *only*, *all*, *any*, and *much*). We also predicted that number words would behave differently from all the adjectives except for *big* and *little*, which, due to their semantics, almost always appear with count nouns. The results are shown in figure 9.1.

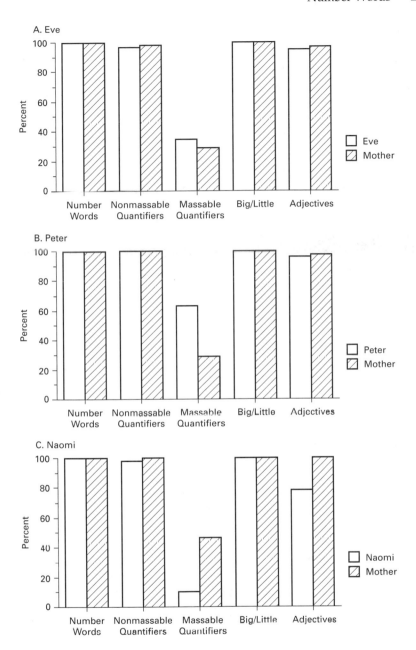

Figure 9.1
Percentage of utterances in which target words preceded a count noun, out of the total number of utterances in which target words preceded a count or mass noun (from Bloom & Wynn, 1998)

Each of the dyads showed the same pattern. Eve and her mother, Peter and his mother, and Naomi and her mother used number words exclusively with count nouns and virtually always did the same with the nonmassable quantifiers. The massable quantifiers, in contrast, were used less than half the time with count nouns. We expected that *big* and *little* would be used only with count nouns but, in fact, all the adjectives were used predominantly with count nouns. This does not mean that children or adults use them incorrectly but only that they do not use them in a manner that distinguishes them from number words in this regard.

In sum, number words co-occurred with count nouns, not mass nouns. This provides a cue to the meaning of number words—that they apply to *individuals*. This distinguishes them from certain other quantifiers, although not from adjectives.

Second, do number words appear with modifiers? Since they refer to absolute properties, they should fall into the same class as the non-modifiable quantifiers *some, both, another, any, all, several,* and *only,* and should be distinct from the modifiable quantifiers *much, many, most,* and *few,* as well as from all of the adjectives.

The results are shown in figure 9.2. None of the children or adults ever used modifiers with either number words or with nonmodifiable quantifiers. They were frequently used with the modifiable quantifiers, as well as with adjectives, though this number word versus adjective contrast was significant for only some children and adults (Eve's mother, Peter, and Peter's mother) and not others (Eve, Naomi, and Naomi's mother).

In sum, number words were never used with modifiers. But all of the children and their mothers used modifiers with modifiable quantifiers and, to a lesser extent, with adjectives. This suggests that cues to the semantic distinction between words denoting properties that fall on a continuum (such as size or magnitude) versus words denoting discrete properties (such as being of a certain numerosity) are present in the speech of parents and are understood by children.

Third, do number words occur only before adjectives? For this analysis, we analyzed only those target words that appeared in strings with adjectives and calculated the proportion of these utterances in which the target word appeared before the adjective. The prediction was that number words and quantifiers should appear only in this context.[2]

The results are shown in figure 9.3. It is worth going through these case by case. When number words were used with adjectives, they tended to precede the adjective (Eve: 1/1, Eve's mother: 6/6, Peter: 8/9, Peter's mother: 1/1, Naomi's mother: 1/1). The one error was from Peter, who once said "too big two pockets." Naomi never produced

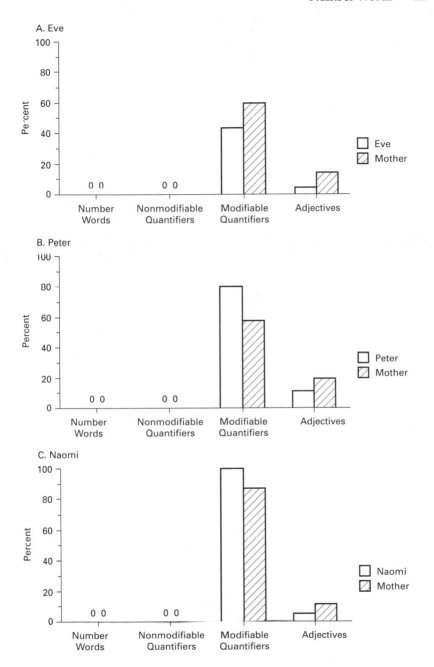

Figure 9.2
Percentage of utterances in which target words were preceded by a modifier (from Bloom & Wynn, 1998)

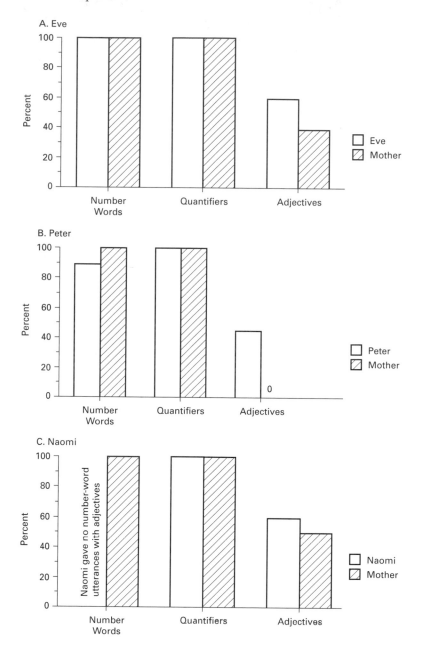

Figure 9.3
Percentage of utterances in which target words preceded an adjective, out of the total number of utterances in which target words either preceded or followed an adjective (from Bloom & Wynn, 1998)

either an adjective-number word string or a number word-adjective string. For all the children and all the adults, quantifiers other than number words always preceded adjectives in adjective-quantifier strings.

These results are significantly different from random variation only for those subjects with a sample size of five utterances or more, and so we can claim better-than-chance performance for only some of the subjects. Nevertheless, the correct order is consistent with our hypothesis. The only error was produced by Peter (assuming that this was not a transcription error), and this was in the context of eight other correct orderings, suggesting that even he has the correct understanding.

Finally, are number words used in the partitive construction? If so, this can serve as information that these words are predicates of sets of individuals and not individuals themselves. In this regard, number words are identical to quantifiers (with the exception of *only*, which we excluded from this analysis) and different from all of the adjectives.

The results are shown in figure 9.4. Partitive usages were relatively rare. Eve used partitives six times, always with quantifiers, never with number words. Eve's mother used them 15 times, with both number words (3) and quantifiers (12). Thus while Eve herself displayed no knowledge that number words can appear in a partitive construction, cues to that effect were present in her input. Peter used partitives 20 times, with both number words (2) and quantifiers (18), and his mother used them 14 times, also with number words (3) and quantifiers (11). The data from Naomi are less revealing; she used the partitive construction only once, with a quantifier. Her mother used this construction 20 times, once with a number word and 19 times with a quantifier. The partitive construction was never used with an adjective.

The frequency of partitive usages is so low that none of these contrasts between number words and adjectives is statistically significant. On the other hand, if children can use the mere presence of a word within the partitive construction as a cue that it is a quantifier, this cue is available for all the children we studied.

The results from these analyses can be summarized as follows:

1. Each child and mother used number words only with count nouns, never with mass nouns. In this regard, they treated number words identically to quantifiers such as *another* but differently from quantifiers such as *all*. They did not show a distinction between number words and adjectives, however, as adjectives were also predominantly used with count nouns.

2. None of the children or their mothers used modifiers with number words or with nonmodifiable quantifiers such as *another*.

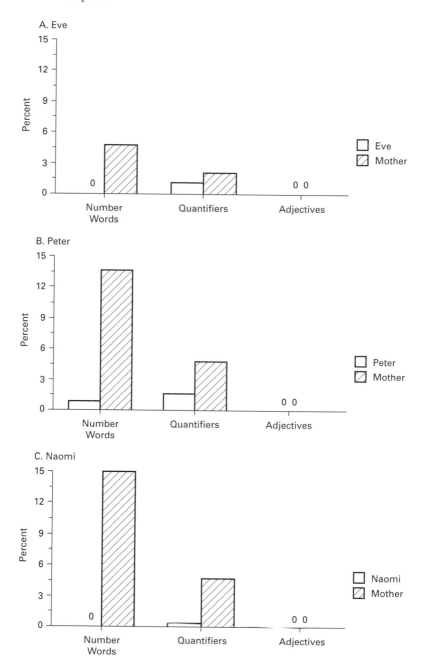

Figure 9.4
Percentage of utterances in which target words occurred in a partitive construction (from Bloom & Wynn, 1998)

Modifiers were used with modifiable quantifiers such as *many*, as well as with adjectives.

3. When number words or other quantifiers appeared with adjectives in the surface string in the speech of the children and their mothers, these words, with a single exception, always preceded the adjectives.

4. The partitive construction was rare, but it occurred only with number words and other quantifiers, never with adjectives.

The analyses above suggest that in both the input to children and in their own speech, number words are used in linguistic contexts that indicate that they apply over individuals, that they denote discrete values that do not permit modification, and that they are quantifiers of sets. These aspects of number-word meaning coincide precisely with the level of understanding that Wynn (1992b) found in her analysis of children's early understanding of the meanings of number words and support the view that through attending to these cues children reach this understanding.

But the study admittedly provides only indirect support for this claim. Such analyses don't show a causal relationship between linguistic cues and children's knowledge. It might be that children reach this level of understanding through some other, as yet unknown, learning mechanism and that the linguistic information present in adult speech and understood by children plays no causal role in the learning process. A more direct test of our hypothesis would involve experimental manipulation, using syntactic cues to try to teach children new number words, along the same lines as the research described in the previous chapter on the role of linguistic cues in the acquisition of nouns and verbs.

It would also be relevant to compare the course of number-word acquisition across different languages. For instance, children acquiring a language such as Straits Salish, in which no syntactic or morphological differences exist between number words and other predicates (Jelinek & Demers 1994), should show a different pattern of emerging knowledge from what we find in children acquiring English. Such children must learn the meanings of number words exclusively through ostension and the counting system of their culture and do not go through an initial stage in which they know there are number words but do not know their precise meaning. Less dramatic cross-linguistic differences, such as those between English and Japanese (which does not draw a grammatical distinction between count nouns and mass nouns), should also have developmental ramifications.

How does this pattern of number word learning relate to other types of word learning? This brings us back to an issue raised in the previous chapter. On the one hand, scholars such as Gleitman (1990) have stressed that syntactic cues play a significant role in word learning, and many empirical demonstrations show that these cues serve to narrow down children's interpretation of the meaning of a novel word and to focus them on the appropriate ontological class. On the other hand—as stressed by Pinker (1989, 1994a)—much of word meaning is *not* reflected in the syntax; no matter how rich the mappings children possess, they cannot solve the problem of word learning.

This tension motivates the view that children can use linguistic cues to determine the broad semantic class of a novel word (kind of individual, quantifier, and so on) and use other nonsyntactic information to determine the word's specific meaning. Number words are unusual because of the clear demarcation between these two processes: the linguistic cues apply about a year before children manage to work out the words' specific meanings.

Learning the Precise Meanings of the Number Words

How do children come to learn the number words' full meanings? From Wynn (1990, 1992b), we know that children first learn the precise meaning of *one*, then *two*, then *three*. Since babies have the capacity to apprehend the numerosity of small sets of items without conscious counting, once they know that these are number words, learning their precise meanings should be straightforward. Children hear "three," appreciate that it is a number word, and realize that it is used to describe a set of entities, typically objects, that has the property of threeness.

But why does it take them so long to learn the words' precise meaning? For instance, once children know that *three* is a number word, why don't they immediately realize that it corresponds to their notion of threeness? Why do many months typically elapse before this understanding emerges?

The answer may have to do with limited exposure to the relevant learning situations. It is not enough that children hear "the three dogs"; they have to hear it in a situation in which they can be certain that the word *three* refers to the numerical property of threeness. Such cases are not as frequent as one would imagine (Durkin et al., 1986). Frequency also explains why the words are learned in ascending order. It might be tempting to see the order in which the number words are learned—*one*, then *two*, and then *three*—as reflecting some inevitable logical progression as in the Peano axioms, in which each number is defined in terms of the one that precedes it. But this ordering has a simpler explanation—word frequency. People use *one* more than *two* and *two* more than *three*. This is true in every language and culture studied (Dehaene & Mehler, 1992). If the frequencies were reversed, children might well learn *three* first, then *two*, then *one*.

After children learn *three*, which corresponds to the largest numerosity that can be apprehended without conscious counting, they experience an explosion in their number-word knowledge: they acquire the precise meanings of *four, five, six*, and larger number words within their counting range all at once. This occurs at precisely the same time that they exhibit an understanding that the result of a count (as in "five, six, SEVEN") can be used to determine the numerosity of a set (that it has seven items) (Wynn, 1992b), which is consistent with Gelman and Gallistel's (1978) proposal that an understanding of the linguistic counting system is crucial for how children acquire the precise meanings of the number words—though only for the bigger ones, not the smaller ones.

But this raises a serious puzzle. Why do children take so long to make the connection between counting and numerosity? That is, why aren't Gelman and Gallistel *right* that counting guides children to the meanings of the smaller number words? After all, even babies have the requisite numerical understanding; they have some notion of oneness and twoness and threeness and know the relative ordering of these numerosities. And young children can count; they can recite the smaller number words in sequence and put them into one-to-one correspondence with entities in the world. It is a mystery, then, why they do not figure out how the counting routine determines numerosity until many months—sometimes over a year—from when they first begin to count. In the next section, I suggest that the solution to this problem emerges from more general facts about how language and number are related.

Language and Number in Human Evolution

Plainly some relationship exists between numerical language and numerical thought. After all, we can use words to communicate our thoughts about number, and I have argued above for a stronger connection—that an understanding of the syntax and semantics of language helps children learn what the number words mean. But some scholars have suggested that there is a much more profound relationship—that our understanding of number is itself the product of the language we possess.

This proposal is sometimes put in an evolutionary context. Noam Chomsky (1988, p. 168) raises the following question: "How did the number faculty develop? It is impossible to believe that it was specifically selected. Cultures still exist today that have not made use of this faculty; their language does not contain a method for constructing indefinitely many number words, and the people of these cultures are not aware of the possibility of counting. But they certainly have the capacity. . . . It is only recently in evolutionary terms, at a time when human evolution had reached its current stage, that the number faculty was manifested."

When Chomsky talks about the "number faculty," he includes knowledge such as the intuitive appreciation of infinity; "children . . . somehow know that it is possible to continue to add one indefinitely" (p. 167). The argument against specific selection for this understanding is reasonable: since some human groups do not use this knowledge, it is unlikely to be a biological adaptation. This in turn raises the possibility that the number faculty is a by-product of some capacity that *has* been selected: "we might think of the human number faculty as essentially an 'abstraction' from human language, preserving the mechanism of discrete infinity and eliminating the other special features of language" (p. 169).

Mechanisms of discrete infinity have a vocabulary of primitive units—rules for combining them—and the potential for using these rules to produce an infinite number of symbol combinations. So defined, discrete infinity can emerge from both iterative and recursive systems, but it has long been known (Chomsky, 1957) that iterative mechanisms such as finite-state Markov processes cannot capture our knowledge of basic aspects of language like subject-verb agreement. As a result, Chomsky argues that language has the property of discrete infinity by virtue of being recursive.

Is it possible that number could have inherited this capacity from language? One problem here is that it is unclear what it means to say that one can abstract away the special features of language and preserve this mechanism of discrete infinity. Recursion is a formal property of some systems of rules; it is a holistic property of systems. One can chip off a piece of blue paint from a Picasso and stick it onto a blank canvas, but it is not sensible to talk of extracting the Picasso's coherence, or asymmetry, or beauty and moving it to another canvas: those properties are not portable. By the same token, it is hard to see how one can take language and strip away all the special features, leaving just recursion (see P. Bloom, 1994a).

A different version of the evolutionary theory is that humans first evolved recursive rules of language that manipulate syntactic categories and, as a subsequent evolutionary development, these rules were extended to manipulate other categories—in particular, symbolic representations of number. But this proposal has problems explaining the existence of people with full-fledged recursive syntax who have severe difficulties with even simple numerical tasks, as well as those who have almost no syntax but nevertheless possess surprisingly good numerical cognition, including idiot savants, who are capable of extraordinary mathematical feats (see Dehaene, 1997, for a review). This double dissociation does not prove that the neural systems underlying syntax and number are separate, but it certainly puts the burden of proof on someone who would argue that they are identical.

I think a more plausible reconstruction of the relationship between language and number makes the connection not in human evolution, but in cognitive development (P. Bloom, 1996c; Dehaene, 1997; Wynn, 1992b).

Language and Number in Cognitive Development

Contemporary neural and computational models of animal capacities do not involve the capacity for generativity. According to the *accumulator model* of counting (Meck & Church, 1983), the same mechanism underlies the ability both to determine numerosity (both of events and of entities) and to measure duration. Described at a functional level, this mechanism works by putting out pulses of energy at a constant rate that are passed into an accumulator by the closing of a switch. When counting, the switch is used to pass a fixed amount of energy into the accumulator for each entity to be counted. When measuring time, the switch is used to pass energy into the accumulator at a continuous rate; the longer the switch is closed, the longer the recorded duration. The final value of the accumulator (the size of the body of pulses transferred into it) can be stored in memory and compared with other values. In support of this theory, certain drugs have been found to affect animal's timing abilities and counting abilities to the same degree, and experiments with rats have found evidence for transfer from the output of timing processes to the output of counting process and vice-versa (Church & Meck, 1984).

This accumulator mechanism seems to be the very same one human babies have, with the same powers and limitations (Dehaene, 1997; Wynn, 1998). There is nothing that babies possess relating to number that is not present in other primates, or even in rats and birds. Contrary to Chomsky, then, the innate foundations for numbers lack the very property that is central to language—discrete infinity, or generativity.

This limitation on the part of humans can explain the long gap between learning to count and relating this knowledge to number. If human children possess a generative understanding of number from the very start, one would expect them to rapidly acquire the generative sequence of counting tags and map it onto their innate knowledge of number. But they don't have such an initial understanding. Children's difficulty in establishing this mapping may therefore derive from the different formats of the representations. The linguistic means of encoding number is through a rule-based symbolic system, while the child's initial nonlinguistic understanding is based on the same analog accumulator mechanism found in other animals (Wynn, 1992b).

How then do humans come to possess a generative understanding of number? One proposal is that the generative nature of human numerical cognition develops only as a result of children acquiring the linguistic counting system of their culture. Many, but not all, human groups have invented a way of using language to talk about number, through use of a recursive symbolic grammar. When children are exposed to the language of number, this causes a dramatic restructuring of their numerical knowledge. Under this view, it is not a coincidence that nonhuman primates lack both generative numerical understanding and a generative language: they lack a generative numerical system just *because* they lack the capacity to develop a generative communication system.

Stanislaus Dehaene (1997, pp. 91–92) discusses the difference language can make:

> Suppose that our only mental representation of number were an approximate accumulator similar to the rat's. We would have rather precise notions of the numbers 1, 2, and 3. But beyond that point, the number line would vanish into a thickening fog. . . . This fuzziness would befuddle any attempt at a monetary system, much of scientific knowledge, indeed human society as we know it.
>
> Linguistic symbols parse the world into discrete categories. Hence they allow us to refer to precise numbers and to separate them categorically from their closest neighbors. Without symbols, we might not discriminate 8 from 9. But with the help of our elaborate numerical notions, we can express thoughts as precise as "The speed of light is 299,792,458 meters per second."

Note that this theory has no problem with people with severe language impairments who might have a rich generative understanding of number. The claim here is not that numerical understanding emerges from language in general but that it emerges from learning the system of number words. Some people might have little knowledge of syntax, but so long as they have learned the system of number words (as is the case for numerical idiot savants), a rich understanding of number is possible. On the other hand, a person needs to have command of a counting system to have a precise understanding of larger numbers or any appreciation of the generative nature of number, regardless of how otherwise sophisticated his or her language is.

If this proposal is true, and we think about number using the symbols of the language we learn, then cross-linguistic differences in counting systems should affect numerical cognition in systematic ways. Some research has been done on the contrast between English and Chinese counting systems. Both are base 10 languages, but Chinese reflects this numerical fact to a greater degree than English. In English, the numbers 11 through 19 are denoted by words (*eleven, twelve*) that are not entirely predictable from the smaller number words. Chinese, in contrast, uses the numbers 1 through 10 exclusively, so that the Chinese word for *thirteen* is literally translated as "ten three." Kevin Miller and his colleagues (Miller, Smith, Zhu & Zhang, 1995) found significant differences in the ability of American and Chinese preschool children to count. The children do equally well when it comes to learning the numbers from one to 10 but profoundly differ once they reach the teens and beyond. The median level of how high a five-year-old could count was 49 for the American children—and 100 for the Chinese children.

Of course, it is one thing to show that properties of a symbol system affect how easy it is to learn and quite another to show that they affect how one thinks about the domain to which it corresponds. Here the evidence is weaker. Chinese children do better than Americans on certain arithmetic tasks that involve an understanding of base 10 (e.g., Fuson & Kwon, 1992; Miura, 1987), but it is hard to know whether this is due to linguistic factors, as opposed to cultural or educational ones.

The differences between the English and Chinese number systems are actually relatively subtle; more radical contrasts can easily be found (Dehaene, 1997; Ifrah, 1985). Aztec, Mayan, and Gaelic languages, as well as modern-day Eskimo and Yoruba, use base 20 systems, and some vestige of this remains in French, in which eighty is "quatre-vingt" (four twenty), as well as in English, which still allows counting in scores (twenties). Some Australian languages have a base 2 system (1 = gamar, 2 = burla, 3 = burla-gamar, 4 = burla-burla). And some languages reputedly don't make it past *two*.

The proposal defended by Dehaene and others makes a strong prediction here: anyone who lacks a symbolic system capable of expressing larger numbers should have problems reasoning about these numbers. In support of this, Peter Gordon (1993) suggests that members of the Piraha tribe, which uses only a "1-2-many" number system, have problems with *nonlinguistic* tasks involving numerical concepts greater than three. If this is true, it would be striking evidence for the role of language in numerical thought.

Finally, let's return to the question of how children come to know that the number system has the property of discrete infinity—that you can keep adding one forever. This can be easily explained in terms of language learning. What children need to know is that a one-to-one correspondence exists between number words and numbers, and that the system of number words allows for the production of an infinity of strings: one can say "a trillion," "a trillion trillion," "a trillion trillion trillion," and so on. Under this view, it is not that somehow children know that there is an infinity of numbers and infer that you can always produce a larger number word. Instead, they learn that one can always produce a larger number word and infer that there must therefore be an infinity of numbers.

This sort of inference is not limited to the domain of number. Someone might figure out that there is an infinity of possible musical compositions by noting the generative nature of musical notation, or that there are only a finite number of potential chess moves on a given turn by recognizing that the notation for expressing these moves is not generative. In general, an inspection of the properties of a symbolic system that refers to the domain can lead to insights about the domain itself.

The Development of Number and Number Words

Many aspects of number-word learning have not been discussed here. The focus has been on the number words as they appear in the counting sequence and in quantificational contexts, but I have little to say about how children learn other meanings of such words, including their ordinal usages (*first, second*) and their usage in contexts such as "two plus two equals four," in which the number word is an NP rather than a quantifier. (This *nominalization* of number words is similar to what goes on when an adjective like *red* is used in a sentence like "Red is a nicer color than blue.") Then there is the question of how children learn the rules of the generative number system—how they come to understand the syntax and semantics of a number word such as *two thousand four hundred and five*. But such a word is not an arbitrary sign in the Saussurian sense; it is the product of morphological rules and so, mercifully, falls outside the scope of this book.

I summarize below the proposed developmental progression in number-word learning with approximate ages based on studies of Western middle-class children acquiring English. This progression is not assumed to be universal. What happens after the age of two, in different languages and cultures, depends on several factors, including the nature of the counting system (if one exists) and the extent to which number words are linguistically distinguished from other parts of speech.

Before 2 years:	An ability to identify small numbers Some understanding of the relationship between these numbers
By about 2½:	An understanding that the smaller number words refer to numbers No knowledge of which numbers they refer to—with the exception of *one* Some ability to count
and then:	Acquisition of the precise meaning of *two* and then *three*
By about 3½:	An understanding of how the counting system determines number An explosion in the understanding of the precise meanings of number words
Sometime later:	An explicit grasp that there is an infinity of number words

This chapter builds on themes introduced earlier in the book, such as the role of linguistic cues in word learning. But I have also raised here for the first time the notion that language itself can play a causal role in conceptual development. This brings up the question of what role word learning plays in the development of mental life more generally, which is the topic of the next chapter.

Notes

1. For at least some dialects of English, exceptions can be found to this generalization. These include phrases such as "a wonderful three weeks" and "the grueling ten miles we walked" (Jackendoff, 1977). Why are these phrases more acceptable than "the brown three dogs"? The answer may lie in the fact that plural count nouns that denote measures of time or space can be construed as establishing reference to a single individual. Thus "three weeks" can denote a single continuous period of time of a certain duration—a temporal individual. (One can say "*a* wonderful three weeks in Thailand *was* just what we needed," using singular noun and verb agreement.) It is different from a phrase that always refers to a set of three distinct individuals, such as "three dogs." If "three weeks" can denote a single individual more readily than "three dogs," then it follows that "a wonderful three weeks" should be more acceptable than "the brown three dogs."

2. We also predicted that the adjectives we analyzed should be equally distributed, but this is virtually a preordained result, as most of the strings of more than one adjective we found in our transcripts contained only those adjectives we were searching for. In such cases, one adjective gets counted as preceding an adjective, the other as following one—leading to a roughly 50 percent distribution.

Chapter 10
Words and Concepts

In *One Hundred Years of Solitude*, Gabriel García Márquez tells how the people of Macondo, struck with the plague of insomnia, coped with its worst effect, the loss of memory. One of the villagers used an inked brush to mark everything with its name—*table, clock, wall, cow, hen, banana*. But he soon realized that as the plague grew worse, the day would come when he would forget not only the names of objects but also their use. So he wrote detailed instructions on the cow: *This is the cow. She must be milked every morning*. But this too would be only a temporary solution, since soon he would forget how to read.

Implicit in this story is the idea that knowing the name for something is separate from knowing about the thing itself. It is one thing to know what the cow is called; it is quite another to know what to do with the cow. The assumption has intuitive appeal. On at least some occasions when children learn a new word, it is clear that they already have the right concept. They might know, for instance, about shoes—what they are for, what they look like, and so on. Learning the word *shoe* lets them talk about shoes and understand when others talk about them, but it has no other effect on their mental life.

In accord with this perspective, scholars have often assumed that before learning language, children already know about the kinds and individuals that occupy their world. They just don't know their names. As Jerry Fodor (1975) has put it, under this view all language learning is actually *second*-language learning. Before being exposed to words in a language such as English, infants possess the concepts that these words correspond to, as part of what Fodor calls *mentalese* or *a language of thought*.

This is not currently a popular view within the cognitive sciences. Many philosophers reject the idea that thought, or at least all thought, can exist without language. Many linguists and anthropologists claim that the language one learns has a profound influence on how one thinks. And many developmental psychologists have been struck by the correlation between language development and cognitive development: a 12-month-old has few words and a limited mental life; a 24-month-old has many words and a much richer mental life. The idea that words are a catalyst to mature thinking is one way to explain this correlation.

A similar claim has been made about human evolution. Nonhumans have no words and a relatively limited mental life; humans have many words and a much richer mental life. This might be no accident. Charles Darwin (1874, p. 128) suggests: "If it could be proved that certain high mental powers, such as the formation of general concepts, self-consciousness, etc., were absolutely peculiar to man . . . it is not improbable that these qualities are merely the incidental results of other highly-advanced intellectual faculties, and these again are mainly the result of the continued use of a perfect language."

Following Darwin, many modern scholars have argued that the unique aspects of human thought (creativity, the ability to think about the past and future, powers of logical thought, and so on) are made possible through language (e.g., Bickerton, 1995; Carruthers, 1996; Corballis, 1992). Daniel Dennett (1996, p. 17) sums up the strongest version of this proposal in admirably stark terms: "Perhaps the kind of mind you get when you add language to it is so different from the kind of mind you can have without language that calling them both minds is a mistake."

This chapter reviews different versions of this proposal. I argue that some of the weaker versions are true; in certain ways the words one learns affect the nature of thought. But in the end, the commonsense view implicit in García Márquez's story is the right one: rich abstract thought is possible without words, and much of what goes on in word learning is establishing a correspondence between the symbols of a natural language and concepts that exist prior to, and independently of, the acquisition of that language.

Language, Thought, and Structured Thought

The most radical proposal about the relationship between language and thought is that all thinking is done in natural language. Most readers of this book think in English, someone who speaks only Dutch thinks in Dutch, and someone with no language does not think at all. Steven Pinker (1994b) raises some serious concerns with this view: Do chimpanzees, dogs, aphasics, and babies really have no mental life at all? Are they *unconscious*, like bricks, sand, and slime molds? This seems to be an absurd conclusion. If all our thoughts were in the words that we speak, how could we ever have difficulty finding the right words to express an idea? If you need a word to have a concept, how could anyone ever coin a new word? Furthermore, under any theory of word learning, children need to have *some* mental capacities to start with, and so there must be some thought without language.

Perhaps nobody would deny this. After all, even Edward Sapir (1921) and Benjamin Lee Whorf (1956), the strong proponents of *linguistic determinism*, were adamant that language and thought are distinct. But they claimed that in the absence of language, thought is an unstructured mess. As Whorf (pp. 213–214) puts it, "The categories and types that we isolate from the world of phenomena we do not find there because they stare every observer in the face; on the contrary, the world is presented as a kaleidoscopic flux of impressions which has to be organized by our minds—and this means largely by the linguistic systems in our minds."

And one way in which languages imposes this structure is through words (p. 240): "Languages differ not only in how they build their sentences but also in how they break down nature to secure the elements to put in those sentences. This breakdown gives units of the lexicon. . . . By these more or less distinct terms we ascribe a semifictitious isolation to parts of experience."

Linguistic determinism is not an exclusively American preoccupation. Ferdinand de Saussure (1916/1959, p. 110) asserts the following as simple fact: "Philosophers and linguists have always agreed were it not for signs, we should be incapable of differentiating any two ideas in a clear and constant way. In itself, thought is like a whirling cloud, where no shape is intrinsically determinate. No ideas are established in advance, and nothing is distinct, before the introduction of linguistic structure."

Under the strongest version of this claim, children start with none of the concepts that language-using adults have. It is wrong, then, to say that children first know what a shoe is and then learn the word for it. Instead, by hearing the word *shoe* they come to know about shoes. In fact, the very notion of a solid object is sometimes argued to derive from exposure to the words and grammar of natural language (Quine, 1960).

There are several ways in which words might conceivably structure thought. Imagine a long horizontal line. Suppose you were shown the leftmost third of the line and told that it is *zoop* and then shown the rest of the line and told that it is *moop*. You had not initially thought of the line as having structure, but now you do. This has cognitive consequences. For instance, if you had to cluster three equally spaced dots where two are in the zoop region and one is in the moop region, you might use this linguistically induced categorization as a cue and put the two zoop ones together.

Or imagine that someone dumped in front of you 50 small objects of different colors and textures and the person pointed to all the red and soft object and called them "doops." This would cause you to view the red soft objects as falling into a distinct category, and forming the category might affect how you reason about and recall other sets of objects you encounter, even in contexts that have nothing to do with communication.

Another way in which language could affect thought is that it could provide an alternative representational format for the storage of information. Imagine seeing a cluttered room and then, much later, having to remember what was in it. A creature without language could access only its visual memory of the scene, but a creature with language might also be able to access a linguistic description that was generated when the room was first seen—something that might make a substantial difference.

So language *could*, at least in principle, have an influence on nonlinguistic thought. But does it? The problem with radical linguistic determinism is its premise that human thought is unstructured prior to language. This just isn't true; as reviewed in previous chapters, babies have a rich mental life. For instance, they know a lot about objects. They expect them to continue to exist even when they go out of sight, can predict their trajectories, can determine the numerosities of small arrays of objects, and can compute the results of simple additions and subtractions performed over these arrays. They do *not* see the world as a "kaleidoscopic flux of impressions" (or the "blooming buzzing confusion" of William James). And so Whorf was wrong when he said that the categories we see in the world do not "stare every observer in the face." Actually, at least some of them do.

Cross-Linguistic Differences

Whorf and Sapir were most interested in the effects of cross-linguistic variation on adult cognition. If our thoughts are shaped by language, and if languages differ in major ways, it follows that adult speakers of different languages should differ in how they think.

Under the most plausible version of this view, this effect of language applies to conscious experience. For instance, one might be able to unconsciously distinguish different types of dogs but only consciously attend to this distinction on hearing the types described with different words. Or perhaps continued use of a language in which verbs differ according to the shape of the object that is acted on (as in Navajo, in which one verb is used for describing the giving of a long thin object like a stick and another for a spherical object like a rock) might lead language users to think about object shape, more so than they would if using a language like English that doesn't make such a distinction.

Does this actually happen? Whorf presented several case studies that were said to support this view. Most famously, he suggested that Hopi speakers, just by virtue of having learned Hopi, think about time and space in a very different way than speakers of languages such as English. Part of the attraction of this claim is its cultural generosity. Whorf claimed that, as a result of the languages that they have learned, individuals in Western societies have a stodgy and linear Newtonian perspective on space and time, while the Hopi have an up-to-date funky Einsteinian view. The Hopi are natural physicists; we are not.

Whorf's empirical claims have not weathered well. On more careful scrutiny, the languages are not nearly as dissimilar as Whorf made them out to be (Malotki, 1983). Furthermore, Whorf never actually presented evidence that Hopi think any differently about time and space than Americans do; he simply came to this conclusion that they *must*— because, after all, their languages are different (Brown, 1958b). This sort of circular reasoning is not unprecedented in contemporary discussions of linguistic determinism. Gregory Murphy (1996, p. 183) provides the following parody:

> *Whorfian:* Eskimos are greatly influenced by their language in their perception of snow. For example, they have N words for snow [N varies widely; see Pullum, 1991], whereas English only has one, *snow*. Having all these different words makes them think of snow very differently than, say, Americans do.
>
> *Skeptic:* How do you know they think of snow differently?
>
> *Whorfian:* Look at all the words they have for it! N of them!

Subsequent psychological research has provided little support for the Whorfian hypothesis in domains such as the perception of color and counterfactual reasoning. Such studies have found either that speakers of different language have identical nonlinguistic capacities (e.g., Au, 1983; Brown, 1958b) or that they differ only in tasks that are themselves language dependent, such as those that rely on explicit verbal memory of words (e.g., Kay & Kempton, 1984). As a result, many psychologists have viewed the Whorfian claim as being decisively refuted.

More recent studies are sometimes said to resuscitate the Whorfian view. Lucy and Gaskins (in press) report a series of experiments in which subjects are shown a target object and two alternatives—one of the same shape but a different material from the target, the other of a different shape and the same material. When simply asked which of the alternatives was most similar to the target—without the introduction of any novel word—the dominant response by English-speaking adults is to choose the object of the same shape. Such findings support the claim that adults have a bias toward shape in object categorization (see chapter 6). But Lucy and Gaskins also tested native speakers of Yucatec Maya, a classifier language spoken in southeastern Mexico. These adults did not show the same shape bias; instead, they tended to generalize to the material match.

Lucy and Gaskins suggest that this is an effect of language: English describes the shape match using the same word that describes the target, while Yucatec describes the substance match with the same expression. For instance, a long thin candle would usually be described in English as *candle*, a word that would be extended to other entities on the basis of shape and function. But the same candle would be described in Yucatec with a classifier plus a mass noun, an expression akin to "one-long-thin wax," and this mass noun would be extended to other entities on the basis of substance. It might be, then, that judgments of similarity are affected by the language one knows.

But other ways can be found to explain these findings. One is that subjects explicitly use their linguistic knowledge when doing such a task. That is, they use the strategy of naming the target object to themselves and then look toward the other objects and see which gets the same name. Alternatively, the effect might be due to cultural factors independent of language; these might have to do with how people from different cultures behave when asked to make similarity judgments or (more interestingly) might reflect differences in how they think about simple artifacts. The reason to favor such alternatives is that Lucy and Gaskins also tested seven-year-olds on the same task and found no difference across the two groups: *all* subjects showed a strong shape bias. Since the seven-year-olds already know English and Yucatec, this suggests that the adult difference is not an effect of language.

Another set of studies has been carried out by Steven Levinson (1996). When describing the spatial relations between objects, languages typically use multiple frames of reference and choose the frame according to the situation. Dutch, like English, tends to use either an *intrinsic* frame that employs the spatial properties of objects in the scene (as in "The boy is in front of the truck") or a *relative* frame based on the viewer's own position (as in "The boy is to the left of the truck"). But this is not universal. A dialect of Tzeltal, a Mayan language spoken in the community of Tenejapa within Chiapas, Mexico, uses an *absolute* system. The Tenejapans describe the spatial relations between objects using three main expressions: *downhill* (roughly north), *uphill* (roughly south), and *across* (roughly, east and west). So the same situation that would be described by a Dutch speaker as the equivalent of "The boy is in front of me" might be described by a Tzeltal speaker as the equivalent of "The boy is uphill of me." Phrases such as "Take the first right turn" are simply untranslatable into Tzeltal; that language has no way to express spatial notions that are entirely independent of absolute location.

Levinson predicted that Dutch speakers would think about objects in close proximity in terms of relative notions like right and left, while Tzeltal speakers would think about them in terms of absolute notions such as north and south. In one study, four toy animals (cow, pig, horse, sheep) were placed on a table in a random order—such as in left-to-right order or in north-to-south order. Subjects were asked to remember the array, were rotated 180 degrees to face another table, and were asked to recreate the array "exactly as it was." Dutch speakers tended to preserve relative order; they would put cow, pig, horse, and sheep on the table in left-to-right order. The Tenejapans tended to do the opposite: they violated relative order but preserved absolute location by putting the sheep, horse, pig, and cow on the table, in left-to-right order.

In another study, Tenejapan subjects were asked to face north and then shown a cartoon in which movement occurred from east to west. The subjects were then moved to another room and asked to tell someone else about the cartoon, and their spontaneous gestures were surreptitiously observed. Unlike Dutch subjects, who preserved the relative direction of the movement (left to right), the Tenejapans tended to preserve the absolute east-to-west movement in their gestures, and so they either gestured from right-to-left or left-to-right, *depending on which direction they were facing when telling the story.*

It is unlikely that such results are due to the conscious use of linguistic strategies, and so Levinson (1996, p. 125) concludes that "The frame of reference dominant in the language, whether relative or absolute, comes to bias the choice of frame of reference in various kinds of nonlinguistic conceptual representation."

Just as with the Lucy and Gaskins studies, however, one needs to rule out the possibility that some third factor explains both the linguistic and the nonlinguistic differences between members of the two cultures. It might be, for instance, that the physical environment in which the Tenejapans live encourages *both* the use of an absolute spatial system in Tzeltal *and* an absolute spatial encoding of objects, but that there is no direct effect of learning Tzeltal on the Tenejapans' spatial thought.

It is not impossible to rule out this alternative; more convincing would be research into the potential effects of linguistic variation in human groups from more similar physical and cultural environments, such as between English and Japanese speakers raised in Japan or between English and Spanish speakers in the United States. Such research is in progress by Levinson and others.

But what if Levinson's explanation of these effects is right? That is, what if language per se, not culture, really causes the difference? This would be a striking finding, but it is important to acknowledge its scope. It would be a mistake to take this finding as showing that language somehow *creates* systems of spatial thought. After all, both relative and absolute systems are encoded in brain mechanisms that underlie the navigation of species other than humans and hence are independent of language (O'Keefe & Nadel, 1978; Peterson, Nadel, Bloom & Garrett, 1996). Furthermore, Dutch speakers can think in absolute terms, and Tzeltal speakers can think in relative terms (and, in Levinson's studies, some do): it is just that they tend not to. If language does have a role to play in spatial cognition, then, it is not in creating new ways of thinking of space but in determining which of the available methods of spatial thought gets used the most.

Inner Speech

A related version of linguistic determinism focuses on what is sometimes called *inner speech,* though deaf signers have a visual equivalent called *inner sign.* Under this view, the inner voices some of us perceive as we think actually reflect processes of thought. To put it in a more formal way, the acquisition of a natural language may give rise to an alternative representational medium with which to carry out certain computations. Babies have only a language of thought; adults have a language of thought plus a natural language such as English.

The most obvious use of inner speech is in cognitive tasks related to language, such as planning what to write or imagining what someone else will say in the course of a conversation. But many scholars have argued that inner speech plays a larger role. Peter Carruthers (1996) has suggested that certain types of thought, such as causal reasoning and social cognition, require the support of an internalized natural language. For instance, when I try to anticipate the reactions the behavior of others (how will Jane react if I don't go to her party?), I might do so in *English;* a language of thought is not sufficient. Similar proposals have been made by Dennett (1996) and Vygotsky (1962).

It is clear that knowledge of a natural language cannot be necessary for all causal and social reasoning, since nonlinguistic creatures, such as babies and chimpanzees, have competence in these domains and, if the arguments in chapter 3 are correct, some social reasoning capacities are necessary to explain how word learning starts in the first place. But certain limitations on the part of children might be explained by this proposal, particularly with regard to complex tasks involving theory of mind.

Consider the false-belief task (Wimmer & Perner, 1983). In one version of this, the experimenter shows children a Smarties container (the American equivalent to Smarties is M&Ms) and shakes the container, making a rattling noise. The children are asked "What is inside?" and they inevitably reply "Smarties." Then the container is opened, and they are shown that it actually contains small pencils. They are then asked how another child who has not seen the opened container will answer when he is asked the same question "What is inside?" By the age of about four, children answer as do adults, saying "Smarties." But younger children tend to answer "pencils" and will give the same answer when asked what they themselves had previously thought was in the container before it was opened (Perner, Leekham & Wimmer, 1987).

The explanation for this developmental difference is a matter of some debate, and many scholars have blamed children's difficulties with task demands, not actual lack of competence (e.g., Leslie, 1994). But Carruthers raises the possibility that young children's poor performance is due to their failure to encode the situation into natural language (see also de Villiers & de Villiers, 1997).

Evidence from adult aphasics is relevant here (Varley, in press). Many aphasics suffer from serious cognitive impairments. This could be due to an intrinsic connection between language and thought or to anatomical accident because lesions that damage language might damage other capacities. But other aphasics demonstrate a dissociation between language and thought. They give the impression of being rational people struggling to communicate. They are not retarded or deranged but instead act as we would act if our primary ability to communicate was stripped from us. They can find their way around, use tools, drive cars, and show appropriate behavior in social situations. As one would expect, they are frustrated by their problems with language and try to compensate by communicating in other ways, such as drawing and gesture. In some cases, their impairment extends to inner speech, as indirect evidence suggests that some aphasics lack the subjective experience of an inner voice in their heads (e.g., Goodglass, Denes & Calderon, 1974).

Such cases provide an excellent opportunity to explore Carruther's claim. Rosemary Varley (in press) tested a severely aphasic man on tasks involving causal reasoning and an understanding of false beliefs (a variant of the Smarties task above). He was unable to produce or comprehend anything more than strings of isolated words, but he nonetheless did perfectly well at such tasks. This doesn't show that language is irrelevant for the understanding of these notions (after all, he had *once* had language). But it does suggest that the online computation of causal and intentional inferences does not require the possession of a natural language.

The inner-voice proposal might be right about one domain, however. It was argued in the last chapter, following Dehaene (1997), that the ability to reason about the larger numbers—to understand, for instance, that if you remove two objects from 20 objects, 18 will remain—is impossible without the possession of a natural language. This makes a prediction about acquisition: only people who have learned a generative number system can reason about these larger numbers. But a stronger version of this theory makes the prediction that only people who can *access* the language of numbers can reason about them. Without language, all that remains is the approximate accumulator mechanism that humans share with rats and other animals.

If so, then the man with aphasia studied by Varley (assuming that he lacks the linguistic number system) should find it impossible to judge, for instance, the precise number of pencils that would remain if he was presented with an array of 20 and then saw two of them removed. In fact, there is evidence for a clinical dissociation between precise numerical reasoning (arguably the product of language) versus approximate numerical reasoning (arguably the product of the accumulator mechanism) (Dehaene, 1997). But as yet no evidence bears on the important issue of whether the loss of the number words has a specific effect on precise numerical reasoning.

Language and Concepts

A different way in which language can affect thought is not by shifting one's focus of attention or creating a new format for mental computation but by actually creating new concepts. Many developmental psychologists propose that exposure to words might serve to establish the boundaries of novel concepts (e.g., Bowerman, 1996; Gentner & Boroditsky, in press; Gopnik & Meltzoff, 1987, 1997; Waxman & Markow, 1995; Waxman & Thompson, 1998).

What would count as evidence for this proposal? It is important to distinguish between showing that words can create categories and showing that they can draw attention to existing ones. For instance, Markman and Hutchinson (1984) find that if you show young children a novel object and just say "See this one. Find another one," they will typically choose something that has a spatial or thematic relationship to that object, such as finding a bone to go with a dog. But if you use a new word, as with "See this fendle. Find another fendle," they typically seek something from the same category, such as another dog.

This shows that the presence of a word can motivate categorization. But, of course, the children *already* know that the two dogs belong to the same category; the concept of dog exists prior to their hearing the new word. As Markman and Hutchinson conclude, the role of the word is to tell the child that the category, and not some spatial or thematic relationship, is relevant in this context. It draws attention to a category already in the child's mind; it doesn't cause one to exist.

More generally, abundant evidence shows that hearing words (and later, hearing words that belong to certain syntactic categories) can draw children's attention to kinds. But more is needed to show a causal role of language on concept formation. To take a trivial example, babies who suffer from recurrent ear infections sometimes have an operation in which tubes are put in their ears to drain out fluid. I used to call these "tubes in the ears," but, on talking with a pediatrician, I learned that they actually have a name; they are *grommets*. Learning this word didn't motivate the creation of a new concept. I already knew about the category; I just didn't know its name. If all word learning worked like this, there would be no interesting sense in which words shape or create novel concepts.

It is sometimes argued that cross-linguistic differences in spatial language do have a corresponding effect on spatial cognition. Consider a cup on a table, a handle on a door, and an apple in a bowl. In English, the first two are deemed to be in the same relationship—contact and support—described with the spatial preposition *on*, while the third relationship of containment is described by *in*. But Finnish treats the handle on the door and the apple in the bowl as instantiating the same relationship (collapsing both containment and attachment as highly intimate relations), which is distinct from the support relationship present in the cup on the table. Dutch names each of the three relationships with a different expression, and Spanish collapses them all into a single expression.

Melissa Bowerman (1996) reports a series of studies suggesting that, in this spatial domain and in others, children very quickly come to grasp the specific spatial system to which they are exposed. She concludes (p. 422) that "We have to appeal to a process of learning in which children *build* spatial semantic categories in response to the distribution of spatial morphemes across contexts in the languages that they hear."

This is one interpretation of the results. But Mandler (1996) points out another. Perhaps multiple nonlinguistic categorization schemes serve to carve up space and are available to children. Language learning involves not creating new semantic categories but establishing the conventional mappings between the words of a given language and the particular spatial categorization scheme to which they correspond. To take a potentially parallel example, an array of objects could be talked about in many ways—the red ones versus the blue ones, the squares versus the circles, the wet ones versus the dry ones. Suppose a child quickly learned all of these categorization schemes; she learned the words *red, square, wet,* and so on. This would not prove that the concepts were "built" through interaction with language, as the notions of red, square, wet, and so on could possibly have been available prior to the learning of the words. The same point holds if three children are each learning a different language—one that has only the words *red* and *blue,* another that has only *square* and *circle,* and a third that has only *wet* and *dry.* If each of the children quickly learns the words of their language, this *might* be because language is shaping thought—but it could also mean that the concepts are there already and that languages differ in the concepts that they have words for. By the same token, then, children's quick learning of distinct spatial expressions does not show that language shapes spatial cognition.

This alternative is plausible only to the extent that one doesn't have to posit a new set of nonlinguistic spatial notions for every language we look at; the variation that exists should be highly constrained (see Bowerman, 1996; Landau & Jackendoff, 1993). It would also bear on this issue if there was evidence for these putatively non linguistic spatial categories in babies and in other species. I see this as an open question. It might turn out that Bowerman's conclusion is correct; the point here is that the rapid acquisition of different spatial systems is not decisive evidence in favor of it.

Susan Gelman and her colleagues have done several studies that bear directly on the question of how words influence conceptual structure. As discussed in chapter 6, Gelman and Markman (1986, 1987) found that sameness of category can override sameness of appearance when children are inferring hidden properties that objects possess. For instance, children were told that a brontosaurus has one property (cold blood) and a rhinoceros has another property (warm blood) and were then asked which property a triceratops has. Both the brontosaurus and the triceratops were described as belonging to same kind: they were both described as "dinosaurs." Under these conditions, children tend to infer that the triceratops has cold blood, even though it looks more like the warm-blooded rhinoceros.

One concern, however, is that children might draw the same inference even if they hadn't been given the labels. Children's assumption that the brontosaurus and the triceratops have the same sort of blood might be based solely on their knowledge that both are dinosaurs; their having the same label might have been irrelevant. Davidson and Gelman (1990) explored this issue in a series of experiments in which four- and five-year-olds were taught hidden properties of *unfamiliar* animals. In one condition, the target animal was given a familiar label (such as "cow"). Children tended to generalize the hidden properties to other animals that were given the same label, even if these animals were perceptually dissimilar from the target (see also Gelman & Coley, 1990). This shows that language really does affect children's categorization; it can serve as a cue that different objects belong to the same kind.

In another condition, however, the animals were given novel labels. For instance, the target animal might be described as "This is a zav. This zav has four stomachs." Then children would be shown other animals some which were "zavs," others which were "traws"—and asked which of these also have four stomachs. The results were surprising. When the objects were perceptually dissimilar, there was no effect of sameness of label. In other words, if two objects didn't look alike, then their having the same novel name did not motivate children to treat them as belonging to the same category.

This caution about using words as a cue to conceptual structure makes sense. After all, there is an excellent reason for children *not* to automatically assume that if two objects get the same name, then they belong to the same category. One word (or more precisely, one phonological string) can correspond to many concepts. Flying mammals and instruments for hitting baseballs are both *bats*, and so a child who had the assumption of same-word-equals-same-concept would end up with a strange concept indeed. Because of this, children cannot lean too heavily on words; hearing two objects receive the same name might be a *cue* that they belong to the same category, but it is not definitive.

I don't want to be overly skeptical here. After all, Davidson and Gelman looked at only basic-level kinds; it might be that words play more of a role for subordinate kinds. These carry more information than basic-level kinds (at the cost of being harder to tell apart) and are more associated with expertise in a given domain (Murphy & Lassaline, 1997). As an example, consider going to a wine-tasting class. If you are a wine novice, all wines might taste pretty much the same, and might be categorized, and named, solely as *wine*. But because linguistic cues are repeatedly provided in the context in this class—"This is a *Merlot*, this is a *Beaujolais*"; "This is *dry*, this is *sweet*"—you might come to organize the "flux of impressions" that you experience into discrete categories and to appreciate the ways in which wines differ. As a result, you can acquire the functional ability to distinguish the wines and also come to have a different, richer, phenomenal experience of their taste (though see Solomon, 1997, for an alternative view).

It might be that wine-tasting classes really do have such effects, at least sometimes, and that language plays an important causal role. After all, evidence suggests that exposure to category labels in artificial learning tasks can increase one's sensitivity to certain perceptual properties (Goldstone, 1994), and that the mere presence of labels causes people to exaggerate differences between groups (Tajfel & Wilkes, 1963). But note there is nothing special about words in this situation; any other distinctive signal would work as well. One might run a wine class by holding up different colored cards to denote the different wines or putting them in distinctively shaped glasses. Words are just particularly convenient ways of drawing distinctions; there is nothing magical about them.

The argument so far can be summed up as follows. It is often proposed that the words we learn guide our patterns of habitual thought (as in the domain of spatial reasoning), enable us to perform abstract inferences (as in the domain of theory of mind), and help us carve the external world into distinct categories (as in the domain of object categorization). Such proposals might be true, but as yet no strong evidence exists for any of them. Instead, we find that spatial reasoning, theory of mind, and object categorization can all apply independently of language.

None of this is to deny that exposure to language can create new concepts. This would be crazy; *of course* it can. If you are a hockey novice, you might not know what a hat trick is. Someone might helpfully tell you that "A hat trick is when someone scores three goals in a row," and now you know. What goes on here? You didn't already have the notion of hat trick and simply learn what it was called; this isn't like the *grommet* example above. Instead, the concept was created through the vehicle of language. As discussed in Chapter 8, this is likely to hold for the acquisition of many abstract words.

But this is not a Whorfian process in which words give structure to a previously undifferentiated conceptual space. The creation of new concepts instead results from language conveying ideas. It is not the *form* of language that causes the concepts to emerge; it is the *content* that the language conveys.

A World without Words

In the end, how important are words to thought? How far can one get without them? If you try to answer these questions by comparing normal language-using adults with babies and nonhuman animals, you risk overestimating the importance of words. After all, the limitations of babies and animals are due in part to factors other than language. On the other hand, studies of aphasics might lead one to underestimate the role of words. Aphasics *once* knew words, after all, and these might guide their structure of thought in the sense that blueprints guide the construction of a house: after the house is built, it doesn't matter if the blueprints are lost.

One way to explore this issue is to look at otherwise normal people who have never been exposed to a natural language. Some such cases arise through conditions of terrible neglect. These are so-called wild children, such as the Wild Boy of Aveyron, who was raised by animals in the woods (Lane, 1976), and Genie, who was kept in a closet until puberty by her mad father (Curtiss, 1977). But these wild children have been deprived of much more than language, and so the extent to which their cognitive limitations (which are often profound) are caused by other factors is unclear.

A better group to look at is congenitally deaf adults who have been raised within a hearing society and have grown up without exposure to sign language. As Oliver Sacks (1988) reviews, throughout much of European history, the languageless deaf were thought of as imbeciles. Many modern commentators would draw a similar conclusion. A deaf isolate is, in Sacks's own words, "severely restricted in the range of his thoughts, confined, in effect, to an immediate, small world" (p. 41). Others have said that such isolates lack the capacity for abstract thought (Church, 1961) or suffer from a (curable) form of mental retardation (Rapin, 1979).

This is not an unfounded view. Sacks describes Joseph, a boy who was born deaf and was misdiagnosed first as retarded and then as autistic. When his deafness was finally recognized, he was categorized as "deaf and dumb." No attempt was made to expose him to sign language. By the time Joseph was 11, he *was* retarded and showed no sign of any ability to cope with abstraction, to think about the past, or to plan the future. Such cases support the view that exposure to language is essential for abstract and mature cognition.

But two qualifications should be made. The first is that Joseph and others in a similar situation are often, like wild children, deprived of more than language. They also miss out on everything that language typically conveys. Susan Schaller (1991, pp. 35–36) discusses the plight of another deaf isolate named Ildefonso:

> Ildefonso was sane after twenty-seven years of a mental isolation worse than any solitary confinement in prison. His cell had open windows; he could experience everything in he world—touch it, feel it, taste it, watch it—but only in total isolation.

No one had ever agreed or disagreed with him, mirrored, confirmed, or argued with his impressions. He had only his own mind to connect experiences, find patterns, imagine meanings, and fit together semantic puzzles. Even with shared meaning, feedback, and help in interpreting the world, many people have trouble with reality. How does one stay sane when all interpretation is generated by one's self alone?

But as Schaller later discusses, there are means of communication other than language. People who have no language in common can make some progress at getting ideas across to one another. It is unclear how much of Joseph's plight really was inevitable and how much he would have benefited from the careful attention and support of people who might have used other means to communicate with him.

Second, it is hard to know what goes on in the mind of someone without language. Imagine suddenly being stripped of your ability to use and understand words, and consider how hard it would be to convince a skeptical audience of language users that you are capable of full-blown abstract thought. Who really knows what Joseph is thinking? This is the dilemma that arises more generally when studying people and animals without language. Often it is only when clever experimental studies are done—as with Varley's work with aphasics, Hauser's work with monkeys, or Spelke's work with babies—that one learns how smart these individuals really are.

One somewhat unusual source bears on the question of the abilities of people without language—autobiographical accounts. One interesting account came from the deaf artist and photographer, Theophilus d'Estrella, who did not acquire a formal sign language until the age of nine. After he had acquired language, he wrote a letter to William James that contained an account of his early experience. This letter described elaborate ruminations that he had had about religion and other matters. This greatly impressed James, who wrote (1893, p. 144), "His narrative tends to discountenance the notion that no abstract thought is possible without words. Abstract thought of a decidedly subtle kind, both scientific and moral, went on here in advance of the means of expressing it to others."

Helen Keller is also interesting in this regard. She became deaf and blind at 17 months of age. She most likely had learned several words by then, though the only word she remembered later was *water*. Keller learned no other language until the age of six, when she was first exposed to a tactile language by a talented and persistent teacher. She was later able to read and write, eventually attending college and writing several books, including an autobiography entitled *The Story of My Life* (1909).

Keller's autobiography is often cited as evidence for the position that no thought exists prior to language. After all, this was Keller's own view; she described herself "at sea in a dense fog" and doubted that her "wordless sensations" could really be called "thoughts." But I think that even a cursory reading of the events that Keller recounts from that period shows that her skepticism was misplaced. She was able to develop a simple nonlinguistic communication system, using both simple signs (nodding to mean yes, shaking her head for no, a pull meaning "come") and more complicated ones (shivering to request ice cream). She could anticipate future events, noticing when her mother dressed to go outside and demanding to join her. She soon learned that she was different from other people, that they somehow talked with their mouths—and the fact that she could not communicate this way caused her terrible frustration. She would play practical jokes, using a key to lock her mother in a pantry and laughing with glee as she pounded to get out. (Mother was rescued by servants hours later.)

Then there is the famous story of how Helen Keller (1909, pp. 23–24) came to realize that the proddings of her teacher were instances of the act of naming: "As the cool stream gushed over one hand she spelled into the other the word *water*, first slowly, and then rapidly. I stood still, my whole attention fixed upon the motions of her fingers. Suddenly I felt a misty consciousness as of something forgotten—a thrill of returning thought; and somehow the mystery of language was revealed to me. I knew then that w-a-t-e-r meant the wonderful cool something that was flowing over my hand."

"I learned a great many new words that day," she concludes. This story might not convince a skeptic. After all, it is reasonable to distrust autobiographical reports. Many of James's contemporaries rejected his conclusion for this reason, and both the d'Estrella and Keller autobiographies—like most autobiographies, from St. Augustine to Larry King—contain episodes that strain credulity. But as support, consider the testimony of her teacher, Anne Sullivan, from a letter she wrote on the next day (Keller, 1909, p. 316): "She has learned that *everything has a name, and that the manual alphabet is the key to everything she wants to know.* . . . All the way back to the house she was highly excited, and learned the name of every object she touched, so that in a few hours she had added thirty new words to her vocabulary. Here are some of them: Door, open, shut, give, go, come, and a great many more. . . . Helen got up this morning like a radiant fairy. She has flitted from object to object, asking the name of everything."

In a sense this episode is more impressive, and informative, than what occurs with word learning. Normal children go quite a while hearing words before starting to use them, and a Whorfian might argue that this early exposure provides the conceptual foundation for their own first words. And besides, when normal children first start to use words, these words are learned very gradually; no normal one-year-old has ever learned 30 words in a day. But Keller was a different story. In the years before her epiphany, she had been exposed to no words at all. And so her rapid learning of these tactile signs is clear evidence that the relevant concepts were already present in her mind.

Finally, Schaller (1991) studied adult deaf isolates in the United States, many of them illegal immigrants from Mexico. Some showed profound limitations in their cognitive and social abilities. But others, such as Ildefonso, did not; they showed all signs of possessing a rich mental life. They had elaborate spatial knowledge and skills, including the ability to repair complicated machinery, and they could handle money: in fact, some of them did well enough to live on their own. They could also describe events from the past, using pantomimed narratives.

In sum, no support can be found for the view that words are necessary for thought. Instead, a continuum of abilities includes some people without language who are like Joseph and others without language who are like Ildefonso. This shouldn't be surprising. Language is the main way we transmit and store culture. Unless one is lucky enough to be in a supportive community that can compensate for the lack of language, the results can be tragic.

A useful analogy can be made here with vision, which is also an excellent tool for the transfer of information. People who are blind find it harder than people who can see to pick up certain aspects of human culture because they lack the same access to books, diagrams, maps, television, and so on. And without a supportive community that provides alternative means of information transfer—such as Braille—blind people will lose out on social and cultural interaction, which might have cognitive consequences. But this does not mean that vision makes you smart or that explaining how vision evolves or develops is tantamount to explaining the evolution and development of abstract thought. Language may be useful in the same sense that vision is useful. It is a tool for the communication of ideas. It is not a mechanism that gives rise to the capacity to generate and appreciate these ideas in the first place.

This book can be seen as a long argument for just this conclusion. Consider the sorts of capacities that underlie early word learning—an understanding that the world contains objects, events, and relations, kinds and individuals; an appreciation that the nature of some categories does not reduce to their superficial features; an ability to appreciate the referential intentions of others, to understand what they are referring to when they communicate. These are precisely the abilities that many scholars have argued to be the products of language learning. But they are not: they are its prerequisites.

Words are not necessary for thought. Structured and abstract thought occurs without them. Words are important because they are the building blocks of language, and language allows us to express our thoughts and understand those of others—to become full-fledged members of the human community.

Chapter 11
Final Words

It looks simple. A 14-month-old toddles after the family dog, smacking it whenever she gets close. The dog wearily moves under the table. "Dog," the child's mother tells her. "You're chasing the dog. That's the dog." The child stops, points a pudgy hand at the dog, and shrieks, "Daw!" The mother smiles: "Yes, dog."

It looks simple—but it isn't. This book began with a discussion of why word learning requires cognitive capacities of considerable richness (chapter 1). These include the ability to learn and store arbitrary mappings (chapter 2), theory of mind (chapter 3), an understanding of concepts corresponding to kinds and individuals (chapters 4 to 7), and, for at least some words, an appreciation of syntactic cues to meaning (chapters 8 and 9). These abilities—with the exception of the appreciation of syntax—exist prior to language learning; they are not the result of it (chapter 10). This theory was applied to the acquisition of different kinds of words, including common nouns, pronouns, proper names, adjectives, verbs, number words, and (if only in passing) determiners and prepositions.

Most of the specific proposals made in the preceding chapters—for instance, about how children name visual representations or how they learn the precise meanings of the smaller number words—can be easily refuted or modified by further empirical work, and no doubt some of them will be. Also, as discussed in the first chapter, the more general position that children learn words by means of conceptual, social, and linguistic capacities that are not special to the task of word learning is also falsifiable.

There are two ways in which this position could be wrong. It might attribute too much to young children. For instance, the findings of Dare Baldwin, Eve Clark, and Michael Tomasello might be better explained in terms of capacities that do not involve theory of mind. (It would be decisive evidence for such an alternative if some children with severe theory of mind deficits had little or no problems with word learning.) Alternatively, this account might err in the opposite direction: perhaps it attributes too little to young children. Perhaps, as proposed by scholars such as Roberta Golinkoff, Kathy Hirsh-Pasek, and Linda Smith, once children begin to acquire words, they quickly come to learn special biases or constraints that make them more effective learners. Or, as Ellen Markman and Sandra Waxman have suggested, some such constraints or biases might be necessary for word learning to start in the first place.

It should be stressed that contemporary theories of word learning, including the one outlined in this book, are—to put it kindly—in their initial stages. Nobody knows how children learn the meanings of words. Any adequate theory needs to cover a range of phenomena that have been ignored in this book and in most of the literature as well. The most obvious one concerns word learning in languages that differ radically from English. In the course of this book, I have reviewed the available cross-linguistic research, but we know little about how this process works in languages such as Yucatec Mayan, in which all names are similar to English mass nouns, or in agglutinating languages such as Turkish, in which complex meanings can be conveyed through the formation of novel words.

Then there is the question of the effect of cultural differences. We know, for instance, that children who are raised in environments in which they are not explicitly taught words nevertheless come to develop language, but, as Elena Lieven (1994) stresses, we know little about *how* they do so. Are some words harder to learn, and some easier? Do certain systematic misinterpretations emerge in the absence of careful tutelage?

And what about the different words themselves? The majority of word-learning experiments are restricted to artifact names (names for real-world artifacts such as chairs or novel objects created by experimenters), natural kind terms (usually animal names), and verbs that describe physical actions. This happens in part because it is relatively easy to teach new words that fall into these kinds. But relatively little experimental research has explored how children learn other parts of speech, such as connectives and modals. What cues do children use when learning such words? What sorts of constraints exist on their meanings?

Another domain worth exploring is the learning of words that refer to abstract entities within structured domains (like the names for the days of the week or the names for the individuals, activities, and properties that have to do with games like hockey, such as *goalie, puck, checking,* and *period*). A particularly interesting domain is the acquisition of moral terms like *fair* and *wrong.* An examination of how children learn such words would enlighten us not only about language development but also about the nature and development of moral thought. But with the exception of a fascinating discussion by Macnamara (1991), this domain of word learning has been ignored in the developmental literature.

A final question is how children cope with polysemy. When children hear *bat* used to describe a baseball bat and *bat* used to describe a flying mammal, they come to know that these are different words, but when they hear *bird* used to describe a robin and *bird* used to describe a pelican, they come to know it is the same word. How? This might seem like a technical concern, but, as discussed in the previous chapter, it is intimately related to the deeper issue of how the learning of words might shape and modify concepts in the course of cognitive development.

An adequate theory of word learning should not only be broader; it must be deeper. One needs to say more about the capacities that underlie this process—how they develop, how they are instantiated in the brain, and how they evolve. Perhaps the most needs to be said about the role of theory of mind, which is a domain that includes everything from the ability to track eye gaze to an understanding of sarcasm. Some of this is necessary for word learning, but some of it plainly isn't: two-year-olds (as well as certain older autistic children) are able to learn words, even though they may lack the full understanding of other minds that older children and adults possess (see chapter 3). An important question, then, concerns the precise nature of the theory-of-mind capacities that are essential for different types of word learning.

Hedgehogs and Foxes

Isaiah Berlin (1954) used the distinction between hedgehogs and foxes to distinguish two sorts of theories. A hedgehog does one thing and does it well: it has quills for protection. In contrast, a fox succeeds by doing many things and modifying its behavior according to the situation. Berlin suggested that some philosophers approach the world in a hedgehog way and that others are more foxlike in their theorizing.

Michael Maratsos and Gedeon Deák (1995) maintain that the same distinction can be applied to psychological processes. Hedgehog processes are well captured by algorithms and involve a relatively small set of capacities; fox processes are harder to make explicit and involve a relatively large and diverse set of capacities. Most models of syntax, and particularly parameter-setting theory of syntax acquisition, involve hedgehog processes, while theories of discourse tend to be much more foxlike. Looking at the extremes, a reflex is very hedgehog; making up a joke is exceedingly fox.

Maratsos and Deák point out that most contemporary theories of word learning see it as a hedgehog process. As examples of this, they discuss the work of theorists who posit dedicated constraints on word learning, such as the whole object and mutual exclusivity assumptions proposed by Ellen Markman. But a very different hedgehog proposal is made by Linda Smith and her colleagues (1996), who posit that "dumb attentional mechanisms" underlie word learning, at least in young children. They explicitly reject the foxlike alternative that children sometimes engage in "slower, more conscious and deliberate weighting and ignoring of different aspects of the situation" (Gelman & Medin, 1993, p. 164).

Why do so many scholars from diverse theoretical perspectives expect word learning to be a hedgehog process? As Smith et al. (1996) note, one advantage of such processes is that they tend to be fast and accurate; they avoid Hamlet's problem of becoming lost in deep thought (see also Fodor, 1983). Given how good children are at learning words, then, it is reasonable to propose that they do so through simple encapsulated mechanisms. It might be, as proposed by Maratsos and Deák, that hedgehog processes work for an important subset of words—basic-level object names, words like *dog* and *chair*. Fox processes apply for all the rest of the lexicon—words such as *story*, *game*, and *dreaming*, which are harder to learn and less constrained by perceptual systems.

The view defended in this book is quite different. Word learning is never done through a hedgehog process. No constraints, biases, or assumptions are special to figuring out the meanings of words, and word learning is not a mental organ, module, or instinct. Even the learning of basic-level object names involves the exercise of foxlike capacities, including an understanding of the referential intentions of others.

How can we reconcile this foxlike complexity with the legendary speed and efficiency of children's word learning? Well, as discussed in chapters 2 and 3, children's speed and efficiency are sometimes overstated. Children are impressive word learners, but their abilities develop over the course of years, reaching their peak sometime in adolescence. Just like the exercise of other foxlike processes—everything from planning a vacation to understanding a joke—the ability to learn new words improves with practice.

Developmental psychologists have another reason for being so enamored with hedgehog processes. Just as it is easier to understand the activities of a hedgehog than those of a fox, the successful theories in psychology tend to address hedgehog capacities such as reflexes, low-level vision, and phonological processing. We know considerably less about fox capacities such as constructing explanations, choosing friends, and making up jokes. It would be better for psychologists if word learning—and language development more generally—actually was a hedgehog process and could be explained through a small set of special constraints or the workings of a simple connectionist network. But as has often been pointed out, the human mind was not created for the convenience of psychologists.

My view is that a complete theory of word learning will develop in the context of an understanding of other aspects of human mental life, including how we think about material and abstract entities and how we reason about the thoughts of other people. The good news is that the opposite is also true: the study of how children learn the meanings of words promises to tell us a great deal about the nature and development of the human mind.

References

Adams, A.K., & Bullock, D. (1985). Apprenticeship in word use: Social convergence processes in learning categorically related nouns. In S.A. Kuczaj & M.D. Barrett (Eds.), *The development of word meaning*. New York: Springer-Verlag.

Adamson, L.B., Tomasello, M., & Benbisty, L.L. (1984). An "expressive" infant's communicative development. Paper presented at the International Conference on Infant Studies, New York.

Aitchinson, J. (1994). *Words in the mind: An introduction to the mental lexicon* (2nd ed.). Oxford: Blackwell.

Akhtar, N., Dunham, F., & Dunham, P.J. (1991). Directive interactions and early vocabulary development: The role of joint attentional focus. *Journal of Child Language, 18,* 41–49.

Amis, K. (1994). *You can't do both*. London: Random House.

Andersen, E.A., Dunlea, A., & Kekelis, L.S. (1983). Blind children's language: Resolving some differences. *Journal of Child Language, 11,* 645–666.

Andersen, E.S. (1978). Lexical universals of body-part terminology. In J. Greenberg (Ed.), *Universals of human language*, Vol. 3, *Word structure*. Stanford, CA: Stanford University Press.

Anglin, J. (1993). Vocabulary development: A morphological analysis. *Monographs of the Society for Research in Child Development, 58* (10, Serial No. 238), 1–166.

Aristotle (1941). *Metaphysics*. In R. McKeon (Ed.), *Basic Works of Aristotle*. New York: Random House.

Armstrong, S.L., Gleitman, L.R., & Gleitman, H.G. (1983). On what some concepts might not be. *Cognition, 13,* 263–308.

Asperger, H. (1944). Die Autistichen Psychopathen' im Kindesalter. *Archiv fur Psychiatrie Nervenkrankheiten, 117,* 76–136 [translated by Uta Frith in U. Frith, (1991), *Autism and Asperger's syndrome*. Cambridge: Cambridge University Press].

Atran, S. (1998). Folk biology and the anthropology of science: Cognitive universals and cultural particulars. *Behavioral and Brain Sciences, 21,* 547–609.

Au, T.K. (1983). Chinese and English counterfactuals: The Sapir-Whorf hypothesis revisited. *Cognition, 15,* 155–187.

Au, T.K., Dapretto, M., & Song, Y-K. (1994). Input vs. constraints: Early word acquisition in Korean and English. *Journal of Memory and Language, 33,* 567–582.

Au, T.K., & Glusman, M. (1990). The principle of mutual exclusivity in word learning: To honor or not to honor? *Child Development, 61,* 1474–1490.

Augustine, St. (398/1961). *The Confessions of Saint Augustine*. New York: Random House.

Baillargeon, R., Spelke, E.S., & Wasserman, S. (1985). Object permanence in five-month-old infants. *Cognition, 20,* 191–208.

Baldwin, D.A. (1989). Priorities in children's expectations about object label reference: Form over color. *Child Development, 60,* 1289–1306.

Baldwin, D.A. (1991). Infants' contribution to the achievement of joint reference. *Child Development, 62,* 875–890.

Baldwin, D.A. (1992). Clarifying the role of the shape assumption. *Journal of Experimental Child Psychology, 54,* 392–416.

Baldwin, D.A. (1993a). Early referential understanding: Infants' ability to recognize referential acts for what they are. *Developmental Psychology, 29,* 832–843.

Baldwin, D.A. (1993b). Infants' ability to consult the speaker for clues to word reference. *Journal of Child Language, 20,* 395–418.

Baldwin, D.A. (1995). Understanding relations between constraints and a socio-pragmatic account of meaning acquisition. Paper presented at the Biennial Meeting of the Society for Research in Child Development, Indianapolis, Indiana.

Baldwin, D.A., Bill, B., & Ontai, L.L. (1996). Infant's tendency to monitor other's gaze: Is it rooted in intentional understanding or a result of simple orienting? Paper presented at the Tenth Biennial International Conference on Infant Studies, Providence, RI.

Baldwin, D.A., Markman, E.M., Bill, B., Desjardins, R.N., Irwin, J.M., & Tidball, G. (1996). Infants' reliance on a social criterion for establishing word-object relations. *Child Development, 67,* 3135–3153.

Baldwin, D.A., & Moses, L.M. (1994). Early understanding of referential intent and attentional focus: Evidence from language and emotion. In C. Lewis & P. Mitchell (Eds.), *Children's early understanding of mind: Origins and development.* Hillsdale, NJ: Erlbaum.

Baron-Cohen, S. (1995). *Mindblindness: An essay on autism and theory of mind.* Cambridge, MA: MIT Press.

Baron-Cohen, S., Baldwin, D.A., & Crowson, M. (1997). Do children with autism use the speaker's direction of gaze strategy to crack the code of language? *Child Development, 68,* 48–57.

Baron-Cohen, S., Leslie, A.M., & Frith, U. (1985). Does the autistic child have a "theory of mind"? *Cognition, 21,* 37–46.

Barwise, J., & Cooper, R. (1981). Generalized quantifiers and natural language. *Linguistics and Philosophy, 4,* 159–219.

Bates, E., Bretherton, I., & Snyder, L. (1988). *From first words to grammar: Individual differences and dissociable mechanisms.* Cambridge: Cambridge University Press.

Bates, E., & Carnevale, G.F. (1993). New directions in research on language development. *Developmental Review, 13,* 436–470.

Bates, E., Marchman, V., Thal, D., Fenson, L., Dale, P., Reznick, J.S., Reilly, J., & Hartung, J.P. (1994). Developmental and stylistic variation in the composition of early vocabulary. *Journal of Child Language, 21,* 85–124.

Beal, C.R., & Flavell, J.H. (1984). Demonstration of the ability to distinguish communicative intention and literal message meaning. *Child Development, 55,* 920–928.

Beals, D.E. (1998). Sources of support for learning words in conversation: Evidence from mealtimes. *Journal of Child Language, 24,* 673–694.

Beals, D.E., & Tabors, P.O. (1995). Arboretum, beurocratic, and carbohydrates: Preschooler's exposure to rare vocabulary at home. *First Language, 15,* 57–76.

Becker, A.H., & Ward, T.B. (1991). Children's use of shape in extending novel labels to animate objects: Identity versus postural change. *Cognitive Development, 6,* 3–16.

Behrend, D.A. (1990). Constraints and development: A reply to Nelson (1988). *Cognitive Development, 5,* 313–330.

Beilin, H., & Pearlman, E.G. (1991). Children's iconic realism: Object vs. property realism. In H.W. Reese (Ed.), *Advances in child development and behavior* (Vol. 23). New York: Academic Press.

Bellugi, U., Marks, S., Bihrle, A.M., & Sabo, H. (1988). Dissociation between language and cognitive functions in Williams syndrome. In D. Bishop & K. Mogford (Eds.), *Language development in exceptional circumstances.* London: Churchill Livingstone.

Benedict, H. (1979). Early lexical development: Comprehension and production. *Journal of Child Language, 6,* 183–200.

Berlin, B., & Kay, P. (1969). *Basic color terms: Their universality and evolution.* Berkeley: University of California Press.

Berlin, I. (1954). *The hedgehog and the fox.* London: Weidenfeld & Nicholson.

Bickerton, D. (1995). *Language and human behavior.* Seattle: University of Washington Press.

Biederman, I. (1987). Recognition-by-components: A theory of human image understanding. *Psychological Review, 94,* 115–147.

Blewitt, P. (1983). *Dog* versus *collie:* Vocabulary in speech to young children. *Developmental Psychology, 19,* 602–609.

Block, N. (1986). Advertisement for a semantics for psychology. In P.A. Rench, T.E. Uehling, Jr. & H.K. Wettstein (Eds.), *Midwest Studies in Philosophy,* Vol. 10, *Studies in the Philosophy of Mind.* Minneapolis: University of Minnesota Press.

Bloom, L. (1970). *Language development: Form and function in emerging grammars.* Cambridge, MA: MIT Press.

Bloom, L. (1973). *One word at a time: The use of single word utterances before syntax.* The Hague: Mouton.

Bloom, L. (1993). *The transition from infancy to language: Acquiring the power of expression.* New York: Cambridge University Press.

Bloom, L. (1994). Meaning and expression. In W. Overton & D. Palermo (Eds.), *The ontogenesis of meaning.* Hillsdale, NJ: Erlbaum.

Bloom, L., Hood, L., & Lightbown, P. (1974). Imitation in language development: If, when and why. *Cognitive Psychology, 6,* 380–420.

Bloom, L., Tinker, E., & Margulis, C. (1993). The words children learn: Evidence against a noun bias in early vocabularies. *Cognitive Development, 8,* 431–450.

Bloom, P. (1990). Syntactic distinctions in child language. *Journal of Child Language, 17,* 343–355.

Bloom, P. (1994a). Generativity within language and other cognitive domains. *Cognition, 51,* 177–189.

Bloom, P. (1994b). Possible names: The role of syntax-semantics mappings in the acquisition of nominals. *Lingua, 92,* 297–329.

Bloom, P. (1994c). Semantic competence as an explanation for some transitions in language development. In Y. Levy (Ed.), *Other children, other languages: Issues in the theory of language acquisition.* Hillsdale, NJ: Erlbaum.

Bloom, P. (1996a). Intention, history, and artifact concepts. *Cognition, 60,* 1–29.

Bloom, P. (1996b). Possible individuals in language and cognition. *Current Directions in Psychological Science, 5,* 90–94.

Bloom, P. (1996c). Word learning and the part of speech. In R. Gelman & T. Au (Eds.), *Handbook of perceptual and cognitive development.* New York: Academic Press.

Bloom, P. (1998). Theories of artifact categorization. *Cognition, 66,* 87–93.

Bloom, P. (1999). Semantics and the bootstrapping problem. In R. Jackendoff, P. Bloom & K. Wynn (Eds.), *Language, logic, and concepts: Essays in honor of John Macnamara.* Cambridge, MA: MIT Press.

Bloom, P., & Kelemen, D. (1995). Syntactic cues in the acquisition of collective nouns. *Cognition, 56,* 1–30.

Bloom, P., Kelemen, D., Fountain, A., & Courtney, E. (1995). The acquisition of collective nouns. In D. MacLaughlin and S. McEwen (Eds.), *Proceedings of the nineteenth Boston University conference on language development.* Somerville, MA: Cascadilla Press.

Bloom, P., & Markson, L. (1997). Children's naming of representations. Poster presented at the Biennial Meeting for the Society for Research in Child Development, April 4–6.

Bloom, P., & Markson, L. (1998). Intention and analogy in children's naming of pictorial representations. *Psychological Science, 9,* 200–204.

Bloom, P., Markson, L., & Diesendruck, G. (1998). Origins of the shape bias. Unpublished manuscript, University of Arizona.

Bloom, P., & Wynn, K. (1998). Linguistic cues in the acquisition of number words. *Journal of Child Language, 24,* 511–533.

Bloomfield, L. (1933). *Language.* New York: Holt.

Bolinger, D. (1967). Adjectives in English: Attribution and predication. *Lingua, 18,* 1–34.

Bowerman, M. (1978). The acquisition of word meaning. In N. Waterson & C. Snow (Eds.), *Development of communication: Social and pragmatic factors in language acquisition.* New York: Wiley.

Bowerman, M. (1996). Learning how to structure space for language. In P. Bloom, M.A. Peterson, L. Nadel & M.F. Garrett (Eds.), *Language and space.* Cambridge, MA: MIT Press.

Boysen, S.T., & Berntson, G.G. (1989). Numerical competence in a chimpanzee, *Pan troglodytes. Journal of Comparative Psychology, 103,* 23–31.

Bregman, A.S. (1990). *Auditory scene analysis: The perceptual organization of sound.* Cambridge, MA: MIT Press.

Bretherton, I. (1992). Social referencing, intentional communication, and the interfacing of minds in infancy. In D. Frye & C. Moore (Eds.), *Children's theories of mind: Mental states and social understanding.* New York: Plenum Press.

Brown, A.L. (1990). Domain-specific principles affect learning and transfer in children. *Cognitive Science, 14,* 392–416.

Brown, P. (1993). The role of shape in the acquisition of Tzeltal (Mayan) locatives. In E. Clark (Ed.), *The proceedings of the twenty-fifth annual child language research forum.* Stanford, CA: CSLI.

Brown, R. (1957). Linguistic determinism and the part of speech. *Journal of Abnormal and Social Psychology, 55,* 1–5.

Brown, R. (1958a). How shall a thing be called? *Psychological Review, 65,* 14–21.

Brown, R. (1958b). *Words and things.* New York: Free Press.

Brown, R. (1973). *A first language: The early stages.* Cambridge, MA: Harvard University Press.

Brown, R., & Hanlon, C. (1970). Derivational complexity and order of acquisition in child speech. In J.R. Hayes (Ed.), *Cognition and the development of language.* New York: Wiley.

Burns, T., & Soja, N.N. (1995). The case of NP-type nouns: Support for semantic theories of acquisition. In E.V. Clark (Ed.), *The proceedings of the twenty-sixty annual child language research forum.* Stanford: CSLI.

Butterworth, G. (1991). The ontogeny and phylogeny of joint visual attention. In A. Whiten (Ed.), *Natural theories of mind: Evolution, development, and simulation of everyday mindreading.* Oxford: Blackwell.

Cabe, P.A. (1980). Picture perception in nonhuman subjects. In M.A. Hagen (Ed.), *The perception of pictures.* New York: Academic Press.

Call, J., & Tomasello, M. (1994) The production and comprehension of referential pointing by organutans (*Pongo pygmaeus*). *Journal of Comparative Psychology, 108,* 307–
317.

Callanan, M.A. (1985). How parents name objects for young children: The role of input
in the acquisition of category hierarchies. *Child Development, 56,* 508–523.

Callanan, M.A., & Markman, E.M. (1982). Principles of organization in young children's
natural language hierarchies. *Child Development, 53,* 1093–1101.

Carey, S. (1978). The child as word-learner. In M. Halle, J. Bresnan & G.A. Miller (Eds.),
Linguistic theory and psychological reality. Cambridge, MA: MIT Press.

Carey, S. (1985). *Conceptual change in childhood.* Cambridge, MA: MIT Press.

Carey, S. (1988). Conceptual differences between children and adults. *Mind and Language,
3,* 167–181.

Carey, S. (1994). Does learning a language require the child to reconceptualize the world?
Lingua, 92, 143–167.

Carey, S., & Bartlett, E. (1978). Acquiring a single new word. *Papers and Reports on Child
Language Development, 15,* 17–29.

Carey, S., & Spelke, E.S. (1994). Domain specific knowledge and conceptual change. In
L.A. Hirschfeld & S.A. Gelman (Eds.), *Mapping the mind: Domain specificity in cognition and culture.* New York: Cambridge University Press.

Carruthers, P. (1996). *Language, thought, and consciousness.* Cambridge: Cambridge University Press.

Casati, R., & Varzi, A.C. (1994). *Holes and other superficialities.* Cambridge, MA: MIT Press.

Caselli, M.C., Bates, E., Casadio, P., Fenson, L., Fenson, J., Sanderl, L., & Weir, J. (1995).
A cross-linguistic study of early lexical development. *Cognitive Development, 10,*
159–200.

Cheney, D.L., & Seyfarth, R.M. (1990). *How monkeys see the world.* Chicago: University
of Chicago Press.

Choi, S., & Gopnik, A. (1995). Early acquisition of verbs in Korean: A crosslinguistic
study. *Journal of Child Language, 22,* 497–529.

Chomsky, N. (1957). *Syntactic structures.* The Hague: Mouton.

Chomsky, N. (1975). *Reflections on language.* New York: Pantheon.

Chomsky, N. (1981). *Lectures on government and binding.* Dordrecht: Foris.

Chomsky, N. (1988). *Language and problems of knowledge: The Managua lectures.* Cambridge,
MA: MIT Press.

Chomsky, N. (1993). *Language and thought.* London: Moyer Bell.

Chomsky, N. (1995). Language and nature. *Mind, 104,* 1–61.

Church, J. (1961). *Language and the discovery of reality.* New York: Random House.

Church, R.M., & Meck, W.H. (1984). The numerical attribute of stimuli. In H.L. Roitblat,
T.G. Bever & H.S. Terrace (Eds.), *Animal cognition.* Hillsdale, NJ: Erlbaum.

Clark, E.V. (1973). What's in a word? On the child's acquisition of semantics in his first
language. In T.E. Moore (Ed.), *Cognitive development and the acquisition of language.*
New York: Academic Press.

Clark, E.V. (1978). From gestures to word: On the natural history of deixis in language
acquisition. In J.S. Bruner & A. Garton (Eds.), *Human growth and development.* Wolf-
son College Lectures 1976. Oxford: Clarendon Press.

Clark, E.V. (1987). The principle of contrast: A constraint on language acquisition. In B.
MacWhinney (Ed.), *Mechanisms of language acquisition: The twentieth annual Carne-
gie symposium on cognition.* Hillsdale, NJ: Erlbaum.

Clark, E.V. (1993). *The lexicon in acquisition.* Cambridge: Cambridge University Press.

Clark, E.V. (1997). Conceptual perspective and lexical choice in acquisition. *Cognition,
64,* 1–37.

Cohen, L.B., & Strauss, M.S. (1979). Concept acquisition in the human infant. *Child Development, 50*, 419–424.

Cohen, S.M. (1996). *Aristotle on nature and incomplete substance.* Cambridge: Cambridge University Press.

Collins, G.M. (1977). Visual co-orientation and maternal speech. In H.R. Schaffer (Ed.), *Studies in mother-infant interaction.* London: Academic Press.

Corballis, M. (1992). On the evolution of language and generativity. *Cognition, 44*, 197–226.

Corkum, V., & Moore, C. (1995). Development of joint visual attention in infants. In C. Moore & P. Dunham (Eds.), *Joint attention: Its origin and role in development.* Hillsdale, NJ: Erlbaum.

Cosmides, L., & Tooby, J. (1992). Cognitive adaptations for social exchange. In J. Barkow, J. Tooby & L. Cosmides (Eds.), *The adapted mind: Evolutionary psychology and the generation of culture.* Oxford: Oxford University Press.

Courtney, E. (1994). Children's first parses and syntactic rules: A proposal. Unpublished manuscript, University of Arizona.

Cox, M. (1992). *Children's drawings.* London: Penguin Books.

Curtiss, S. (1977). *Genie: A psycholinguistic study of a modern-day "wild child."* New York: Academic Press.

Danto, A. (1981). *The transfiguration of the commonplace.* Cambridge, MA: Harvard University Press.

Danto, A. (1992). The art world revisited: Comedies of similarity. In A.C. Danto (Ed.), *Beyond the Brillo box: The visual arts in post-historical perspective.* New York: Farrar, Straus, Giroux.

Darwin, C.R. (1874). *The descent of man and selection in relation in sex* (2nd ed.). New York: Hurst.

Davidson, N.A., & Gelman, S.A. (1990). Inductions from novel categories: The role of language and conceptual structure. *Cognitive Development, 5*, 171–196.

Davies, S. (1991). *Definitions of art.* Ithaca, NY: Cornell University Press.

Davis, H. (1984). Discrimination of the number three by a raccoon (*Procyonlotor*). *Animal Learning and Behavior, 12*, 409–413.

Dehaene, S. (1997). *The number sense: How the mind creates mathematics.* New York: Oxford University Press.

Dehaene, S., & Mehler, J. (1992). Cross-linguistic regularities in the frequency of number words, *Cognition, 43*, 1–29.

DeLoache, J.S. (1995). Early understanding and use of symbols: The model model. *Current Directions in Psychological Science, 4*, 109–113.

DeLoache, J.S., & Burns, N.M. (1994). Early understanding of the representational function of pictures. *Cognition, 52*, 83–110.

DeLoache, J.S., Miller, K.F., & Rosengren, K.S. (1997). The credible shrinking room: Very young children's performance with symbolic and nonsymbolic relations. *Psychological Science, 8*, 308–313.

DeLoache, J.S., Strauss, M., & Maynard, J. (1979). Picture perception in infancy. *Infant Behavior and Development, 2*, 77–89.

Dennett, D.C. (1987). *The intentional stance.* Cambridge, MA: MIT Press.

Dennett, D.C. (1990). The interpretation of texts, people, and other artifacts. *Philosophy and Phenomenological Research, 50*, 177–194.

Dennett, D.C. (1996). *Kinds of minds.* New York: Basic Books.

De Villiers, J.G., & De Villiers, P.A. (1997) Linguistic determinism and theory of mind. Paper presented at the Biennial Meeting for the Society for Research in Child Development, Washington, DC.

Dickinson, D.K. (1988). Learning names for materials: Factors limiting and constraining hypotheses about word meaning. *Cognitive Development, 3,* 15–35.

Diesendruck, G. (under review). Essentialism and word learning: A cross-cultural investigation.

Diesendruck, G., Gelman, S.A., & Lebowitz, K. (1998). Conceptual and linguistic biases in children's word learning. *Developmental Psychology, 34,* 823–839.

Diesendruck, G., & Markson, L. (under review). Children's interpretation of word meanings: Lexical constraints or pragmatics?

Di Sciullo, A.M., & Wiliams, E. (1987). *On the definition of word.* Cambridge, MA: MIT Press.

Dockrell, J., & Campbell, R. (1986). Lexical acquisition strategies in the preschool child. In S. Kuczaj & M. Barrett (Eds.), *The development of word meaning* (pp. 121–154). Berlin: Springer-Verlag.

Dollaghan, C. (1985). Child meets word: "Fast mapping" in preschool children. *Journal of Speech and Hearing Research, 28,* 449–454.

Donnellan, K.S. (1977). Speaking of nothing. In S.P. Schwartz (Ed.), *Naming, necessity, and natural kinds.* Ithaca, NY: Cornell University Press.

Dore, J. (1978). Conditions for the acquisition of speech acts. In L. Markova (Ed.), *The social context of language* (pp. 87–111). New York: Wiley.

Dromi, E. (1987). *Early lexical development.* Cambridge: Cambridge University Press.

Durkin, K., Shire, B., Reim, R., Crowther, R.D., & Rutter, D.R. (1986). The social and linguistic context of early number word use. *British Journal of Developmental Psychology, 4,* 269–288.

Dutton, D. (1979). Artistic crimes: The problem of forgery in the arts. *British Journal of Aesthetics, 19,* 304–314.

Ekman, P., & Friesen, W.V. (1975). *Unmasking the face.* Englewood Cliffs, NJ: Prentice-Hall.

Elman, J., Bates, E.., Johnson, M., Karmiloff-Smith, A., Parisi, D., & Plunkett, K. (1996). *Rethinking innateness: A connectionist perspective on development.* Cambridge, MA: MIT Press.

Fenson, L, Dale, P.S., Reznick, J.S., Bates, E., Thal, D., & Pethick, S.J. (1994). Variability in early communicative development. *Monographs of the Society for Research in Child Development, 59* (5, serial no. 242).

Fernald, A., & Morikawa, H. (1993). Common themes and cultural variation in Japanese and American mothers' speech to infants. *Child Development, 64,* 637–656.

Fink, J.S. (1997). *If he lived: A modern ghost story.* London: Vintage.

Fisher, C. (1996). Structural limits on verb mapping: The role of analogy in children's interpretations of sentences. *Cognitive Psychology, 31,* 41–81.

Fisher, C., Gleitman, H., & Gleitman, L.R. (1991). On the semantic content of subcategorization frames. *Cognitive Psychology, 23,* 331–392.

Fisher, C., Hall, D.G., Rakowitz, S., & Gleitman, L. (1994). Why it is better to receive than to give: Syntactic and conceptual constraints on vocabulary growth. *Lingua, 92,* 333–375.

Fodor, J.A. (1975). *The language of thought.* New York: Crowell.

Fodor, J.A. (1981). The current status of the innateness controversy. In J.A. Fodor (Ed.), *Representations.* Cambridge, MA: MIT Press.

Fodor, J.A. (1983). *The modularity of mind.* Cambridge, MA: MIT Press.

Fodor, J.A. (1998). *Concepts: Where cognitive science went wrong.* Oxford: Clarendon.

Fodor, J.A., & LePore, E. (1992). *Holism: A shopper's guide.* Oxford: Blackwell.

Freeman, N.H. (1991). The theory of art that underpin children's naive realism. *Visual Arts Research, 17,* 65–75.

Frege, G. (1892). On sense and reference. Reprinted in D. Davidson and G. Harmon (Eds.), (1975), *The logic of grammar*. Encino, CA: Dickerson.

Frege, G. (1893). *The foundations of arithmetic*. Evanston, IL: Northwestern University Press, 1980.

Frith, U., & Happé, F. (1994). Language and communication in autistic disorders. *Philosophical Transactions of the Royal Society of London B, 346*, 97–104.

Fukui, N. (1987). A theory of category projection and its implications. Unpublished doctoral dissertation, MIT.

Fuson, K.C. (1988). *Children's counting and concepts of number*. New York: Springer-Verlag.

Fuson, K.C., & Kwon, Y. (1992). Effects of the system of number words and other cultural tools on children's addition and subtraction. In J. Bideaud & C. Meljac (Eds.), *Pathways to number: Children's developing numerical abilities*. Hillsdale, NJ: Erlbaum.

Fuson, K.C., Richards, J., & Briars, D.J. (1982). The acquisition and elaboration of the number word sequence. In C.J. Brainerd (Ed.), *Children's logical and mathematical cognition: Progress in cognitive development research*. New York: Springer-Verlag.

Gallistel, C.R. (1990). *The organization of learning*. Cambridge, MA: MIT Press.

Ganger, J., Pinker, S., & Wallis, E.G. (1997). Genetic contributions to vocabulary development. Poster presented at the Biennial Meeting for the Society for Research in Child Development, Washington, DC.

García Márquez, G. (1972). *One hundred years of solitude*. New York: Harper.

Gardner, H. (1980). *Artful scribbles: The significance of children's drawings*. London: Jill Norman.

Gardner, J., Winner, E., & Kircher, M. (1975). Children's conception of the arts. *Journal of Aesthetic Education, 9*, 60–77.

Gasser, M., & Smith, L.B. (1998). Learning nouns and adjectives: A connectionist approach. *Language and Cognitive Processes, 13*, 269–306.

Gathercole, V.C. (1986). Evaluating competing linguistic theories with child language data: The case of the mass-count distinction. *Linguistics and Philosophy, 9*, 151–190.

Gathercole, V.C. (1987). The contrastive hypothesis for the acquisition of word meaning: A reconsideration of the theory. *Journal of Child Language, 14*, 493–532.

Geach, P. (1962). *Reference and generality*. Ithaca, NY: Cornell University Press.

Gelman, R., & Gallistel, C. R. (1978). *The child's understanding of number*. Cambridge, MA: Harvard University Press.

Gelman, R., Meck, E., & Merkin, S. (1986). Young children's numerical competence. *Cognitive Development, 1*, 1–29.

Gelman, S.A., & Coley, J.D. (1990). The importance of knowing a dodo is a bird: Categories and inferences in two-year-olds. *Developmental Psychology, 26*, 796–804.

Gelman, S.A., Coley, J.D., Rosengren, K.S., Hartman, E., & Pappas, A. (in press a). Beyond labeling: The role of maternal input in the acquisition of richly structured categories. *Monographs of the Society for Research in Child Development*.

Gelman, S.A., Croft, W., Fu, P., Clausner, T., & Gottfried, G. (in press b). Why is a pomegranate an "apple"? The role of shape, taxonomic relatedness, and prior lexical knowledge in children's overextensions of "apple" and "dog." *Journal of Child Language*.

Gelman, S.A., & Diesendruck, G. (in press). What's in a concept? Context, variability, and psychological essentialism. In I.E. Sigel (Ed.), *Theoretical perspectives in the development of representational thought*. Hillsdale, NJ: Erlbaum.

Gelman, S.A., & Ebeling, K.S. (1998). Shape and representational status in children's early naming. *Cognition, 66*, 835–847.

Gelman, S.A., & Hirschfeld, L.A. (1999). How biological is essentialism? In S. Atran & D. Medin (Eds.), *Folkbiology* Cambridge, MA: MIT Press.

Gelman, S.A., & Markman, E.M. (1985). Implicit contrast in adjectives vs. nouns: Implications for word-learning in preschoolers. *Journal of Child Language, 12*, 125–143.

Gelman, S.A., & Markman, E.M. (1986). Categories and induction in young children. *Cognition, 23*, 183–208.

Gelman, S.A., & Markman, E.M. (1987). Young children's induction from natural kinds: The role of categories and appearances. *Child Development, 58*, 1532–1541.

Gelman, S.A., & Medin, D.L. (1993). What's so essential about essentialism? A different perspective on the interaction of perception, language, and concrete knowledge. *Cognitive Development, 8*, 113–139.

Gelman, S.A., & Taylor, M. (1984). How two-year-old children interpret proper and common names for unfamiliar objects. *Child Development, 55*, 1535–1540.

Gelman, S.A., & Wellman, H.M. (1991). Insides and essences: Early understandings of the non-obvious. *Cognition, 38*, 213–244.

Gentner, D. (1978). What looks like a jiggy but acts like a zimbo? A study of early word meaning using artificial objects. *Papers and Reports on Child Language Development, 15*, 1–6.

Gentner, D. (1982). Why nouns are learned before verbs: Linguistic relativity versus natural partitioning. In S. A. Kuczaj II (Ed.), *Language development*, Vol 2, *Language, thought, and culture*. Hillsdale, NJ: Erlbaum.

Gentner, D. (1983). Structure-mapping: A theoretical framework for analogy. *Cognitive Science, 7*, 155–170.

Gentner, D., & Boroditsky, L. (in press). Individuation, relativity and early word learning. In M. Bowerman & S. Levinson (Eds.), *Conceptual development and language acquisition*. Cambridge: Cambridge University Press.

Gergely, G., Nádasdy, Z., Csibra, G., & Biró, S. (1995). Taking the intentional stance at twelve months of age. *Cognition, 56*, 165–193.

Gerken, L.A., Landau, B., & Remez, R.E. (1989). Function morphemes in young children's speech perception and production. *Developmental Psychology, 27*, 204–216.

Gibbs, R.W. (1983). Do people always process the literal meanings of indirect requests? *Journal of Experimental Psychology: Learning, Memory, and Cognition, 9*, 524–533.

Gibbs, R.W., & Nayak, N.P. (1989). Psycholinguistic studies on the syntactic behavior of idioms. *Cognitive Psychology, 23*, 100–138.

Gillette, J., Gleitman, H., Gleitman, L., and Lederer, A. (1997). Human simulations of lexical acquisition. Unpublished manuscript, University of Pennsylvania.

Ginsberg, H. (1977). *Children's arithmetic*. New York: Van Nostrand.

Giralt, N., & Bloom, P. (in press). Individuation by young children: Reasoning about objects, parts, and holes. *Psychological Science*.

Girouard, P.C., Ricard, M., & Decarie, T.G. (1997). The acquisition of personal pronouns in French-speaking and English-speaking children. *Journal of Child Language, 24*, 311–326.

Gleitman, L.R. (1990). The structural sources of verb meanings. *Language Acquisition, 1*, 3–55.

Gleitman, L.R., & Gleitman, H. (1997). What is language made out of? *Lingua, 100*, 29–55.

Gleitman, L.R., & Wanner, E. (1982). Language acquisition: The state of the state of the art. In E. Wanner & L. Gleitman (Eds.), *Language acquisition: The state of the art*. Cambridge: Cambridge University Press.

Goldfield, B.A. (1993). Noun bias in maternal speech to one-year-olds. *Journal of Child Language, 17*, 171–183.

Goldfield, B.A., & Reznick, J.S. (1990). Early lexical acquisition: Rate, content, and the vocabulary spurt. *Journal of Child Language, 17*, 171–183.

Goldin-Meadow, S., & Mylander, C. (1984). Gestural communication in deaf children: The effects and noneffects of parental input on early language development. *Monographs of the Society for Research in Child Development, 49* (serial no. 207).

Goldstone, R.L. (1994). Influences of categorization on perceptual discrimination. *Journal of Experimental Psychology: General, 123,* 178–200.

Golinkoff, R.M. (1986). I beg your pardon? The preverbal negotiation of failed messages. *Journal of Child Language, 13,* 455–476.

Golinkoff, R.M, Hirsh-Pasek, K., Mervis, C.B., Frawley, W.B., & Parillo, M. (1995). Lexical principles can be extended to the acquisition of verbs. In M. Tomasello & W.E. Merriman (Eds.), *Beyond names for things. Young children's acquisition of verbs.* Hillsdale, NJ: Erlbaum.

Golinkoff, R.M., Mervis, C.B., & Hirsh-Pasek, K. (1994). Early object labels: The case for a developmental lexical principles framework. *Journal of Child Language, 21,* 125–155.

Golinkoff, R.M., Shuff-Bailey, M., Olguin, R., & Ruan, W. (1995). Young children extend words at the basic-level: Evidence for the principle of categorical scope. *Developmental Psychology, 31,* 494–507.

Golomb, C. (1993). Art and the young child: Another look at the developmental question. *Visual Arts Research, 19,* 1–15.

Gombrich, E.H. (1960). *Art and illusion: A study in the psychology of pictoral representations.* New York: Pantheon.

Goodglass, H., Denes, G., & Calderson, M. (1974). The absence of covert verbal mediation in aphasia. *Cortex, 10,* 264–269.

Goodman, N. (1968). *Languages of art: An approach to the theory of symbols.* Indianapolis: Hockett.

Goodman, N. (1983). *Fact, fiction, and forecast.* Cambridge, MA: Harvard University Press.

Gopnik, A., & Choi, S. (1995). Names, relational words, and cognitive development in English and Korean speakers: Nouns are not always learned before verbs. In M. Tomasello & W.E. Merriman (Eds.), *Beyond names for things: Young children's acquisition of verbs.* Hillsdale, NJ: Erlbaum.

Gopnik, A., & Meltzoff, A.N. (1986). Words, plans, things, and locations: Interactions between semantic and cognitive development in the one-word stage. In S. Kuczaj & M. Barrett (Eds.), *The development of word meaning.* New York: Springer-Verlag.

Gopnik, A., & Meltzoff, A.N. (1987). The development of categorization in the second year of life and its relation to other cognitive and linguistic developments. *Child Development, 58,* 1523–1531

Gopnik, A. & Meltzoff, A.N. (1997). *Words, thoughts, and theories.* Cambridge, MA: MIT Press.

Gordon, P. (1988). Count-mass category acquisition: Distributional distinctions in children's speech. *Journal of Child Language, 15,* 109–128.

Gordon, P. (1992). Object, substance, and individuation: Canonical vs. non-canonical count/mass nouns in children's speech. Unpublished manuscript, University of Pittsburgh.

Gordon, P. (1993). One-two-many systems in Amazonia: Implications for number acquisition theory. Paper presented at the Biennial Meeting of the Society for Research in Child Development, New Orleans, March 25–28.

Grice, H.P. (1975). Logic and conversation. In P. Cole & J.L Morgan (Eds.), *Syntax and semantics 3: Speech Acts.* New York: Academic Press.

Grimshaw, J. (1981). Form, function, and the language acquisition device. In C.L. Baker & J.J. McCarthy (Eds.), *The logical problem of language acquisition.* Cambridge, MA: MIT Press.

Gropen, J., Pinker, S., Hollander, M., & Goldberg, R. (1991). Syntax and semantics in the acquisition of locative verbs. *Journal of Child Language, 18,* 115–151.

Gupta, A.K. (1980). *The logic of common nouns.* New Haven: Yale University Press.

Gutheil, G., & Rosengren, K. (in press). A rose by any other name: Preschoolers' understanding of individual identity across name and appearance changes. *British Journal of Developmental Psychology.*

Hall, D.G. (1991). Acquiring proper names for familiar and unfamiliar animate objects: Two-year-olds' word-learning biases. *Child Development, 62,* 1142–1154.

Hall, D.G. (1994). Semantic constraints on word learning: Proper names and adjectives. *Child Development, 65,* 1291–1309.

Hall, D.G. (1995). Artifacts and origins. Unpublished manuscript. Department of Psychology, University of British Columbia.

Hall, D.G. (1996a). Naming solids and nonsolids: Children's default construals. *Cognitive Development, 11,* 229–265.

Hall, D.G. (1996b). Preschoolers' default assumptions about word meaning: Proper names designate unique individuals. *Developmental Psychology, 32,* 177–186.

Hall, D.G. (1998). Continuity and the persistence of objects: When the whole is greater than the sum of the parts. *Cognitive Psychology, 37,* 28–59.

Hall, D.G. (1999). Semantics and the acquisition of proper names. In R. Jackendoff, P. Bloom & K. Wynn (Eds.), *Language, logic, and concepts: Essays in honor of John Macnamara.* Cambridge, MA: MIT Press.

Hall, D.G., & Graham, S.A. (1997). Beyond mutual exclusivity: Children use form class information to constrain word-referent mapping. In E. Clark (Ed.), *Proceedings of the twenty-ninth Stanford child language research forum.* New York: Cambridge University Press.

Hall, D.G., Waxman, S.R., & Hurwitz, W.M. (1993). How two- and four-year-old children interpret adjectives and count nouns. *Child Development, 64,* 1651–1664.

Hampton, J.A. (1995). Testing prototype theory of concepts. *Journal of Memory and Language, 34,* 686–708.

Happé, F. (1996). *Autism: An introduction to psychological theory.* Cambridge, MA: Harvard University Press.

Harris, M., Jones, D., & Grant, J. (1983). The nonverbal content of mothers' speech to infants. *First Language, 4,* 21–31.

Hauser, M.D. (1997). Artifactual kinds and functional design features: What a primate understands without language. *Cognition, 64,* 285–308.

Hauser, M.D., MacNeilage, P., & Ware, M. (1996). Numerical representations in primates: Perceptual or arithmetic. *Proceedings of the National Academy of Sciences USA, 93,* 1514–1517.

Heath, S.B. (1986). What no bedtime story means: Narrative skills at home and school. In B.S. Schieffelin & E. Ochs (Eds.), *Language socialization across cultures.* Cambridge: Cambridge University Press.

Heibeck, T.H., & Markman, E.M. (1987). Word learning in children: An examination of fast mapping. *Child Development, 58,* 1021–1034.

Higginbotham, J. (1983). Logical form, binding, and nominals. *Linguistic Inquiry, 14,* 395–420.

Hirsch, E. (1982). *The concept of identity.* New York: Oxford University Press.

Hirschfeld, L.A. (1996). *Race in the making.* Cambridge, MA: MIT Press.

Hirsh-Pasek, K., Gleitman, H., Gleitman, L.R., Golinkoff, R., & Naigles, L. (1988). Syntactic bootstrapping: Evidence from comprehension. Paper presented at the Boston University Conference on Language Development, Boston, MA.

Hobbes, T. (1672/1913). *Metaphysical system of Hobbes in twelve chapters*. Chicago: Open Court.

Hobson, R.P. (1994). Through feeling and sight to self and symbol. In U. Neisser (Ed.), *The perceived self: Ecological and interpersonal knowledge of the self*. New York: Cambridge University Press.

Hochberg, J., & Brooks, V. (1962). Pictorial recognition as an unlearned ability: A study of one child's performance. *American Journal of Psychology, 75*, 624–628.

Hoffman, D.D., & Richards, W.A. (1984). Parts of recognition. In S. Pinker (Ed.), *Visual Cognition*. Cambridge, MA: MIT Press.

Horton, M.S., & Markman, E.M. (1980). Developmental differences in the acquisition of basic and superordinate categories. *Child Development, 51*, 708–719.

Hull, D.L. (1965). The effect of essentialism on taxonomy: Two thousand years of statis. *British Journal for the Philosophy of Science, 15*, 314–326.

Hume, D. (1739/1978). *A treatise on human nature*. Oxford: Clarendon.

Huntley-Fenner, G., & Carey, S. (1995). Individuation of objects and portions of nonsolid substances: A pattern of success (objects) and failure (nonsolid substances). Poster presented at the Biennial Meeting of the Society for Research in Child Development, Indianapolis, IN, April.

Hurford, J.R. (1989). Biological evolution of the Saussurian sign as a component of the language acquisition device. *Lingua, 77*, 187–222.

Hurford, J.R. (in press). The interaction between numerals and nouns. In F. Plank (Ed.), *Noun phrase structure in the languages of Europe*. Berlin: Mouton de Gruyter.

Hutchinson, J.E. (1986). Children's sensitivity to the contrastive use of object category terms. Paper presented at the 1986 Stanford Child Language Research Forum, Stanford, CA.

Hutchinson, J.E., & Herman, J.P. (1991). The development of word-learning strategies in delayed children. Paper presented at the Boston University Conference on Language Development, Boston, MA.

Huttenlocher, J., Haight, W., Bryk, A., Seltzer, M., & Lyons, T. (1991). Early vocabulary growth: Relation to language input and gender. *Developmental Psychology, 27*, 236–248.

Huttenlocher, J. & Smiley, P. (1987). Early word meanings: The case of object names. *Cognitive Psychology, 19*, 63–89.

Ifrah, G. (1985). *From one to zero: A universal history of numbers*. New York: Viking.

Imai, M., & Gentner, D. (1997). A cross-linguistic study of early word meaning: Universal ontology and linguistic influence. *Cognition, 62*, 169–200.

Imai, M., Gentner, D., & Uchida, N. (1994). Children's theories of word meaning: The role of shape similarity in early acquisition. *Cognitive Development, 9*, 45–75.

Ittelson, W.H. (1996). Visual perception of markings. *Psychonomic Bulletin and Review, 3*, 171–187.

Jackendoff, R. (1977). *X-bar syntax: A study of phrase structure*. Cambridge, MA: MIT Press.

Jackendoff, R. (1989). What is a concept, that a person may grasp it? *Mind and Language, 4*, 68–102/3.

Jackendoff, R. (1990). *Semantic structures*. Cambridge, MA: MIT Press.

Jackendoff, R. (1992). Mme Tussaud meets the binding theory. *Natural Language and Linguistic Theory, 10*, 1–31.

James, W. (1893). Thought before language: A deaf-mute's recollections. *American Annals of the Deaf, 38*, 135–145.

Jelinek, E., & Demers, R.A. (1994). Predicates and pronominal arguments in Straits Salish. *Language, 70*, 647–736.

Johnson, S., Slaughter, V., & Carey, S. (in press). Whose gaze will infants follow? The elicitation of gaze following in twelve-month-olds. *Developmental Science*.

Jones, S.S., & Smith, L.B. (1993). The place of perception in children's concepts. *Cognitive Development, 8*, 113–139.

Jones, S.S., Smith, L.B., & Landau, B. (1991). Object properties and knowledge in early lexical learning. *Child Development, 62*, 499–516.

Jusczyk, P.W. (1997) *The discovery of spoken language.* Cambridge, MA: MIT Press.

Kagan, J. (1981). *The second year.* Cambridge, MA: Harvard University Press.

Kahneman, D., Treisman, A., & Gibbs, B.J. (1992). The reviewing of object files: Object-specific integration of information. *Cognitive Psychology, 24*, 174–219.

Kanner, L. (1943). Autistic disturbances of affective contact. *Nervous Child, 2*, 217–250.

Karmiloff-Smith, A., Klima, E., Bellugi, U., Grant, J., & Baron-Cohen, S. (1995). Is there a social module? Language, face processing, and theory of mind in individuals with Williams syndrome. *Journal of Cognitive Neuroscience, 7*, 196–208.

Katz, N., Baker, E., & Macnamara, J. (1974). What's in a name? A study of how children learn common and proper names. *Child Development, 45*, 469–473.

Kay, P., & Kempton, W. (1984). What is the Sapir-Whorf hypothesis? *American Anthropologist, 86*, 65–79.

Keil, F.C. (1979). *Semantic and conceptual development: An ontological perspective.* Cambridge, MA: Harvard University Press.

Keil, F.C. (1989). *Concepts, kinds, and cognitive development.* Cambridge, MA: MIT Press.

Keil, F.C. (1994). Explanation, association, and the acquisition of word meaning. *Lingua, 92*, 169–196.

Kelemen, D., & Bloom P. (1994). Domain-specific knowledge in simple categorization tasks. *Psychonomic Bulletin and Review, 1*, 390–395.

Keller, H. (1909). *The story of my life.* London: Hodder & Stoughton.

Kellman, P.J., & Spelke, E.S. (1983). Perception of partly occluded objects in infancy. *Cognitive Psychology, 15*, 483–524.

Kemler-Nelson, D.G. (in press). Attention to functional properties in toddlers' naming and problem-solving. *Cognitive Development*.

Kemler-Nelson, D.G., and eleven Swarthmore College students (1995). Principle-based inferences in young children's categorization: Revisiting the impact of function on the naming of artifacts. *Cognitive Development, 10*, 347–380.

Klahr, D., & Wallace, J.G. (1976). *Cognitive development: An information-processing view.* Hillsdale, NJ: Erlbaum.

Kolstad, V.T., & Baillargeon, R. (1990). Context-dependent perceptual and functional categorization in 10.5-month-old infants. Unpublished manuscript.

Kripke, S. (1980). *Naming and necessity.* Cambridge, MA: Harvard University Press.

Lakoff, G. (1987). *Women, fire, and dangerous things.* Chicago: University of Chicago Press.

Landau, B. (1994). Where's what and what's where: The language of objects in space. *Lingua, 92*, 259–296.

Landau, B. (1996). Multiple geometric representations of objects in language and language learners. In P. Bloom, M.A. Peterson, L. Nadel & M.F. Garrett (Eds.), *Language and space.* Cambridge, MA: MIT Press.

Landau, B., & Gleitman L. (1985). *Language and experience: Evidence from the blind child.* Cambridge MA: Harvard University Press.

Landau, B., & Jackendoff, R. (1993). "What" and "where" in spatial language and spatial cognition. *Behavioral and Brain Sciences, 16*, 217–238.

Landau, B., Smith, L.B., & Jones, S.S. (1988). The importance of shape in early lexical learning. *Cognitive Development, 3*, 299–321.

Landau, B., Smith, L.B., & Jones, S.S. (1998). Object shape, object function, and object name. *Journal of Memory and Language, 38,* 1–27.

Landau, B., & Stecker, D. (1990). Objects and places: Syntactic and geometric representations in early lexical learning. *Cognitive Development, 5,* 287–312.

Lane, H. (1976). *The wild boy of Aveyron.* Cambridge, MA: Harvard University Press.

Langacker, R.W. (1987). Nouns and verbs. *Language, 63,* 53–94.

Langer, S.K. (1942). *Philosophy in a new key.* Cambridge, MA: Harvard University Press.

Lefebvre, C., & Muysken, P. (1988). *Mixed categories: Nominalizations in Quechua.* Dordrecht: Kluwer.

Leslie, A.M. (1982). The perception of causality in infants. *Perception, 11,* 173–186.

Leslie, A.M. (1994). ToMM, ToBy, and Agency: Core architecture and domain specificity. In L. Hirschfeld & S. Gelman (Eds.), *Mapping the mind: Domain specificity in cognition and culture.* Cambridge: Cambridge University Press.

Leslie, A.M. (1995). Pretending and believing: Issues in the theory of ToMM. *Cognition, 50,* 193–200.

Leslie, A.M., & Thaiss, L. (1992). Domain specificity in conceptual development: Neuropsychological evidence from autism. *Cognition, 43,* 225–251.

Levin, B. (1993). *English verb classes and alternations: A preliminary investigation* Chicago: University of Chicago Press.

Levinson, J. (1993). Extending art historically. *Journal of Aesthetics and Art Criticism, 51,* 411–423.

Levinson, S.C. (1996). Frames of reference and Molyneux's question: Crosslinguistic evidence. In P. Bloom, M.A. Peterson, L. Nadel & M.F. Garrett (Eds.), *Language and space.* Cambridge, MA: MIT Press.

Levy, Y. (1988). On the early learning of formal grammatical systems: Evidence from studies of the acquisition of gender and countability. *Journal of Child Language, 15,* 179–187.

Lewis, D. (1969). *Convention.* Cambridge, MA: Harvard University Press.

Lewis, D. (1972). General semantics. In D. Davidson & G. Harmon (Eds.), *The logic of grammar.* Encino, CA: Dickerson.

Lewis, S. (1997). *Zen and the art of fatherhood.* New York: Plume.

Leyton, M. (1992). *Symmetry, causality, mind.* Cambridge, MA: MIT Press.

Lieven, E.V.M. (1994). Crosslinguistic and crosscultural aspects of language addressed to children. In C. Gallaway & B.J. Richards (Eds.), *Input and interaction in language acquisition.* Cambridge: Cambridge University Press.

Lifter, K., & Bloom, L. (1989). Object knowledge and the emergence of language. *Infant Behavior and Development, 12,* 395–423.

Liittschwager, J.C., & Markman, E.M (1993). Young children's understanding of proper versus common nouns. Paper presented at the Biennial Meeting of the Society for Research in Child Development, New Orleans, LA, March 25–28.

Locke, J. (1690/1964). *An essay concerning human understanding.* Cleveland: Meridian Books.

Lodge, D. (1994). *The art of fiction.* New York: Penguin.

Lucy, J.A., & Gaskins, S. (in press). Grammatical categories and the development of classification preferences: A comparative approach. In M. Bowerman & S. Levinson (Eds.), *Conceptual development and language acquisition.* Cambridge: Cambridge University Press.

Macario, J. (1991). Young children's use of color in classification: Foods and canonically colored objects. *Cognitive Development, 6,* 17–46.

Macnamara, J. (1972). Cognitive basis of language learning in infants. *Psychological Review, 79,* 1–13.

Macnamara, J. (1982). *Names for things: A study of human learning.* Cambridge, MA: MIT Press.

Macnamara, J. (1986). *A border dispute: The place of logic in psychology.* Cambridge, MA: MIT Press.

Macnamara, J. (1991). The development of moral reasoning and the foundations of geometry. *Journal for the Theory of Social Behavior, 21,* 125–150.

Macnamara, J., & Reyes, G.E. (1994). Foundational issues in the learning of proper names, count nouns and mass nouns. In J. Macnamara & G.E. Reyes (Eds.), *The logical foundations of cognition.* Oxford: Oxford University Press.

MacWhinney, B., & Snow, C. (1990). The Child Language Data Exchange System: An update. *Journal of Child Language, 17,* 457–472.

Maddy, P. (1990). *Realism in mathematics.* New York: Oxford University Press.

Malotki, E. (1983). *Hopi time: A linguistic analysis of temporal concepts in the Hopi language.* Berlin: Mouton.

Malt, B.C. (1991). Word meaning and word use. In P. Schwanenflugel (Ed.), *The psychology of word meanings* (pp. 37–70). Hillsdale, NJ: Erlbaum.

Malt, B.C. (1994). Water is not H_2O. *Cognitive Psychology, 27,* 41–70.

Malt, B.C., & Johnson, E.C. (1992). Do artifact concepts have cores? *Journal of Memory and Language, 31,* 195–217.

Malt, B.C., & Johnson, E.C. (1998). Artifact category membership and the intentional-historical theory. *Cognition, 66,* 79–85.

Mandler, J.M. (1996). Preverbal representation and language. In P. Bloom, M.A. Peterson, L. Nadel & M.F. Garrett (Eds.), *Language and space.* Cambridge, MA: MIT Press.

Mandler, J.M., & McDonough, L. (1993). Concept formation in infancy. *Cognitive Development, 8,* 291–318.

Maratsos, M. (1991). How the acquisition of nouns may be different from that of verbs. In N. Krasnegor, D. Rumbaugh, R. Schiefelbusch & M. Studdert-Kennedy (Eds.), *Biological and behavioral determinants of language development.* Hillsdale, NJ: Erlbaum.

Maratsos, M.P., & Chalkley, M. (1981). The internal language of children's syntax: The ontogenesis and representation of syntactic categories. In K. Nelson (Ed.), *Children's language* (Vol. 2.) New York: Gardner Press.

Maratsos, M., & Deák, G. (1995). Hedgehogs, foxes, and the acquisition of verb meaning. In M. Tomasello & W.E. Merriman (Eds.), *Beyond names for things: Young children's acquisition of verbs.* Hillsdale, NJ: Erlbaum.

Marcus, G.F. (1993). Negative evidence in language acquisition. *Cognition, 46,* 53–85.

Marcus, G.F., Pinker, S., Ullman, M., Hollander, M., Rosen, T.J., & Xu, F. (1992). Overgeneralization in language acquisition. *Monographs of the Society for Research in Child Development, 57* (serial no. 228), 1–182.

Markman, E.M. (1989). *Categorization and naming in children.* Cambridge, MA: MIT Press.

Markman, E.M. (1992). Constraints on word learning: Speculations about their nature, origins, and domain specificity. In M.R. Gunnar & M.P. Maratsos (Eds.), *Modularity and constraints on language and cognition: The Minnesota Symposium on Child Psychology.* Hillsdale, NJ: Erlbaum.

Markman, E.M., Horton, M.S., & McLanahan, A.G. (1980). Classes and collections: Principle of organization in the learning of hierarchical relations. *Cognition, 8,* 227–241.

Markman, E.M., & Hutchinson, J.E. (1984). Children's sensitivity to constraints on word meaning: Taxonomic versus thematic relations. *Cognitive Psychology, 16,* 1–27.

Markman, E.M., & Wachtel, G.F. (1988). Children's use of mutual exclusivity to constrain the meaning of words. *Cognitive Psychology, 20,* 121–157.

Markson, L. (1999). *Mechanisms of word learning in children: Insights from fast mapping.* Unpublished doctoral dissertation, University of Arizona.

Markson, L., & Bloom, P. (1997). Evidence against a dedicated system for word learning in children. *Nature, 385,* 813–815.

Marr, D. (1982). *Vision.* San Francisco: Freeman.

Marslen-Wilson, W.D., & Tyler, L.K. (1980). The temporal structure of spoken language understanding. *Cognition, 8,* 1–71.

Masur, E.F. (1997). Maternal labeling of novel and familiar objects: Implications for children's development of lexical constraints. *Journal of Child Language, 24,* 427–439.

Mayr, E. (1982). *The growth of biological thought.* Cambridge, MA: Harvard University Press.

McCarrell, N.S., & Callanan, M.A. (1995). Form-function correspondences in children's inference. *Child Development, 66,* 532–546.

McCarthy, D. (1954). Language development in children. In L. Carmichael (Ed.), *Manual of child development.* New York: Wiley.

McPherson, L. (1991). "A little" goes a long way: Evidence for a perceptual basis of learning for the noun categories COUNT and MASS. *Journal of Child Language, 18,* 315–338.

McShane, J. (1979). The development of naming. *Linguistics, 17,* 79–90.

Mechner, F., & Guevrekian, L. (1962). Effects of deprivation upon counting and timing in rats. *Journal of the Experimental Analysis of Behavior, 5,* 463–466.

Meck, W.H., & Church, R.M. (1983). A node control model of counting and timing processes. *Journal of Experimental Psychology: Animal Behavior Processes, 9,* 320–334.

Medin, D.L., & Ortony. A. (1989). Psychological essentialism. In S. Vosinadou & A. Ortony (Eds.), *Similarity and analogical reasoning.* Cambridge: Cambridge University Press.

Meltzoff, A.N. (1988). Infant imitation after a one-week delay: Long-term memory for novel acts and multiple stimuli. *Developmental Psychology, 24,* 470–476.

Meltzoff, A.N. (1995). Understanding the intentions of others: Re-enactment of intended acts by eighteen-month-old children. *Developmental Psychology, 31,* 838–850.

Merriman, W.E., & Bowman, L.L. (1989). The mutual exclusivity bias in children's word learning. *Monographs of the Society for Research in Child Development, 54* (serial no. 220): 1–132.

Merriman, W.E., Marazita, J., & Jarvis, L. (1995). Children's disposition to map new words onto new referents. In M. Tomasello & W.E. Merriman (Eds.), *Beyond names for things: Young children's acquisition of verbs.* Hillsdale, NJ: Erlbaum.

Mervis, C.B., & Bertrand, J. (1995). Acquisition of the novel name-nameless category (N3C) principle. *Child Development, 65,* 1646–1663.

Mervis, C.B., & Crisafi, M.A. (1982). Order of acquisition of subordinate, basic, and superordinate level categories. *Child Development, 53,* 258–266.

Mervis, C.B., Golinkoff, R.M., & Bertrand, J. (1994). Two-year-olds readily learn multiple labels for the same basic-level kind. *Child Development, 65,* 1163–1177.

Messer, D. (1981). Non-linguistic information which could assist the young children's interpretation of adult's speech. In W.P. Robinson (Ed.), *Communication in development.* London: Academic Press.

Mill, J.S. (1843). *A system of logic ratiocinative and inductive.* London: Longmans.

Miller, G.A. (1996). *The science of words.* New York: Freeman.

Miller, G.A., & Gildea, P.M. (1987). How children learn words. *Scientific American, 257,* 86–91.

Miller, G.A., & Johnson-Laird, P. (1976). *Language and perception* Cambridge, MA: Harvard University Press.

Miller, G.A., & Wakefield, P.C. (1993). On Anglin's analysis of vocabulary growth. *Monographs of the Society for Research in Child Development, 58,* (serial no. 238), 167–175.

Miller, K.F., Smith, C.M., Zhu, J., & Zhang, H. (1995). Preschool origins of cross-national differences in mathematical competence: The role of number counting systems. *Psychological Science, 6,* 56–60.

Miura, I.T. (1987). Mathematics achievement as a function of language. *Journal of Educational Psychology, 79,* 79–82.

Morales, M., Mundy, P., & Rojas, J. (1998). Following the direction of gaze and language development in six-month-olds. *Infant Behavior and Development, 21,* 373–377.

Murphy, C.M., & Messer, D.J. (1977). Mothers, infants, and pointing: A study of gesture. In H.R. Schaffer (Ed.), *Studies in mother-infant interaction.* London: Academic Press.

Murphy, G.L. (1991). Meaning and concepts. In P.J. Schwanenflugel (Ed.), *The psychology of word meanings.* Hillsdale, NJ: Erlbaum.

Murphy, G.L. (1996). On metaphoric representation. *Cognition, 60,* 173–204.

Murphy, G.L., & Lassaline, M.E. (1997). Hierarchical structure in concepts and the basic level of categorization. In K. Lamberts & D.R. Shanks (Eds.), *Knowledge, concepts and categories.* Cambridge, MA: MIT Press.

Murphy, G.L., & Medin. D.L. (1985). The role of theories in conceptual coherence. *Psychological Review, 92,* 289–316.

Naigles, L.R. (1990). Children use syntax to learn verb meanings. *Journal of Child Language, 17,* 357–374.

Naigles, L.R., Fowler, A., & Heim, A. (1992). Developmental shifts in the construction of verb meanings. *Cognitive Development, 7,* 403–427.

Naigles, L.R., Fowler, A., & Helm, A. (1995). Syntactic bootstrapping from start to finish with special reference to Down syndrome. In M. Tomasello & W.E. Merriman (Eds.), *Beyond names for things: Young children's acquisition of verbs.* Hillsdale, NJ: Erlbaum.

Naigles, L.R., & Gelman, S.A. (1995). Overextensions in comprehension and production revisited: Preferential looking in a study of "dog," "cat," and "cow." *Journal of Child Language, 22,* 19–46.

Naigles, L.R., Gleitman, H., & Gleitman, L.R. (1993). Children acquire word meaning components from syntactic evidence. In E. Dromi (Ed.), *Language and cognition: A developmental perspective* (pp. 104–140). Norwood, NJ: Ablex.

Naigles, L.R., & Hoff-Ginsberg, E. (1995). Input to verb learning: Evidence for the plausibility of syntactic bootstrapping. *Developmental Psychology, 31,* 827–837.

Naigles, L.R., & Hoff-Ginsberg, E. (1998). What are some verbs learned before other verbs? Effects on input frequency and structure on children's early verb use. *Journal of Child Language, 25,* 95–120.

Naigles, L.R., & Kako, E. (1993). First contact in verb acquisition: Defining a role for syntax. *Child Development, 64,* 1665–1687.

Nagy, W.E., & Herman, P.A. (1987). Breadth and depth of vocabulary knowledge: Implications for acquisition and instruction. In M.G. McKeown & M.E. Curtis (Eds.), *The nature of vocabulary acquisition.* Hillsdale, NJ: Erlbaum.

Namy, L.L., & Waxman, S.R. (1998). Words and gestures: Infants' interpretations of different forms of symbolic reference. *Child Development, 69,* 295–308.

Needham, A., & Baillargeon, R. (1997). Object segregation in eight-month-old infants. *Cognition, 62,* 121–149.

Nelson, K. (1973). Structure and strategy in learning to talk. *Monographs of the Society for Research in Child Development, 38* [serial no. 149]: 1–137.

Nelson, K. (1976). Some attributes of adjectives used by young children. *Cognition, 4,* 1–31.

Nelson, K. (1988). Constraints on word meaning? *Cognitive Development, 3,* 221–246.

Nelson, K., Hampson, J., & Shaw, L.K. (1993). Nouns in early lexicons: Evidence, explanations, and implications. *Journal of Child Language, 20,* 61–84.

Newport, E. (1990). Maturational constraints on language learning. *Cognitive Science, 14,* 11–28.

Nice, M.M. (1926). On the size of vocabularies. *American Speech, 2,* 1–7.

Ninio, A. (1980). Picture-book reading in mother-infant dyads belonging to two subgroups in Israel. *Child Development, 51,* 587–590.

Ninio, A., & Bruner, J. (1978). The achievement and antecedents of labeling. *Journal of Child Language, 5,* 1–15.

Nosofsky, R.M. (1988). Exemplar-based accounts of relations between classification, recognition, and typicality. *Journal of Experimental Psychology: Learning, Memory, and Cognition, 14,* 700–708.

O'Keefe, J., & Nadel, L. (1978). *The hippocampus as a cognitive map.* Oxford: Clarendon Press.

O'Neill, D.K. (1996). Two-year-old children's sensitivity to parent's knowledge state when making requests. *Child Development, 67,* 659–677.

Oshima-Takane, Y. (1988). Children learn from speech not addressed to them: The case of personal pronouns. *Journal of Child Language, 15,* 94–108.

Oshima-Takane, Y. (1999). The learning of first and second person pronouns in English. In R. Jackendoff, P. Bloom & K. Wynn (Eds.), *Language, logic, and concepts: Essays in honor of John Macnamara.* Cambridge, MA: MIT Press.

Oshima-Takane, Y., Goodz, E., & Derevensky, J.L. (1996). Birth order effects on early language development: Do secondborn children learn from overheard speech? *Child Development, 67,* 621–634.

Oviatt, S.L. (1980). The emerging ability to comprehend language: An experimental approach. *Child Development, 51,* 97–106.

Parfit, D. (1984). *Reasons and persons.* Oxford: Clarendon.

Pelletier, F. (1979). Non-singular reference: Some preliminaries. In F. Pelletier (Ed.), *Mass terms: Some philosophical problems.* Reidel: Dordrecht.

Pepperberg, I.M. (1987). Evidence for conceptual quantitative abilities in the African grey parrot: Labeling of cardinal sets. *Ethology, 75,* 37–61.

Perception. (1994). *23* (4–5). Special issues on perceptual organization and object recognition.

Perner, J. (1991). *Understanding the representational mind.* Cambridge, MA: MIT Press.

Perner, J., Leekham, S., & Wimmer, H. (1987). Three-year-olds' difficulty with false belief: The case for conceptual deficit. *British Journal of Developmental Psychology, 5,* 125–137.

Peterson, M.A., Nadel, L., Bloom, P., & Garrett, M.F. (1996). Space and language. In P. Bloom, M.A. Peterson, L. Nadel & M.F. Garrett (Eds.), *Language and space.* Cambridge, MA: MIT Press.

Petitto, L.A. (1987). On the autonomy of language and gesture: Evidence from the acquisition of personal pronouns in American Sign Language. *Cognition, 27,* 1–52.

Petitto, L.A. (1992). Modularity and constraints in early lexical acquisition: Evidence from children's first words/signs and gestures. In M.R. Gunnar & M. Maratsos (Eds.), *Modularity and constraints in language and cognition: The Minnesota Symposia on Child Psychology,* (Vol. 25). Hillsdale, NJ: Erlbaum.

Piaget, J. (1929). *The child's conception of the world.* London: Routledge and Kegan Paul.

Piaget, J. (1952). *Origins of intelligence in children.* New York: IUP.

Pine, J.M., & Lieven, E.V.M. (1990). Referential style at thirteen months: Why age-defined cross-sectional measures are inappropriate for the study of strategy differences in early language development. *Journal of Child Language, 17,* 625–631.

Pinker, S. (1984). *Language learnability and language development.* Cambridge, MA: Harvard University Press.

Pinker, S. (1989). *Learnability and cognition: The acquisition of argument structure.* Cambridge, MA: MIT Press.

Pinker, S. (1994a). How could a child use verb syntax to learn verb semantics? *Lingua, 92,* 377–410.

Pinker, S. (1994b). *The language instinct.* New York: HarperCollins.

Pinker, S. (1997). *How the mind works.* New York: Penguin.

Plunkett, K. (1997). Theories of early language acquisition. *Trends in Cognitive Sciences, 1,* 146–153.

Plunkett, K., Sinha, C., Møller, M.F., & Strandsby, O. (1992). Symbol grounding or the emergence of symbols? Vocabulary growth in children and a connectionist net. *Connection Science, 4,* 293–312.

Posner, M.I., & Keele, S.W. (1968). On the genesis of abstract ideas. *Journal of Experimental Psychology, 77,* 353–363.

Poulin-Dubois, D., Graham, S., & Sippola, L. (1995). Early lexical development: The contribution of parental labeling and infants' categorization abilities. *Journal of Child Language, 22,* 325–343.

Povinelli, D.J., Reaux, J.E., Bierschwale, D.T., Allain, A.D., & Simon, B.B. (1997). Exploitation of pointing as a referential gesture in young children, but not adolescent chimpanzees. *Cognitive Development, 12,* 327–365.

Prasada, S. (1993). Learning names for solid substances: Quantifying solid entities in terms of portions. *Cognitive Development, 8,* 83–104.

Prasada, S. (1997). Sentential and non-sentential cues to adjective meaning. Paper presented at the Biennial Meeting of the Society for Research in Child Development, Washington, DC, April 3–6.

Prasada, S. (1999). Names for things and stuff: An Aristotelian perspective. In R. Jackendoff, P. Bloom & K. Wynn (Eds.), *Language, logic, and concepts: Essays in honor of John Macnamara.* Cambridge, MA: MIT Press.

Pullum, G.K. (1991). *The great Eskimo vocabulary hoax, and other irreverent essays on the study of language.* Chicago: University of Chicago Press.

Pustejovsky, J. (1995). *The generative lexicon.* Cambridge, MA: MIT Press.

Putnam, H. (1975). The meaning of "meaning". In H. Putnam (Ed.), *Mind, language, and reality: Philosophical papers* (Vol. 2). Cambridge: Cambridge University Press.

Putnam, H. (1988). *Representation and reality.* Cambridge, MA: MIT Press.

Quine, W.V.O. (1960). *Word and object.* Cambridge, MA: MIT Press.

Rapin, I. (1979). Effects of early blindness and deafness on cognition. In R. Katznman (Ed.), *Congenital and acquired cognitive disorders.* New York: Raven Press.

Rescorla, L.A. (1980). Overextension in early language development. *Journal of Child Language, 7,* 321–335.

Reznick, J.S., & Goldfield, B.A. (1992). Rapid change in lexical development in comprehension and production. *Developmental Psychology, 28,* 406–413.

Rice, M.L. (1990). Preschooler's QUIL: Quick incidental learning of words. In G. Conti-Ramsden & C. Snow (Eds.), *Children's language* (Vol. 7). Hillsdale, NJ: Erlbaum.

Richards, D.D., & Goldfarb, J. (1986). The episodic memory model of conceptual development: An integrative viewpoint. *Cognitive Development, 1,* 183–219.

Rips, L.J. (1989). Similarity, typicality, and categorization. In S. Vosinadou & A. Ortony (Eds.), *Similarity and analogical reasoning.* New York: Cambridge University Press.

Robinson, E.J., Nye, R., & Thomas, G.V. (1994). Children's conceptions of the relationship between pictures and their referents. *Cognitive Development, 8,* 165–191.

Rosch, E., & Mervis, C.B. (1975). Family resemblances: Studies in the internal structure of categories. *Cognitive Psychology. 7,* 573–605.

Rosch, E., Mervis, C.B., Gray, W.D., Johnson, D.M., & Boyes-Braem, P. (1976). Basic objects in natural categories. *Cognitive Psychology, 8,* 382–439.

Sachs, J. (1983). Talking about there and then: The emergence of displaced reference in parent-child discourse. In K.E. Nelson (Ed.), *Children's language* (Vol. 4). Hillsdale, NJ: Erlbaum.

Sacks, O. (1988). *Seeing voices: A journey into the world of the deaf.* Berkeley: University of California Press.

Sapir, E. (1921). *Language.* New York: Harcourt, Brace, and World.

Saussure, F. de. (1916/1959). *Course in general linguistics:* New York: McGraw Hill.

Savage-Rambaugh, S., Murphy, J., Sevcik, R., Brakke, K., Williams, S., & Rumbaugh, D. (1993). Language comprehension in ape and child. *Monographs of the Society for Research in Child Development, 58* (serial no. 233): 1–256.

Saxe, J.B., Guberman, S.R., & Gearhart, M. (1987). Social processes in early number development. *Monographs of the Society for Research in Child Development, 52* (serial no. 216): 1–162.

Scaife, J.F., & Bruner, J.S. (1975). The capacity for joint visual attention in the infant. *Nature, 253,* 265–266.

Scarr, S., & Weisberg, R.A. (1978). The influence of "family background" on intellectual attainment. *American Sociological Review, 43.* 674–692.

Schacter, P. (1985). Parts-of-speech systems. In T. Shopen (Ed.) *Language typology and syntactic description,* Vol. 1, *Clause structure.* New York: Cambridge University Press.

Schaller, S. (1991). *A man without words.* New York: Summit Press.

Schieffelin, B.B. (1985). The acquisition of Kaluli. In D.I. Slobin (Ed.), *The crosslinguistic study of language acquisition* Vol. 1, *The data.* Hillsdale, NJ: Erlbaum.

Schwartz, S.P. (1978). Putnam on artifacts. *Philosophical Review, 87,* 566–574.

Seashore, R.H., & Eckerson, L.D. (1940). The measurement of individual differences in general English vocabularies. *Journal of Educational Psychology, 31,* 14–37.

Shepard, R.N., & Metzler, J. (1971). Mental rotation of three-dimensional objects. *Science, 171,* 701–703.

Shipley, E.F., Kuhn, I.F., & Madden, E.C. (1983). Mothers' use of superordinate category terms. *Journal of Child Language, 10,* 571–588.

Shipley, E.F., & Shepperson, B. (1990). Countable entities: Developmental changes. *Cognition, 34,* 109–136.

Shipley, E.F., & Shipley, T.E. (1969). Quaker children's use of thee: A relational analysis. *Journal of Verbal Learning and Verbal Behavior, 8,* 112–117.

Shore, C.M. (1995). *Individual differences in language development.* London: Sage.

Siegler, R.S., & Robinson, M. (1982). The development of numerical understandings. In H.W. Reese & L.P. Lipsitt (Eds.), *Advances in child development and behavior* (Vol. 16). New York: Academic.

Simon, T.J. (1997). Reconceptualizing the origins of numerical knowledge: A "non-numerical" account. *Cognitive Development, 12,* 349–372.

Simons, D.L., & Levin, D.T. (1998). Failure to detect changes to people during a real-world interaction. *Psychonomic Bulletin and Review, 5,* 644–649.

Skinner, B.F. (1957). *Verbal behavior.* New York: Appleton-Century-Crofts.

Skyrms, B. (1996). *Evolution of the social contract.* Cambridge: Cambridge University Press.

Smith, L.B., Jones, S.S., & Landau, B. (1992). Count nouns, adjectives, and perceptual properties in children's novel word interpretations. *Developmental Psychology, 28,* 273–286.

Smith, L.B., Jones, S.S., & Landau, B. (1996). Naming in young children: A dumb attentional mechanism? *Cognition, 60,* 143–171.

Smolak, L., & Weinraub, M. (1983). Maternal speech: Strategy or response? *Journal of Child Language, 10,* 369–380.

Soja, N.N. (1991). Young children's difficulty with solid substance words. Unpublished manuscript, Northeastern University.

Soja, N.N. (1992). Inferences about the meanings of nouns: The relationship between perception and syntax. *Cognitive Development, 7,* 29–45.

Soja, N.N. (1994). Evidence for a distinct kind of noun. *Cognition, 51,* 267–284.

Soja, N.N., Carey S., & Spelke, E.S. (1991). Ontological categories guide young children's inductions of word meaning: Object terms and substance terms. *Cognition, 38,* 179–211.

Soja, N.N., Carey, S., & Spelke, E.S. (1992). Perception, ontology, and word meaning. *Cognition, 45,* 101–107.

Solomon, G.E.A. (1997). Conceptual change and wine expertise. *Journal of the Learning Sciences, 6,* 41–60.

Sophian, C. (1987). Early developments in children's use of counting to solve quantitative problems. *Cognition and Instruction, 4,* 61–90.

Sophian, C. (1995). *Children's numbers.* Madison, WI: Brown & Benchmark.

Sorrentino, C. (1997). The role of mental state attribution in young children's interpretation of proper nouns. Paper presented at the Biennial Meeting of the Society for Research in Child Development, Washington, DC.

Sorrentino, C. (1999). Individuation, identity, and proper names in cognitive development. Unpublished doctoral dissertation, MIT.

Sowell, T. (1997). *Late-talking children.* New York: Basic Books.

Spelke, E.S. (1994). Initial knowledge: Six suggestions. *Cognition, 50,* 443–447.

Spelke, E.S., Breinlinger, K., Jacobson, K., & Phillips, A. (1993). Gestalt relations and object perception: A developmental study. *Perception, 22,* 1483–1501.

Spelke, E.S., Phillips, A., & Woodward, A.L. (1995). Infant's knowledge of object motion and human action. In D. Sperber, D. Premack & A.J. Premack. (Eds.), *Causal cognition.* New York: Oxford University Press.

Sperber, D. (1997). Metarepresentations in an evolutionary perspective. Paper presented at the Hang Seng Workshop on Evolution of Mind and Language, University of Sheffield, September 20.

Sperber, D., & Wilson, D. (1986). *Relevance: Communication and cognition.* Cambridge, MA: MIT Press.

Starkey, P., & Cooper, R.G., Jr. (1980). Perception of numbers by human infants. *Science, 210,* 1033–1035.

Starkey, P., Spelke, E.S., & Gelman, R. (1990). Numerical abstraction by human infants. *Cognition, 36,* 97–127.

Sternberg, R.J. (1987). Most vocabulary is learned from context. In M.G. McKeown & M.E. Curtis (Eds.), *The nature of vocabulary acquisition.* Hillsdale, NJ: Erlbaum.

Sternberg, R.J., Chawarski, M.C., & Allbritton, D.W. (1998). If you changed your name and appearance to those of Elvis Presley, who would you be? Historical features in categorization. *American Journal of Psychology, 111,* 327–351.

Stevens, T., & Karmiloff-Smith, A. (1997). Word learning in a special population: Do individuals with Williams syndrome obey lexical constraints? *Journal of Child Language, 24,* 737–765.

Stromswold, K. (1994). Language comprehension without language production: Implications for theories of language acquisition. Paper presented at the eighteenth Annual Boston University Conference on Language Development, January.

Tajfel, H., & Wilkes, A.L. (1963). Classification and quantitative judgement. *British Journal of Psychology, 54,* 101–114.

Talmy, L. (1985). Lexicalization patterns: Semantic structure in lexical forms. In T. Shopen (Ed.), *Language typology and syntactic description,* Vol. 3, *Grammatical categories and the lexicon.* New York: Cambridge University Press.

Taylor, M., & Gelman, S.A. (1988). Adjectives and nouns: Children's strategies for learning new words. *Child Development, 59,* 411–419.

Thal, D., Bates, E., & Bellugi, U. (1989). Language and cognition in two children with Williams syndrome. *Journal of Speech and Hearing Research, 32,* 489–500.

Thomas, G.V., Nye, R., & Robinson, E.J. (1994). How children view pictures: Children's responses to pictures as things in themselves and as representations of something else. *Cognitive Development, 9,* 141–164.

Tolman, E.C., & Brunswik, E. (1935). The organism and the causal texture of the environment. *Psychological Review, 42,* 43–77.

Tomasello, M. (1992). *First verbs: A case study of early grammatical development.* Cambridge: Cambridge University Press.

Tomasello, M. (1998). Uniquely primate, uniquely human. *Developmental Science, 1,* 1–16.

Tomasello, M., & Akhtar, N. (1995). Two-year-olds use pragmatic cues to differentiate reference to objects and actions. *Cognitive Development, 10,* 201–224.

Tomasello, M., & Barton, M. (1994). Learning words in non-ostensive contexts. *Developmental Psychology, 30,* 639–650.

Tomasello, M., & Kruger, A. (1992). Joint attention on actions: Acquiring verbs in ostensive and non-ostensive contexts. *Journal of Child Language, 19,* 311–333.

Tomasello, M., Mannle, S., & Kruger, A.C. (1986). Linguistic environment of one- to two-year-old twins. *Developmental Psychology, 22,* 169–176.

Tomasello, M., & Mervis, C.B. (1994). The instrument is great, but measuring comprehension is still a problem. *Monographs of the Society for Research in Child Development, 59* (2, serial no. 242), 174–179.

Tomasello, M., Strosberg, R., & Akhtar, N. (1996). Eighteen-month-old children learn words in non-ostensive contexts. *Journal of Child Language, 23,* 157–176.

Tomasello, M., & Todd, J. (1983). Joint attention and lexical acquisition style. *First Language, 4,* 197–212.

Tomikawa, S.A., & Dodd, D.H. (1980). Early word meanings: Perceptually or functionally based? *Child Development, 51,* 1103–1109.

Uller, M.C., Carey, S., Huntley-Fenner, G.N., & Klatt, L. (in press). What representations might underlie infant numerical competence? *Cognitive Development.*

Valian, V. (1986). Syntactic categories in the speech of young children. *Developmental Psychology, 22,* 562–579.

Valian, V. (1990). Null subjects: A problem for parameter-setting models of language acquisition. *Cognition, 35,* 105–122.

Van Geert, P. (1991). A dynamic system model of cognitive and language growth. *Psychological Review, 98,* 3–53.

Varley, R. (in press). Aphasic language, aphasic thought: an investigation of propositional thinking in an apropositional aphasic. In P. Carruthers & J. Boucher (Eds.), *Language and thought: Interdisciplinary themes.* Cambridge: Cambridge University Press.

von Loosbroek, E., & Smitsman, A.W. (1990). Visual perception of numerosity in infancy. *Developmental Psychology, 26,* 916–922.

Vygotsky, L.S. (1962). *Thought and language.* Cambridge, MA: MIT Press.

Wales, R. (1979). Deixis. In P. Fletcher & M. Garmen (Eds.), *Language acquisition.* New York: Cambridge University Press.

Ward, T.B., Becker, A.H., Hass, S.D., & Vela, E. (1991). Attribute availability and the shape bias in children's category construction. *Cognitive Development, 6,* 143–167.

Waxman, S.R. (1990). Linguistic biases and the establishment of conceptual hierarchies: Evidence from preschool children. *Cognitive Development, 5,* 123–150.

Waxman, S.R. (1994). The development of an appreciation of specific linkages between linguistic and conceptual organization. *Lingua, 92,* 229–257.

Waxman, S.R., & Gelman, R. (1986). Preschoolers' use of superordinate relations in classification and language. *Cognitive Development, 1,* 139–156.

Waxman, S.R., & Kosowski, T. (1990). Nouns mark category relations: Toddlers' and preschoolers' word-learning biases. *Child Development, 61,* 1461–1473.

Waxman, S.R., & Markow, D.B. (1995). Words as invitations to form categories: Evidence from twelve- to thirteen-month-old infants. *Cognitive Psychology, 29,* 257–302.

Waxman, S.R. & Thompson, W. (1998). Words are invitations to learn about categories. *Behavioral and Brain Sciences, 21,* 88.

Werner, H., & Kaplan, H. (1963). *Symbol formation.* New York: Wiley.

Whorf, B.L. (1956). *Language, thought, and reality.* Cambridge, MA: MIT Press.

Wiggins, D. (1980). *Sameness and substance.* Oxford: Basil Blackwell.

Wimmer, H., & Perner, J. (1983). Beliefs about beliefs: Representation and the containing function of wrong beliefs in young children's understanding of deception. *Cognition, 13,* 103–128.

Wisniewski, E.J., & Medin, D.L. (1994). On the interaction of theory and data in concept learning. *Cognitive Science, 18,* 221–281.

Wittgenstein, L. (1953). *Philosophical investigations.* Oxford: Basic Blackwell.

Woodward, A.L. (1998). Infants selectively encode the goal object of an actor's reach. *Cognition, 69,* 1–34.

Woodward, A.L., & Hoyne, K.L. (1999). Infants' learning about words and sounds in relation to objects. *Child Development, 70,* 65–77.

Woodward, A.L., & Markman, E.M. (1997). Early word learning. In W. Damion, D. Kuhn & R. Siegler (Eds.), *Handbook of child psychology,* Vol. 2, *Cognition, perception, and language.* New York: Wiley.

Woodward, A.L., Markman, E.M., & Fitzsimmons, C.M. (1994). Rapid word learning in thirteen- and eighteen-month-olds. *Developmental Psychology, 30,* 553–566.

Wynn, K. (1990). Children's understanding of counting. *Cognition, 36,* 155–193.

Wynn, K. (1992a). Addition and subtraction by human infants. *Nature, 358,* 749–750.

Wynn, K. (1992b). Children's acquisition of the number words and the counting system. *Cognitive Psychology, 24,* 220–251.

Wynn, K. (1995). Origins of numerical knowledge. *Mathematical Cognition, 1,* 35–60.

Wynn, K. (1996). Infants' individuation and enumeration of actions. *Psychological Science, 7,* 164–169.

Wynn, K. (1998). Psychological foundations of number: Numerical competence in human infants. *Trends in Cognitive Sciences, 2,* 296–303.

Wynn, K., & Bloom, P. (1992). The origins of psychological axioms of arithmetic and geometry. *Mind and Language, 7,* 409–416.

Wynn, K., Bloom, P., & Chiang, W-C. (under review). Enumeration of non-object individuals by five-month-old infants.

Xu, F. (1997). From Lot's wife to a pillar of salt: Evidence that *physical object* is a sortal concept. *Mind and Language, 12,* 365–392.

Xu, F., & Carey, S. (1996). Infants' metaphysics: The case of numerical identity. *Cognitive Psychology, 30,* 111–153.

Zaitchik, D. (1990). When representations conflict with reality: The preschooler's problem with false beliefs and "false" photographs. *Cognition, 35,* 41–68.

Zarbatany, L., & Lamb, M.E. (1985). Social referencing as a function of information source: Mothers versus strangers. *Infant Behavior and Development, 8,* 25–33.

Author Index

Subject Index